The Unmaking of Arab Socialism

Anthem Frontiers of Global Political Economy

The **Anthem Frontiers of Global Political Economy** series seeks to trigger and attract new thinking in global political economy, with particular reference to the prospects of emerging markets and developing countries. Written by renowned scholars from different parts of the world, books in this series provide historical, analytical and empirical perspectives on national economic strategies and processes, the implications of global and regional economic integration, the changing nature of the development project and the diverse global-to-local forces that drive change. Scholars featured in the series extend earlier economic insights to provide fresh interpretations that allow new understandings of contemporary economic processes.

Series Editors

Kevin Gallagher – Boston University, USA
Jayati Ghosh – Jawaharlal Nehru University, India

Editorial Board

Stephanie Blankenburg – School of Oriental and African Studies (SOAS), UK
Ha-Joon Chang – University of Cambridge, UK
Wan-Wen Chu – RCHSS, Academia Sinica, Taiwan
Alica Puyana Mutis – Facultad Latinoamericana de Ciencias Sociales (FLASCO–México), Mexico
Léonce Ndikumana – University of Massachusetts–Amherst, USA
Matías Vernengo – Bucknell University, USA
Robert Wade – London School of Economics and Political Science (LSE), UK
Yu Yongding – Chinese Academy of Social Sciences (CASS), China

The Unmaking of Arab Socialism

Ali Kadri

ANTHEM PRESS

Anthem Press
An imprint of Wimbledon Publishing Company
www.anthempress.com

This edition first published in UK and USA 2019
by ANTHEM PRESS
75–76 Blackfriars Road, London SE1 8HA, UK
or PO Box 9779, London SW19 7ZG, UK
and
244 Madison Ave #116, New York, NY 10016, USA

First published in the UK and USA by Anthem Press 2016

Copyright © Ali Kadri 2019

The author asserts the moral right to be identified as the author of this work.

All rights reserved. Without limiting the rights under copyright reserved above, no part of this publication may be reproduced, stored or introduced into a retrieval system, or transmitted, in any form or by any means (electronic, mechanical, photocopying, recording or otherwise), without the prior written permission of both the copyright owner and the above publisher of this book.

British Library Cataloguing-in-Publication Data
A catalogue record for this book is available from the British Library.

ISBN-13: 978-1-78527-122-9 (Pbk)
ISBN-10: 1-78527-122-9 (Pbk)

This title is also available as an e-book.

To the memory of Arthur K. Davis

CONTENTS

List of Illustrations	ix
Acknowledgements	xi
Introduction From Arab Socialism to Neo-liberalism: The Politics of Immiseration	1
1. Arab Socialism in Retrospect	29
2. The Devastation of Peace in Egypt	77
3. The Infeasibility of Revolution in Syria	117
4. Iraq – Then and Now	159
5. The Perverse Transformation	201
6. Permanent War in the Arab World	249
Bibliography	285
Index	303

ILLUSTRATIONS

Tables

1.1	Yearly average real GDP per capita growth, real GDP growth and output per worker growth rates in constant local currency units for the periods 1960–1979 and 1980–2011	74
1.2	High and low points for the periods 1960–1979 and 1980–2011 followed by modal range for inflation rates	74
1.3	Average unemployment rates for the periods 1960–1979 and 1980–2011	75
1.4	Average total debt service as a percentage of Gross National Income for the periods 1960–1979 and 1980–2011	75
1.5	Average for the difference between the rate of investment and the rate of saving as a percentage of Gross National Income for the periods 1960–1979 and 1980–2011	75
4.1	Major economic and social development indicators in the economy over selected years	183
4.2	Inflation and market exchange rates: 1990–2003	183
4.3	Gross Domestic Product at 2002 prices by sectors (in millions of US dollars)	184
4.4	Estimates of GDP and selected components at constant 1990 prices (in millions of US dollars)	185
5.1	Share of agricultural investment in total investment in Egypt	206
5.2	Rural and urban populations of Arab countries, 1980–2020 (percentages)	235
5.3	The agriculture sector's contribution to employment and as a share of GDP (%), selected countries and years	235
5.4	Distribution of rural and urban poverty	235

Figures

3.1	General Price Level Index for 1960–2010	146
3.2	Income inequality index for some available years between 1987 and 1995	146

ACKNOWLEDGEMENTS

Thanks to Adam Cornford for his attentive reading of my manuscript and many helpful suggestions.

Introduction

FROM ARAB SOCIALISM TO NEO-LIBERALISM: THE POLITICS OF IMMISERATION

At the time of writing this introduction, in early 2016, the richest countries on earth, the Gulf States, were bombarding Yemen, possibly the poorest of all countries. Conditions of malnutrition, conflict, or a combination of both, characterise most Arab countries today. But things were not always as bad. As in much of the developing world, the immediate post-independence period represented an age of hope and relative prosperity. Yet, imperialism does not fall asleep while the Third World develops. No sooner than it could intervene with the assistance of its class allies to destroy Arab post-independence achievements, imperialism did so in a big way. Two principal defeats by, and losses of territory to, Israel in 1967 and 1973, and many others that followed, left behind more than mere destruction of assets and loss of human lives; the Arab World (hereinafter the AW) lost its ideology of resistance, Arabism, and its associated socialism. This book is a modest attempt to understand why Arab development declined from its peak in the heyday of Arab socialism to the present desolate conditions.

Reversing this defeat and ideological defeatism requires a metamorphosis of the multitude into the masses and of the working class into a proletariat. It requires people who espouse an ideology – the actualisation of which, through policy, assigns a greater share of wealth to the security of the working classes. A living security, nonetheless, which obtains from an anti-imperialist struggle because the higher share of wages in the aristocratic nations have for long created the colonial mercenaries who pillaged the developing world. Undoubtedly, all ideologies will represent a system of thought shaped by the conditions of the class struggle. Revolutionary theory regards reigning ideology, even its own, as involving a biased perception of real processes. Capitalistic ideologies, however, are either the prefab social dicta meant to discipline labour or the unexamined assumptions upon which theory is built to strengthen the rule of capital. Deciphering positive from negative ideology requires more than just the Debord (1967) criterion: the true is a moment of the false. In revolutionary praxis, the true is not any moment of the false; the true is its determining moment; the true is its state of becoming in continued anti-imperialist struggle and all-round development.

The consensus on the significance of ideological shifts to policy turnarounds dates back millennia.

> The Annunaki of the sky
> Made the Igigi (lower-class gods assigned hard work) bear the workload
> They were counting the years of loads
> For 3,600 years they bore the excess
> Hard work, night and day
> They groaned and blamed each other
> Grumbled over the masses of excavated soil:
> Let us confront our Warden
> And get him to relieve us of our hard work!
> Then Kingu, (a rebellious god) made his voice heard
> And spoke to the gods (the Igigis), his brothers:
> Now, cry battle! (Atrahasis, eighteenth-century BCE, as compiled by Lambert, 1999)

It has taken the Igigis 3,600 years to rise up, win their war and retire to leisurely activities. However, as production came to depend on higher circulation of exchange value, which entailed an 'annihilation of space by time' (Marx [1877] 1973), ideological shifts and revolts became all the more frequent. With the growth of socialising space and communication, people unexpectedly change their views and 'theory becomes a material force as it grips the masses' (Marx 1844). The exercise of realising the necessity for change, or of socialising what is socially produced – as opposed to privatising – is also an exercise in individual freedom on the way to emancipation. The ethical connotations of such an ideological process may be summed up in the set of policies that negate private property (Truitt 2005).

In the Marxian sense, it is the experience of the masses in the course of the class struggle that shapes their consciousness. The recent experience of Arab working classes in the neo-liberal age is an extreme version of war, poverty and underdevelopment. The combination of armed conflicts, petrodollar-funded civil society, and neo-liberalism has deconstructed working-class organisations, tarnished their symbols and engendered widespread despondency, catapulting a significant mass of working people into the lap of reactionary fatalism. But, for Marxism change is the only constant, and class war never comes to rest. It is always fought, in practice and in theory. Subjected to systematic imperialist assault, the AW has lived through an extraordinary experience in which the weapon of criticism is yet to replace the criticism of the weapon (as paraphrased from

Marx 1844). The practice of revolutionary theory in war and, especially, the war of ideas, is what resituates class struggle on an emancipatory path.

More so than in the past, the future of class struggle in the AW appears to be taking the shape of armed struggle. One is painfully aware of the fact that this would not need to be as protracted had there been advances in socialist–internationalist ideology; but that is a far cry from the way things are. In this historical epoch, Arab death rates due to hunger, disease and war rose significantly. The prevailing state of consciousness associated with war, the rise of the war economy in several Arab states and its associated war-indigent proletariat seem to prolong intercommunal conflicts and the policies that have bred abjection.[1] More and more, worldly phenomena acquire religious interpretations. The delusions of theocratic mysticism infiltrate and set back every aspect of social development. There are probably millions of examples that could illustrate the ebbing of revolutionary symbols and practice in class conflict, but one instance may be worth mentioning. When an Iraqi woman parliamentarian was asked why she ran for office in the National Assembly erected by Paul Bremer, she answered: 'I really cannot care less for parliamentarianism, but my husband told me to run for office because the US-drawn constitution designated seats by quota in parliament for women, so I am doing this for my husband; otherwise the role of women is to be at home with the children'.[2] Non-secular or imperialistically constructed states in which social and legal representation occurs through the sectional-identity form, as opposed to working-class citizenry, cannot intermediate social contradictions. They become the terrain of easily ignitable wars. The case is doubly relevant

---

1 A war economy has at its disposal real and financial resources that are put to work to produce a service, which is the outcome of the war and its power balances. It also has a ruling class composed of the relationship of the inter-fighting factions that appropriate their surplus product via the pillage of the national economy at the behest of imperialism and the regimentation or workers-soldiers, the war-indigent proletariat employed in war or war effort. The war-indigent proletariat group solidarity is established around some form of identity politics that utterly conceals the joint class lines. Although each warring section of the war bourgeoisie competes with the other for moneyed and real resources, their competition dollarises and draws down the values and resources of the national economy. In the process of the war bourgeoisie's self-reproduction, which involves dollarisation, destruction and cheapening of third world resources and values and, ultimately, the eradication of revolutionary ideological power, the principal benefactor becomes the superior bourgeois relation of US-led international financial capital and its practice of imperialism. The transformations of the nationalist state bourgeoisie from the days of Arab socialism into a structurally imperialist-allied merchant class bourgeoisie and later into a war bourgeoisie that is consuming the life and labour of its own working class, all occur as successive concessions to defeat to the power of imperialism.
2 Discussion with M. Hage Ali of the London School of Economics.

when the developing region in question, the Arab region, is subjected to persistent imperialist offensives.

The imperialist objective of setting on course the self-destruction of Arab society is as easy as devolving funds to the working class along identity demarcation lines or applying the darker side of the Drucker thesis (1964) of management by objectives (creating incentives for agents to willingly engage in the act of self-destruction). At any rate, the practice of survival by identity-based value grab in a state whose authority over its own territory is questionable becomes tantamount to permanent inter-working class conflict. The residues of petrodollars, or only the pittance of what remains in the AW after the bigger shares of Gulf oil wealth have gone to circulate in the global money markets, underwrite the phenomenon of spiritual underdevelopment manifested in American-sponsored political Islam. In contrast to this most recent period, between 1950 and 1980, the AW experienced faster and healthier growth and social development in spite of lower earnings in oil revenues. This divergence in performance between then and now requires an even-handed explanation that steers clear of the hallucinatory constructs of individualistic freedom and choice. It does not make sense to speak of individual choices when the choice is often a single one, handed down by the class in command of history to the majority. This book is one attempt to understand these perplexing issues without resort to such ideological legerdemain. Obviously, one cannot cover all areas related to the topic, but in the present work I focus on the concept of Arab socialism in general, its application to three Arab states – Iraq, Syria and Egypt – and two cases of perverse transformation under neo-liberalism: the creation of a huge mass of redundant labour as a result of dispossessions in the hinterland; and the persistence of what amounts to permanent war in the AW. By the end, I hope to define and qualify the way the AW has become articulated with the global economy.

An Overview of the AW

Once a relatively equitable group of societies, the AW has come to be characterised by acute income inequality (nearly the highest rate, according to the Texas Income Inequality Database 2012). Several military losses shook up these societies and metamorphosed the ruling nationalist Arab bourgeoisie into a comprador–merchant class fully integrated with international financial capital. Between 1970 and 2010, the shares of manufacturing in Syria, Egypt, Algeria and Iraq went down from 19 to 5, 21 to 15, 10 to 2, and 12 to 4 per cent respectively (UNIDO, various years). With the material grounds for the reproduction of the wealth of the ruling classes shifting from national industry to the international dollar-denominated financial space, social integration, both national and regional, faced insurmountable difficulties. Arab merchant classes – sprouting like toxic mould on the back of military defeat and socialist ideological defeatism, and owning the state apparatus – constructed openness policies that acted as conduits for the usurpation of national wealth. The bulk of regional oil revenues, especially in the Gulf, fly abroad into US T-bills, affluent consumption and military and regime security spending (defence spending alone is twice the world share from GDP, according to the World Bank (WB), with American military aid to the Arab region ranking the highest). In 2004, the Inter-Arab Investment Guarantee Corporation (IAIGC) estimated that Arab assets abroad are at $1.4 trillion. This is likely a crude underestimate. In the same year, the Union of Arab Banks (UAB) estimated the figure at $21 trillion.[3] The intra-regional disparities are also glaring: in contrast with the rich Gulf States, Yemen, Sudan, Somalia and Mauritania are among the poorest countries in the world. While Egypt and Morocco are not in an open-conflict condition, their working families spend 60 per cent of their income on food (WB 2011).

The Gulf States are an oddity, with citizens earning some of the highest incomes globally. The rich Gulf economies represent around 5 per cent of the total Arab population (Gulf citizens number around 20 million) but earn 1.6 per cent of world income (World Development Indicators (WDI) 2012). In less oil-endowed Arab economies, around 350 million people earn 0.9 per cent of world income, of which the labour share is estimated at 0.3 per cent of world income (WDI 2012). This figure is only slightly higher than the sub-Saharan Africa rate. Gulf industrialisation centres on costly oil derivatives or on facilities that exhibit few positive technological linkages to the rest of the economy. By reducing modern industrial expansion and its associated space for worker socialisation, the ruling merchant capital contributes to holding back the production of knowledge as the practice that engenders the development of society.

Nearly all Arab states are oil exporters and price their oil in dollars. They also peg the national currency to the dollar, despite the fact that most of their trade takes place outside the dollar zone (China and Europe). For dollar-pegging states, monetary policy becomes ineffective; because the majority cannot export enough oil to earn foreign currency and pay for imports, their fiscal policy (under neo-liberal austerity) has to contract – save for the Gulf States, of course. It is not just because the exchange and interest rates do not adjust to calibrate the demands of savings or trade accounts; it is more because pegging in an open-capital-account context hands over monetary

---

3 Arab funds invest $21 trillion abroad, 2004. Online: http://www.albawaba.com/business/arab-funds-invest-21-trillion-abroad (viewed 9 October 2015).

policy to the country of the stronger partner to whom the currency is being pegged – in this case the United States. Also, apart from the Gulf, Arab states experience a balance-of-payments constraint and exercise an inflation-targeting monetary policy under open capital accounts leading to de facto dollarisation of the national currency. The impact of dollar fluctuations on the domestic price level has been negative, as seen in the rise of food prices in 2008 that caused death on bread queues in Egypt (Slackman 2008).

It is not easy to measure unemployment in the least-developed or war-torn Arab countries. Where unemployment has been measured, the official rate may appear as somewhere around 10 per cent, but in actuality, with absolute poverty (below 2 dollars a day) being higher than 50 per cent (AMF 2011), the true unemployment rate is also closer to the 50 per cent mark. People who are forced to eke out a living at below-subsistence levels in informal employment cannot be counted as employed. Aside from the Human Rights Bill edict on the right to work, counting them as employed contradicts the Decent Work clause of the International Labour Organisation (ILO). In some Gulf States, unemployment hits the 20 per cent mark, but given their wealth profile, the unemployed do not face the same conditions of poverty prevalent elsewhere. Yet, in the Gulf, one observes nearly 20 million foreign workers who occupy local jobs. With elastic supplies of rights-deprived Asian workers, more will be hired by profit-driven commerce because investment in local labour is much less lucrative for the ruling merchant class: they neither depend on the industrial skills of the labour force nor on a rising productivity-wage internal demand component. The synergy between labour and industry that may promote rising-productivity-led development is central to building security capabilities and, as such, it represents a threat to US-led hegemony. Merchants, their neo-liberal policy patrons and their institutions engineer the necessary mismatch between capital and labour at every stage of the labour process. Many highly skilled workers emigrate, while foreign labour competes with unskilled national labour for low-paying jobs. Productivity growth often exhibits negative signs (KILM 2014). Although one may posit that productivity growth has fallen as a result of a substitution effect (cheaper labour replacing capital), the principal cause is to be found in a combination of slow endogenous technology growth and a ruling class with no commitment to capitalising the national economy.

While AW countries are deindustrialising and slowing down the rate of decent job creation, the numbers of poverty-wage service-sector jobs naturally swell. Simply put, new entrants or laid-off working people have no other source of income apart from informal/poverty work. A highly capitalised oil sector has created few jobs relative to its capital stock, and decent job expansion initially arose in the public sector – but only initially, because public-sector wages later fell, spearheading wage compression for the economy (UN 2006). Together, deindustrialisation, poverty-wage employment and the shrinking of decent job creation resulted in enormous unemployment (measured by the minimum level of decent income). The capping of resource flows to the working class, the erection of constitutional frameworks that sanctify working-class dividedness by identity and the limiting of social spaces or proxy factory floors that unify labour's position, together resulted in inter-working class divisions that eclipsed the development of revolutionary-class consciousness.

With comprador-merchant capital rising to power in Arab states – gradually, beginning with Egypt's swerving to the US imperialist side after the Camp David Accords of 1978 – oil revenues were purposefully used to sow divisions in societies. Moreover, besides being a precondition for internal war, deepening working class differentiation – working class differentiation bears little or no resemblance to the apolitical 'labour market segmentation' of the mainstream – combined with uncertainty, also enhances short-term returns in all sectors. For economic agents holding moneyed wealth, the present becomes more valuable than the future. Above all, geopolitical uncertainty and the threat of war, conjointly with institutional brittleness, shape inter-temporal investor preferences (Do investors think they make more or less money in the future?). Investment lodges in finance or short-gestation projects. However, it is not the individual decision that matters for investment, but the overall geopolitical context. Class disarticulation in both consciousness and spatial demarcation lines associated with conflicts, in addition to deepening income divisions and rural–urban disparities, also fuels identity-based conflicts. The capacity of the working class to steer the circuit of capital for its benefit becomes estranged and demolished by sectarian or tribal politics. Working-class politics becomes a self-defeating goal as the cycle of inter-working class violence and the consequent weakening of the state continuously tip the balance in favour of US-led imperialism and its regional class allies.

For comprador-merchant capital, more-equitable redistribution in the form of presumptive income and capital gains taxation (as opposed to the predominant form of indirect taxation) and greater interest in regional development via a stronger demand side, are anathema. The merchant class reproduces itself via a commerce almost bereft of national industrial production. The social contract that brokers class differences nationally shifts from one between the national ruling and ruled classes to one between international financial capital and the ruling Arab merchant class. In the circulation of value within the triad of state, capital and labour, the policy outcome of the new external social contract is to reduce the cost of the social reproduction of the working class by a combination of dispossession, undermining public services, and raising unemployment.

In retrospect, the divide between pan-Arab secularism and monarchism-Islamism has mirrored the US–Soviet rift during the Cold War and continues to form the basis for the 'rights of the working class versus charity to the working class' debate. The Gulf States, whose security and sovereignty are maintained by US imperial coverage, propagate and fund free-market adhering political Islam or Salafist ideologies and movements: their funding of the Afghan jihadists is one historical watershed. After the occupation of Iraq and the rise of Iranian backed Shiite militias, US-led imperialism capitalised on such sectarianism to fuel indefinite regional conflicts sponsored by the funds and ideology of Wahhabism. The power that US-led capital amasses from rearing the Sunni–Shiite divide, the rising terror threats worldwide shifting control into the hands of capital's security apparatuses, and the ensuing militarisation are the real loot from its invasion of Iraq.

Throughout the AW, a rise in obscurantism and identity schisms has weakened the foundation of the state as the principal body that could negotiate the position of the working class in the global economy. Given socialist ideological decline and much of the working class eking a poverty-stricken living, it takes an insignificant share of Gulf petrodollar revenues to fund unrest. In a strategic region such as the AW, political considerations eclipse short-term economic cost considerations. Nonetheless, the total volume of petrodollar flows from the Gulf (second to East Asia in size) are worthwhile to Western financial markets. The Gulf's sovereign funds are too substantial to be controlled (not just managed) by Gulf sheikhs, and the imperialist edict to arrest Arab industrial development ensures that these assets remain unrequited transfers or uncashed cheques.

The Gulf's earning-without-work model had served, by the demonstration effect, to disrupt the industrious and regulated Arab economies of the 1970s and had thwarted work incentives. Petrodollar remittances to non-Gulf Arab countries distorted exchange-rate regimes and had Dutch-disease–like effects on the national industry, especially on the protected economies of Syria and Egypt. These remittances did not, however, fall outside the destabilising geopolitical-rents component of imperialist intervention; they came laced with the ideological poison of colonially and American-groomed political Islam. That said, capital outflows from the majority of Arab countries (non-Gulf) are insignificant in global terms. Most non-Gulf Arab countries exhibit balance-of-payment constraints. The flows from these non-Gulf countries are gauged, not according to their money value, but according to their impact in destabilising national states and, conversely, buttressing the position of US-led imperialism, regionally and globally.

When oil prices fell at the beginning of 1981 and remained low until 2002, the biggest economy in the Gulf – Saudi Arabia – could not maintain its previous living standards as did the smaller and richer per-capita Gulf States. Saudi's real per-capita income fell from around $18,000 in 1981 to about $8,000 in 2000 (WDI, various years). By the late 1990s, the Saudis had borrowed more than $200 billion in short-term, high-interest loans to cover fiscal shortfalls (WDI 2002). In 2003, poverty reports from Saudi Arabia indicated that nearly 25 per cent of the population subsisted at below the national poverty line.[4] The oil price hike, beginning in 2003, leveraged the Saudi economy; however, under the neo-liberal policy package, power delegated to private actors grew, channelling more resources away from labour. The recent fall in oil prices beginning in January 2015 may precipitate yet another, even more serious lowering of the standard of living.[5]

In the early 1980s, neo-liberal policies effected under the name *infitah* (Arabic for 'openness') came into operation. Two significant military losses in 1967 and 1973 had already raised national social tensions and risks and had lured investors to the safety of US-dollar markets. As is typical under structural adjustment, policymakers deregulated trade and capital accounts. National industry started to shrink because of falling investment and increased

---

4 See 'Poverty in the Oil Kingdom: An Introduction', 2010. Online: http://www.jadaliyya.com/pages/index/202/poverty-in-the-oil-kingdom_an-introduction- (viewed 12 March 2014); and '[i]n wealthy oil-rich countries: a quarter of Saudis under poverty line' (Arabic), 2013. Online: http://middle-east-online.com/?id=146523 (viewed 6 April 2015).

5 It was not difficult to foresee that the regional macroeconomic trends were headed for collapse. The following passages from the work of the Economic Analysis team at the Western Asia office had forewarned of decline or violent transition.

'But only three years after the decline in oil prices in the first oil boom, per capita income fell drastically and certain States resorted to short-term borrowing from private banks at high interest rates to redress their fiscal deficits. Recently, moreover, speculative elements have accounted for a significant proportion of the oil price. If speculative pressures subside, a fall could occur again, yet this time at a higher rate (UN 2008b).'

'The full repercussions of the war in Iraq and the stalemate in the peace process are yet to be seen. In addition, and as always, continued insecurity in the Near East threatens more than just the region and raises the security premium of the member countries. If and when the very volatile oil price tumbles, a whole mode of development that is based mainly on oil revenues will be held in check (UN 2005a).'

'The likelihood that major macroeconomic and demographic variables will, inevitably, collide means that there is little space for argument over whether or not change is avoidable. The buildup of imbalances in a regional economy that does not expand at a rate commensurate with the demands of the demographic transition means that, unless the system experiences a chance occurrence of heavy oil rent fallout, change cannot be gauged in terms of degree (UN 2003).'

competition from scale-enhanced foreign industry. On average, economic growth rates fell for everyone, but more so for the Gulf. The combination of shrinking public-sector revenues, lower public investment, and shrivelling national industries lowered the rate of job creation even as labour-force growth rates were not as high as those of the post-independence period. In contrast, under Arab socialism, population growth rates had reached the high plateau of 2.5 per cent as of the late 1950s, and job-creation nearly matched workforce growth (AMF 2005). Ironically, neo-liberals lay the blame for high unemployment on the demographic transition and supply-side elements (as in inapposite education), in spite of the fact that population pressure tapered off as of 1990 and neo-liberally imposed cyclical contraction crushed the previously enacted decent job-creation rate.

Economic growth rates were on average higher under state *dirigisme* in the 1960s and 1970s (WDI, various years).[6] Unemployment rates were lower as well. In the two decades between the first and second oil booms (1980–2000), the AW exhibited the highest unemployment rates, the lowest average real per-capita growth rates, and the widest gap in income distribution within and across regional countries (UN 2005). With lower oil revenues, funding to the social infrastructure retrenched, causing the quality of public services to follow suit. As for economic infrastructure, in 2002 investment rates were the lowest of all regions, at 16 per cent (WDI 2002). Intra-Arab trade remained low, between 7 and 8 per cent, with much of the Gulf's excess savings channelled abroad (UN 2008b). With shrinking investment in plant and equipment and the hollowing-out of capital (in other words, with reduction of the technical composition of capital) for a good two decades (1980–2000) the AW was the global record-holder in malperformance. As evidenced by the pre-Arab Spring social disaster, when the new oil boom arrived in 2003, the policy of freer markets had already distorted resource-allocation mechanisms and most growth resulted in anti-development outcomes. In 2003, Saudi Arabia needed to sell its oil at $18 per barrel to balance its budget (UN 2005). In 2015, a $100 price per barrel is required for the Saudis to offset their government spending (Hallinan 2015). Rough estimates indicate that Saudi Arabia will draw down its financial reserves within a period of ten years, given oil prices hold steady at around $50 per barrel. For a state to quintuple its rate of dependency on oil revenues in the span of decade is indelible proof of massive industrial and developmental failure.

---

6 All Arab states adopted a high degree of dirigisme, or government intervention, in their economies. Arab socialism represented a higher degree of dirigisme combined with pre-distribution and nationalisation/socialisation of assets and key sectors in the economy.

Whole cities in the Gulf ('Cities of Salt', as per the metaphor of Saudi novelist Abdul Rahman Munif, 1987) that were constructed with little concern for energy conservation serve as monuments of the type of low output to capital ratio investment that the rest of the AW copied. Imported technology neither linked up with local industry nor deepened the production value chain (Krogstrup and Matar 2005). The combination of cultural retreat related to the sinking knowledge attendant to the development of national industry and unemployment in the absence of socialist ideological alternatives facilitated the growth of spiritual fatalism. With capital becoming more united across borders (universalising through financialisation), and its organisation becoming more effective through international financial institutions, the old–new cultural phenomenon of political, and later Salafi, Islam – beginning with colonial backing for the objectification of constructed forms of identity into states – splintered working classes. The schism in consciousness – between what it takes for the working class to grasp a higher share of the social product and the illusory ideas that sanctify private property and expropriation as entitlements – gaped further.

In the 1960s and 1970s, oil revenues funded the social and productive infrastructure through a high rate of public investment. As of 2002, rising oil revenues had leveraged speculative activities on poorly regulated stock markets that had grown several-fold in the previous ten years (WDI, various years). Hollow growth meant that the official unemployment rate for Arab countries went down cumulatively by around 3 percentage points for some 50 percentage points of growth between 2002 and 2011 (WDI, various years). A comparison between economic *dirigiste* regimes and the 'free market' shows that it is in the diminishing role of national agents in development and consequent declining public investment that the difference lies. As public investment fell, private investment failed to fill the gap left behind. As the former national agents of development – the military in alliance with broad sections of the professional working class and bureaucratic elites – integrate with international financial markets, a class emerges whose task is not to industrialise and trade within the region but rather to gradually dismantle the state. This class (the newly evolved merchant/comprador class) effectively becomes part of the international financial class, albeit a subordinate partner in the imperialist relationship, for whom (the combined comprador and imperialist) war is not only a profitable endeavour, but also a condition of its very existence as capital. The AW is a peculiar case; the high frequency of conflicts in a strategic region such as this turns war-for-the-sake-of-war into a medium of accumulation. The Arab wars and their associated war economy are more relevant to imperialism than buying and selling dates, cars and so forth to a part of the global working class whose income is a mere one third of 1 per cent of global income. Accumulation by wars of encroachment, the imperialist wars that strip nations of their autonomy and resources, as opposed to market realisation is now the mode of integration of the AW into the global economy. The implications of war to finance, imperialist power repositioning and imperial rents, as will be seen later, necessitates the disempowerment of Arab working classes and their states.

The AW as a whole has undergone shrinkage in output per worker, and the quantity and quality of the consumption bundle of the working class has deteriorated relative to the rise in the historically determined level required for working-class reproduction. The AW's ruling classes have become fully articulated with world capital as subordinate partners willing to set their own nations ablaze as their wealth becomes dollarised. This class alliance with imperialism is a form of apoptosis, the internationally conjoined class of capital killing part of itself to maintain its strength. The Arab losses in successive wars and the severely tilted balance of military forces against their nations leave working classes with little room to exercise their civil and national rights. These stark quantitative and qualitative divergences from the development path of the rest of the world newly characterise the way the AW is integrated with the global economy. These divergences did not spring from the reification-driven policies of neo-liberalism (reification is Georg Lukacs's term for the process, described by Marx in Capital vol. I, in 'The Fetishism of Commodities and the Secret Thereof') by which relations between human beings appear as relations between things – *thingification* of social processes.[7] Rather, they emerge from intermediated human agency in historical time or, more aptly, from shifts in Arab class structure. Policies are mere instruments that serve class interests. What are the new classes that shifted policies, and how did conditions deteriorate as such?

From Arab Socialism Onwards

Something striking when reading Arab economic history is the dictum that import substitution or *dirigiste* policies have somehow 'run their course'. Policies do not run things; people organised along class lines do. During the post-independence years, development in Arab socialist states was led by an alliance of the military and the working class. The army

---

7 As a synonym of 'thingification', the inverse of personification, reification refers to the transformation of human properties, relations, processes, actions, concepts etc. into things that act as pseudo-persons, endowed with a life of their own'. F. Vandenberghe (2001) 'Reification: History of the Concept', *Logos*, vol. 14, no. 1. See also Section I 'Reification and the Consciousness of the Proletariat' in Georg Lukács (1967) *History & Class Consciousness* (London: Merlin Press).

was the dominant partner in this relationship and played a progressive role by placating populist aspirations for a more egalitarian distribution. The army, the state bureaucracy and the leadership of the working class formed a state bourgeois class and exercised collective ownership of the state, characterised as what Hussein and Abdel-Malek termed a *proxy bourgeoisie* (Abdel-Malek 1967; Hussein 1971). Under Arab socialism, the predominant relationships remained capitalist, and the exploitative control of the labour process necessary for value creation persisted. However, by creating the financial space for the expansion of state-led industrial investment, investing in social infrastructure and undertaking vast land reform and redistribution measures, the Arab socialist model dramatically outperformed the current neo-liberal model in economic and social dynamism. Beginning with the neo-liberal model, however, the military re-allied itself with the merchant class and global financial capital. In the new ethos, 'generals aspired to be merchants', which weakened the national security front considerably. The old state bourgeois class transformed itself into a full-fledged comprador class. In this new ruling class alliance, the nationalist army no longer held sway. The Arab ruling class became a subordinate partner of imperialism. Social conditions in Arab states have since worsened, contributing to massive uprisings at a time when socialist ideology as an alternative is no longer readily comprehendible. As a result, social formations collapsed and states crumbled, and Islamists of various sorts rose to authority, enrobing neo-liberal usurpation in divine fiat.

Setting aside for a moment the much-discussed disaster of neo-liberalism: wars upon the AW act as the instrument by which social and non-monetised resources and labour are coercively engaged in the formation of value under capitalist accumulation. Wars on an *already defeated* AW have served multiple overlapping functions:

- to maintain US control of oil supplies through military hegemony;
- to stabilise a financial order in which the dollar remains the world reserve currency and wealth-holding medium;
- to reinforce militarism and religious and ultranationalist ideologies;
- to assist in the compression of the global wage and, ultimately,
- to hold at bay ascendant and competing imperialist powers with US-led capital.

The violence of imperialism boosts capital's principal ideological drive to achieve the division of the working class by fanning hatred. Materially, imperialist wars cheapen capital inputs and labour power supplies. To date, the US still assumes surrogate sovereignty over the whole of the Gulf – Iran excluded, although its ruling class wishes to partner with a reluctant US-led imperialism. This control itself affords US-led financial circles seignorage rights and imperial rents that exceed petrodollar flows from the AW and extend their sources of revenue far beyond its boundaries.

However, the economic mainstream posits that private earnings in non-warring periods hold steady, and that even military industries can still perform profitably in peacetime conditions. More salient mainstream commentators point out that much of the Third World is trivial money-wise to the West – it is too poor to trade with – and therefore the West can prosper without it. Both views, though, are falsifications of fact. The grim social conditions, the battered countries and labour organisations that pave the way for higher profits, do so at various lags. Fuller conceptualisation of events is not only about where to draw the timeline of the points at which various inputs, such as the initial securing of cheapened labour and raw materials by capital, increase production and profits; but also the recognition of the fact that war is a permanent feature of the global capitalist condition. One might also suggest that the West could do without colonisation or imperialist intervention, but there has never been a time without imperialist intervention. Such scenarios are counterfactual, and the study of history disallows the inclusion of the hypothetical except where it serves as an analytical illustrative tool to elucidate a fact (Hobsbawm 1998).

The capital-production process is an integrated whole. One must assess its parts in relation to the whole picture. In any first-year psychology textbook, the symptoms of a certain class of severe schizophrenic depressions are said to include the oddity of partial vision. Instead of seeing the whole picture at once, the patient sees only a skewed section of the whole. If the patient is viewing the painting of a human body, for example, that patient is seeing only a foot or a head although he or she is at an adequate distance from the image to see the entire body. One of many causes for such a strand of mental illness is said to be spitefulness. In much the same way, Eurocentric economic thinking (including some versions of Marxism) claims to be unable to 'see' value extracted from the Third World (because it is too small in price terms) while simultaneously writing off much of the world and its history from the global production picture. But value is formed by a historical process of dispossession.

> By the time a commodity has gone through numerous nodes of a global chain to arrive at the doorstep of the consumer, it has incorporated not only the inputs of low-paid labour-power but also massive amounts of underpaid and unpaid labour and ecological inputs. Capitalists drain hidden surpluses from household and informal-sector activities. A long dark-value chain of food producers and informal-sector activities is needed to generate the productive capacity and the

survival maintenance of every waged labourer. This flow of dark value lowers the reproduction costs of peripheral labour and, thus, the wage level that capitalists pay. These household and informal sectors are not outside capitalism, but are intrinsic components of global commodity chains. (Lauesen and Cope 2015)

In the context of the AW (also Africa), one may add that the darkest of the dark value is generated by colonial and imperialist wars. Money values reflect deep-seated social and political processes. For example, if workers are banned from organising and imprisoned for seeking higher wages, their share of income will decline over time. Similarly, for Europe to self-develop, it had to obstruct the Third World's autonomy and block its industrialisation. As happens in countries in which labour representation is weak, European colonialism and later imperialism also reduce Third World countrywide representation and its share of income in money value. To juxtapose the final money-income to the value of people is to not see the history of commercial exploitation.[8] In exactly the same manner as a mentally ill person imbued with hate sees only a part of a whole picture, mainstream social science refuses to assign value and determinacy to Third World labour's contribution to an organic global production process. It is not only a question of how much value the Third World contributed or whether global wealth could have occurred without violent Western interaction with the Third World (throughout this work, Western is an ideological descriptor and *not* a geographic one); wealth is the result of a determining stepping stone, the pedestal by which the West rose in Marx's language, which is the commercial exploitation inherent in colonial and imperial wars of aggression.

In an exponentially growing system that metabolises humanity and nature at progressively higher rates, the social relations that enhance economic growth in its money-form aspect piggyback on the most aggressive of capitalist relationships: imperialism. Wars, as an exercise of violence and as major events that generate the symbolism of power, entail *imperial rents*. These rents

---

8 The concept of commercial exploitation can best be illustrated with Marx's remark when addressing the genesis of capitalism in *Capital*, vol. 1 (1867): '[T]he veiled slavery of the wage workers in Europe needed, for its pedestal, slavery pure and simple in the new world'. It is about reducing the social relationship of subject-object to object only, or to grab resources whose collective ownership was dismantled. Just like slavery: imperialism grabs resources for nothing; similarly as slaves cannot negotiate their wages and work for no wages, countries could be reduced to slave like position when their will to rule themselves is sapped. Another way to put forth the point in terms of value relations is to say that the quantification of value in imperialist constructed prices leaves out all the grabbed resources and unpaid and low-paid Third World labour whose slave-like poverty conditions are the product of colonialism and imperialist policy. In the tradition of Marx, Smith (2016) highlighted that the super-exploitation of the periphery provides the foremost mitigating factor against the declining rate of profit.

are the totality of benefits, economic, cultural and otherwise, that the empire enjoys – not only by exploiting the Third World but also by limiting its development. Although Amin (2012) attempts a quantitative assessment of imperial rents, he underestimates the value because he does not take into account the historical momentum of imperialist power building that keeps shifting the playing field in favour of imperialism and, hence, the totality of the benefits accruing as historical surplus value (as per Abdel-Malek [1963] 1981). Abdel-Malek's chapter on the definition of historical surplus value includes the following:

> Historical surplus value designates the looting of all major continents as of the fifteenth century and the accumulation of their wealth in the then rising bourgeoisies of the West. The roots of violence and the roots of global war lie in the historical restructuring of the international order, that is, the formation of western hegemony, rooted in the historical surplus value from the fifteenth century onwards. This strangely ignored condition by western academia considers capitalist surplus value as if it was a product of the last stage of the history of mankind and or a product of the of the last phase of the class struggle, during which the bourgeoisies were to exploit the working class. The historical surplus value is not limited to economics, raw material, energy, resources, land and space etc., it above all provided Europe with the means to secure world hegemony. Historical surplus value provided the grounds for the rise of the scientific and technological revolution. Its geopolitics furnished Europe with the means of control of the world via sea routes while the dissemination of ideas from the centre via communication technologies dictated the theories and conceptions for the third world to grow into. As such, the ethical-normative position by which the Western liberal left judges violence as a pathology of the system, or as an exogenous syndrome, conceals the fact that the historical context and its colonial policies were laid down by the violence of European imperialism, and that Asia, Africa and Latin America could only develop along the lines suggested by Western schools of thought. Imperialism as a central factor in the power structure of modern times was viewed in its immediacy and not as a contemporary expression of a historical process. (Abdel-Malek 1981, 71–73)

The United States, for instance, still imposes upon many parts of the world an amount of American television drama time that national visual media must air, even if against their wishes. Imperial rents cannot easily be reversed with protectionist Third-Worldist policies alone; they also require civilisational turnarounds (Abdel-Malek 1981; Frank 1998). In one aspect of imperial rents, as conflicts around the world escalate and risk premiums rise in dollarised transactions, the creation of financial wealth attendant on dollar-money growth and its flows into the US-led financial market gain speed. Wars abet the process of world dollarisation. They shock and expand the money supply, providing more credit to financial institutions. It is not just in oil or weapons sales that the bulk of profits is made; it is in the trillions of dollars of debt issued to finance wars and the power structure that releases value back to empire by dollarisation and financial flows. The combined cost of the Iraq and Afghan wars is nearly six trillion dollars (Bilmes 2013), which constitute a great part of the revenues of the US-led capitalist class. Estimates of the service of war debt in total American debt vary according the method of measurement. Foster et al. (2008) estimate that a little over half of US government debt-service finances past wars, nearly 60 per cent of tax dollars in discretionary US government spending funds current militarism, and in 2007, real total US military spending amounted to about 8 per cent of GDP. By 2015, Lindorff (2015) estimates that 69 per cent of each tax dollar supports military spending. He explains that the media presents a smaller figure 'by sleight of hand, because it does not break out just the discretionary budget, or point out the parts of the budget that are outside the Pentagon but that are still really military-related, and then lump the huge outlays for Social Security benefits and Medicare into the overall spending budget, although the latter are partly auto-funded by a Trust fund of some $1.7 trillion, which was created over the years by specially dedicated payroll taxes separately paid by workers and their employers over the working life of each person'.[9] Although countervailed by the hegemony and the wealth drawn from the dollarisation of the world economy, as government, private and corporate US debts are added, the total in 2011 would 'indeed exceed 350 per cent of GDP and is much more than double what it was in the early 1970s' (Goodwin et al. 2015).

So much liquidity was available prior to the 2007–2008 crisis that the leverage power in finance allowed a speculator to borrow nearly fifty dollars for every dollar he or she deposited in the banks (Liu 2008). Almost-free money was loaned to institutional investors without collateral, yet the 2007–2008 crisis is blamed on poor home owners. The creation of unwarranted supplies of money to satisfy higher financial profit rates necessitate future wars to underwrite superfluous dollar debts.

An economy in hypothetical space (approaching a steady state) tends to exhibit steadily lower growth rates. Shocks represented by fiscal or monetary expansions or new technical discoveries may lift such an economy out of its

---

9 According to the Congressional Budget Office (CBO) the discretionary budget is about 40 percent of total government spending. https://www.cbo.gov/sites/default/files/114th-congress-2015-2016/graphic/51112-discretionaryspending.pdf (Viewed 2 March 2016)

slump. Also, tautologically, a rising profit rate entails a larger share of the income pie for capital vis-à-vis labour's income share, especially as the political power of labour wanes. A lower wage share lowers consumption demand and output. Left to uninterrupted expansion, growth rates will fall unless demand and supply are managed simultaneously to keep labour's share of income rising uninterruptedly. To achieve this not only requires stabilising opposing political forces (capital versus labour) but also obliges a plan to manage resources throughout the supply chain by setting production prices at values that address income imbalances within the working class and the needs of a just society. For example, low-paid agricultural workers would have their produced commodities priced higher and their wages rise to comparably higher wages within the national economy. This is obviously more than Keynesian demand management; it is edging toward an equalising tax structure imposed on production, or perhaps even planning. For this to work, it entails rising incomes and equalisation of product revenues by workers across sectors.

Demand management or its ultra-version in planning are anathema to free-market doctrine (only theoretical comparisons are given here; ideologically, demand management is a capitalist measure, and planning is a step up to end capitalism). Anyway, these Keynesian and socialist policy designs are also ideologically defunct at the present historical stage. The anarchy of the free market and the ideological hold of capital have generated highly inequitable income shares and suppressed the demand drivers of the economy. Hence, along with interest-rate reduction – which, as a result of the crisis of confidence underpinned by weak demand under-financialisation no longer has the immediate bearing on growth it used to enjoy – imperialist war becomes the chief strategic shock instrument, whose success in undervaluing developing nations' resources dynamises the US-led global business cycle. Wars stimulate credit expansion and technological innovation and restructure power and income shares, leading to higher profit rates. Even if war is fought by proxies of empire and appears to have no monetary bearing on the economy, the shifting balance of forces in international relations alone adds to imperial standing and subsequently to imperial rents.

On its own, money – and its value signification – cannot explain itself: how it came to be or how the world transitions from one state into another. If money accounts could explain social transitions, the world would be too simple to explain; it would need only accountants and not social scientists. Money is a mediated manifestation of deeper social relationships of production and exchange. For the money-rents to flow to empire, the ruling class and its decision structures must reproduce the power undergirding their position – using both violent and nonviolent means. Staying ahead requires the use of power, especially ideological power. US leadership in the international division of labour, to which the contribution of technology – much of which derived from military R&D – is foundational, implies that the formalised agencies of capital – that is, nearly all effective national and international institutions – will promote war and its associated industry, save the agencies resisting and escaping the ideological hegemony of capital. The justification for war is often framed as an existential threat, as in the requirement to respond to some peripheral nation threatening the American way of life. However, underneath the rhetoric there is a sequence of events that determines the value circuit and capital flows: these events constitute the US-led imperialist power endorsing the dollar money supply and its capacity for the production of knowledge (militarily induced technology), which together act as the purveyors of financial wealth through war and technology rents.

If one relies on the current profits amassed in money-form to explain why there were colonial or imperial wars in the AW or Africa, the reasons one finds would be insignificant. In the latter stages of colonialism, the money-value extricated from the poorer corners of the developing world became negligible in comparison to incomes and trade volumes circulating within the more industrialised regions. In fact, if one counts aid, it is possible that the developed nations may appear to be unnecessarily charitable toward their undeveloped partners. With exceptions like the works of Baran (1957), Amin (1974 [1957]) Emmanuel (1972) and others, notably Abdel-Malek (1961), Eurocentric accounts have judged imperialism by the superficial appearances of money and have concluded that the money-profits from the Third World are neither worth the effort nor serve as justification for colonial wars. On the basis of such mistaken assessments, the cause of war can be avidly assigned to a civilising mission. That the West credulously undertakes war to civilise others – and persistently makes blunders resulting in unintended consequences – speaks volumes about its 'naiveté': one pleads, when can the ruling Western classes stop being such good folk?

In addition to mediating the contradiction between use value and exchange value, money-value resolves a series of social, political and production-exchange relationships-cum-contradictions, which include colonisation, bombing for raw material, co-opting unions and so on. Without the suppression of labour as a political force and the dislocation of peripheral peoples, money would not possess the value it bears in the West vis-à-vis its value in the AW and Africa. The ceaseless propping-up of the power platforms underpinning exchange is a shifting process that assigns value by force or by stripping the owners of commodities of their power to negotiate. The whole idea that the West can survive or has survived in trade isolation from the poorest countries is too absurd to discuss. An oft-cited proverb in the weekly souks of Mount Hermon says that if one bargains to buy something for a very cheap price, one ought to make sure that the owner of the item for sale is dead. The war process drives the class power restructuring, the auto-conflicting relationship between different national capitalists, which cements the hold of imperialist classes on property and, as such, it is inseparable from the necessity of value destruction and value creation under capitalism.

Imperialist assaults are necessary and mediate the contradictions at the root of global capital. The strategic value of the Arab region brings us ever closer to a condition where the primacy of politics (or the subordination of economic concerns to political ones) is realized for the purpose of firming up the capital relationship. Imperialist oil control and war objectives intertwine to rain down one blow after another upon the working peoples of the region. War saps resources, and the loss of a war is a watershed event that remoulds the dominant ideology (the objective stock of knowledge instrumentised to serve the interest of capital). The chain 'defeat-destroy-disengage assets' is the form of articulation of the Arab formation with US capital. It issues from outright US military superiority and hegemony, and the reproduction of wars of encroachment, to diminish Arab state sovereignty – that is, working-class representation mediated in national and policy autonomy. Continuous defeats are followed by the decline of nationalist ideology. This decline accompanies the ruling classes accommodating the terms of surrender by instilling a perverse rationale whereby society justifies its own dismemberment. To reverse Badiou's (2014) optimism regarding events, wars as events are ruptural in relation to the dominant order, destroying the dominant state of the situation and writing off constructive alternatives.

From a people who, in the era of Arab socialism, believed in a shared Arab identity with egalitarian goals, the Arab masses' negative ideology – as per an extreme version of Larrain (1983), which is a distorted view of the real processes enacted in sectional identity politics – permits them again and again to re-elect to power the same ruling class, under neo-liberalism. This is more than just a case of false consciousness instilled by the cultural arsenal of Islamist politics; it is an unthinkable perversion of reality, in which the alternative of a better world has disappeared, and the masses of people are left to compete for imperialistically imposed limited resources, or for resources that are plentiful but that are made scarce by the distributional policies of capital. In the present epoch, there is precious little in the cultural debate to delegitimise the transfers of value away from the working class or, similarly, to condemn the rising death rate from war and disease in the Third World. This vanishing of alternatives to capitalism and its agendas is a hideous novelty in modern history.

Emerging in a state of war in the second half of the twentieth century, the Arab states spent double the world average on defence (WDI various years). But it is not higher rates of defence spending that in themselves constitute national security; far more important is the totality of cultural-cum-productive structures that secure the needs of the working class. When arming the Egyptian army prior to the Six-Day War in 1967, the Soviets worried that so many Egyptian soldiers were illiterate and would not be able to operate their weapons systems. Security, per se, is a condition derived from better livelihoods and cultural and industrial development. As regimes weaken after defeat, their policies and security spending veer away from working-class security (or the security of people and state as a whole) and toward regime stability and the security of the class controlling the state apparatus. The changes in resource flows involve ideological revisions, which, as elsewhere around the world, correlate with the rise of neo-liberalism as the ideology of capital. It is at this conjunction of military defeats and neo-liberalism that wars begin to raise the cost of maintaining the security of the working class. The earliest break with the nationalist ideological status quo became manifest with the reforms of Anwar Sadat in Egypt in May 1971, which, by 1977 resulted in the first popular anti-regime protests, known as the 'Bread Riots'.[10] Since then, social conditions have been deteriorating across the AW. To make matters worse, as the crisis deepened, its neo-liberal ideology rose to occupy a policy position to which there was no other alternative. Maldistribution and war – or at least war's inevitable threat – weakened the state as the agency of development. In this book, I follow the descent of development from the days of Arab socialism, focusing on the conditions of three former Arab socialist states: Egypt, Syria and Iraq. I begin by defining and exposing the Arab socialist development experience vis-á-vis neo-liberalism. I then turn to specific development patterns in these three states and examine their different processes of developmental descent. In the last two chapters, the focus shifts to the perverse transformation under neo-liberalism, whereby a huge reserve army of labour was created, and ends with a discussion of what it means to be integrated into global economy via the combined channels of war and oil; the latter being a form of commercial exploitation, which reduces subject-object to object (resources without owners) and enslaves whole countries.

Chapter 1: Arab socialism in retrospect

Prior to the ongoing counter-revolutionary phase, the neo-liberal Arab state depressed wages, lifted its protection of national industry, set single exchange and interest rates and opened up trade and capital accounts with the intention of readying cheapened national resources for transfer abroad. This chapter

---

10 '36 Years after the "Bread Uprising": Egypt's Struggle for Social Justice Lives On', 2013. Online: http://english.ahram.org.eg/NewsContent/1/64/62785/Egypt/Politics-/-years-after-the-Bread-Uprising-Egypts-Struggle-fo.aspx (viewed 5 November 2015)

traces the metamorphosis of the state bourgeois class in Arab socialist countries, namely Egypt and Syria, into the neo-liberal-cum-comprador class. With the exception of Iraq, which was crushed from without by the force of outright occupation, the other states experienced gradual social erosion leading to uprisings from within. This chapter reassesses the social and economic development under Arab socialism and examines how, as neo-liberalism dawned, the state bourgeois class underwent a transformation from a surrogate national bourgeoisie to a surrogate international financial bourgeoisie.

Chapter 2: The devastation of peace in Egypt

This chapter begins with the premise that a disempowered Egypt is relevant for value transfers from Africa to the AW. A brittle Egyptian social formation contributes to imperial rents being more than they would be in an Egypt developing along industrial lines which, under the appropriate policy interface, would empower its working population. Low historically determined subsistence levels for broad sections of the working class were brought about by Egypt's loss of two principal wars, the signing of the Camp David Accords, and the introduction of a process of economic liberalisation that began in the 1980s. But instead of a post–Camp David peace dividend leading to further development, Egypt slid further into misery. By applying neo-liberal policy, Egypt was paying the conqueror tribute derived from the resources that otherwise would have strengthened its working class and, by implication, national security. The systematic weakening of Egypt and its incorporation into the US-led imperialist orbit was part of US-led imperialism achieving its broader goals in Africa and the Middle East. Economic stabilisation arrangements, as in US or Gulf aid, are secondary in relation to the broader US-led imperialist hegemony.

Chapter 3: The infeasibility of revolution in Syria

This chapter assesses the policies of the Arab socialist experience and investigates the history or the social class that precipitated the social disaster in Syria. There is an ideological blame game that vulgarly personalises class relations with the aim of exonerating this or that side in the war. This chapter attempts to dispel the mystification attendant upon such facile explanations. The subject of history is the social force that moulds ideological and social relationships to ensure an outcome favouring its class interests. The chapter focuses on the circulation of capital under Arab socialism and later under neo-liberalism as it veered away from the Syrian working class. Under neo-liberalism, the regime abandoned the old Arab socialist strategy of combining development with security objectives. It formally split the economics of resistance from the politics of resistance and, instead, destructively pursued resource-grabbing. With this transformation, the Syrian state became only secondarily the Syrian regime's means of repression and exploitation; that means was principally imperialism. This chapter argues against the perception that a small clique in a somewhat isolated state like Syria makes history. The social forces that produced the conditions for blind accumulation (short-termism competition for profits without concern for social stability) when the Syrian regime combined absolute political and economic power are the imperialistically imposed terms on which the regime engages in economic activity. As socialist ideology ebbs and labour, as an internationalist power, fragments, US-led capital continues to be the uncontested subject of history. This chapter concludes that given Syria's geostrategic position and the political mileage that imperialist forces gain from having a foothold there, it is presently impossible for a social democratic revolution to succeed.

Chapter 4: Iraq then and now

This chapter examines the historical causation behind the destruction of the Iraqi state. In the two decades after 1958, Iraq made considerable social and economic advances. Yet, despite rising oil revenues since the 2003 invasion, violence, poverty and destitution are rampant. The windfall profits from oil have entrenched a divisive social mode that has been put to the service of global capital. While the AW rebels against abjection in favour of civil liberties, in Iraq the sectarian divide preempted the grounds for revolt. In point of fact, there is no true singular state with a government to rebel against; there are many 'Iraqs'. The decapitation and immiserisation of Iraq strengthened American hegemony over the global accumulation structure.

Chapter 5: The perverse transformation

Much has been said about the neo-liberal fiasco in the AW and elsewhere. The Arab Spring exposed the disaster. In this chapter, I re-examine the capital process by looking into its most defining constituent, the labour process and, specifically, into rising proletarianisation under neo-liberalism. I examine how wars and neo-liberal polices served as the means of massive labour-force dislocation at a time when job creation was decelerating at a tremendous rate. Evicting the peasants from the land, making them into wage labourers and depriving them of their private means of subsistence combine into a process of socialisation that intensifies the contradictions of capitalism. Massive socialisation of the labour force was accompanied by increasing privatisation of output and rising inequality. I show how redundancy and working-class insecurity are even more necessary to financially integrated capital. The abundance of the reserve army of labour implies that the horror of a wage system devoid of labour representation works itself more aggressively into the labour process, which circularly determines the global structure of capital and its power. When there is a need for an excessive and low-priced labour-power commodity, and when that commodity stands above people and rules over them, for capital to dispose of that commodity it has to render human lives more dispensable than they already are.

Chapter 6: Permanent war in the Arab World

In the final chapter, I pay a closer look at the operation of imperialism in an Arab context. Intertwined with oil control, imperialist-sponsored wars in the AW have become an ends in themselves. Every economic process has social and political underpinnings that render the making of exponential profits possible. These social and political relationships are labour's expropriation, disciplining and regimentation, which assume the form of wholesale pillage in the AW and Africa.[11] The intensity of repression in these corners of the globe is related to the law of value (the mediation of use and exchange values through power-derived price systems) inseminating the easily penetrable social formations. Cheapened human and natural resources extracted from insecure formations along with ways of controlling crucial territories and strategic resource flows also reinforce imperialist positioning. The rates of exploitation appear to not contribute very much to value creation from the productivity (relative surplus value) side, but surplus value per se would not have existed without primitive accumulation *cum* commercial exploitation, which involved the consumption of the labourer along with his or her labour power. The drainage of historical social wealth is accomplished as the accumulation of surplus value from the moment the debilitation of the colony begins. The value derived from inhibiting industrialisation in the colony, and the impetus that the rate of destruction of wealth in the periphery realises since primitive accumulation, never comes to rest, together contributing to an iterative wealth-making process that requires not only living labour to be consumed in production, but also living labourers to literally perish in the

---

11 The process of recurring forms of primitive accumulation, meaning the socialising of the workforce, in the insecure periphery of the AW does not displace labourers from the land to rehire them in industry as happened in England; primitive accumulation in the war-integrated areas such as the AW leads not to factory-type exploitation; it rather leads to commercial exploitation.

colonies, or on the periphery where forms of primitive accumulation resolved into commercial exploitation persist. Measuring values by the sum of prices is like squaring the circle, especially in the peripheral economy, where these prices are determined by imperialist fiat. Value creation as such becomes a derivative of human annihilation set against an exponentially rising metabolic rate of capital accumulation. Seen from the point of commercial exploitation, whose first instantiations involved slavery and genocide, wars in the AW are a necessary by-product of the crisis of global capital.

Postscript

State-led as opposed to market-led development under neo-liberalism did not just appear on the world stage circa 1980 out of nowhere. Its recent history is rooted in the decline of the world 'socialist' camp and its ideology, which began with the Sino-Soviet split in the early 1960s.[12] At that time, Nikita Khrushchev taunted the United States that the Soviet Union had reached outer space first and would soon put more sausages on East European tables. The 'more sausage' line drew both ridicule and critique from hardline Communists. The emphasis implied by Kruschev's remark on diverting resources to consumption at home in the Soviet Union and away from supporting national liberation movements abroad implied that the Soviets wanted to build a more affluent 'socialism' at home and to peacefully compete with the United States in improving standards of living. But it was not only the inapposite belief in peaceful competition with the United States upheld by sections of the Soviet ruling class or the exorbitant costs of the military arms race that ushered in the decline of the idea of state control of the economy; it was also the ideological rift that divided the world 'socialist' camp. In retrospect, one can see that a combination of Cold War costs, relative loss of

12 The idea of neo-liberalism itself dates back to the Austrian school of economics. It was later heralded by Milton Friedman in his 'Neo-Liberalism and Its Prospects', Farmand, 17 February 1951, http://0055d26.netsolhost.com/friedman/pdfs/other_commentary/Farmand.02.17.1951.pdf (viewed 15 March 2016). Although Friedman assumed that the early fifties were the right time for a turn in events by which the billions of people begin to choose what to consume guided by a 'system of prices that will allocate resources efficiently,' the end of collectivist ideology dawned when the Soviets and other national liberation movements began to place their ruling class interests above commitment to internationalism, and it later peaked with the collapse of the Soviet Union. The 'prices' of which Friedman speaks are the product of power relations intended to deprive the working classes of the living security gains achieved via collective struggle. Ideas do not assume a real living shape unless victorious historical forces resurrect them in form, but not in content, to meet their historically specific requirements.

first-strike capability and a class of social imperialists using the metaphor of the sausage to acquire more wealth via the medium of the state – these together brought the Soviet Union to ruination, and with it the utopia of socialism. I want to state very cautiously, knowing the difficulty of the subject, that for the sake of continuity in the argument it was essentially the shift in the ideological foundation of the Soviet ruling class from commitment to internationalism to commitment to their own prosperity that unravelled the Soviet socialist experiment.

More sausages on the table entailed the idea that some sort of moneyed incentive is required to mobilise individual productivity that would raise the standard of living in the Soviet camp. This pernicious myth of individual money incentives – the central pillar of 'free market' propaganda – would feed Soviet class antagonisms and the rise of neo-liberalism as the nouveau ideology of capital. While support for the industrialisation of China and the developing world was attenuated by the cliché of US–Soviet peaceful coexistence, capitalism was, in in the background, beginning to devour socialism. Initially, Soviet 'socialism in one country' created a huge anti-imperialist state that would catalyse national liberation movements in the developing world. The process of introversion (socialism in one country would be criticised by the European left for delaying the onset of revolution in Europe, but later would be praised in the Third World for creating a viable anti-imperialist bloc under whose shade many national liberation movements gained independence. As of the split with China in the early 1960s, the Soviets began to shift more resources to peacetime consumerism at the expense of supporting the potential rise of Third World resistance and autonomy.

Tangentially, one should not draw conclusions on the basis of the argument that Europe was more developed or technologically readier to make the transformation to socialism than was less-developed Russia or the Third World, as in Deutscher (1964 or 1967). The Eurocentric bent reeks of chauvinism even when it originates in Marxism. Speaking of China's fast 'descent into Bolshevism' because of its lack of a European cultural heritage, Deutscher (1964) remarked that 'the archaic structure of Chinese society was impermeable to European ideological ferments, and Western imperialism was unable to fructify the mind of China with any vital liberating idea'. There possibly is a 'Chinese Mind booklet' that guides US State Department work in China, a publication similar to the notoriously racist 'Arab Mind' manual that owes its conceptual grandiosity to Deutscher. Apart from the ignorance of revolutionary and egalitarian moments in Eastern history, which is often shrouded under the blanket label of 'Oriental Despotism', the idea that one society is more receptive than another to socialism because of its level of technological development contradicts Marx's views; it was not the stock of wealth and technology that Marx had in mind, it was the mode of social organisation governing the reproduction of society. Capitalist progress measured by an analytical scale of the sort that 'Europe killed hundreds of millions of natives but the remaining few can have electric showers', is not a method that Marx used to supplement his historical approach. Capitalism and its more violent form, imperialism, are born in crisis and only impart misery by the absolute general law of development of capitalism, which transcends national borders. Marx recognised the growing class-cum-wealth rift between the colonising and colonised nations and proposed that communal forms of social organisation (especially Russia) could just as equally become platforms readied for the development of socialism (Hobsbawm 1964). It is not the technological level of development proper that would ensure socialist construction, but the direct social and popular hold on the means of production that engenders a civilisation of communal social responsibility.

Many are the reasons for the fall of the Soviet Union, but as in any system that falters, the Achilles heel is ideological decline or the loss of the hold of the ruling class on the state. That fall accounts for today's rise in unfettered capitalism under the guise of neo-liberalism. Against this broader context, the downward Arab developmental spiral is conditioned by the reigning neo-liberal ideology that has hijacked working-class consciousness. Internationalist ideological retreat reproduces laggard nationalist development and invokes the worst symbols and superstitions from the cultural heritage as a way for society to cope with the diminishing opportunities for work and worsening living standards. The perceived unreliability of alternative socialist models and institutions, and the defeat and marginalisation of the international left, can only further the retrogression.

Chapter 1

ARAB SOCIALISM IN RETROSPECT

Early in the post-independence years, major socialist Arab states such as Iraq, Syria and Egypt undertook massive land reform measures, nationalised industry and financial institutions, provided universal healthcare and education and clamped down on the cycle of resource usurpation.[1] This class of Arab states sought self-sufficiency in production, endorsed import-substituting industrialization and effected public investments in heavy industry while synchronizing the demands of a growing industry with adequate human skills. In social and economic dynamics, the Arab socialist model has outperformed the ongoing neo-liberal model, which began to be implemented in the early 1980s (see Annex to this chapter for tables on economic growth records and other economic indicators for three major Arab socialist countries: Egypt, Iraq and Syria). In popular culture, this period is dubbed *Alzaman Aljamil*: 'beautiful times'. Although standards of living are historically determined, the period 1960–1980 represented an epoch in which Arab countries exhibited dynamic performance in terms of real wages growth, more equal income distribution and improvements in infant mortality and life expectancy as well as many other social indicators. Arab socialist regimes in particular have not only outshone the rest of the Arab countries, but also scored high growth averages in social and economic indicators relative to the rest of the world. With the beginning of the Arab Spring in 2011, nearly all the previous Arab socialist states experienced collapse, save Algeria, which staggers along depending more on oil revenues than on auto-development or an economy that grows and develops by relying on its own productive capabilities. The Arab socialist model may not have been super but, in comparison, neo-liberalism had stripped the working population of its previous social gains and raised the measure of repression.

Development outcomes depend on the commitment of the social class in power to real-resource mobilisation. This chapter addresses the issue of Arab

1 In addition to the three countries mentioned above, Algeria, Sudan, South Yemen and Libya are also states that followed the Arab socialist model. For the purpose of illustration, I will draw examples from only the three states and, in the chapters to follow, examine their recent developments.

socialism and investigates the structure of the class formation that shaped development in the post-independence years. The class of military officers and its adjunct ally, the intermediate stratum – composed of professionals, small capital holders, including sections of the small land-holding peasantry, which together formed the state bourgeois class (by virtue of their control over state resources) – assumed the role of agent of development during the Arab socialist phase.

As a social relationship, the intermediate stratum is codetermined by its relationship to other classes and to its sources of material and ideological reproduction. This stratum is not the middle class in the Weberian sense, or a categorisation by income, as opposed to being related to the mode of creation and appropriation of productive capital assets in their various forms. In its relationship with other classes, a social class historically acquires, in memories, symbols, institutions and forms of organisation. It is decisively defined by its forms of control over, and its property relationship with the means of production. In terms of structure, petty property owners without control, or those with access to smaller forms or amounts of productive capital, do not constitute capital. It is not theoretically sufficient to limit the definition of the working class to the absence of ownership of productive capitals or to working for capital owned by the capitalist class. It is also not sufficient to classify self-exploiting workers with petty ownership of capital as not 'working class'. Concretely, workers may be defined by their particular relationships with particular forms of capital. Moving back from the analytics of this, and seeing class as a historical relationship – one not determined by the inflated 'I' of mainstream social science realised in the ideologically slanted system of bourgeois democracy, but by the intermediated political agency arising from inherited forms of social organisations and the state of play in working-class ideology – would allow us to sufficiently grasp the real process that is intermediate class *cum* modern petty bourgeoisie. The weight of history cannot be written off; and it is not only the forms of property but also the systems of control via mediated political agency and ideology that make the appearance and evolutions of social classes the fluid historical moments that they are.

Both Poulantzas and Labica stress the difficulty of giving analytical shape – a structure – to the petty bourgeoisie. Poulantzas (1978) observes that there is no clear demarcation line between the old and the new forms of the petty bourgeoisie; their relationship in terms of the structure arising therefrom is intertwined and complex. Labica (1985) posits that *petty bourgeoisie* is a malleable concept, difficult to grapple with, but still one with bourgeois undertones that slot it within the tier with the least self-consciousness among the more definitive working social classes. This concept's variable identity, unlike the more stable proletariat or the peasantry, oscillates between the two words that compose it: petty and bourgeois (Labica 1985). The petty bourgeoisie's position in several disparate social groups is mediated as part of the contradiction between the working class and the ruling class. Meillassoux (1998) aptly uses the term 'social corps', those who are not significant proprietors but whose services are required for capital to rule. They are the service groups generated as functional to the forms of capital in question.

In an Arab context, modern class formation was born within the limping process of transformation to capitalism and under the colonial yoke; it retained many of the characteristics of the pre-capitalist class structure. However, it did so only in terms of appearance rather than essence (the dialectical category), for the latter is determined by the historically specific material and ideological circumstances underpinning the class.[2] As neo-liberal openness began to take its toll, and the earnings of the intermediate class moved from relying on rents raised by national productivity growth to geopolitical or financial rents, the intermediate class, or the old 'corps social', ceased to exist. As aptly observed by Sourani (2015), these intermediate classes could have only survived under Arab socialist regimes and, indeed, vanished as soon as the nationalist economic system was exposed to the vagaries of the international market. For very practical reasons related to activism under occupation in Gaza, Sourani delineates the successor class as the new petty bourgeoisie composed, albeit in a socially engineered order, of three echelons: high, medium and low – ranging from professionals to shopkeepers to self-employed menial workers whose power in the state is negligible. This classification issues from broad quantified averages and aids to clarify the grounds for activism – Sourani is an activist in the Occupied Gaza Strip. To Sourani, the new petty bourgeois order is more befitting of lagging production conditions under openness that predisposes many who make ends meet to do so with their own meagre means of production or subsistence.

2 The dialectical category of essence does not mean a trait that is innate to culture across history (a definition that is currently fashionable), but it is the law of motion in its totality. It is not, for instance, an essential characteristic of Islam to suppress civil liberties and that, subsequently, for Islam to be realised it would actually require a form of organisation similar to an IS caliphate. There are as many ideas and forms of thought as the infinitude of thought meeting practice; but for a certain idea from Islamic history to be resurrected in the twenty-first century requires a current form of social practice rooted in the necessities of the current era. Ideas may still share the same name, but their historical content and meaning have become something totally different. Apart from lacking respect, the current definition of essentialism is 'past alive in the present'. In such notions of essentialism, there is utter disregard for the diachronic development of concepts or the social relationships that underlie forms of social organization, which makes them more racism than social science.

Taking Labica to an extreme, Sourani also extends the variability of the petty bourgeois class position to the development of its consciousness in a reflexive manner. Because of its oscillation between working and ruling classes, the petty bourgeoisie's position swings wildly and has never been able to attain a mature class consciousness of its own (Sourani 2015). In other words, there is some ideal consciousness that is only attainable through the definiteness of being engaged in socialised wage–labour activity. The value-creating working class as the totality of a multitude of social relationships incorporates the disengaged and the self-exploiting strata as well as the 'factory employed'. It (the working class) is an organic state of being and becoming mediated by the developments in working-class organisation and consciousness. Such consciousness, however, is rooted in the historically borne organisational power of global labour and its ideological counterweight to the neo-liberal doctrine of capital – obviously more so than the isolated development in national ideological conditions. The objective basis of repression attendant upon capitalist exploitation is the immutable condition of being (there is always repression and exploitation under capital), whereas the subjective sphere or the ideological development whose ideal end is realising the demise of the wage system is historically contingent upon the class struggle despite being necessary and emancipatory. These ideological developments cannot pertain to a preenvisaged linear or nonlinear path; they are socio-historical and uncertain. Take, for instance, the recent crisis, the deaths and hunger culminating in the revolts known as the Arab Spring, in view of the uncontested avalanche of neo-liberalism: Arab misery elicited none of the measures that would even slightly dent the drudgery of the wage system.

In terms of structure, Petras (1976) points out that the intermediate stratum comprises skilled professionals – such as schoolteachers, university professors, civil servants, accountants, military officers, medical doctors, engineers and lawyers – whose status is not dependent on the ownership of property and wealth, but on their training and performance. The intermediate stratum refers to a differentiated relationship within the working class distinguished from the less-privileged working-class on the basis of salary, education, skill and, more decisively, by the degree of control over the means of production delegated to it by the military. Note that in a war context with weak institutions resulting from the potential insecurity of the state, the military emerged as the key player on the Arab political scene. The rise of the Arab bourgeoisie can be dated to European and, specifically, to early nineteenth-century Napoleonic changes to landholding laws empowering individual capitalists, but the embryonic formation of the intermediate stratum (the state bourgeois class) took hold as Arab industry in the early twentieth century grew under the shadow of European industry and war (Abdel-Malek 1968). The history of modern Arab states, like European history in the nineteenth and twentieth centuries, is a history of national movements (Rodinson 1978). Alongside the national struggle for liberation, there existed a social struggle against a national bourgeoisie that had already become an appendage to Western colonial interests and industry (Abdel-Malek 1968).

Because of the underdeveloped capacities (lacking in finance and real capital) of the national bourgeoisie at the time of independence after World War II, the state bourgeois class assumed the role of a surrogate national bourgeoisie (Hussein 1971; Abdel-Malek 1971). Accounts of the detailed aspects of the interface between national policies and their developmental outcomes show that the broad determinants of the relative success of the Arab socialist regimes stem from the fact that they tackled *security* and developmental concerns jointly. In terms of definitions, development policies remain the resource-channelling mechanisms that direct wealth flows to the social class in command. *Security* is a totality that encompasses communal and national securities, knowledge-related productive capacity, including health and education, with working-class security being the backbone of national sovereignty.

In the Arab World (AW), US-led imperialist control of oil is pivotal to maintaining the global accumulation process. In this context, Arab autonomy with respect to territory, resources and policy becomes the *sine qua non* for development. Subsequently, the reverse development or *lumpen* development, as used by A. G. Frank (1972, 17) incurred by the AW in the ongoing neo-liberal phase can be mainly attributed to the structural terms of surrender to imperialism. The neo-liberal phase did not end with the beginning of the Arab Spring. If anything, failure to redistribute plundered assets through bourgeois power in the state and continuing adherence to 'free-market' policies indicate that many of the dispossessory tendencies of the past will gain momentum under the elected or unelected governments that have resulted.

As with state-socialist or dirigisme models elsewhere around the world, the turnaround from Arab socialism to neo-liberalism occurred as a result of the retreat of socialist ideology, peaking with the demise of the Soviet Union. With successive Arab military defeats and the sinking-in of defeatism, the ideological conditions developed for the state bourgeois class in power to manifest apostasy and lead the assault on working-class security. The end of the Arab socialist project had more to do with a shifting of class alliances that structurally absorbed the terms of surrender, and with the global ideological move away from socialism, than with mass dissatisfaction with socialist measures. Egypt succumbed first, as it signed the Camp David Accords; Syria followed, with its second phase of neo-liberal reform introduced in 2000; and in the case of Iraq, despite many concessions offered by the regime to avert war, the precipitous and wholesale destruction of the social formation was necessary to capital, as opposed to the gradual descent into the neo-liberal quagmire experienced by the other countries in this study. The metamorphosed ruling class, the disarticulation of hierarchically structured factions looting the national economy, which presided over the current neo-liberal social disaster has ceased to be a surrogate national bourgeoisie; it has become a proxy for the rule of the more aggressive facet of imperialism associated with international financial capital.

As already noted, strong state intervention and state-led investment during the 1960s characterised the path of Arab socialist development. The state bourgeois class supplanted the national entrepreneurial class, promoted investment in heavy industry and, in general, built productive capacity. The rise of this class is premised on the absence of a nationalist bourgeois class, which could have acted as an agent of development (Amin 1976; Petras 1976). Not that the case of the AW is peculiar: in most of Africa and the Middle East, the postcolonial capacity debacle and the inability of the entrepreneurial business class to promote development paved the way for the rise of a ruling class made up of an alliance of the military, small landholding peasantry and the middle class, or a state bourgeois class. This mishmash of alliances led by the military became the subject of the postcolonial development project in many of the newly independent Arab states.

To further clarify: in much of the immediate post-independence AW, an entrepreneurial class was not totally absent. In Iraq, Syria and Egypt, prior to independence, sections of the national bourgeoisie with limited ties to the colonialists took part in ferocious anticolonial struggles. Yet, as soon as independence was won, the social frailty of the national bourgeoisie became evident, especially as their umbilical cords with the colonialists (through merchandise trade) were severed. From the ashes of the old classes – such as the *Wafd* in Egypt and the national block in Syria – there arose a set of military dictatorships competing in populist and genuine anti-imperialist positions. The old, colonially reared sections of the bourgeois classes were politically subjugated in the process of strengthening national independence. In an ideological tidal wave of equity and national liberation, the social inequities of colonialism were scornfully rejected and egalitarian measures were implemented to redress what was perceived to be odious development under colonialism.

Whether it is a bourgeois class per se or a state bourgeois class, the common denominator of *bourgeois* implies a similar substance to both of these classes. In an oil-producing or geopolitical rent-driven context, given the pull of a cross-border class alliance, the state bourgeois class is innately predisposed to surrender under imperialist pressure. As a bourgeois class, it can offer concessions to the working classes but cannot provide them with the civil liberties that would undermine capital as a social relationship. Braverman

(1959) foresaw the bifurcation in development lying ahead and warned that unless the working population politically participated in the making of socialism, that is it hegemonised the political process to ensure a growing share of the surplus product, the whole process of egalitarian distribution undertaken by Arab socialism could be easily reversed. The repression attendant upon the labour process implied that socialisation and egalitarian distribution could be easily overturned from above without much resistance from below once historical conditions were ripe. When frequent military routs (the 1948, 1967 and 1973 wars with Israel, to name a few) instilled a state of defeatism in the upper layers of society, and working class and civil society organisations remained appendages to one-party regimes, the class in power easily overturned the gains acquired by working people under Arab socialism.[3] That it is impossible to militarily defy nuclear-powered imperialism was the thought that encapsulated the *état d'esprit* motivating the process of de-socialisation.

By the time the uprisings occurred in 2011, the state of social devastation in the AW was so severe that the masses poured into the streets without a revolutionary plan. Their principal aim was to change the status quo, but with what? These were revolutions with neither a party vanguard nor social programs. The only organised groups were free-marketeer Islamists already operating in Gulf-funded and US-funded civil society.

The political relationships of different ruling classes to imperialism as well as their control of the means of production, including informal forms of property control via the medium of the state, underscore the transition from socialisation to privatisation. The underlying conditions for the social mutation of the ruling classes from national bourgeoisie to agent of global financial capital occurred as a result of ideological and military defeat that, in any case, has engulfed much of the world's left-leaning national movements. Defeatism erased armed struggle from the nationalist agenda and replaced it with institutions that promote 'peaceful resolutions' to the conflict with imperialism – especially in the Arab-Israeli conflict. Once the politics of compromise steer the political strategy, the natural end is for the nationalist class to fall into the lap of imperialism (Frank 1982). Time after time, armed resistance against a better-armed enemy was touted as futile. To make matters worse, under the blows of international financial capital, which prefers a higher income share

---

3 The swift defeat of Arab armies to Israel in the 1967 and 1973 wars represented an attestation to the superiority of United States' conventional weaponry. In such a strategic region, these highly publicized wars contributed to the power standing of the United States vis-à-vis the Soviet Union. The ideological impact of such military routs propped up the ideological position of the United States, offsetting its retreat elsewhere, demonstrating its industrial superiority and the efficacy of its market economy.

by seizure, it became difficult for a national alliance of classes in the AW to maintain a nationalist predisposition. Gradually, but also willingly, the Arab ruling classes internalised the terms of surrender as dictated by the Bretton Woods institutions. They have realised their potential as a bourgeois class subordinated by world capital and become modern suzerains of empire.

In exploring the subject of this chapter, the argument will pursue the shifting class structures and the changing mode of appropriation in imperialistically aggressed formations. All by itself, the topic is broad, and a single chapter will not do it justice. Capital accumulation in a developing context cannot be read using either a neoclassical outline of voluntary employment or a Keynesian full-employment framework. Under capitalism of any sort – predatory or 'docile' – a full-employment hypothesis does not even apply in a developed context, let alone in a developing one. Although necessary, demand-side (Keynes and Kalecki) approaches are also inadequate on account of frail capacity in the developing world. What is there to demand when there is little productive capacity with which to meet demand? Developmental capital accumulation is not solely the incremental rise in capital stock over time; it is primarily based on the social relationship that underpins the decision to build and recirculate the social product nationally. In Marxian phraseology, the degree of development is the degree of independence from wage slavery or 'how well off people are' even when not engaged in wage employment. Hence, the point is to explore the primacy of the social class in charge of development. In the socialist AW, as the state bourgeois class represented an alliance of the intermediate class with the military, one witnessed a marked developmental impact. However, when the class alliance became that of the military with a capitalist class that moved from industry to externally tied commerce, the result is developmental retrogression. The underlying hypotheses are: (a) changes to the class structure in the group of Arab socialist countries occurred under the weight of consecutive Arab defeats and a concomitant rise of neo-liberal ideology globally; (b) the state bourgeois class structurally fulfilled the conditions of surrender and underwent a transformation from national bourgeoisie to surrogate international financial bourgeoisie, and: (c) situated in a context of accumulation by wars of encroachment and commercial exploitation, the social formations holding by the ideology of modern nationalism are destined to come undone if US-led imperialism holds sway in the sphere of international power relations.

The line of thought in this chapter tracing the changing nature of the state bourgeois class from nationalist to comprador will be structured as follows. In what follows, I examine the relevance, to a developing Arab context, of the concept of state capitalism and state-led development. In the section titled 'The State Bourgeois Class', I investigate the state bourgeoisie, its frailty and its predisposition to capitulate to imperialism. The colonial legacy and its weak entrepreneurial class in the AW will be analysed in the sections 'Colonial Plunder and Beyond' and 'A Frail Arab Bourgeois Class'. No discussion of this specific Arab experience in development can proceed without exploring the dominant role of the military in power; hence, in the section titled 'The Military in Power', the rise of the military to power, its transformation into a comprador segment of the ruling class and the versatility it exhibited when faced with successive defeats are detailed. The section 'Arab Socialism' deals with the historical achievements of the Arab socialist experience and the reasons for its collapse.

State-Led Development

In characterising socio-political entities like Arab socialist states, Kalecki (1972) employed the concept of 'intermediate regimes'. He describes those regimes as being neither strictly capitalist, as foreign influence on them was limited, nor truly socialist. On an international level, intermediate regimes obtained credits from both socialist and imperialist camps. In the case of Egypt's Nasser regime, for instance, the archives of the US State Department from 1958 to 1961 reveal how Nasser acquired American Hawk missiles in addition to being tempted with credit from the United States in an effort to dissuade him from forming an alliance with the Soviet Union.[4]

Gramsci ([1928] (1978)) tackled class formations in peripheral Eastern and Southern European societies and noted the conspicuous rise of an intermediate stratum that occupied middle-of-the-road functions between the state and the workers or peasant populations. A broad spectrum of intermediate classes stretches between the proletarian and capitalist classes and seeks to carry on policies of their own, with ideologies that influence broad layers of the proletariat but that particularly affect the peasants and rural communities.

The intermediate strata in the AW had partnered with the military in an Arab-Israeli war context but did not own significant properties apart from those for personal use. The power afforded to these strata during the Arab socialist age was delegated to them by the military. Though subordinated to the military, they effectively became part of the ruling nomenclature as a result of the expanding bureaucracy and by means of their indirect control of the economy via the state bureaucracy. At the beginning of the neo-liberal period, defiant sections of these intermediate strata rejected the neo-liberal

---

4 *Foreign Relations of the United States, 1958–1960*, vol. XII, Near East Region; Iraq; Iran; Arabian Peninsula, Document 210, 1959. Online: https://history.state.gov/historicaldocuments/frus1958-60v12/d210 (viewed 11 February 2015)

transition and were ruthlessly suppressed by the newly transformed ruling class. The military then (under neo-liberalism) parted with the intermediate strata and allied itself with the local merchant class. This alliance became a subservient partner of global financial capital, at first implementing the recipes of structural adjustment and neo-liberalism later.

Within the class of intermediate regimes, a narrower band of regimes closely resembling the Soviet model, to which the Arab socialist states also belonged, were dubbed state-capitalist (Petras 1976). This was more or less a general label for any socialist regime that still drew surplus value from wage labour but also exhibited a higher degree of equitable distribution as a result of asset distribution as compared to the salient capitalist regime with heavy state intervention. The same concept, however, as developed within various tendencies of Northern Marxism after World War II had carried a pejorative connotation in line with the imperialist ideological assault on the Soviet Union (Binns 1986; Binns and Hallas 1976; Cliff ([1955] 1974). The state-capitalist states were not as socialist when compared to the utopia that Western socialists had in mind. This strand of thought proposes that the Bolsheviks (Communist Party of the Soviet Union) had, by 1929, crushed workers' democracy, or the original content of the *soviets* or workers' councils. Democracy here is understood in the abstract Western sense of individual freedoms (bourgeois democracy) and not in the derived civil liberties wrought through victories of working classes over imperialism (working class freedom from want). The consolidation of the lines of defence in conditions of war involve the application of communal or class freedom and not abstract individual liberty. Socialist humanism is best expressed in terms of class dictatorship rather than in terms of personal freedom (Althusser 1964). The argument also assumes in a counterfactual roundabout that, had the workers themselves remained in power and consolidated the soviet system, many problems would have been overcome despite the low level of development in productive forces. One need not argue the counterfactual; however, when interrelatedness is introduced as opposed to formal compartmentalisation, the reversion of the Soviet Union to stricter forms of regimentation tally with the retreat of socialist forces as Western social democracy turned to *social fascism*, a term publicised by Browder (1933). Dropping interrelatedness in the form of assessment of the historical moment and the balance of forces poised against the Soviet Union internationally – including imperialist wealth buying the conscience of its working class as the majority of humanity remained colonised – is selective and pernicious science.

The Soviet Union was isolated in the midst of a hostile capitalist world. It did not possess the means and capabilities for the construction of an immediate modern economy that would bolster its security. Industrial modernisation was more about self-defence than ensuring a socialised working class (proletariat) more prone to a transformation to socialist values than was the small landholding peasantry. But the pre-Soviet MIR (collective non-owning peasantry) was predominant vis-à-vis a minority of Kulaks (landholding peasantry) by comparison (*History of the CPSU*, 1939). The transition to a modern economy (the building of national security) required massive industrial transformation. At first, the Bolshevik leadership believed that completing socialist construction in the Soviet Union would need the unfolding proletarian revolution in the more advanced capitalist formations of Western Europe (Germany especially), which would later supply Russia with the prerequisites needed to develop a socialist workers' state. For several years after the 1917 October Revolution, the dominant language of the Comintern (the Communist International) remained German in the hope that Germany would become the next socialist revolution. The extinguishing of socialist transformation in Western Europe by social fascism (social democracy) and the budding of fascism forced the Soviet Union into the position of building socialism in one country. The real rift that occurred within the internationalist socialist movement is not the one between proponents of permanent revolution and Stalinism, the former group was puny in armed and organisational capacity and inconsequential globally. On the ideological plane, Western Marxism piped the same anti-Soviet cant as bourgeois democracy. Behind this propaganda there lingered the sort of chauvinist Eurocentric valorisation of human lives, which really trailed from the unquestioned ethos that capitalism was historical progress in spite of its many genocides in the colonies: one Westerner's life is more valuable than many Africans or Asians. Value theory is not only about the moneyed surplus labour time, but more so about the real human lives from the Third World wrested by violence to produce the commodity since the birth of commodity production. The real fissure in the socialist movement is the Soviet shift from China (early 1960s), which weakened national liberation movements, allowed colonialism to position itself geostrategically by reconciliation across bourgeois classes alliances, and contributed to weakening the building power momentum of many nations in the Third World.

Extensive socialisations in land and social resources, which were carried out under Arab socialist regimes, indeed resemble the Soviet model. However, Arab socialist regimes did not extirpate the old bourgeois class as did the Soviet and Chinese models. In their five-year plans, their inter-industry prices were not fully set at cost (as in social costing under the Soviet system), and where the private sector was involved in the production chain, a price markup that generated profits was permitted up to a capped level. A limit on the prices of goods provided by the private sector mirrored the depth and the power of this sector's involvement in the broadly socialised economy. Until 1980, these price caps were only slightly above production cost and restricted private-sector expansion. In the neo-liberal era, price-capping was gradually removed, except in Iraq, which was at war and had to ration food and other commodities. As will be seen in chapter 3, when Assad liberalised prices and removed price caps, the private sector assumed full control of the Syrian economy beginning in 2007. Egypt's Sadat began the process of liberalisation as early as 1980, and the results of neo-liberal growth were socially disastrous, as will be shown in chapter 2.

The very notion of state capitalism, however, can be simplistic or a sort of one-size-fits-all concept. It is unlikely that any state in transition out of capitalism can escape the totality of capital as a social relationship. The abolition of capital as a social relationship under state ownership of national resources, although possible (if only on account of structural shifts in history), is unlikely to occur precipitously and in a single developing country, particularly if the country in question is subjected to imperialist aggression. This is so even if civil liberties and working-class participation in the political process are freed from state control. Imperialist assaults aimed at snuffing out successful socialist models and the unevenness inherent in capitalism would necessitate a calculus of redistribution under which surplus value would still be generated and unequally allocated in the early phases of socialisation. Equalisation payments between sectors or fast-paced industrialisation would imply distorted surplus value distribution even under pristine worker democracy climates. Building security under early socialism, redressing unequal development and maldistribution would also entail exploitation, regimentation and protracted aspects of repression pertaining to a capitalist labour process.[5] These symptoms of early socialism would emerge all the more so in small developing formations whose aim is to buttress security and industrialise simultaneously. An ideal state in which working-class consciousness is based on public property that society internalises as full social responsibility is a historically contingent process[6] that is dependent upon several parameters, the least of which would

---

5 Workers' democracy per se is the working-class' realisation in the state that develops in conditions of struggle limiting the wrath of the operation of the law of value and its more violent mediation, imperialist assault. As a self-conscious working class seizes control of production, its redistribution of surplus-value, its supply lines of needed goods, including diffusion of information and skills to less-developed areas become part of the revolutionary process, which is also a process of ideological self-defense.
6 The very solidarity and collective action that could bring this into being is already the basis of working-class consciousness – it is forged in action and disrupts the circuit of value by direct assertion of collective human need (Luxemburg 1913).

be the level of advancement of productive forces and the efficacy of socialising appropriation through nationalisation, but the most determining would be a civilisational leap (a shift in the basis of the reproduction of knowledge that sustains life through an organisation of man and nature in unison (Davis 1993)). Thus, for capital as a social relationship to promptly self-disband after state ownership of the means of production, is not at all a plausible assumption even under a working-class participatory democracy. The dissolution of capital is a process undertaken by workers and their class allies asserting collective human need and allocating goods and services (and therefore social-labour time and productive resources) according to that imperative. Not that it is impossible to make historical transformations, for the very idea of impossibility is a form of thought that is irrelevant to social agency within a historical process in which change is a state of becoming, otherwise: Whither the science in social science?

Moreover, the traditions and symbols of oppression are not immutable but are historically cast and would, *pari passu*, frustrate the progress of socialisation. The stubborn force of habit 'in millions and tens of millions is a most formidable force' and is a thousand times more difficult to vanquish than the centralised big bourgeoisie because millions of petty proprietors through their ordinary, everyday, imperceptible, elusive and demoralising activities produce the very results that the bourgeoisie needs and that tend to *restore* the bourgeoisie (Lenin 1920). Some half a century later, the internalisation of capitalist daily life as 'ideology materialised', to use Debord's (1967) term, became the assimilation of bourgeois fetishism as one's own rationally discerned conviction. The difficulty is that bourgeois ideology has not only instilled its own images, ideas and symbols as if they were the working classes' own, it has also provided the initial hypothesis, the method of reasoning and the axiology with which to reason. Paradigmatic reasoning reigned, and there was no shortage in the usage of the expression 'paradigm shift' when nothing was shifting so long as the class in power stayed put. There is a lot to overturn if one wants to follow on Marx's advice of 'changing the world', especially, as the method of bourgeois science has become the only irreproachable science.

For the above reasons, the use of the term 'state capitalism' tallies with any state under capitalism or those which are in transition to socialism and, hence, its meaning is only discernible within a specific structure in a given discourse. For the purpose of this chapter, the class that owns the means of production through the state and is in charge of development in the subject group of countries will be referred to as the 'state bourgeoisie'.

The very act of socialising is anti-systemic and a process of self-negation for capital. The social relationships holding capital together as a state of exploitative existence begin to tear at each other once nationalist socialisation of assets bridges internationalist working-class concerns; otherwise it would still be a payoff of one working class against another. In the intermediate term, socialisation can discipline but not abolish capital. Historical experience teaches that nationalising assets, combined with a centralised democracy for the working class, is a requisite step for a socialism growing in the midst of a hostile international milieu. However, within the class of socialist Arab states under discussion, the socialisation of the means of production was incomplete, and the realisation of the working class in the political process, its democratisation, was partial. Arab socialism was in retrospect capitalism held in suspension by Soviet support and also because it did not sufficiently bond together the national front in anti-imperialist struggle. In hindsight too, Arab socialism was moribund from birth; socialism as an ideology was defeated and, subsequently, its more dynamic social performance would not come into question (and rarely brought up in discussions) because the victorious neo-liberal ideology inverts past and present realities. Arab socialism was nonetheless a model that had put into place the necessary measures that were to redress much of the catastrophe of maldistribution and underdevelopment inherited from colonial rule.

Developing-country socialist regimes, including Arab socialist regimes, undertook three vital steps in consolidating their post-independence positions. The first step was the confinement of policy to the remit of the state and its control over natural resources, which would harness the surplus to be redeployed in national development projects (Petras 1976; Amin 1978). The second was agrarian reform, which concurrently limited the political power of the traditional landlord class. The third was economic nationalisation of large-scale financial and industrial institutions. Typically, these regimes supported import-substitution strategies, controlled the capital account and prodigiously invested in manufacturing, heavy industry, and infrastructure. A national modernisation project was carried out by linking the production of knowledge to industrial capacity, including the modernisation of agriculture. Attesting to the latter point, the swift restoration of electric power and partial rebuilding of the infrastructure in Iraq, with indigenous Iraqi engineering capabilities – doing so while under embargo after the 1991 Gulf war – is often given proof of the synergy between the state-guided production of knowledge and its application to national technology.

The Arab socialist state became the chief owner of the means of production and appropriator/allocator of the social product. In Arab socialist states, as earlier noted, the private sector was not wholly superseded. It absorbed a minor proportion of the labour force in services and traditional activities. State ownership existed side by side with this constrained private sector where, with the certitude of hindsight, the private sector's scope for expansion would be reopened after the state bourgeois class in power underwent a metamorphosis into a fully fledged comprador bourgeoisie.

Economic planning and government intervention in relative autarky was the means by which one of the binding constraints of underdevelopment – the financing needed to galvanise national resources – was to be overcome. With low import to GDP ratio and concessional terms for debt service, the national currency circulated without the pressures of the international financial market. Current-account real and capital balances were devised to suit industrial policies. Several interest and exchange rates were put in play to attenuate the impact of foreign-exchange shortages on the national issuance of currency. This was a time when the idea of free markets was ebbing relative to the advance of socialism and national liberation movements around the globe. The threat of Soviet 'socialism' as an alternate model of society helped lay the groundwork for this ideological shift toward socialisation nearly everywhere. Government ownership and massive intervention were premised on the inadequacy and inefficiency of market mechanisms, the need for social control in investment strategy and a more egalitarian redistribution of income (Kalecki 1976). This was all to change under the weight of emergent neo-liberalism and of several Arab defeats that ended with the occupation of Iraq, the rise of monetarism, and the deepening crisis of socialist ideology that assumed catastrophic depth upon the collapse of the Soviet Union. From around 1980 onwards, US-Saudi neo-liberalism eclipsed the Soviet-Nasserite period of Arab history.

The State Bourgeois Class

The state bourgeois class, composed of the military and the intermediate strata, exercised bureaucratic control over the state and economy via a one-party system in which the military had the last word. The state bourgeois class in structural terms consists of the party bosses: the top ranks of the military forces, the uppermost levels of the state bureaucracy and the professionals from the intermediate classes that lead various regime-allied civil society organisations, such as unions and societies for women rights. The litany of scholarship on stratification in the AW, however, pursues a more constricted approach in explaining the autocratic nature of Arab regimes by relating it to the 'cultural mentality' of Arabs. This cultural paradigm, which is a disguised form of racial differentiation collated to the practice of imperialism, presupposes inherent traits in Arab culture. During the proceedings of a conference titled 'The Role of Economic Institutions in the Organization of Middle Eastern Economic Life in the Modern and Pre-Modern Periods' (2011), two presenters were separately running two 1,500-year regressions to show that the Western world appears more stable and more democratic than the AW across 15 centuries, either by the length of time a ruler stays in power or by the number of elected councils (CMES 2011). How is an Arab-type backwardness (ascribed to immutable cultural values and which trails from so far back) not going to call into practice some kind of visual stigma with which an Arab may be singled out? One cannot help but remind the reader – although by now this is probably overemphasised – that the book entitled *The Arab Mind* by Raphael Patai is the manuscript of choice for informing US State Department personnel about the AW and is, of course, the epitome of the cultural-*qua*-racist stance.

In historically concrete definitions of social classes, however, not only in terms of relationship to property but also in terms of their forms of organisation and ideological leanings, especially in relation to modern-day financial imperialism, the AW world exhibits an outstanding particularity. The specificity in the AW is the newly independent state that came under imperialist assault as soon as it proclaimed its independence. This latter contradiction (resulting in the defeat of nationalist forces) around which the character of the national bourgeoisie transmigrates into its opposite – an anti-national social class – is the state of becoming that is discernible from a cursory reading of Arab modern history. The United States changes from being the great evil to an inspirational model. The intersection at which national peripheral classes confront imperialism and to a large extent are redefined by this relationship, involves the diplomatic work of sugar-coating surrender as peace and prosperity under freer markets. In her fieldwork as reported by Matar (2016), the head of industrial promotion policy in 2007 was asked why Syria was dropping the import-protection measures to enter the WTO, when the US vetoes such a step (Syria's accession to the WTO), the top bureaucrat answered that Syria is swerving economically to the right so that later it could move politically to the right, implying a potential peace deal with Israel. In itself, the WikiLeaks-exposed detail level of information that the US State Department receives from the AW about dissent is telling about the organic ties between the different spheres of capitalist social classes. At any rate, the class position of one national group vis-à-vis another and the national interest in a postcolonial Arab context would be determined by its orientation toward imperialism. The political stance of social classes, as in 'for or against' imperialism, is the watershed moment – more so than narrow unionism or commitment to national industrialisation – that defines their political position. Being constantly aggressed upon, the national ruling class is not ruling in relation to its own working class alone; it is also ruling in proportion to the strength of its bonds to imperialism.

This intermediate stratum is a differentiated section of the working class that supplies recruits to the ruling class. It is considered a subsidiary force in the government of society. The stability of a given post-independence Arab political entity partly depended on the efficiency of this stratum. Petras (1976) sees the intermediate stratum as a class-conscious and independent social layer – distinct from both ordinary wage-workers and from traditional landowners – a stratum that is horizontally and vertically anchored in the salaried middle-income strata and has its own political and economic agenda and, whose promotion of market relations and capitalist development is extended under the expansion and shadow of state enterprise. Petras's model closely follows the contours of the Arab socialist ruling class, a joint military and intermediate class that reinforced its grip on power by populist appeal to pan-Arabism and socialism. However, it was a class whose commitment to the broader working classes was shaky given its petty stock of wealth and Veblenian-envious emulation of the bourgeoisie.

The alliance of the intermediate stratum and the military contributed to the partial erosion of some traditional classes (landowners and the colonialist-bred bourgeoisie) and the promotion of others, such as the new and expanded intermediate stratum that grew up as a result of free universal education, subsidised basic necessities, housing and healthcare.[7] These expanded intermediate strata consisted of the professionals who were engaged in technocratic jobs and in running the vast social programs of the state. Immediately after independence, the national industrial bourgeoisie was crippled politically, either because its close ties to the previous colonist were severed or because the post-independence crisis was too deep, and it became feasible for the state bourgeoisie to fill the class power vacuum and consolidate the bureaucracy around the state (Abdel-Malek 1967; Hussein 1971). In these new social relationships of production, the state bourgeoisie maintained not only its relation to the means of production through the state itself, but also distributional arrangements that reinforced the pace of capital accumulation. This was the organised dimension of capital under these regimes: a political process safeguarding capital as a social relationship and the inevitable capitalistic growth of the state bourgeois class. Solidifying control over state power has the goal of entrenching the wealth of this newly developing social class itself. More egalitarian distribution boosted demand, growth and the stock of

7 There was a significant expansion in education in Egypt. Primary enrolment rose from 1.4 million in 1952 to 3.5 million in 1965, and university enrolment increased from 35,000 in 1952 to 123,000 in 1969. The rate of enrolment in higher technical schools that provided recruits for industry rose significantly from 1,320 in 1952 to 34,000 in 1969 (Central Bureau of Statistics Egypt, General Indicators, Cairo, 1952–1970 200–204).

capital. The state, in return, would promulgate the law in tandem with the new class's own expansionary pace. Under more stable conditions, working classes in relation to the dominant military class would have maintained their organisation, nationalist struggles and experiences, which would continue to influence the cohesion of the working population as a whole, including the peasantry. Under conditions of war, workers' rights were curtailed to maintain stricter national defence. The degree of egalitarian redistribution of the social product was proportionate to internal (demands of the working class) and external power considerations (imperialist leverage) meant to maintain regime stability. In the Arab socialist period, national security and developmental objectives were intertwined. The first major schism between development and security was to occur when Egypt signed the Camp David Accords in 1978 and moved into the US orbit. As will be seen in the next chapter, this step weakened an already frail Arab security arrangement, put working-class security at risk and opened a new window for imperialist intervention in much of Africa and the AW.

In privately ordered capitalist markets, the process of capital accumulation is mediated through various legal and political institutions organised by individual capitalists owning shares or property titles; in contrast, the process under Arab socialism was organised by officials of the state or their hired managers (Abdel-Malek 1971). As the contradictions inherent in class society built up as a result of regressive redistribution and successive losses in war to imperialism, an internal clash unfolded between the state capitalist class, which owned state resources, and an increasingly socialised labouring class. The rate of proletarianisation (as in labour becoming socialised) was rising and, in the seventies, the share of the intermediate class from national income gradually began to rise at higher rates than that of the broader working population (Charafeddine 1981). This phenomenon has also been witnessed elsewhere. Kalecki (1976) observed, with respect to the general case of intermediate regimes, that the demands of a growing urban labour force have brought pressure to bear on the state bourgeoisie, and repression has consequently increased against organisations representing the rural and urban poor.

The class fault lines under Arab socialism became progressively more pronounced. In the latter years of the Arab socialist project, access to foreign exchange in the form of petro-remittances permitted sections of society to visibly display signs of wealth, first in Egypt and then in Syria. Iraq, however, is a peculiar case: it was too engrossed in conflict for foreign earnings to weigh on class divisions more than did the conflicts themselves. Under Saddam's regime, the force of the law dealt quickly with shadow-market currency traders.

The initial populist euphoria that accompanied state-bourgeois-led development was followed by more repressive measures against the working class, especially as the walls protecting national industry began to collapse as they were undermined by stealthily infiltrating petrodollars from the oil states. Dollars and petrodinars traded in the black markets allowed similar concrete work, as in engineers performing similar tasks in the Gulf and in the home economy (the Arab socialist country), which is denominated in petrocurrency abroad, to acquire much more wealth at home as a result of repatriation and foreign-exchange dealings. The Arab socialist currency was fixed at high rates against the dollar (a protection measure) and the aspiring intermediate class paid for dollars at several times the official exchange rate (shadow-economy operations) flooding the economy with the national currency, exerting pressure to devaluate and inflate national prices. The protection that the official exchange rate provided was not in setting the exchange rate at the real level or in terms of how much of similar commodities the local currency could buy at home for what the dollar buys in the United States. Not that there is a real level, but the official exchange rate represented a negotiating position, redressing the previous power imbalance with colonialism. It was partly this power that the national economy sought to project in international trade. Since the Camp-David Accords turning point, conditions of uncertainty associated with a combination of political uncertainty and institutions devoid of working-class representation rendered short-term profiteering from commerce, devoid of industry, the principal undertaking of private investors.

Capitalist and merchant classes are not synonymous. The merchant class circulates money rather than converts money into physical elements used for producing wealth (Marx 1867). Its process is that of distribution of goods rather than production of goods and creation of new value. The profits attained by mercantilist practice are effectively a transfer of value from members of society to the merchants through price mark-ups.

However, the lax attitude of the Arab socialist regime toward illicit market operations indicated that certain segments of the military and state bourgeoisie were beneficiaries of such illegal currency-exchange activity. Because of this covert collusion, the walls of the dual exchange-rate regime (it is de facto a multiple rate, but let us just say dual for the sake of perspicuity) that protected national assets from being bought at prices set by the imperialists, collapsed.

These dual exchange-rate structures came into effect to protect the national consumption bundle from foreign-exchange variations and to rebalance the prices assigned to products of differing qualities or to domestically produced versus imported goods. Besides regulating imports, since dollars could only be acquired through the state, the dual exchange rates were correlated with a tariff structure that disproportionally raised the price of imported commodities in order to protect national markets. Dual exchange rates addressed a lopsided power structure left over from the days of colonialism in which the colonising state priced national currencies at low levels to get the most out of the occupied economies with its own currency. Trade unions and less-favoured sections of the working class bore the worst of the assault on the currency when the cohort of the intermediate stratum veered to the political right in pursuit of petrodollars, and class alliances began to shift. But a reminder is in order here; the shift to the right of the intermediate stratum and the ruling military was preceded by a similar shift to the right around the world, while US-led regional military superiority and the Camp David Accords whisked Egypt away from the joint Arab security arrangement.

It may be argued that the emergence of this category of Arab socialist structures is a movement from one type of exploitation to another without a radical shift in the value-extraction process attendant on accumulation (Petras 1976). The increasing mechanisation of production (socialist industrialisation) meant that there was more output per worker compared with the colonial era; obviously, the additional value produced was more equally distributed under Arab-socialist measures. Resource retention within the national economy was also key to the success of socialist performance. The act of recirculating national resources prevented the monetary (waged work) and non-monetary elements that form value (what people need in order to enjoy a certain living standard) from being transferred to the ex-colonialists. As elsewhere in the developing world, prior to independence and the rise of Arab socialism, the colonial circuit of value transfer − by which national resources were appropriated at minimal or no cost − prevailed. The transition from the postcolonialist bourgeois formation to state-ownership-led formation occurred with only cosmetic changes to the fundamental construct of capitalist relations, of which the most fundamental is the wage–labour relationship or labour's ownership of its product. In particular, the key aspect of *workers in control*, which transforms the labour process, did not take root. The appropriation of surplus value proceeded via capitalist-class control through the state as distinct from control through private/titled ownership. One can say that Arab socialist industrialisation drove up relative surplus value by increasing productivity, thereby also increasing incomes and wealth. Until the state bourgeois class switched course, rising wages and reinvestment in the social infrastructure, particularly in health and education, recycled value back as services to the working classes.

Social change − in particular, the leap from colonisation to Arab socialism − can be gauged by the overall betterment of living conditions. Although it is not odd that a fundamental departure from the colonial past in terms of welfare did occur, capital as an exploitative relationship held its ground, which is also not aberrant. What is relevant is the higher degree to which more productivity and egalitarian distribution followed. Concomitantly, despite a reduction in income inequality under Arab socialism, workers and peasants remained passive participants in the political process; their realisation in the state was passed-down as a result of national security concerns as opposed to their dominance in the state through active political struggles. The war effort and the insecurity of the state created a condition of regime paranoia and a race with time. The prioritisation of military security by socialist regimes undermined the impetus that integrates and internalises a working-class culture of resistance. It created masses of workers who were prohibited from autonomously organising or from defending their gains once the neo-liberal phase prevailed.

Hence the post-independence experience of this class of Arab countries was not of radical structural transformation of capitalist relations *proper*, but rather a transition favourable to workers that did not challenge capital as a social relationship governing production. Most significant in this process of maintaining the rule of capital is the regimes' virtual elimination of autonomous working-class organisations by a level of suppression that mirrored the ambitions of sections of the state bourgeois and intermediate classes capitalising on defeat to loosen the spigots of value transfer in their favour. In a sense, what occurred is the opposite of the petty bourgeois suicide that Cabral proposed in 1969 in times of socialist transition. Cabral recognised the class landscape in a developing formation as mainly peasant with a puny industrial working class, a significant petty bourgeoisie and a small elite. He also discerned that colonialism spares few from its wrath, and the petty bourgeois class with the kind of personal experience of colonial oppression will most likely head the revolutionary process (Cabral 1969); however, he pinned revolutionary success on the suicide of the petty bourgeois class or on how it sets aside its servility to capital as a result of safeguards that limit its privileges in the revolutionary age. New social institutions that protect the petty-bourgeoisie leadership from the temptations of power and lead it to give up its positions of privilege are key to direct democracy (Cabral 1969; Meisenhelder 1993). There was a power of ideology, consciousness and will in the days of Arab socialism for the petty bourgeoisie to be circumscribed, but the institutional structures of radical socialist democracy that would stymie the avarice of the petty bourgeoisie were missing.

It is difficult to assess the counterfactual; that is of whether it would have been possible to allow a higher degree of civil liberties under conditions of war; the war-associated losses and the threat to the homeland had never abated. At any rate, while state-led development lifted these economies out of their decrepit postcolonial status, the Arab socialist composite ruling class simply assumed power at the 'positive pole' of the capital relationship. It would later transpire that the rising levels of repression functioned as a prefabricated socioeconomic medium that facilitated surrender and the transition to neo-liberalism.

The accent on an 'Arab' socialism fitting the demands of a national culture was the veil behind which sections of the state bourgeoisies concealed their growing private interests (Charafeddine 1981). The foremost advocate of an Arab type of socialism was the Egyptian jurist Ismat Sayf al-Dawlah. He worked out an elaborate philosophy entitled 'The Dialectic of Man', which was meant to oppose the allegedly barren spiritual grounds of dialectical materialism as the foundation for Arab socialism. Although, his approach replicated Hegel's notion of history as the development of spirit in time, he also reduced materialism to its vulgar usage, as in the debasement of human qualities by consumption, and not the ontological precedence of matter over spirit. In his magnum opus, the *Fundamentals of Arab Socialism* (1965), he stressed the development of a moral code reinforcing the Yugoslav type worker-owners of the means of production. He upheld the belief that autonomous workers freely participating in the political decision-making process will creatively engage with Arab socialism. His was an eclectic socialism, but he also was one of the first anti-openness dissidents to be imprisoned by Sadat (Charafeddine 1981). Arab socialism was a socialism without the Soviet-style historical materialism – allegedly sustaining a higher individual liberty and the rights to small holding ownership (as in the Egyptian land reforms distributing small parcels to peasants as opposed to outright Soviet-like collectivisation) and, ideally, would also part with the exploitation of capitalism. To Charafeddine (1981), the particularity of Arab socialism as envisaged by Sayf al-Dawlah is justifiable given the ravages and alienation of the national culture under colonialism, which had led the nationalist intelligentsia to view foreign social recipes, even Soviet ones, with suspicion.

Colonial Plunder and Beyond

As elsewhere in the developing world, Arab industrialisation was curtailed under colonialism. A classic illustration is Duri's account of the British suffocation of Egyptian textile production in the mid-nineteenth century (Duri 1969). Not that colonial plunder requires much in the way of proof: the splitting up, by newly drawn national frontiers, of Tripoli, Aleppo and Mosul (1917), cities that in the early twentieth century had formed an embryonic industrial hub, corroborates accounts of colonial anti-industrial bias. To industrialise, Europe had to limit the industrialisation of other nations (Emmanuel 1972). As always under colonialism, commerce had been the dominant activity for the capitalist class. And as was common practice, colonialists did not breed an autonomous bourgeoisie. The bourgeois class that they weaned in the immediate postcolonial years was financially weak and, in terms of real resources or productive capacity, incapable of promoting development in scale (modern) economies. If one posits that development is akin to industrialisation, it follows that a national class other than the national bourgeoisie, commandeering the capabilities of the state, had to assume the responsibility for industrial development. Only state resources could have met the challenge of redeeming the damage of colonialism and postcolonial dilapidation.

There is quite a difference between the brutal facts of colonial plunder causing underdevelopment and the convenient theory of 'late-developer syndrome' whereby a country starts from some fictitious underdeveloped point. Late-developer syndrome is said to impose enormous burdens on newly independent countries such that the possibility of solving problems by means of individual entrepreneurial activity all but disappears (Buick and Crump 1986). 'Late developer', however, sounds value-neutral and bereft of politics; as if European barbarism has to be forgotten because many nowadays use a mobile telephone, which is a product of an industrial revolution that was itself the product of colonial pillage. Colonial-type plundering never went away in the AW, and the imperialist assault regained momentum after the fall of the Soviet Union. A constant state of war was endured by alleged Arab 'late developers' – a war that not only forestalled the emergence of a national bourgeois industrial class, but also increased the risks of private investment to the point at which it became almost an act of fatalism to invest over the long term. Since independence, conditions of uncertainty associated with a combination of political risk and institutions devoid of working-class representation rendered short-term profiteering from commerce – devoid of industry – the principal undertaking of private investors.

The normal industrial role played by the bourgeois class had to be passed on to other social classes (the military and the intermediate class), which were no less committed to the accumulation of capital than a run-of-the-mill nationalist bourgeoisie. The new class alliance of military and intermediate strata sought to achieve development by social means, as distinct from individual entrepreneurship (Abdel-Malek 1971). Such a process paved the way for major economic, social and political changes to be carried out from above, either through the state or through an alliance with the Soviet bloc (Turner 1984; Petras 1976). But it is relevant to recall the order of priority. It was not only the vacuum of agency left by a deliberately weakened bourgeoisie that allowed the agent of development to be transplanted in and around the state; imperialistically orchestrated disasters wreaked on the AW – the constant state of war with the newly settled Europeans in ethnically cleansed Palestine, the Suez war of 1956, the French depopulation policies of the Algerian independence war and so forth – have all contributed to the development of an environment that looks for national leadership in nationally committed social classes. In retrospect, the dangers to national security that provided an alibi for the state bourgeois class to separate the working class from the political process were arguably domineering in that historical epoch, but when the neo-liberal landslide commenced, the politics of working-class estrangement from direct representation in the political process also permitted the state bourgeois class to uncontestably transform itself into an imperialist partner.

In the transition from state-led to private-led development, there occurred a rising Gini coefficient (income inequality gaped wider), a trade policy suitable to WTO standards of liberalisation, the annulment of multiple exchange rates, the liberalisation of basic commodity prices (removal of price caps) and the pegging of the exchange rate to the dollar while facilitating capital transfer. Seen together, these measures imply one sordid condition, which is: to facilitate the transfer of value or non-monetised assets and value-forming resources to the ex-colonial powers all over again. Additionally, as a result of the receding power of the Soviet Union and its eventual collapse, the reign of neo-liberal ideology became progressively more complete. The state bourgeois class, which had guarded the fundamental social relationship of capital under the guise of socialism, shifted into full-fledged capitalism, albeit some slowly like Syria, and some in haste like Egypt.

In the financialisation phase of imperialism that accompanied the neo-liberal transition, the social and economic disarticulation endured by Arab societies as a result of gravely imbalanced power structures and resource usurpation, wreaked havoc on nationalist class alliances and structures. At the level of working-class consciousness, the divide between the state of being, rising poverty levels and a historical grasp of that state of being – the mode of knowledge employed by people to understand the reasons for their poverty – spread wide as socialist ideology was in free fall. What people's lives are really like in terms of low wages and services that did not provide for a decent living coincided with the delusions that people adapt to justify such poverty without anti-systemic resistance targeting the capital relationship. Inherent capitalistic tendencies in the partly socialised Arab formation rose anew, pitting the private against the social and further driving integration with global capital. These outcomes were not peculiar to the AW, but they were more biting because of severe military and ideological defeats that rained down on socialising states in the 1980s and were too weighty to be withstood by small developing countries.

A Frail Arab Bourgeois Class

In the two decades that followed World War II, more than half of the AW population remained in the countryside, and the industrial proletariat amounted to a relatively insignificant proportion of the working class (Turner 1984). The commercially engrossed *ancien* bourgeois class circulated capital in a mercantilist fashion. Money returned to money without significant value-added to commodities and with heavy reliance on manufactured imports and few goods produced locally. Entrepreneurial skill swung toward commercial trade as opposed to industry (Turner 1984). Both Berger (1958) and Turner (1984) agree that the weakness of entrepreneurship stemmed from the fact that the merchants and small retailers represented a large proportion of the bourgeois class. Moreover, the small number of manufacturers that actually existed emerged from the ranks of the merchant class itself. The vast majority of industrial enterprises were founded by traders or financiers, generally merchants, engaged in foreign trade. No private class on its own had the capital necessary to undertake postcolonial development (Issawi 1955). But it was not entrepreneurial psychology per se that inhibited investments; it was war or the potential of imperialist onslaught premised upon encroachment – the act of dominating the national political process. To the extent that socialist Arab states built their self-defences through alliance with the Soviet camp, redistributed resources nationally and solidified the internal class alliance of workers and peasants, they were capable of redressing the balance of forces with the imperialism and developing.

The social disaster wrought during the neo-liberal era is the result of the structural terms of surrender dictated by imperialism via the interlocution of the World Bank and International Monetary Fund (IMF) policy. Oppression and political persecution in the neo-liberal age have exceeded anything witnessed during the Arab socialist age. One should recall the historical context before judging on the basis of psycho-behavioural assumptions whether a risk-taking entrepreneur can exist in an Arab context. Formalised risk is calculable but uncertainty related to the objective and impersonal social agencies that make war part of their raison d'être is wholly unpredictable. At any rate, prediction is foolhardy in the best of circumstances; to paraphrase the astute American philosopher Barrows Dunham (1955) regarding decision under social uncertainty, any concurrence between prediction and outcome or pronouncement and truth is purely accidental, especially in the temporal order, the world of space and time, which is full of grotesque injustice, stupendous ills, malevolence, murder and McCarthy'.[8] One may add that the AW experiences very few periods of tranquillity and is full of potential for unpredictability and, as such, one need not go as far as relying on philosophy to make the point on the difficulty of prediction. The social and macroeconomic structural shifts driven by defeat and imperialist encroachment wars could not have possibly made the context relatively stable for an actuarial type assessment of the future.

The Military in Power

In the major Arab socialist states, the colonially trained military emerged as a social force after the departure of colonialism (Abdel-Malek 1968; Owen 2004). These militaries had grown after independence, and most officers were recruited from the intermediate strata or smallholding peasantry. Because of the tension generated by imperialist threats and the formation of the state of Israel, armed forces played a central role in the politics of Arab states. Coups and the recycling of military regimes were a common feature of postcolonial Syria and, to a an equal extent, Iraq. Although, because of the popularity of Nasser, such coups did not in occur in Egypt the 'May Corrective Movement' (1971) undertaken by Sadat was in many respects similar to a putsch. The higher frequency of coups in Syria and Iraq may be attributed to a fiercer international struggle over both states as well as self-induced factors of instability (Picard 1988). Khuri (1982) posits that in some developing regions, the military seemed to act outside class relations as a moderator as it intervened in civilian affairs only to put things in order then return to the barracks, but not so in the AW. The idea that contingently any group, including the military, may fall outside class relations assumes that classes are static constructs and not the historically set social relationship into which people are born, react to through organised political agency and are socially situated. The armed forces in the AW amassed authoritarian power at the behest of shifting class forces, especially the subservient partnership of the national bourgeoisie with colonialism, and not in spite of class relations. Class relations are makers of history, and the rise of the armed forces was a historical outcome. They intervened directly in civilian affairs and, at later stages, practically commandeered the economy through the state. In Egypt, Syria and Iraq the military

---

8   Dunham actually says McCarthy in the original because he lost his job at Temple University in 1953 for refusing to 'name names' before the House Un-American Activities Committee.

rose as the principal political actor and instrument of government, but its public visibility varied according to regime stability.

Once the disappointing developmental performance of the national bourgeoisie of non-military postcolonial regimes became apparent, the military took the leading role in 'radical' socioeconomic reform through a revolution from above. Vatikiotis (1972, 12–13) argues that political insurrections, uprisings and rebellions witnessed in the Middle East region often referred to as 'revolution from above', cannot be considered as revolutions and only represented 'middle class dissent'. However, if 'revolution' implies social and political change, then these coups were significant revolutions. Military officers broadened and cemented their hegemony through the state over the social base by espousing the aspirations of broad sections of the masses. Nasserism in Egypt and Ba'athism in Syria and Iraq undertook extensive asset-distributional reforms, infrastructural projects, and heavy-industry development favouring the betterment of conditions for the lower strata (Khuri 1982). Sophistic tweaking of the concept of revolution as some sort of platonic ideal to which real-world processes have to measure up in an instant is more theology than social science.

The broad consensus in the literature presents the military as a progressive social force and an instrument of social change and modernity (Abdel-Malek 1971; Charafeddine 1981). The military is also acknowledged to have partially met the demands of the working class and to have shrunk the influence of the traditional classes of the *ancien regime* – the landed aristocracy and the colonialist-bred bourgeoisie. Unlike the old ruling class, whose origins remained strongly rooted in feudal absolutism, the military acted as a social revolutionary force in the AW, enacting laws that revamped the foundation of civil rights, including the rights of women. Article 45 of the Syrian constitution of 1973, which mimics the Egyptian and Iraqi constitutions, states: 'The state guarantees women all opportunities enabling them to fully and effectively participate in political, social, cultural, and economic life. The state removes the restrictions that prevent women's development and participation in building the socialist Arab society'.[9]

The military's top rank and file were drawn, by and large, from well-to-do sections of the working class and smallholding peasantry. The case may be that the pull of petty property ownership deters social progress; however, the ideological élan of post-independence liberation and Soviet-influenced social ideals/programs prevented vestigial effects or socially regressive traditions from hampering progress. At a later stage, as the military capitulated

---

9 Syria – Constitution Adopted on 13 March 1973 http://www.servat.unibe.ch/icl/sy00000_.html (viewed 7 June 2014)

to imperialist diktat, it was not the resurrection of some inert cultural value originating in small property holding that swayed it to become a comprador class; it was pliancy induced by military and ideological defeat. Although the alleged inertness (à la Bernard Lewis) of reactionary traits among Arabs occupies a huge space in the colonial–imperialist imagination, this approach should not be admitted into proper social science simply because the 'transhistorical ethos' of peoples explains almost all there is to know about them. The abstraction of the Arab as an inherently regressive type is ahistorical and too absurd to discuss – and is in any case contradicted by the real changes in social norms and behaviour that occurred under Arab socialism.

To assess the shifting class allegiance of the military, one needs to examine the key alliances that the armed forces undertook at different historical periods. The firm articulation between the military and the newly expanding intermediate strata in the socialist radicalisation phase of the 1960s strengthened the hegemony of the armed forces over the social base (Leca 1988). As of the early 1980s, weakened national security implied weaknesses at all security levels, including working-class security – that is, first of all, security from want. By the early 1980s, petrodollars began to seep into the semi-autarkic economies of Arab socialism, and signs of conspicuous consumption emerged. The state bourgeois class became noticeably capitalistic and abandoned its populist working-class rhetoric. At first sight, it appears as if this bourgeois predisposition is driven by the dynamic of inequity under any capitalistic mode of development. However, upon a closer look, these changes were decisively determined by the onslaught of militarised imperialism against this crucial oil region.

By the 1980s, Egypt had already switched camps, and Syria was left alone facing Israel, while Iraq had just entered another war. Evidently, these quagmires along with the advent of neo-liberalism pressured socialist institutions and expanded the potential for private accumulation – taking the faster route to profit-making. A litany of defeatist literature as of the Camp David Accords stressed the faults of autarky and socialism and the reasonability of pragmatism (Hassan 2005). With the ideological interlocking of national ruling classes and imperialism afoot, the determining moment in the transition had little to do with the tendency of national capital to grow by accentuating unequal conditions, and a lot to do with the implicitly enshrined terms of surrender to imperialism. Recalling that imperialism has engaged the region through the war and oil channels, and growth occurred under conditions of increasing inequality. The drive to recolonise in order to commercially exploit, or to draw strategic power, also meant that US-led imperialism had to pauperise and disempower Arab working classes. The mode of integration of the AW through the combined channels of oil and war requires the articulation of the

AW with the global economy via a pattern of destructiveness or a deconstruction of popular forms of working-class organisation. Gaining imperial rents from war required the creation of more war-prone social conditions, and – as will be argued in chapter 6 – under a persistent global overproduction crisis, the disengagement of Arab national assets was under way.

In Iraq, the embargo and the never-ending state of war necessitated heavy state involvement in the economy. The regime rationed scarce goods and could not have possibly embarked on neo-liberal policies that would structurally weaken the economy in times of war. Iraq's form of Arab socialism, the indepnendent position of its leadership and its vast reserves of oil implied that its surrender could only be brought about by invasion and re-colonisation. At one point prior to the second Gulf war in 2003, the Iraqi leadership nearly pawned its oil output to French and Russian cartels in order to draw them to its side in the war, but that was not enough to deter the United States from aggression. As will be seen in chapter 4, the subjugation of Iraq was pondered by the United States during the Cold War, but Soviet nuclear capabilities acted as deterrent at the time. For imperialism, Iraq is too strategic to be left standing; its dissolution into several antagonistic territories and continuous internal strife is an imperialistic model that will stifle popular sovereignty for years to come. The collapse of Iraq as a state appears to have been necessary to tilt the balance of power securely in favour of militarised imperialism. The rise of Islamist terror and its associated military-financial rent *premia* is but a case in point. It is fallacious to comprehend the goal of the United States in terms of a desire to set up a stable social formation in Iraq. The continued state of violent flux militarises the globally crucial Gulf region and hollows out the social formation of Iraq so that it is no longer able to sustain itself. In a narrow sense, and relative to a degree of working-class representation in the state, to disengage Iraqi resources and dislocate people cheapens them, which is profitable to capital because it can harness cheaper inputs and sell its excess goods to unproductive regions. However, the destruction of the Iraqi state attendant on the social formation as a viable political entity and the rise of Israel as a regional superpower enhance the clout of the US-led imperialist camp. Whereas working people stand to benefit from inter-capitalistic divisions and from the retreat of extractive and militarised capital, such a state of play hinders the potential progress of the international working-class movement.

While, as noted, there was political repression under Arab socialism, it was during the neo-liberal period that the intelligence agencies (or secret police) in these three countries, the *mukhabarat*, became the most powerful institution and main instrument of social control. With the retreat of social benefits and lower wages, the suppression of organised labour and other civil-society organisations assumed new intensity (Belqaziz 2003). State bourgeois classes, which had capped affluent consumption and funnelled resources into public investment, would in the 1980s come to mimic Western consumption patterns and, conjointly, to rely more heavily on coercion. The postcolonial crisis of underdevelopment, which was bolstered by a crisis of inequitable distribution and was partly redressed by Arab socialism, re-emerged under the rule of the newly established military-global financial elite-merchant class alliance. Income inequality rose at an increasing rate (University of Texas Inequality Project UTIP, various years).[10] In this new order, the military concentrated more power in its hands and became strictly the subject of development (or rather de-development). The military's rule in Egypt since the uprising remains unbroken. The military's top ranks have linked themselves closely with vested interests in the commerce of their respective economies. They did so in relation to an import-led mode of development that slowly displaced national industry. Upon retirement, the brigadier was destined to enjoy a state patent over a certain imported product or economic undertaking. The public sector was fated to become privately owned.

Arab Socialism

Arab socialism, as it has been discussed so far, was led by the class alliance between the military and an intermediate stratum. However, a formal characterisation borrowed from the mainstream implies that it was the rule of a middle class, or a class considered as distinct from the working class, as per the putative usage of the term in the United States:[11]

> The propertied middle class could not compare in terms of capital, skill, and organisation with the resources and power which governments muster for rapidly overcoming economic backwardness and keeping pace with social change in the Middle East [...] only the new, salaried middle class, clustered around a core of civilian and military politicians and administrators, seems capable of leading the quest for status, power, and prosperity by taking control of the state apparatus. (Halpern 1962, 279)

10 There is extreme paucity of data from official sources on income distribution. Knowing that the UTIP score itself may not be an adequate representation of income inequality, in this estimate I consider only variations along a trend, which shows a steep rise in income disparity.
11 Actually, the term has been used to mean roughly a stably employed worker who can afford to buy a house and appliances. However, a class is the resultant vector of relationships to other classes whose actualisation is presented by the historical forms and power structures with which people interact and which, in the absence of organised labour, emit time and again through the politics of the class struggle the poorer conditions for livelihood and for job instability or stability.

This distinction between strata within the working class on the basis of differing skill levels and amounts and modes of wage payment (monthly or weekly salary versus hourly wage, for instance) is a politically constructed falsification. The compartmentalisation does not genuinely define a social class in relation to other classes or, more specifically (in an Arab context), in relation to imperialism. It one-sidedly measures the materialisation of class in the income position of a group at a specific moment, as distinguished from the historically given social relationship reproducing the incomes via the process of capital accumulation. The latter is a class-defined process. The degree of cohesion of a working class depends on its position vis-à-vis the ideological power of capital. The share of wages, which is the share of the working class from the social product denominated in money form, is unevenly distributed between sections of the working class on the basis of a false science that reduces socially emitted productivity to personal effort and promotes differentials such as skill, marginal productivity and so forth and always in relation to the power of capital. In broader terms, capital elevates absurd particular conditions such as individual productivity to the position of a fetish, while the particular could not come into being without the general condition, which is social productivity.

It was not the reasoned discourse of capital that conquered the AW; as I discuss in chapter 4, winning hearts and minds was never the purpose of US-led aggression anywhere in the region. It is brutal imperialism, a formidable force by which workers' lives are crushed, their value is destroyed and their submission is wrought. The US military bases scattered around strategic resources all over the world are the embodiment of international financial classes in actual physical form. None of the Arab class structures can any longer be said to exist outside this militaristic relationship to imperialism. In the 1960s, with colonialism retreating, imperialist clout over national social classes was waning, and anti-imperialist fronts were buoyant, placing working-class strategy above narrow sectional identities. However, inasmuch as Arab modern states were remoulded by imperialism, so were their bourgeois classes. As soon as the Arab socialist project succumbed to a combination of imperialist assault and internal fracturing, the ties of bourgeois 'national' classes with the previous colonists *cum* imperialism were re-established. The ideology of the imperialist victor blamed debts, import substitution policy and war fatigue for the failure of Arab socialism. But in actuality, socialism had outperformed the neo-liberal model on economic dynamics and social measures. Deficits, inflation and unemployment were all at lower and tolerable levels (see annex to this chapter). What was intolerable was the state of military and ideological defeat that shifted the allegiances of bourgeois, military and sections of the intermediate strata from the national base to foreign pursuits.

It may well have been the so-called frustration of the new educated 'middle class' that emerged after the colonial period that escalated the sentiments of anti-Westernism, but the real reasons for the anti-Western stance are far more complex and multilayered. They cannot be reduced to the undulating feelings of a social substratum. Anti-imperialist positions gained momentum in response to the practice of imperialism and the abject conditions that were created by the colonialist forces. The rising tide of socialist ideology and national liberation movements in this post–World War II epoch earmarked the anti-imperialist struggle. The Arab bourgeois class, on the other hand, composed of merchants and large retailers, was deeply integrated into the capitalist system during the pre- and postcolonial period. This class acted as an appendage to imperialism (Amin 1978). It served foreign interests by colluding with the West and by stifling resources (al-Hamsh 2004, 40). In the more general case, Petras (1976) argues that the global expansion of imperial capital into the developing formations has incorporated the national bourgeoisie into its international network through trade, joint ventures, patents, loans and credit. These linkages strengthened the dependency of host economies on foreign capital in financial and technical support once independence came through.

In addition to insufficient financial and material resources to build productive capacity in the immediate postcolonial phase, the Arab bourgeoisie also failed to garner legitimacy. The lingering postcolonial inequality and underdevelopment laid the groundwork for discharging the old land-owning and comprador classes once the tide of socialist ideology took root. With the Soviet Union exemplifying the social model of state-led development, the new ruling alliance of military and intermediate strata emulated Soviet-style socialism. While the scale and form of state intervention in political, economic and social activities varied from one country to another, the trend of the post-independence years was for growing state ownership of the economy. As shown by the statistical record in the annex to this chapter, even mainstream scholars such as Anderson (1987) had to attest to the fact that the Arab socialist models acted as engines of growth. The fabrications spun around rising debts and trade deficits breaking the advance of socialism are not borne out by the data as shown in the Annex to this chapter. The only valid reason for the academic assault on the socialist measures was to further the debilitations of the Arab socialist states in favour of imperialist strategy. The state bourgeois class led the process of development by focusing on industrialisation and infrastructure. In the mid-1960s, the Syrian Ba'ath carried out massive land reforms. In Iraq, the Ba'ath nationalised oil in the 1970's and redistributed land and oil revenues in more equitable ways. In Egypt, state-owned enterprises accounted for about 60 per cent of value-added in manufacturing, and in Syria they accounted for about 55 per cent. The output of these newly established public enterprises recorded 13 per cent of GDP in Egypt and 11 per cent of GDP in Syria (Richards and Waterbury 1990). Land reform accompanied these achievements, and increasing agricultural productivity partly stemmed rural–urban migration.[12] Until 2006, Syria was exporting cereals (AMF 2007). With extensive social investment, standards of living rose significantly (Ayubi 1995; Anderson 1987).

The regional as well as the particular Arab socialist growth rates of the pre neo-liberal period as compared to the more recent neo-liberal one were higher.[13] In the uncertain immediate post-independence environment, the state acted as a guarantor of long-term investments in plants and equipment. State-owned industrial and agricultural banks lent to national projects at concessional long-term rates. A so-called blacklist protected national industry from foreign competition. A tightening of the capital account and a multiple interest-and-exchange-rate policy galvanised national resources and provided exchange-rate stability. Subsidies and price controls in essentials raised the standard of living for the rural population. Land reforms, which have since been rolled back, raised food production considerably (FAOSTAT, various years).

As already discussed, unlike in Soviet socialisation, the private sector remained partially active under Arab socialism. Cooper (1983), for instance, argues that there is a tendency among scholars to dismiss public–private oscillations that characterised what he terms 'state capitalist' regimes of the Arab region. He concludes that state capitalist regimes failed to transform the fundamental structure of their societies, either into a dynamic capitalist form or into a non-capitalist one; hence they oscillated between various mixes of public and private, that is, mixed or joint-sector structure in which the public sector was inefficient. Moreover, Cooper (1983, 458) presents Egypt as a case model, whereby 'state control did not obviate the role of private ownership'.

---

12 The state bourgeois class under Arab socialism reasoned that food security is part of national security. It glorified farming and invested substantially in agriculture. Of course, rural–urban differences remained, but not to the degree seen under colonialism. When the neo-liberal age dawned, investment in agriculture fell, and so did agricultural output. As will be seen in chapter 5, under neo-liberalism, nearly 100 million people left the countryside for urban areas between 1980 and 2010 only to find themselves faced with poverty once again. The uprising cohort during the 2011 Arab Spring was principally composed of descendants of pauperised rural migrants.
13 Also, the whole region performed at higher rates prior to neo-liberalism. GDP and GDP per capita growth rates of the Middle East region registered 7.5 per cent and 4.8 per cent respectively for the 1964–1974 period. These rates dropped to 2.9 per cent and 0.3 per cent during 1985–1995 (World Bank 2009).

Cooper notes that the incentive to accumulate was always present and strong, both in the agrarian sector, where the incentive was to escape from state control, and the non-agrarian sectors, where efforts were made to maximise one's ability to gain from the state's economic development. The problem with this doctrinal line that dubs the public sector inefficient is the sloppiness of branding any form of state intervention as 'state capitalist' and then assuming that privately motivated profiteering is something innate to human nature and runs against the grain of socialism. The pursuit of private interest pitted against public welfare was conditioned by the form of social organisation, which was principally the hegemony of capital through the state. Hence, rent-seeking around the state counter to the public interest is a consequence of the ideological strength of the capital relationship. When the supposedly inefficient public sector was curbed under neo-liberalism, the whole of the social structure in these countries went into a tailspin. Efficiency is a value criterion related to class interests. In the absence of unemployment insurance, the public sector served as a welfare cushion when job creation declined and fell far below the rate of growth of the labour force. Under capitalism, in whichever form it appears, private incentives and habits are not going to immediately disappear. The stubborn fact remains that during the immediate post-independence period, no individual incentive framework motivating the private sector could have carried out the task of development given its structural incapacitation in terms of resources and finance. Incentive or not, the private sector was puny, in actual productive capacity and finance. Moreover, the comprador-class' tolerance of imperial intervention in national affairs discredited it as a subject worthy of carrying out the task of development.

When former Arab socialist countries followed the neo-liberal mantra of free markets and private-led investment, as noted in the Introduction, the investment rate in general fell from a high plateau of nearly 30 per cent in 1980, to a low of around 20 per cent in 2010 (WDI, various years). More important, the quality of investment worsened in terms of output per capita (see annex to this chapter). That private investors in the AW cannot lead in capacity building is not only due to lack of finance or to geopolitical uncertainty, but also to the broader imperialist objective of controlling oil by disempowering and pauperising the population in an oil-abundant region. In the socialist phase, the private sector was free-riding on the success of the state interventionist model. In Egypt and Syria, what remained of the private sector after massive socialisation in the mid-1960s grew in tandem with growth in public investment. The private sector parasitically survived at all stages of the socialist project. The same private sector would infect the state capitalist class that metamorphosed into the new owning class of the neo-liberal era with the culture of neo-liberalism. It became the fermenting agent that would contribute to converting the state-capitalist class into the new comprador class. The fact that the Arab socialist transformation was not more radical, especially when the working class were alienated from direct participation in political life, does not mean that the socialist state-led developmental experience did not bring about structurally and historically positive social transformation. The welfare outcome of socialisation is not wholly irreversible, but to date, it has proven difficult to completely eradicate.

The case of Iraq is, however, different because higher oil revenues provided the socialising state with leverage to finance welfare with foreign exchange. Iraq is also different in the way its terms of surrender were imposed by military devastation rather than through neo-liberalism leading to indigence or war, as was the case of Syria. Criticism of the regime that arose from a leftist perspective appears retrospectively to have been displaced and hid an ulterior motive that abetted the imperialist drive.[14]

Al-Khafaji (1986), for instance, argues that the 'socialist' state in Iraq strengthened the private sector and the economy's transition toward a capitalist state. He describes the Iraqi genre of Arab socialism throughout the 1970s and 1980s as the state's incubation of Iraqi capitalism whereby the state supported and monitored its development in a controlled manner. That may as well have been the case in Syria, but in the context of the Iraqi state

---

14 Unethicality and the aesthetic category of the ugly, to borrow from György Lukács, are omnipresent under a market economy and capitalism. Nearly all is unethical except the anti-systemic struggle against the rule of capital understood as political sequences of criminality initiated by US-led imperialism whose economics and politics are 'utterly destitute of ingenuity and value' (Badiou 2001). Ethics is discerned as truth from the concrete, which is the ideology, organisational forms and practice of the international financial class and its imperialism. The concrete is not the spectacular event of Iraqi regime crimes or the 'shock and awe' of Iraq's bombardment; that is a false non-truth-invoking event to continue using the terms of Badiou. The moral position is to arrest the growth of capital, the 'singularity' of which differs little from Nazism as practiced in the Third World (Badiou 2001). Current imperialism does not avow a racial motive for war, however: it reconstitutes its power by killing indiscriminately by ad hoc reversion to all sorts of alibis, and foremost in these are its own generated class morality and human rights. Ethics exists in the realm of the universal, whose truth derives from the event that is capital, which in the Marxian characterisation 'drips in blood from head to toe'. Ethics, if it is to materialise, using Badiou's language, is not a question of human rights and morality but a question of the fundamental battle for equality of all people against the law of profit. In hindsight, it was not naïve, but the utmost evil to demonise the Iraqi regime as justification for invasion. From where we stand, one could easily see that isolating and flaunting the transgressions of the Iraqi regime as a singularity similar to Nazism was more Nazi-like propaganda in order to justify and reinforce the US invasion that has strengthened militarism as the basic avenue for accumulation at the global level.

such observation is irrelevant in view of the devastation of the social formation by invasion. The Iraqi opposition was so engrossed in its allegiance to imperialism that in one rather stupendously ludicrous work, the poverty and misery under the US-imposed embargo was blamed on the monetary policy of the Saddam regime. The state over which the old Iraqi state bourgeois class presided is not the Iraqi state of today. To put it facetiously, if there was an incubation of the private sector in socialist Iraq, it did not generate the rise of private bourgeois class; instead it hatched recolonisation and the destruction of the society.

In Iraq, the conditions of surrender were not laid down gradually through structural adjustment programmes; they were imposed by guns and the policies of Paul Bremer. Juhasz (2004) noted that before his departure, Bremer issued 100 orders to dramatically restructure Iraq's economy to fit free-market ideals, and no Iraqi, including future elected officials, can undo them. Bremer tore down what was left of national industry and agriculture that the bombardments had not already destroyed. The majority of the left in Iraq purposefully underestimated imperialist intent and tempered their critique of imperialism to justify imperialist expansion.[15] A nationalist social class in a former colony is nationalistic by virtue the working-class alliances it holds and the distance it keeps from the imperialist centre. To use Althusserian phrasing: anti-imperialism holds primacy in the overdetermined whole because the principal contradiction is between the integrity of the national state against US-led imperialism. Underestimating the significance to imperialism of the destruction of Iraq or, worse yet, relegating the whole US assault on Iraq to a mistake based on misinformation, guides the scope of research into the absurd. The historically relevant condition rests in the deepening crisis of capital that drives powerful trends toward further imperialist expansion, oil control and resource grabs. To condemn the preservation of the private sector in Iraq is off the mark. It assumes that with more radical forms of socialisation, Iraq could have escaped the war and the oil-control agenda of imperialism. Deconstructing global capital is not an analytical process but a real anti-systemic process in which class struggles, especially those stemming from the struggle against imperialism in the periphery, politically pressure capital into making further reforms and concessions in favour of working people in poorer nations.

In all Arab socialist countries, the state-centred economy protected certain niches occupied by the private sector. Private-sector activities were concentrated on retail and construction rather than large-scale manufacturing.

---

15 'I did not want to be a collaborator', said Issam al-Khafaji, a former member of the Iraqi reconstruction council, explaining his decision to resign (al-Khafaji 2003).

Their inputs were state-subsidised and the prices they passed on to consumers were capped to moderate their profits. The tariff walls that were designed to protect public enterprises also protected private enterprises from foreign competition. The state extended supply and construction contracts to the private sector, and private-sector profits were amassed through subcontracting. The latter gave rise to patron–client relationships between state officials and businessmen. However, Batatu (1986) notes that the leveraging power that the private sector enjoyed under the government of Saddam Hussein was minimal. This particular point could be made for all the Arab socialist regimes by the degree to which they upheld an anti-imperialist position that required a fortification of national social cohesion through redistribution. The post-independence imperialist assault on these formations also conditioned domestic economic and social policies. Until their capitulation, these socialising states were at risk of war or in a state of war, and as the cost of essential commodities peaked as a result of shortages during conflict, the private sector would naturally voice its concern by critiquing the inefficacy of the public sector's seeking a broader role in the economy. Judging by the private sector's failure as of the Arab Spring, not only its inefficiency measured from the social side, but more so from the way it created the objective grounds for national dissolution, these states may have been theoretically better off had they extirpated the private concerns.

With the exception of Iraq, which was shattered by imperialist aggression, the remnants of the private sector in Arab socialist states did indeed serve as the embryo for broader private-sector-led development at the later stage of neo-liberalism. The very class in power under socialism moved into the private sector and formalised its control of state property in titled form during the neo-liberal stage. The immense growths in the private wealth of the ruling classes in Egypt and Syria, in contrast to misery, are irrefutable testimonies to this public-to-private wealth transfer. In view of the way imperialism had engaged in wars of destruction against sovereign states in this region, it is very likely that in the case of Egypt, and later Syria, submitting to the diktat of imperialism proceeded in a way that may have pre-empted or delayed imperial aggression, Iraqi-style, upon their territory. The proclivity of the bourgeoisie to grow without public regulatory restrictions and shift into the merchant mode, away from industrialisation, had already been groomed by colonialists paving the way to cement the objective divides that engender state implosion.

Underneath the potential of US-led aggression, imperialism unleashed neo-liberal openness in an institutional context, which is skewed and anti-labour, instead of bombs (as was the case in Iraq). To be sure, the destruction of Iraq cannot be attributed to the stubborn position of its leadership, or its refusal to partly surrender to the conditions of capital laid down in neo-liberal policy; no liberalisation program was seriously presented to the Iraqi authorities to follow. The modern history of Iraq is a history of wars, or history has presented Iraq with the one alternative, which is war. The regional balance of forces and the end of the Cold War presented imperialism with a window of opportunity that it could have not forfeited. Short of re-colonisation, US-led imperialism would have not taken an Iraqi 'yes' for an answer. Notice that as of late (since the 2003 invasion of Iraq) the global and the regional balance of power, including the positions of Russia and China on Syria, do not make of Iran the current soft spot that Iraq represented then. Iraq's destruction proper engenders more enhanced power standing for the US. It will be argued in chapter 4 that in view of the dynamic growth of US-led capital, which requires restructuring power and value relations by seizure continuously, it was indispensable for US-led imperialism to turn the balance of power in its favour by demolishing the whole of the Iraqi social formation. The current protracted process of destruction in Syria follows a similar rationale in terms of raising the scale of accumulation by militarism and devalorisation in easily penetrable formations exhibiting low calculated risks to US-led imperialist forces. To speak in the colloquial media stance that was once employed during the invasion of Iraq: The destruction of Syria costs less than a cakewalk and shooting fish in a barrel.

The debate concerning equitable distribution between the state and the national bourgeoisie during the 1950s addressed the crisis of inequity bequeathed by colonialism. The state had to force through equalisation measures such as land reform given the highly unequal distribution of post-colonialism. However, the idea flaunted during the socialist days – that the private sector constituted an indispensable constituent of the national front in the struggle against imperialism – has not been borne out by the facts. The weakening nexus of development and security in the neo-liberal era is ipso facto proof that private-led policy was a failure. The state bourgeoisie later used the private sector to carry through the conditions of capitulation to imperialism and relaunched itself as a full-fledged private capitalist class and a partner of the old bourgeoisie. The defeat of Arab socialist states to Israel in two major blitzkriegs was manifold, but the further retreat in socialist ideology following the Soviet collapse provided the state bourgeoisie with the ideological pretext for the *volte face*. Without the condition of Soviet collapse, which resembles a *force majeure*, the ease with which these social transformations and class restructurings were carried out by the autocratic regimes may not have been so unproblematic or implemented without effective opposition from the working classes, as they evidently appear so in hindsight.

At the time of independence, the private sector was submerged in crisis, its reputation tarnished by the stigma of a shifty national allegiance, and its structural shortcoming, which is its lack of capacity to tap into the substantial resources needed for development, was evident. During the Arab socialist phase, the determining moment in the course of development was not merely in superficial squabbles between party bosses and merchants, but crucially in joint Israeli–American pressures which were kept up by military force to drain the capacities of the noncompliant states. Had the state not intervened in the economy, it is doubtful that any meaningful net additions to modernise the capital stock and real development would have followed.

It is an intractable task to dissociate policies and development outcomes by attributing them exclusively either to internal national class formations or to the external meddling of the imperialist camp in national affairs. The mainstream often employs an analytical frame of reference that is freighted with neo-liberal ideological bias. It adopts a language of blaming national forces for the shortcomings in development policies in order to exonerate imperialism from its wrongdoings. Corruption is the mainstream's oft repeated refrain. But external involvement in national affairs forms part of the class structure that constitutes the state and its policies. Corruption requires a context conducive to the illegal funnelling of public assets to private ends – a context that has been provided by the introduction of neo-liberal policies, especially pegging the currency to the dollar in open capital and trade accounts and, in an institutional context, already hijacked by the state bourgeois class. To question whether the Arab developmental disaster is the fault of national elements or of imperialism, subjects social science to the banality of crude empiricism that overlooks contingency as the outward manifestation of determinacy in class–power relations or to the whim of empire. This cross-border class relationship is not an analytical object per se; it is a process of history. Whatever class alliance existed in the socialist Arab state, it was developmental or anti-developmental according the distance it kept from the US-led imperialist centre. Depending on the centripetal strength of the working class, national class formations shape the condition that combines the struggle against imperialism and development outcomes in real and ideological forms. This strength ultimately secures the flow of resources within the national economy and clamps the venues of resource outflows or regulates the context that is conducive to the ultimate in corrupt conduct, which is the intertwined act of cheapening and dollarising national physical and human assets.

The chapter on Latin American Structuralism and Dependency Theory by Saad-Filho in Jomo (2005) proposes that the national bourgeoisie was responsible for the poor developmental outcomes; its message is that subordination to a world market seals the fate of nations and that is squarely the doing of the national class in charge of development. Not that there is much national in weakly sovereign countries, especially Arab countries, but the fate of nations in an increasingly interconnected world remains contingent upon the existence and relative strength of an anti-imperialist international class alliance. On balance, the nature and behaviour of a national bourgeoisie is determined by its mode of integration with global capital and its mode of appropriation from the national economy. The class in its impersonal and objectively specified historical relationships, transcends the national context. The roots of its material appropriation and reproduction provide the objective grounds occupied by the national class. Unfettered expansion denominated in dollars in a macro context of openness, fiscal austerity, dollar pegged currency, dwindling capacity and rising import dependency, will inevitably convert the national bourgeois class into a compradorial one. A social class cannot be defined in terms of the passport it holds. Historically, a social class supersedes the modern form of the nation-state. The bourgeoisie organises the pursuit of profit through the state, and the state is only a means to an end. The agent of development, which is a social class not principally defined by ethnicity or skin colour, but by its relation to the appropriation of surplus from social production, is the subject of history and of social science. Accordingly, to expect that a national bourgeois class in defeated social formations will oppose imperialism on nationalistic grounds or because it is committed to its own national working class over the long term on the basis of nationalist affinity is a supposition that runs counter to the materialist logic of social class reproduction, especially so in the dollar-dominated financialised age, or when the class has become the historically given inter-conflicting relationship destroying its own national base as tribute to imperialism.

From the standpoint of Arab working classes alienated from their states and subjected to the threat of US-led or induced bombardment, the present global structure appears immutable. Change is class-determined, and the victorious imperialist capitalist class with military bases across the Middle East forms the determining constituent of Arab states. Historically, Western anti-war protest movements have been unsuccessful in arresting war. The Northern labour aristocracy nationalised, as opposed to internationalised, the struggle and sought an end to wars as if it were a form of charity by the rich North to the poor South and not a historical imperative. The creation of social wealth by more productive means in the North became possible by usurping and destroying the productive means of the South. The dominant social democratic stance has given wealth creation a Western nationality proper; it severed the organic ties of international labour. To date there is no recognition of the failure and, in light of the ties of theory to practice, Western social democracy theorised the wrong object and practised the wrong theory. There is not even a semblance of recognising the responsibility for a history of genocide in the colonies, which if it had really existed the world would be completely different. Such a Eurocentric approach, which is often upheld by Western Marxism, represents a distortion of value relations wherein Western lives are dearer than those of the rest according to the criteria of a nationalism invariably laced with racism. It is neither through the nationalist structure scope nor through the atomised-individualistic perspective that an understanding of the issue forms; it is through understanding that the social ties of the working classes are real and transcend the fiction of national borders.

The above discussion has summarised the reasons why the state bourgeois class, which in the postcolonial period assumed the position of anti-imperialism under Arab socialism, was later to become more alienated from its own social base under *infitah* (literally 'openness', the Arabic equivalent of neo-liberalism) and a close ally of imperialism. *Infitah* was no ordinary neo-liberal model. It was capitulation to every conditionality imposed by the Bretton Woods institutions. Opening up national markets along with geopolitical rents levelled the national productive capacity, brought down the protective dual-exchange rate arrangement and enacted the Saudi model of earning without effort. US–Saudi administered geopolitical rents were accompanied by obscurantist (Islamist) ideology, which is already noted as a quintessentially capitalist framework of resource allocation.[16] The blame game – trying to decide whether this retreat was the fault of the AW or the fault of the centre that caused developmental disasters – is a disingenuous debate; it misses the point that global accumulation is an interconnected social process, which is valued and monetised subject to the *rapports de force* in international class relations.

16 Modern Islamic economics, which bears only superficial resemblance to pre-capitalist Islamic practice, exceeded neo-liberalism in its penchant for laissez faire economics. Consider for example the twisting of the meaning of Islamic justice by modern Islamists that assumes new heights as justice becomes equated with the trickle-down effect of neoliberal markets: (a) obstructions of unrestricted trade, free capital flows and market openness become a violation of Islamic justice (Chapra 2014); (b) free movement of goods, people and capital accelerate development and further cement solidarity and integration, which are among the important objectives of Islam (Chapra 2001, 7); (c) the neoliberal recipe is central to development, and it is (Islam-wise) unjust to stand in the way of such development (Chapra 2001). The projection of old Islamic thought upon the modern world without major qualifications can be meaningless because under capitalism commodification prevails and, at least in one area of fundamental difference with past modes of production, there is a necessity to disengage assets that did not exist in Islamic times. Modern Islamic economics, like neoclassical economics, falsely constructs history as a set of homogenous commercial relations continuous across time. The modern capitalist market little resembles the Islamic market of the past. In the time of the caliphates the market extended narrowly to luxury goods and barter, such that when disrupted, it resulted in no major perturbance of day-to-day existence. By contrast, under capitalism, market activity determines most of social life.

Closing Comment

From a culturalist perspective, limited industrialisation and development in the Third World has been ascribed to the lack of a spirit of entrepreneurship or the 'problematic of the missing middle class' (Turner 1984, 44). However, Poulantzas (1973) thinks little of this alleged problematic. Poulantzas argues that, although the capitalist class plays a dominant role in capital accumulation, it nonetheless is not to be found in a vacuum. To him, the totality of the mode of production, in which the state is central, constitutes the determining relationship of social and economic transformation. One cannot accurately identify or define social classes without prior identification of the mode of production – Poulantzas (1973), drawing on Marx 101 so to speak. The case of the AW is especially acute, since the capitalist system incorporated the Arab region in terms of production, exchange and cultural relations via colonisation and raw material extraction (Amin 1978). The entrepreneurial spirit said to be bred by and within the capitalist social formation was here constrained by a national structure commanded by colonising foreign capitalists. And as Baran (1973, 385) rightly points out: 'in the absence of industrial capitalism there are no industrial capitalists'. The existence of an 'entrepreneurial role' is sociologically determined, not generated by the genius of abstract individuals. The contemporary class formation in the AW is the product of an oil-and-war co-determined articulation, which is instantiated first by militarisation. It is this militarised articulation that forbade not only the evolution of a vibrant entrepreneurial class, but also precipitated the planned abortion of development in the AW. This condition is not unique to the AW, but it is certainly glaringly obvious in the war zones of developing regions (Africa, for example). It becomes visible at the point where the metabolic rate of the reproduction of capital imposes social dislocation to a degree that meets the depth of its crisis of accumulation.

Real developmental achievement leaves its imprint in real time, which is one continuous socially reinforced whole and not the formalised short-term/long-term neoclassical travesty it is often made out to be. The positive developmental impact of the socialist Arab state was real and lasting. Lumping together Arab socialist states and their later mutations, the neo-liberal regimes, on the grounds that they were both capitalist is self-delusional or, to rephrase Hegel's parable: in the dark night, all cows are black. In real terms no socialism could be created overnight, and the socialist leadership must grapple with the strategic goal of how to remove the last traces of capital, not only concerning the abolition of the wage system but, equally important, as a civilisational turnaround whose defining feature is transforming private responsibility into social responsibility. Gauged against an ideal socialist state, these Arab socialists could only have been capitalists parading under the logo of socialism, but that would be a hollow comparison against an idealism yet to be achieved. To be sure, the Arab socialist investment and egalitarian redistribution undertaken in the early stages of independence left a lasting impact. To have drastically raised living standards, health and education is in itself a significant accomplishment.

Different starting points of development lead to different paths of development afterwards. Thus, a socialism emerging in a less-developed Arab formation, threatened by belligerent imperialism, was in terms of its populism a democracy responding to the demands of the working class. That was also a time of global victory of labour over capital allowing for a closer interface of socialist theory and practice. The state fiats of 'equalise assets and lands, industrialise and grant women rights' could have only been the encapsulation of the demands of a working class that had already waged a combined war of independence and a class war. Yet, the concordance of theory and practice at the socialist Arab level can also be ascribed to the global working class that emerged stronger after World War II. Western imperialism was on the defensive as colonialism was dismantled and the global ideological debate had, at its ceiling, full employment and the eradication of poverty via state intervention. There cannot be a current re-enactment of that history – unless one inflates the puny size of socialist organisation to the megalomaniacal stature of academics who think that they can achieve humanitarian socialism through the channels of bourgeois democracy. No small country will be successful in socialising on its own. More so in the neo-liberal era than before, socialist theory and practice in the AW will meet or depart from each other by the outcome of international class struggle than by any nationally confined class struggle.

The reading of class transformation in this chapter is based on the premise that it was submission to imperialism that revamped class structure in order to absorb the successive terms of surrender. Arab socialist regimes went from being led by an alliance of the military and the intermediate strata to an alliance of the military with a more aggressive and domineering international financial capital. A telling drawback of Arab socialist regimes, however, is that the working population was not afforded adequate civil liberties to partake in the political process. This repression came in handy for capital when the turn to neo-liberalism took place at a later stage. Critiques of this experience from the far left exhibit a moral overtone that indicts the Arab socialist model on the grounds that it had maintained the relationship of capital under partial collectivisation along with state bureaucratisation and capped western style democratisation. The argument implicitly reifies the bourgeois democratic experiment and meets with concerns of the liberal right. Osman (2013) summarises these critiques in that the Nasser experience, for instance, is said to have supplanted the liberal experiment and halted a transformation to a genuine liberal democracy.

True enough, a working class is itself the agent of social transformation and should not be excluded from control of that transformation by a state bureaucracy. The realisation of the working class in the state as democracy and the organisation/implementation of the socialist plan via the bureaucracy are expected as the working class assumes power. The question, however, remains: How is it possible for a weakly armed working class, both in terms of munitions and cultural hegemony – in an underdeveloped country, where the cost of making ballot boxes may come at the expense of bread – to erect a democratic model by quasi-universal suffrage without losing out to more powerful imperialist meddling? Can one presume that imperialism will respect the will of Third World working classes? Not even remotely will imperialism acquiesce to a modicum of socialist activity. The European–US bourgeois democratic processes and their election models are anathema to working class democracy and rule. Judging by the state socialist organisational collapse along with a corresponding ideological collapse, Western social-democratic reform, with its organising and door-to-door canvassing for votes, resulted in social fascism – not revolution. It failed because it theorised the wrong subject, a nationally partitioned working class or, it had placed its nationalism before internationalism and compromised on principle with capital.

Bourgeois democracy is capital's key resilience mechanism. Where the chief contradiction of capital, the rising private appropriation at the expense of the social would bring down the system, the payoff to parts of the Western working classes via a sectional election process, would restabilise it. In relation to global accumulation, such a 'democratic' measure becomes the fundamental point of departure for fuelling North–South working-class divisions and the imperialist drive. The strength of capital's ideology in obscuring the insidious Western democratic process is multifarious, but I will name two:

(1) The promotion of Western-style democracy in the Third World, the application of the very contrivance that props capital in the North, cannot be implemented as a reform and redistribution channel in the South because it homogenises labour. Said differently, the absolute general law of capitalist accumulation implied under historically determined living standards, or the rate of surplus drain from the South that must buttress both Northern profit and wage rates, cannot admit political reform measures that would equalise the disparate global wage rate, revalorise Third World labour upward and decrease both the rate of the metabolic consumption of man and nature, which would lower the rate of profit (more on this in chapter 6).
(2) Of the conceptual paraphernalia of mainstream social science, democracy and the right to vote stand atop the pyramid in sacred sainthood.

That a context of legal and social inequality redelivers through the voting booth the same condition time and again is irrelevant to the alleged moral position that without the individual right to vote, there will be suppression of freedom or free speech. This mainstream individual is both abstracted from his or her own social being and de-contextualised from his or her social relationships. Seen socially however, the individual, necessarily but not exclusively, acts in line with the vested interest of the social group to which he or she belongs and mediates the position via the politics of the given historical structure; figuratively speaking, in the absence of a biting crisis and alternative socialist ideology, the two-party system will repeatedly be re-elected by the central working classes that partake in the spoils of imperialism (Emmanuel 1972). Such a scheme that omits the real – as in global interrelatedness, value transfers from the sweatshops of the South, war deaths of the Third World, and de-historicises social development by packaging fascist-like platitudes as science – is an advanced form of bourgeois ideological reconstruction. It achieves its goal not only by mystifying and convoluting language and facts in bamboozling the working class, but also by continuously distorting the means of perception by fortifying the hegemony of a false science. As the dominant ideology fans Western democracy into dogma and dogma into science, a system of knowledge collapses into a system of belief. This phantasmagorical fabrication of democracy and the tribute paid out in bribes to Western classes are at the heart of the stabilising mechanism of capital. It is this crucial area that mainstream social theory rarely theorises.

That is why central to the movement of the working class is its self-activity in a context of its own dictatorship. Practically, for a democracy to work it has to be a democracy for the working class only. The real movement that is communism/socialism is inseparable from this self-activity, which is the dictatorship of the proletariat as unity of means and ends. As such, the issue of democracy is not an ethical point but a philosophical and practical one.

> Communism is for us not a state of affairs which is to be established, an ideal to which reality [will] have to adjust itself. We call communism the real movement which abolishes the present state of things. The conditions of this movement result from the premises now in existence. (Marx 1845)

Ethical evaluation begins at the intersection of theory with practice, and not of theory with theory (Dunham 1955). Capitalist social relations are entrenched, and radical socialist change would have required more than a simple commitment to socialism in some corner of the Third World, such as the AW. Given the low level of development in Arab states and their traces of semi-feudal despotism, Arab socialism on its own could not have speedily attenuated the repression attendant upon the labour process. The failure of the Arab socialist model is more related to the loss of socialism in general rather than to its particular Arab brand of socialism.

Annex

Table 1.1 Yearly average real GDP per capita growth, real GDP growth and output per worker growth rates in constant local currency units for the periods 1960–1979 and 1980–2011

	1960–1979	1980–2011
GDP per capita growth rates		
Syria	3.8%	1.2%
Iraq	6.8%	2.1%
Egypt	3.5%	2.3%
GDP growth rate		
Syria	7.1%	4.0%
Iraq	10%	4.9%
Egypt	5.5%	4.3%
Output per worker		
Syria	4.5%	0.5%
Iraq	8.6%	1.2%
Egypt	3.3%	2.2%

Due to data availability prior to 1980, the rates are calculated using at least 10 consecutive observations for Iraq, 15 for Egypt, and 20 for Syria. Post-1980, the economic performance of Syria and Egypt depended more on oil revenues. The data demonstrate that in terms of growth and output per worker, the Arab socialist period was by far the better performer.
Source: The Penn Tables (Feenstra et al. 2015).

Table 1.2 High and low points of inflation for the periods 1960–1979 and 1980–2011 followed by modal range and average for inflation rates

	1960–79	1980–2011
Egypt	−1.6 and 10% (modal range 4–5%), average 5.6%	5 and 25% (modal range 12 13%), average 14.5 %
Iraq	−1 and 4% (modal range 3–4%), average 4.5%	5 and 450% (modal range 23 26%). average 65%
Syria	−4 and 10% (modal range 4–5%), average 5.5%	7 and 60% (modal range 13 15%), average 12.2%

The data from this table show that inflation rates were on average lower and steadier during the Arab socialist period. Because of high variations in inflation rates, the mode or modal ranges are better measures of centrality.
Source: World Bank, WDI, various years.

ARAB SOCIALISM IN RETROSPECT

Table 1.3 Average unemployment rates for the periods 1960–1979 and 1980–2011

	1960–79	1980–2011
Egypt	5.2%	13.2%
Syria	4.2%	10.9%

Iraq is not included in this table because much of Iraq's data have been removed from the WDI database. Obviously, the unemployment rate under Arab socialism is much lower. The measurement of the unemployment rate under Arab socialism was more accurate because the labour resource was surveyed regularly in planning procedures and input-output models.
Source: World Bank, WDI, various years.

Table 1.4 Average total debt service as a percentage of Gross National Income for the periods 1960–1979 and 1980–2011

	1960–79	1980–2011
Egypt	3%	4%
Syria	2%	4%

The time series for Syria ends in 2007.
Source: World Bank, WDI various years.

Table 1.5 Average for the difference between the rate of investment and the rate of saving as a percentage of Gross National Income for the periods 1960–1979 and 1980–2011

	1960–79	1980–2011
Egypt	4%	7%
Syria	5%	5%*

Although the difference in Syria remains the same before and after, the dependency on foreign aid and loans grew under neo-liberalism because the state under open capital accounts was no longer as credible or effective in issuing new credit substantiated by national means. *The series for Syria ends in 2007.
Source: World Bank, WDI various years.

Chapter 2

THE DEVASTATION OF PEACE IN EGYPT

In Egypt, the internationally integrated ruling class imposes a schismatic relationship on the development of society, the symptom of which is the growing gap between the working and the ruling classes. The rift deepens by the extent to which the ruling class submits to US-led imperialism. The sources of growth in such a disjointed economy after 30 years of liberalisation (1980–2010) depend little on standard macroeconomic recipes or whether the interest rate or the currency is undervalued or overvalued. Growth originates in the United States sponsored geopolitical rents, financial flows and trade considerations needed to stabilise, or to destabilise if need be, the socioeconomic formation. In any case, principal macroeconomic variables have become the tools for imperialist plunder.

The mainstream's economic concept of efficiency derived via prices obscures the workings of economic-transfer mechanisms. More than elsewhere, in Africa and the AW prices are generated by repressive power structures, and much of value is snatched by forcible dislocation of people and resources or by aborting the gelling of working class revolutionary consciousness and organisations. The means of fiscal or financial intermediation between the public and private spheres in the forms of redistributive taxation and recirculation of rents/profits within the national economy are calibrated to imperialist desires. The tax base of the state depends less and less on direct or progressive taxation, and the assets of the public and private sectors are de facto dollarised as a result of openness, multiple internal and external deficits and the informally pegged exchange rate. In 2010, the year of the uprising, Egypt's indirect taxes were at 8 per cent of GDP, more than twice the rate of direct taxation (UN 2015). Under neo-liberalism, Egypt developed two economies over its territory – one national and the other extra-national – with very few welfare-promoting linkages between them. To have arrived at the point where value usurpation undermines basic subsistence, Egypt lost two principal wars, entered into the Camp David Accords and introduced a process of economic liberalisation, beginning roughly in 1980, which eviscerated the nation of its nationalism. Instead of a post–Camp David peace dividend leading to development, Egypt experienced a slide into misery: hence, the title for this chapter. All along, Egypt was paying the imperialist conqueror tribute derived from the resources that would have otherwise strengthened its development, especially the living security of its working class and, by implication national security.

In this chapter, I posit that the process of social disarticulation under way in Egypt is related to the broader goals of US-led imperialism in Africa and Middle East, to which a weakened Egypt, situated in the US-led imperialist orbit, contributes. Subsequently, financial stabilisation arrangements, such as US aid or Gulf funds to steady the exchange rate, are secondary in relation to the broader goal of US-led imperialist hegemony. Because of the historical surplus value and other value transfers (through the indigence of the working population, primary resource transfers and also through the premature death of people by imperialist policy and aggression), which continue to be wrought by commercial exploitation, forfeiting a money premium in the form of anesthetising US or Gulf aid so as to consolidate the power of Egypt's comprador class is insignificant when compared to the circuitous returns stemming from the disempowerment of Egypt. Commercial exploitation is not restricted to capturing individual slaves and putting them to work; it is about driving the whole nation into a condition of slavery. In between fomenting civil strife and stabilisation, imperialism opted for processes that would pre-empt any nationalist class restructuring that would, by implication, re-empower the working classes of the African/Arab continents. US-led hegemony and the extraction of value by violence wrought upon the African/Arab region released tremendous cheapened resources for imperialist grab. In a nutshell, a disempowered Egypt experiencing lumpen development buttresses imperial rents more than an Egypt developing by industrialisation that would have otherwise empowered its working population.

As of late, the Egyptian uprising occurred in an epoch of crisis in humanist philosophy and its ideological progeny, socialism. The absence of internationalism in working-class ideology and the decline of worldly socialist utopia may condemn the already puny Egyptian left along with its progressive social agenda to failure or to an existence on the margin of society.

The argument for the descent of Egypt from the days of its socialist accomplishments into a model of lumpen development will be structured as follows. The first section provides a glimpse into Egypt's economic history with an emphasis on the transition from a socialised to privatised economy. In the section entitled 'Recent Empirical Observations', the present economic woes and mainstream fabrications are exposed. Section three follows the rise of merchant capital and the consequent necrotrophic relationship between the private and social spheres. Section four deals with the difficulties facing the transition from uprising to revolution. Section five covers the issue of how the crisis in socialist ideology blocks revolutionary transformation. With an ever-higher velocity of exchange value circulation forcing technological innovations to compress time and space and to shift a socialising factory floor into cyberspace, the Closing Comments suggest that the conditions for another insurrection are already forming. To invert Althusser's aphorism: the future may no longer last a long time, and the success of the next revolt will be tied to how the policies of the alternative popular model will be received contingently upon the strength of socialist ideology.

A Glimpse into Economic History

Egypt's recent economic and social history could be split into two phases: a socialised phase of high and equitable growth, which ended in the late 1970s, and a neo-liberal period of inequitable growth beginning shortly thereafter. Although standards of living are historically determined, the post-independence period, as mentioned in the previous chapter, represented a better model of development and growth (World Bank 1995, Bush 2004). The Arab socialist states in particular outperformed the other AW nations in employment creation, output per worker, and average real growth (Refer to the annex to chapter 1; also a cursory review of the World Development Indicators (WDI) would bear similar results). Egypt's growth exhibited a lower average in the neo-liberal phase, but it remained high relative to other developing countries (developing world average of about 4 per cent as per the WDI). As calculated from national sources, the real per-capita growth rate was closer to 4 per cent under the Arab socialist period, then fell by almost half to 2 per cent between 1985 and 2000 (these national figures concur with those of the WDI); it subsequently rose to slightly more than 3 per cent over the last decade prior to the uprising (2000–2010). One ought to note the population growth rate was higher around the 1960s. By 1960 it was at 2.8 per cent, but it fell to 1.6 per cent in 2010, while the rate of new entrants into the labour market also declined from about 1990; it expectedly dropped at a lower rate than that of the population growth rate, according to the Egyptian Central Agency for Public Mobilization and Statistics (CAPMAS). The socialist phase comprised a tightly controlled economy with concentrated spending on social and industrial projects financed principally by national means; all the while Egypt was in a state of war with

Israel until 1978. The neo-liberal phase, principally the post–Camp David Accords phase, represented a period of reliance on the free market, unconditional openness and social debilitation.

Initially, it was Sadat's *infitah* (openness, which involved the gradual liberalisation of the trade and capital accounts) that caused the exchange rate to fall and prices of basic necessities to rise, while wages rose sluggishly without catching up with inflation (CAPMAS, various years). The *infitah*, which immediately began to pauperise the working class, was blamed on Nasser's autarkic policies, debt related to war,[1] and the impossibility of financing welfare in view of Egypt's allegedly 'feeble' current account position. However, the current account position was not weak. The data in the Annex to chapter 1 shows that the rates of dependence on foreign savings and rate of debt service were lower on average prior to 1980. The terms of trade for Egypt (export to import price levels) held steady until 1980 and then began to decline principally in relation to deindustrialisation, the rising importance of primary product export and a global open-trade environment pressuring downward the unit labour cost of tradable goods.[2] The balance of payments difficulties that were encountered as a result of the 1967 and 1973 wars were offset by rising geopolitical aid (dependence on foreign saving was lower as seen in the Annex to chapter 1). The bulk of the debt, which was minimal in the late 1970s compared to later external debt developments, was owed to the Soviet Union and denominated in the national currency at concessional interest rates, or partly repaid through barter agreements (CAPMAS, various years). The eclipse of the Soviet Union (1990) and the rise of *laissez-faire* ideology further shored up the drive for the *infitah*. Sadat's *infitah*, however, did not only target price liberalisation, free trade and capital movement, but it was also about reversing socialisation, restructuring social classes and relinquishing state sovereignty to a class fully integrated

---

1 The cost of war of the 1967 with Israel was overly exaggerated to prepare the stage for openness. In the collection of articles entitled 'The Egyptian Economy in a Quarter of a Century 1952–1977', Issawi (1978, 8) estimates the losses of the 1967 Six-Day War to be between 20 and 24 billion Egyptian pounds, nearly five times the actual GDP in 1967. According to the WDI, there was almost a 1 per cent real growth in GDP in 1968. The damage to the infrastructure was minimal and the war materiel was replaced by Arab and USSR funding. It is highly unlikely that an economy could have sustained such losses to infrastructure and GDP and still maintain a positive growth rate in the year after.

2 The terms of trade are calculated price levels of exports and imports from the Penn Tables (Feenstra et al. 2015). The slope of the trend line between 1952 and 1978 is flat, showing no decline. As of 1978, the trend line exhibits a downward slope, implying a deterioration in the terms of trade.

with global capital. The terms of surrender, not so discreetly embedded in the Camp David Accords, unlocked the value spigots of the Egyptian social formation for draining down. The neo-liberal 'openness' paradigm became the conveyor belt of war booty.

Prior to the Camp David Accords, Nasser's social reforms, land reforms, universal healthcare and free education in a country that had ranked poorly on the development scale under King Farook, catapulted the nation into the modern age (Haseeb 2002). Growth of literacy, life expectancy and real incomes soared in the first 15 years of the Nasser revolution (Haseeb 2002). In the collection of articles entitled 'The Egyptian Economy in a Quarter of a Century 1952–1977', published in 1978 by the Egyptian Society for Political Economy, several authors critique past performance, but it was nowhere near the scale of the disaster that unfolded under neo-liberalism. Translated excerpts follow:

1. Although military spending rose significantly between 1964 and 1975, private consumption was not undercut and steadily rose between 1952 and 1977 (Altayib 1978).
2. Altoukhi (1978) attributes the success of employment policy in the Nasser period to high investment in industry, metallurgy and construction accompanied with a planned programme to educate graduates in economic activity foreseen to expand in the future.
3. In industry and agriculture, Ibrahim (1978) notes significant improvements in agricultural production per acre as result of Nasserite land reforms,
4. Handoussa (1978) disparages the accusations of inefficiency levied against public-sector management of industry and proposes that in terms of social efficiency criteria and real value contribution to the economy, social gains and protection, the public sector scores high on the efficiency scale.

In 2013, illiteracy, which had been on the way to being eliminated under Nasser, reached 26 per cent for people over ten years of age (UNESCO 2015). In 2015, CAPMAS stated that poverty and illiteracy were on the rise in Egypt with 'the vast number of poor concentrated in the south of the country with as many as 43.7 per cent of the population living under [the] poverty line'. CAPMAS has also revealed that illiteracy among poor families has increased to 41 per cent.[3] Khamis estimates real adult illiteracy in

---

3 See also: Egypt: Population Growth Overtakes Literacy Rise, IPS Inter Press Service News Agency, March 12 2010. http://www.ipsnews.net/2010/03/egypt-population-growth-overtakes-literacy-rise/, viewed March 2015. Poverty and illiteracy on the rise in Egypt: new study Ahram Online, Tuesday 13 September 2011,

2015 at 50 per cent.[4] Although the quality of health and educational services was being degraded, Abernethy (2000, 42) claimed that US aid had lifted the quality of health and primary education to the top ranks of the Third World.[5] This sort of blatant mendacity misled many about Egypt's real state of development.

During the *infitah* (beginning early 1980s), the share of manufacturing shrank under the combined assault of low-priced imports and petrodollar inflows, which incidentally lowered the exchange rate in ways that could have boosted competitiveness had industrial capacity risen. However, official statistics indicate a fall in the share of industry from 22 per cent in 1970 to 16 per cent in 2013 (UNIDO, various years).[6] In the early stages of the *infitah*, remittances from the Gulf exchanged on the black market had much higher purchasing power and created a work model of earning without effort. In 1976, the dollar black market rate exchanged for five times the official rate.[7] The same engineering position in Kuwait, for instance, paid several times more in terms of purchasing power in Egypt. There were more Egyptian pounds chasing fewer goods or goods rationed by the war effort when national capacity was being neglected. Prices rose, and Egypt's socialised housing, subsidised transport and fixed-price food staples were thirsting for more resources (Abdel Fadil 2000). By the late 1970s, the dual exchange rate was coming undone as a result of the huge quantity of petrodollars circulating in the local economy, and national money creation rose to meet the conversion demands drawn on the black market in favour of foreign wage earners and importers. The process of deconstructing the protected basic consumption bundle itself

> http://english.ahram.org.eg/NewsContent/1/64/21158/Egypt/Politics-/Poverty-and-illiteracy-on-the-rise-in-Egypt-new-st.aspx, viewed September 2015.
> 4 S. Khamis spoke of the declining knowledge economy in Egypt at the NUS-MEI Media Conference on 3 September 2015
> 5 United States aid to Egypt is principally military aid with the remainder fostering intelligence platforms that contain resistance and inculcate defeatism (Haseeb 2002).
> 6 One ought to caution that apart from balance of payment figures, the data is quite distorted. Labour productivity in the manufacturing sector for the year 2007 shows Egypt's data to be five times higher than Syria's, and Oman's about seven times higher than Egypt (UN 2014, 12), when in fact the difference between Egypt and Syria is minimal while Oman is far less industrialised, yet it possesses a high dollar-revenue-yielding petrochemical industry that is highly capital intensive. Egypt's manufacturing share, at 15 per cent, appears much higher than Syria's, at 5 per cent, because the capital-intensive and high-dollar revenue of foreign-owned firms in Egypt raise the share of industrial value in national output. But both, the faulty method of measurement linking productivity to dollarised output instead of to national real currency and the ownership composition of globally integrated firms in Egypt artificially boost the numbers.
> 7 Discussion with economist Mohamad Dowidar, of Alexandria university.

could not have been achieved without the complicity of vast sections of the regime's bureaucracy.

Two historical circumstances assisted Sadat and his class in rolling back development. One was the half-hearted nature of the Nasser revolution, in which Egyptian workers did not fully partake in the political process of social reform to later safeguard progressive achievements – the general case for all Arab socialist states. Harry Braverman was somewhat prophetic in 1959 when he stated:

> Nasser's regime is certainly a dictatorship masquerading as a revolution, but it is also a dictatorship fulfilling some of the obligations of a revolution, and initiating the trends and processes which will make for more revolution in Egypt. So long as the military can effectively substitute itself for the social struggle, keep the pot boiling, and give at least the impression of forward motion, it can hold sway. If it falters, the dispossessed nobles and landowners are on hand to take over again, with imperialist help, unless the Egyptian working class and peasantry have in the meantime so matured as to be able to make the Nile Valley the scene of Africa's first experiment in socialism. (Braverman 1959)

This is not to say that there were no mass resistance movements opposing the initial neo-liberal steps. In 1977, working people in Cairo rose up in a bread riot, but the rebellion was brutally crushed by the army. The revolt was centred in Cairo and not organised nationwide. The detachment of the working class from direct political representation through autonomous institutions under Nasser facilitated the process of quelling the uprising. Nasser's measures to shore up national security were used to undermine the combined security of the nation and its working class.

The second more decisive circumstance that crushed Nasserist socialisation was US-led imperialist war and intervention. After Egypt's second major military defeat to Israel in 1973, the encirclement of its armies and the Israeli threat of non-conventional warfare, the daunting weight of imperialist military forces stacked against Egypt became even greater. Fearing to follow a strategy of arming the working class to conduct people's warfare, which might turn the army against the rising bourgeoisie, the sacrifices required to redress the imbalance with imperialism were grossly exaggerated by the Sadat-reared intellectual elite. Resistance was said to be futile, and 'peace' with Israel was adumbrated as a bright future of plenty when, in fact it became a veneer under which the spoils of imperialist victory in war were stealthily withdrawn from the national economy.

Egypt's experience with modern Western imperialism began with the short-lived Napoleonic conquests, and later the British conquests of the last quarter of the nineteenth century that terminated the Egyptian textile and other embryonic industry, which employed nearly 40,000 wage labourers around 1840 (Lutsky 1969). The British removed barriers to trade that would later erode prospects for the take off of any nascent industry, which marked the first phase of Egyptian industrial decline (Duri 1969).

In fact, the era following the Camp David Accords that surrendered Egypt to US-led imperialism significantly resembles the late nineteenth-century period when taxes (imperial booty) collected from Egypt went to service Ottoman debt and pauperised the population, leading to the Orabi Pasha revolt (1882). Around 1880, prior to the Orabi revolt, Egypt had to deliver a million pounds in yearly taxes to service Ottoman debts (Lutsky 1969).[8] Modern neo-liberal policies siphoned resources as if they were a tax by colonial fiat. The Camp David Accords' 'peace dividend' was only forthcoming in terms of aid consolidating comprador rule, maldistribution policies, and a higher rate of privatisation and expropriation, which have only exacerbated Egypt's economic problems. The positive rates of 'growth' (as measured in mainstream economic terms) witnessed since 1980 – nearly 5 per cent real average growth over 30 years (1980–2010) – do indicate the existence of a dividend; but this was a privatised growth benefiting the comprador and US-led financial capital and conversely lowering the incomes of the working class.[9]

It is not so straightforward to point out a surplus drain from Egypt to the US-led empire when the United States has provided Egypt with around two billion dollars in aid annually since 1979. One may say that as of 2011 the US-sponsored Gulf funds pumped into Egyptian reserves and capital flight have been significant, but the upshot of these flows is unimportant to US-led capital. However, one may also add that the value wrought from cheapened wages and the blocking of Egypt's indigenous industrialisation effort is historically significant. This value may be roughly signified by the trend in the gaping divide (opening scissors)[10] between capital and labour shares, or by measuring

---

8 Abdel-Malek (1968) relegates the rise of the Egyptian bourgeoisie to the Napoleonic law of 16 July 1798, which allowed Egyptians to own land, and to the step taken by Mohammad Ali to distribute two million acres between 1813 and 1816 to state officials. The Orabi Pasha military insurrection was ignited by higher taxes cutting into the wages of the military officer class and capitalized on popular discontent to combat the British. Although the army putsch of Sisi in 2014 drew strength from popular discontent, it enacted a process of comprador class re-strengthening that cemented ties with imperialism.
9 This could be said in two other ways: first, the rate of income maldistribution outstripped the growth rate or, second, the rate of profit outgrew the rate of growth.
10 When viewed along a trend, the declining share of labour vis-à-vis that of capital looks like opening scissor blades with the former dipping and the latter rising, signifying (albeit within the national boundary) the size of their value shares in the social product.

the fall in labour's income share in relation to the rise of capital's share and the outflow of national assets to the international financial markets. The estimates of the distribution of the income pie in Egypt indicate that labour share has fallen from a high plateau of nearly 45 per cent between 1963 and 1975 to a low plateau of 25 per cent between 1996 and 2008 (ILOSTAT 2009; Marquetti and Foley 2011). Since 2008, an average inflation rate of about 10 per cent and non-indexed wages have further lowered labour share.

Yet, these nationally bounded estimates do not do justice to the broader picture of value transfers to US-led empire, especially circuitous transfers from the rest of the region and the globe as a result of the weakening of Egypt. It may be worthwhile to underline that about two-thirds of US aid to Egypt since 1979 was destined for military purposes, and much of the remaining third went into research aimed at ideologically buttressing the comprador's hold on power – basically intelligence platforms to conscript the intelligentsia: e.g., as in social research into what would cause a revolution and whether the political alternatives would bring back any form of working-class representation to power (Sayed 2003, Sharp 2015). Firstly, it is relevant to recall that Egypt was a major Arab and African power, and its contributions to the Non-Aligned Movement (NAM) and national liberation struggles were weighty. Its subordination requires a weakening of national development, which circularly leads to working-class and national insecurity. US-led imperialism requires a dependent and passively consuming Egyptian working class that will not re-empower itself by gains in knowledge and living standards associated with rising productivity (Amin 2015). US-led imperialism also requires an Egypt subdued such that it will not question the pillage of Africa and the AW or rethink the practice of Arab regionalism. By the time of the uprising in 2011, the state of degradation in social assets as a result of imperialist grab in Egypt and, more pertinently, the losses sustained by Africa and the AW as result of unfettered liberalisation since 1980, attest to the significance of value usurpation and the forgone opportunity of development if a nationalist Egypt had exercised more power on the regional level.

In the past three decades, Africa and the AW could not have seriously bettered their development (no matter how they tinkered with macroeconomic variables) partly because of the distorted balance of forces resulting from Egypt's co-option. Even when the African and the AW economies grew by rising commodity prices between 2000 and 2010, the growth was hollow or devoid of developmental gains.[11] In Egypt, particularly, the growth of

---

11 In the essay 'We Must Address Political Economy of Growth without Development in Africa' 23 October 2015 by Jean-Luc Stalon', one spots an excellent example of how the UNDP, similar to other international capital-linked institutions, jumps at

privatisation hit a delicate point involving the basic right to healthy nutrition with the rolling back of land reforms in the early 1990s (Bush 2015), which released a mass of property-less labour from the land only to meet the reality of shrinking industry, productive capacity and decent jobs (more on this perverse transformation in chapter 5).

If security imparts development, which it tautologically does, then it is understandable why for the last 30 years the AW and Africa have experienced lumpen development. A process of accumulation by colonial wars of encroachment that had receded after independence took hold once again over much of Africa and the AW beginning in 1979, immediately after the Camp David Accords. The decades of the 1980s and 1990s are known as the lost decades for sub-Saharan Africa and the AW. One explanation for this poor performance may follow from the fact that the neo-liberal context altogether was outperformed by the state intervention measures of the postwar years. However, the average negative per capita growth rates for these two decades (negative 2 to 3 per cent as per the WDI) and the faulty distributional mechanism that took hold of these economies once the commodity boom arrived in 2002 cannot be simply relegated to some global statistic when wars and dislocation were tearing at these continents. Egypt's shift to the side of the United States, and the imperialist encroachment process, were partly the cause of the Congo holocaust and the invasions of Lebanon and Iraq, among other disasters. Events may so progress such that the insatiability of US-led capital will soon devour other nations, as is happening in Yemen. As world integration with the Arab economy became less based on trade in manufactured goods and more on the export of raw materials, class cross-border alliance between comprador Arab classes and US-led capital became yet more fortified for the simple reason: the comprador depended more on the international market for wealth accumulation.

The bonding process of cross-border ruling class alliances is not simply economic, but also sociological, involving the falsification of old development experience, the resurrection of royal symbols and the creation of new representations arising out of the neo-liberal school to solidify the economic bond. Under neo-liberalism, the Arab state gradually morphed into a security

> the opportunity to mollify the cause of African de-development by citing nearly every secondary symptom of imperialist aggression, its history and its modern forms of aggression. What he really wants is to raise taxes, increase revenues and, worse of all, get population growth restrained, which is, in the context of fracturing states, a form of demographic engineering that usually occurs by inter-communal violence. The imperialists' bombings and interventions, pauperising policies and arming civil wars and genocides, destruction of states like Libya are a statistical outlier of sorts, one presumes. See http://www.theeastafrican.co.ke/OpEd/comment/Address-political-economy-of-growth-without-development-Africa/-/434750/2910370/-/t1s6bdz/-/index.html, viewed 3 January 2015.

apparatus with less and less of popular consent arising from social investment. Figuratively, the head of the state could be reduced to the head of the internal security ministry. The ideological apparatuses of the state would mostly tout the ideal of free markets and the inherent backwardness of local culture, which is allegedly to blame for the failure to meet the lofty goals of modernity. In personified institutions of this sort, economic growth that generates wealth would not trickle down, certainly not in substantive amounts to improve welfare. The guiding light and partners of the comprador class, the Bretton Woods institutions, were much like Egypt and other Arab states undemocratically governed (namely, governed by the United States and Europe); these institutions knew very well that Arab states were nothing but vessels for impaired working-class participation and, hence, incapable of effecting socially stabilising redistribution or peaceful democratic transitions. Their cant of the possibility of Egyptian or Arab 'good governance' was part of the bonding exercise they undertook to boost the ratings of their partnering regimes.

Capital's international institutions projected an image of goodness upon imperialist partnering regimes by implying that good governance by these regimes – whose formation was guided for precisely the opposite purpose – was a possibility. The ideological grip of capital through administrative machination suppressed any sign of serious intellectual challenge from the heterodoxy. In one example of such clampdown, a 2009 UN report that hinted at the depth of the crisis before the Arab Spring was blocked before publication. In one paragraph of the report, the study highlighted the difference between the concepts of crisis in the developed world and the AW.

> There is a Eurocentric tone to the word crisis in an underdeveloped region that has had the highest rates of conflicts globally. In the totality of existence, which is called underdevelopment, where wars and displacement rage in countries like Iraq, Sudan, Yemen and Palestine, and where after some three decades of high positive growth rates nearly a third of Egyptian children suffer from malnutrition, the word crisis has little or no meaning for it is an everyday occurrence. [...] But, the case may be that if economic wealth for the more developed world can be created by non-economic factors, by dispossession and dislocation of peripheral formations, then that could mean that the creation of wealth in the centre is positively related to pauperisation of the periphery. If even remotely or partially true, then the road to peace should begin here. (UN 2009)

In explaining the modus operandi of developing conditions and the relationships that were driving them, a published summary of the above report (the summary appeared first, after which the report was in small part bowdlerised, but more generally suppressed), which had gone through to publication despite the many hurdles, noted the following.

> Certain Arab countries have been locked into a particular orbit of de-development. De-development depends on the extent to which the interplay between national and international forces allows for the retention of a bigger share of the social surplus in the national economy for the sake of industrialization and development. Certainly, cross-border class ties have come into play, facilitating the process of surplus usurpation. The development of the region in relation to security is therefore an outcome of the multi-tiered power structure; the continuing flux of international relations has thus far situated many Arab countries on the dispossession side of capital accumulation. Of the two paths of capital accumulation – accumulation by commodity realisation and accumulation by dispossession – the region is subject to the diktat of the latter process. (UN 2009)

And as to how this Arab/African de-development became distinguished from other Third World processes: for reasons of diplomatic discretion, the report shies away from naming the hegemony of American imperialism in the region and the brutality of its sponsored dictatorships that accounted for the collapse of development. Analytically, the report stresses imperialist overdetermination in general, and how the terms of power preceded the making of the terms of trade.

> Terms of power in lieu of terms of trade offer us a new perspective for analysing the determinants of the autonomy structure of Arab States. Those terms of power are determined by the interplay of national comprador forces and international forces within a context in which capital accumulation, rent-seeking and profiteering are predicates of, and hold primacy over, nationalistic forms of social organizations. Security arrangements in the Arab region are rarely the result of domestic developments or even of regional developments; they have to be understood in the context of the international division of political power, of which the AW represents the periphery. The geostrategic importance of the area has meant that the international powers have, to a large extent, an interest in determining its security arrangements and thus its autonomy over its own policy. Such a focus on the international roots of the security arrangements in the AW does not, however, negate the effect of domestic and historical factors. Nevertheless, it provides a rudimentary framework which enables these factors to be distilled and reorganized for a better understanding of the issues. (UN 2009)

As the report notes, the reasons for the pervasively poor developmental showings can best be understood from the standpoint of imperialist power relations. Foremost among these relationships is the set of social relations geared toward generating divisiveness along constructed and imperialistically funded identities that differentiate working classes. The condition of decaying global labour solidarity had reached such a low point such that the Muslim-Copt clashes of the 2011 revolt mirrored the ideological retreat of universal labour. A principal contradiction with capital was diverted into an inter-working class conflict, yet the 'romantic' left never questioned how, with such rifts, the political upheaval will be capable of socially restructuring the power of the dominant class.

In a context devoid of the political power of the working class, it is not so much the effectiveness of monetary or fiscal policy that shapes the development outcome; rather it is the national ownership of such policies; such policy autonomy is missing in the case of Egypt and the broader AW. In Egyptian monetary policy, the history of growth in money supply shows that money expands principally to satisfy foreign exchange demand or the demands of wealthier individuals who will enjoy the benefit of the convertibility of national currency into dollars at fixed rates. The evidence for class-biased credit expansion is jointly supported by the extensive rise in credit to the private sector, the growth in the share of the less liquid elements in the money supply as proxy for (around 13 per cent average yearly growth between 2010 and 2011 as per the WDI) the informal dollar-peg policy and the skewed income and wealth distribution that increasingly favours the moneyed class. As happened elsewhere when financial or speculative bubbles build, the credit from central banks inflates the wealth of financiers.

Prior to the *infitah*, it would be moot to speak of money-supply growth leading to inflation in a protected and semi-closed economy in which most of basic consumption was satisfied by local means. In a sheltered economy with dual exchange rates, as Egypt was in the Nasser period, the money supply grew by the pressure of credit demand stemming from within the national economy and the targeted supply of credit that the central bank produced in relation to the requirements of the five-year plans (Sayf al-Dawlah 1965). National money demand was satisfied by the issuance of local currency and credit, whereas the demand of foreign exchange was controlled by the state, which observed an adequate level of national reserves to stabilise the fixed exchange rate. Recalling that this was an economy of price and capital controls in which the excess or shortfall of the money supply was addressed via open market operations conducted namely at the national level, inflation was tackled by price control, while the treasury soaked up excess money supply. In actuality, there was a dual system of exchange rates whose manifestation was multiple markets with multiple interest rates; that is as if there were multiple currencies, some for national use that are not traded internationally and others for external use. The purpose of these multiple interest rates was to finance domestic investment by domestic means and to protect the necessary consumption bundle from inflation. In Arab socialist Egypt, this was all the more possible because imports (much of which were military materiel bought with cheap loans from the Soviet Union) represented a low 20 per cent of output. Until 1973 the rates of imports were lower than 20 per cent as per the WDI. As of the mid 1970s the share of imports rose and its composition changed with time as more of the basic consumption bundle began to be imported (Abdel-Fadil 2000).

When in the early 1980s petrodollars inflows (Gulf-generated remittances and US aid flows) raised the supply of local currency, and the constraints on price, trade and capital control eased, significant amounts of dollars seeped into the private sector. The exchange of dollars into Egyptian pounds to appropriate assets in the newly liberated market jolted the coordination by which the demand for goods and foreign exchange would not affect everyday commodity price inflation. The flood of dollars raising the supply of national currency on the local market forced an initial fixed exchange rate devaluation in 1980. As the prices of basic necessities to the consumer began to rise, wages followed lethargically, but never caught up. The significant real wage decline occurred in the few years prior to the 2011 uprising.

As imports supplemented national production by the early 1980s, the price rise was not so much attributable to more money chasing fewer commodities (real wages of the working strata did not rise sufficiently to offset inflation given the absence of organised labour), but to price mark-ups as result of limiting local production and freeing licensed imports. Immediately after the first relaxation of import restrictions in the early 1980s, there were no shortages in basic goods (Amin-Ahmad 2007); but the removal of subsidies on national production, along with a monetary policy that shifted credit away from publicly owned industry and agriculture toward the private sector, also rearranged value transfer from the working class to the comprador class.

Empirics and Financial Short-Leashing

It is difficult to reconstruct an empirical macroeconomic profile of Egypt given both the inadequacy of neoclassical market measures when applied to developing formations and the high degree of inaccuracy in the data.[12]

---

12 The Keynesian accounting identity does not designate/separate consumption (as in all that is consumed, including government and investment goods) between labour

Mubarak's successive governments, in cahoots with the World Bank and the IMF, concealed the deteriorating social conditions by reporting a rosy economic picture. The easiest way to view this is to assess the progress of the Gini index as reported by Egypt to the World Bank or as it appears in the World Development Indicators (WDI) database and compare it with another existing measure. Whereas the Gini index as reported by the WDI implied that Egypt was as egalitarian as Austria, and its income distribution remained stagnant over time (as viewed in the WDI on 8 March 2014), the income inequality index constructed by James Galbraith (UTIP 2008) shows that Egypt was becoming more unequal over time: by the start of the uprising it had one of the highest rates of inequality in the world.[13] But the Gini figures are no haphazard falsification. Fabricated figures related to progress achieved under neo-liberalism run through the whole gamut of social variables and provide the grounds for the policy edifice that has so far contributed to the uprisings.[14]

Just prior to the 2011 revolts, only around 5 per cent of Egyptians were reported to be living in abject poverty at below one dollar or so a day (AMF 2009). The figure was revised upward to nearly 20 per cent following the uprising (AMF 2012). However, anthropological research in the countryside reported that the impact of agribusiness biasing changes in land-tenure law on dislocation was significant, and that poverty rates were on average rising (Ayeb 2012). According to H. Kishk of the National Centre for Social

---

and capital, and foremost, it does not measure the contribution of labour to value added, which mollifies the objective conditions upon which the returns to labour and capital follow. For long, the Egyptian growth rates, which were relatively high for some three decades, reflected two measures: (1) the growth rate was mostly the profit rate of capital, and (2) a significant share of the profit rate arose from the consistent lowering of the wage rate.

13 In Guerriero (2012), estimates of the labour share falls from 43 per cent beginning in the mid-1980s to 29 per cent in 2011. The ILO figure for the wage share is at 25 per cent (ILO-KILM 2011). Also, the extended Penn Tables as arranged by Marquetti and Foley (2011) show the labour share to have fallen to 25 per cent by around 2010. The notion that the GINI remained constant while labour share and poverty rates were rising is ludicrous.

14 The misrepresentation of data by international organisations in order to embellish the performance of US-allied regimes can at times take a turn into the phantasmagorical. UN (2014, 17) reports that average yearly wages in Egypt measured in dollars rose from $2,500 in 2006 to $8,133 in 2012, as in the real wages nearly trebling in a span of six years. Between 2011 and 2012, the dollar-denominated yearly wage nearly doubled as it rose from $4,609 to $8,133. Roughly, at this rate of growth in average dollar wages, a worker will be earning $2 million after 40 years of work. The report: *Bulletin of Industrial Statistics for Arab Countries, Eighth Issue*, is forwarded and signed by the undersecretary general for the AW and can be downloaded here: https://www.unescwa.org/publications/bulletin-industrial-statistics-arab-countries-eighth-issue, viewed 12 March 2016.

Research in Cairo, by 2012 more farmers were neglecting the land because successive changes to land-tenure laws made them feel landless. Kishk (2012) also brings up the issue of lower prices and revenues wrought from the sale of locally produced crops, which disincentivised working on the land. At any rate, Egypt, as do most Arab states, imports nearly half of its basic foods (cereals) and is the biggest wheat importer globally (FAO country cereal balance sheet 2015). For Clark (2001), this makes it (and others) vulnerable to US-initiated economic political pressures and food embargoes. Given the shortage of food stocks, sanctions similar to those imposed on Iraq between 1991 and 2003 would, within 90 days, bring Cairo's 12 million people to the brink, of whom 10 million are in real poverty (Clark 2001). As will be seen in chapter 5, food production has fallen further since 2001, and the peasantry, effectively dispossessed by law No. 96 of 1992, which undermined tenancy security, made a gradual exodus from the land. The news item that uncovered the hollowness of supposed growth came at the end of 2009 when UNICEF noted that despite a number of positive economic indicators, Egypt has a hunger problem and that nearly a third of all children are malnourished (IRIN 2009). Despite this grim picture and the fact that informal-sector employment is above 50 per cent (poverty employment is not really employment), the official unemployment rate was reported at below 10 per cent (Hassan 2008). Fabrications, both systemic as a result of the Keynesian accounting identities and blatant, as in data doctoring, are the ideological mainstay of the compradorial class and its international allies.

Moreover, although comparatively significant (at around 5 per cent annually over 30 years), Egyptian economic growth came to depend increasingly on raw material export and foreign sources. Prior to the uprising, Egypt was exporting 500,000 barrels of oil a day, worth nearly 15 billion dollars a year in 2010 (OPEC 2010a). Over the last five years, average workers' remittances were as high as 6 per cent of GDP, and tourism provided an even higher rate of around 10 per cent (IMF-IFS various years). Egypt attracted more than 40 billion dollars in foreign direct investment (FDI) between the years 2005 and 2009 – which, incidentally, is high relative to the rest of the African continent (UNCTAD-WIR, various issues).[15] The country also recorded huge market-capitalisation growth rates; over the five years prior to the 2010 uprising the average yearly value of the stock market was anywhere between $80 and $100 billion, according to the International Monetary Fund (IMF 2009).[16] Public

---

15 According to the Central Bank of Egypt, total FDI in Egypt for the first three quarters of 2011 was only $376 million, compared with the annual inflow for 2010 of $6.4 billion.
16 Portfolio inflow to Egypt over two years 2008–2009 was $1.8 billion (IMF-IFS various issues).

debt as a percentage of GDP went down from 100 per cent in 2005 to around 75 per cent in 2010 (WDI 2011).[17] The current account deficit relative to nominal GDP was also insignificant at just 1 per cent during the penultimate year before the uprising. Just prior to the uprising, Egypt's dollar reserves covered nearly a year of imports, and the inflation rate went from around 18 per cent in 2006 to 10 per cent at the end of 2009. Official unemployment stood at 9 per cent (ILO-KILM 2010). But these were exactly the figures that concealed lumpen development and the building social disaster.

Egypt has steadily liberalised investment, ownership restrictions and trade and capital flow barriers. It further liberalised trade by doing away with many of the quantitative or quota barriers and high tariff levels (Ikram 2006). The onset of heavy liberalisation was ushered by the Paris Club in 1991 in return for a $20.2 billion debt write-off (Human Rights Watch 1991). By 2000, the primary balance resulting from cuts in social spending for an expanding population showed a modest surplus of 1.64 per cent (Ikram 2006, 175). The working class was subjected to fiscal and monetary austerity, whereas the comprador class reaped the benefits of double standards in macroeconomic policy expansion.

A Synopsis of Macro Policy

The state effected a two-pronged macroeconomic policy: first, credit flows to the wealthier class financed in part by foreign sources and a diminution of resource flows to the working class, which reflects the shrinkage of social spending or the austerity associated with addressing an alleged budget deficit (balancing the primary budget);[18] and, second, an implicit or explicit dollar-peg regime that exhausts national moneyed capital, which could otherwise be destined to the working class (building national reserves and servicing debt at the expense of the bread-and-butter basket).[19] This dualist policy reflected the

---

17 Like many of the other economic concerns, debt politics assumes a subsidiary position to the imperialist politics of containment in Egypt. In November 1990, Egypt sought to renegotiate the terms of its debt with the Paris Club, but its request was declined in view of its failing to pursue further liberalisation. In February 1991, rewarding Egypt for its position on the invasion of Iraq, the United States wrote off $6.7 billion, the Gulf states $7billion and the Paris Club $20.2 billion, or half its debts (Human Rights Watch 1991).
18 I would like to thank Korkut Boratav for his insightful remarks on this section.
19 While inflation rates tax the working class by reducing the purchasing power of wages, the higher nominal profits appropriated by the bourgeoisie are exchanged at fixed rates for the dollar from the drawing down of reserves. This is literally a tax on the poor and a subsidy to the rich. In a rough sketch: the single buyer of imports, who happens to be the single seller to the national market, raises prices and pushes

dichotomy between the national productive economy and the internationally integrated comprador and financial sector.

The supply of credit is used in a pernicious manner. The rate of reduction in the labour share is partly determined by the degree to which social spending programmes are cut to meet servicing the internationally imposed debt. The pegged exchange rate also requires a contraction of the supply of money destined to the working class, which tallies with the reduction of real wages. As elsewhere and under open capital accounts, the interest rate is kept artificially high to secure the balance between savings and investment, control inflation and achieve balance of payments equilibrium. Although under standard circumstances, if the interest rate falls either savings will be insufficient, or inflation will start to rise, or the balance of payments will slide into deficit. In cases of political uncertainty such as Egypt's, the interest rate is merely indicative of the risk premium. The key driver of economic stability is not the gradation of the interest rate, but the political guarantees that the United States offers – through the Gulf as well – to support financial and political stability. Another point of departure from the standard in Egypt is that high interest rates over long periods are associated with regressive distributive shifts and financial and balance-of-payments crises (similar to what is in Argitis and Pitelis 2001, Chang and Grabel 2004). Interest rates have to remain high in Egypt on account of openness and risk. Monetary policy has no relevance on consumption given the almost non-existent financial market for the working class. The policy of reducing wages raises the share of capital in the social product, and money supply (that of capital) is determined by its own rising transaction demand. The bank deposits-cum-transactions of the capital class are what drives the creation of money. Pushed by openness, monetary holdings jumped from 33 per cent in 1971 to 90 per cent in 1983 and have remained high since, mirroring the shift in income maldistribution (WDI, various years). In Egypt, the correlation between high interest rates and maldistribution or shortfalls in foreign currency is observable, but at the same time, it is spurious. The failure of industrial policy, capital account openness and risk, along with the primacy of shifting political forces against labour cause income inequality. The principal transfer mechanism hinges on stabilising the exchange rate via cuts to wages and social spending.

Patnaik (2009) explained that under a supply constraint, a rise in government borrowing will more than proportionally raise private surplus 'through

> inflation up, for which the state prints extra cash, which means the nominal profits of the merchants rise. However, because of the fixed exchange rate that the state has to back by depleting its national reserves, the much higher amount of extra cash is converted into a fixed amount of dollars as a result of the pegged exchange rate. It is not the individual who is corrupt; it is the structure of resource flows itself.

profit inflation squeezing out forced savings from the workers'. As the government borrows to spend 'in a situation where the scope for raising output and employment was limited, if government expenditure rises, then there would be inflation that would squeeze workers' consumption, and simultaneously boost profits' (Patnaik 2009). A higher supply of money for which there is not adequate economic activity, would raise prices of workers' consumption goods while the savings and the share of profits of the financiers who had initially lent the state would increase.[20] The capital class benefits from higher levels of nominal GDP and returns on financial assets. Although the financial class should not fear inflation or a worsening balance of payments causing currency depreciation, as spending by borrowing appears to be in its own interest, it nonetheless loathes the idea that the state can boost the economy on its own and, consequently, people may perceive capital's role as unnecessary. This is a sociological explanation that advances the premise that capital's quest for control ranks higher but is not contradictory to fulfilling its profit motive over the long run. However, in Egypt, the capital in question is neither national nor nationalistic. There is an Egyptian capitalist class immersed within imperialism as a secondary relationship. Employing the same sociological relationship of control before profits, imperialism performs a tightrope act between the looting that debilitates Egyptian labour and the aid that keeps Egypt barely afloat for it to circuitously extract value by the power emanating from Egypt's containment.

However, inflation is never an abstract monetary phenomenon, and it must refer to a composite measurement of prices that always denote specific aggregate measures of commodities' prices (Weeks 2014). Historically tracing the workings of inflation on wealth shares in Egypt one finds that inflation did indeed reduce labour share and the real wages and, conversely, raised capital's share by the real growth rate and, obviously, by the lost share of labour from the social product (in value terms and signified in money). That is pretty much what has happened elsewhere in the developing world where labour lacks the muscle to fight capital; but here one must add, there are higher rates of abjection alongside an ideological assault aimed at hollowing the culture of resistance.

In the present epoch, the Egyptian working class is not represented politically by any real form of political organisation of significant weight. As such,

20 In crude estimates for sake of illustration: Only 30 per cent of the total money supply created by the central bank between 2000 and 2010 met the moneyed demands of the labour force; that is additional nominal money supply with which they bought their necessities (WDI various years). Roughly 50 per cent of all new money created between 2000 and 2010, an estimated 70 billion $ went to service the moneyed demands of a tiny capitalist class as it shifted money abroad at fixed exchange rates supported by national reserves or boosted the price of its national assets via speculation and the building of bubbles.

it does not present an economic alternative of its own. Its lower real wages and declining share of GDP should decrease demand and lower prices, but they do not. The fact that prices rise when workers' demand is lower can only be attributed to 'imperfect'[21] markets and monopolies that mark up prices to consumers and, concomitantly but less frequently, as a result of the dollar peg and rising world food prices. If the money supply destined to the working class and wages shrink, prices may be expected to decline; however, the workers' consumption basket includes a combination of demand-determined and cost-determined prices, and the fact that prices tend to rise implies that it is monopolistic decisions that are leading the price hike. The rising price level of basic necessities in Egypt originated in a policy of worker pauperisation concealed behind a monetary phenomenon. The fact that inflation began to taper down in the few years before the uprising could only mean that poverty levels were skyrocketing.

Despite inflation, one notices that prior to the uprising of 2011, the exchange rate held steady and sometimes when floated, it rose slightly. The value of the inflated national assets of the wealthier class remained fixed in terms of dollars. A comprador class that controls the government fears neither inflation nor a worsening of balance of payments because austerity against the workers generates the tax revenue to offset the costs of stabilising the dollar assets of the rich. These forces are at play, and the working class is engaged primarily in terms of how it can be regimented and, secondarily, in terms of the loot that is drawn from its right to decent living. A looted class devoid of resistance ideology is the aim of US-led imperialism.

The dual macroeconomic policy in an open capital account context with pegged exchange rate is a resource-allocation mechanism. When the price level is derived from the product market and the nominal wages are fought for by organised labour, inflation becomes relevant to the unorganised working class and it acts as a supplement to state tax policy. Inflation-targeting monetary policy was accompanied by spending cuts on projects that would expand employment (fiscal contraction) and frequently resulted in a primary

---

21 Perfect markets in which there is free competition and free flow of information in an even playing field context do not and cannot exist. These are simply logical categories without a remote reference in reality. It is a purely Neoplatonic concept. What exists in actuality is a state of flux in which monopolistic competition varies in degree of intensity and according to the hold (primarily ideological, but also reflecting the real organisational power of capital) of the corporate structure on the state. The concept of perfect markets is a deliberate misnomer to create the illusion that free markets lead to an ideal state or a state perfection. A more adequate name for such a market would be the hypothetical market that may assist in illustrating a dynamic point but cannot be basis of departure for theoretical construction.

budget surplus. Debt creation to expand the resources available to the capital class for investment and short-term speculation raised their asset prices and profits by more than the amount of initial spending and its associated debt. The gist of the monetary policy was to index the profit rates to inflation, but not the wage rate, or to augment short-term profit rates in the private sector and to force the working class to pay for it through inflation of wage goods. The money signification of the wealth pie, the total value in the economy, expands in terms of dollars fixed against the national currency by lowering the share of the working class in total income. Thus, in the flux that underlies the making of social conditions for the creation of relative or (inclusive or) absolute surplus value, it is the latter conditions that have come to portray more of the Egyptian capital-accumulation dynamic.

Until the uprising, the trends in selected macro variables such as inflation, unemployment, deficits and so forth were exhibiting an improvement. Despite this World Bank-assessed quasi-crystalline economic performance, Egypt could not be flaunted as a model of neo-liberal success (as in the racist motto 'the golden boy of Africa designated for Tunisia'), as was Tunisia. From the time when the *Economist* Intelligence Unit in 1993 dubbed Egypt as 'Bangladesh on the Med' in one of its fast-sell journalistic scoops, the country's poverty levels remained glaringly visible to visitors and locals alike. Crude estimates situate the 2010 real wage at half of what it was in the early 1990s.[22] Brawls outside a Cairo bakery when bread prices rose in 2008 led to the deaths of many and made major headlines (Slackman 2008).[23] Egypt is one of the few countries in the world where rising food prices have resulted in immediate fatalities. When disguised hidden unemployment and underemployment are considered, the real unemployment rate in Egypt would easily be several times the officially published rate – poverty employment included (more than 50 per cent of private sector employment is in the informal sector). With the economy often recording negative growth in output per worker, energy consumption

22 These are estimates provided informally by the UN regional office for Western Asia. The article 'Egypt wait a generation to eat (2008)', a commentary by a World Bank official, recommends that Egyptians should wait a generation before the effects of growth begin to benefit the poorer population. This was a time when reserves stood at a record high of $31 billion, privatisation was afoot, subsidies were being removed, price of staples rising sharply in a short period and real wages falling. EGYPT: Can't Wait a Generation to Eat, by Adam Morrow, CAIRO, Mar 26 2008 (IPS), http://www.ipsnews.net/2008/03/egypt-can39t-wait-a-generation-to-eat/ (viewed 2 February 2015)
23 Fifteen deaths in the bread queues were reported. There was general shortage, panic and confusion, and many incidents occurred. There was not enough subsidised bread to meet demand (Slackman 2008).

rising only by the rate of population growth (WDI various years) and highly productive sectors like manufacturing shrinking in size, the rate of effective units of labour contributing to production (the kernel of productive employment) could only fall. The broader swath of the labour market was not about the exchange of labour services for a wage; employment was a rigged game in which cronyism and consent were reproduced by a combination of clientelism, coercion or repression. Gradually, the rift resulting from over-regimenting the labour process and restraining national capital expansion widened until it burst open in the uprising. The igniting moment came as a result of ideological disarray within the ruling circles and loss of control over key areas of state functions. Imperialism had noticed the institutional fatigue, the alienation of all social groups from the political process and the overall senility of politics, yet it had not moved to stabilise Egypt. As soon as troubles broke out in 2011, the comprador scrambled to blindly snatch and dollarise national wealth without concern for political stability, depleting reserves.

More than five years after the uprising the flow of funds from the Gulf states and other sources has failed to redress the dwindling of Egyptian national reserves. Reserves fell by around $2 billion a month in October, November and December 2011 and in January 2012. Since February 2012, reserves have fallen by around $600 million a month for a total of $15.2 billion. In late 2012, reserves covered just around three months of imports (UN 2012). Despite the regime's enacting limited controls on dollar withdrawals from national banks, reserves in 2015 remained low, covering around three months of imports.[24]

The currency stabilisation efforts resemble the act of filling a sieve with water. Reserves stood at 3.9 months in 2014 (UN 2015). But subsequent moves to cut spending, raise the interest rate and partially remove subsidies were complemented by increasing flows and aid from the Gulf, except for Qatar, which withheld its aid after President Morsi was deposed. The situation in 2015 still depends on flows that are contingent upon how the United States dictates to the Gulf the necessity to steady Egypt's balance of payments in relation to rising regional tensions (UN 2015).

24 Officially, the Egyptian pound has been floated since 2003. It was not pegged until after the revolt. In actuality, the float was closely monitored so as not to dip into volatile fluctuations. There were times when the pound appreciated slightly against the US dollar. Throughout 2010, the Central Bank led a gradual depreciation of the pound. The currency depreciated from LE5.5/$ to LE6.0/$ during this period (the last of the Mubarak regime). If this depreciation trend had continued, the pound's level today would have been around LE6.6/$ (just below actual official rate of LE6.75/$). However, this gradual devaluation policy was abandoned in February 2011, and the Central Bank in effect pegged the national currency to the US dollar within a narrow range, around LE6.0/$.

Since 2003, the inflation rate grew at a yearly average of around 10 per cent. In the two years after the uprising, the inflation rate registered an average of 11 per cent growth yearly. As noted, the underlying causes of inflation are unrelated to shortages of goods in the local market. For the most part, prices rose in relation to monopolised imports on essential and non-essential goods. Real wages fell in line with the minimal power exercised by politicised trade unionism. Since the uprising, the growth rate has taken a setback. It was 0 per cent in 2011 and 1 per cent in 2012 (however, having grown around 2–3 per cent as a result of considerable Gulf cash inflows, it began to rise slightly again (UN 2015). These are the lowest rates of growth recorded since 1978, the year in which Egypt entered into the Camp David Accords. In the eight years prior to the 2010 uprising, the Egyptian economy grew at an average of around 6 per cent yearly. This growth was also underlain by considerable oil and geopolitical rents (US aid and remittances).

Development-wise, as noted, neo-liberalism was an epoch of inequitable growth and de-industrialisation along the forced removal of peasants from the land without the creation of sufficient (decent) jobs to absorb them. Account taken of the advance in technology over time, the output capital ratio in the period 1960 to 1970 was estimated at a range of 1.1, whereas for the decade of 1998 to 2008, it fell to a median range of .95 (Marquetti and Foley 2011). Investment per worker, measured at constant prices, rose by an average of 9.2 per cent every year from 1963 to 1979, and nearly stopped growing (.08 per cent growth) for the years 1981 until 2008, unchanging from its earlier levels (Marquetti and Foley 2011). Obviously, after 2011 and the collapse the same rate would be negative. In addition to the higher output per worker, these estimates clearly delineate the dynamic efficiency of the socialist economy.

According to the Estimated Household Income Inequality (UTIP 2008), the index of inequality declined at a rate of 1 per cent yearly from 1964 to the late 1970s – roughly the end of Arab socialism – and then rose at the rate of 1 per cent during the Sadat–Mubarak years (UTIP 2008). Linear projections on the Texas Income Inequality database show that by 2010, Egypt would have had one of the highest rates of inequality globally.[25]

Mainstream assessment of Egypt's performance often neglects the fact that although the population growth rates were rising, investments in total (and in agriculture in particular) were declining and creating fewer decent jobs. The demographic argument, which often posits 'Egypt as a rich land

25 I recognise the difficulty of using the absolute measure of the value of the coefficient as an indication of inequality, but I am interested in movement along a trend, in which the systemic data error is less distortive.

that nonetheless has many people beyond its carrying capacity' (Abernethy 2000, 42), assumes that macroeconomic policies have remained dynamic and nationally based. It is rather an ill-informed position as well because macro variables such as growth, job creation and population synergise in terms of rates of growth and not as flat levels. Under healthy macro dynamics, high population growth becomes a blessing. Arguments of this nature completely miss the point that under Arab socialism the economic policy was nationally controlled and served national social interests, as opposed to imperialistically controlled under neo-liberalism.

During the Muslim Brotherhood's (MB) short hold on power (30 June 2012 to 3 July 2013), the previous regime's social and economic policies stayed put. Monetary policy implicitly depends on a dollar-pegged national currency, which varies in relation to the US monetary policy stance and, as such, remains outside the purview of the Egyptian government. The Central Bank of Egypt may intermittently resort to increasing the interest rate with the avowed purpose of stemming the flow of funds and stabilising its national currency. But because of the high degree of risk at home, the interest rate is not the variable that is locking in resources. What is stabilising the national economy and preventing it from going into a tailspin is the political assent of the US administration to the positions and practices of the Egyptian regime. Moreover, the reasons why the national currency would flow out or stay at home have to do with the perception of risk, which is mainly how the United States grades the performance of the Egyptian regime and the ease of convertibility and fund transfers abroad, rather than the minor impact of the difference between world and national interest rates. Since 2012, the Egyptian banking sector's deposit amounts have surpassed its loan amounts (UN 2014). Banks mainly lend what remains in funds after transfers abroad to the public sector (government bonds). In view of the paucity of loans extended to the private sector and the wide latitude of trade and capital account openness, policy interest-rate change would not influence Egyptian domestic demand (fewer loans to national businesses were on offer). With unstable conditions lingering, commercial banks continue to prefer government bonds/bills to private lending. By the way, this is the same rationing of finance to the private sector conducted under Mubarak, but because of the higher recent risks, less credit is afforded to the national private sector.

The Necrotrophic Relationship

Unlike the data reported by UNIDO on the share of manufacturing in total value added, which is close to 16 per cent, the share of manufacturing as reported by the Arab Monetary Fund in 2011 lies slightly below the 10 per cent mark (AMF 2011, 79). The share of manufacturing in GDP for the AW is lower than that in all other developing regions except those in sub-Saharan Africa (World Bank 2011). The AW share of high-technology exports from total manufactured exports is at around 2 per cent, on par with sub-Saharan Africa (World Bank 2011a). The quality of investment in Egypt moved away from high-productivity capital to what is referred to as FIRE (Finance, Insurance and Real Estate) or low productivity capital (UN 2008b). The productivity of capital declined from a ratio of 1.1 in 1963 to .9 in 2008 as per Marquetti and Foley (2011). The share of private investment in total investment went from below 10 per cent in the early 1980s to over 50 per cent in the years preceding the uprising (WDI, various years). Meanwhile, the rate of the tax contribution of the private sector fell while the share of waged private sector labourers went down in relation to GDP (UN National Accounts, various years). The private-sector share of income steadily rose while it continued to tie its national assets to the world dollar market and/or as comprador capital shifted its moneyed assets to international dollar-denominated capital.

Seen from its social side of consuming and allocating resources, capital edged ever closer to a full-scale mercantile mode of accumulation. Much like financial capital, merchants eschew the drudgery of industrial productivity and reinvest little back in society. Merchants proper do not earn their profits from the infusion of knowledge in production; hence, bettering the skills and incomes of workers is not represented in their scope of activities. Because of the high-risk environment, the internationally integrated merchant class *qua* comprador also exacts high borrowing costs on short-term loans while remaining more or less liquid to bail out at short notice when crisis sets in. The whole of the economy mimics the high velocity of exchange associated with hot money (money capital could flow out quickly, busting the economy).

The window of opportunity in which both merchant and financial capital drain the national economy is determined less by the degree of national economic stability or rising demand and more by imperialist acquiescence to regime practices. Recalling: so long as US-led capital consents to regime stability, the geopolitical rents will be on hand to cushion its financial shortfalls. Also, the merchant mode of accumulation is 'growth' without expansion of the productive capacity or a re-skilling of the labour force. Together these processes disengage huge sections of the labour force and, in a time of global socialist ideological retreat, relinquish the social and ideological space to an imperialistically sponsored civil society (Islamist aid organisations funded with Gulf petrodollars), which disguise anti-labour functions as charity.

Around the sixteenth century, when the world began to abandon mercantilism and engaged in productive investment, integrating commerce with industry, a cultural step forward was taken. 'Culture' here does not refer to folk or elite tradition but to the universal store of humanity's knowledge that has accelerated via the engagement of science in technological application. By contrast, what has occurred in Egypt under neo-liberalism is the gradual disengagement of national industrial capital from commerce, after which the latter activity became the dominant mode. Reversion to mercantilist modes was accompanied by cultural regression and loss of socialized knowledge.

Merchant capital exhibits worse outcomes on development than the typical comprador class of Latin America. Whereas a comprador class and a nationalist bourgeoisie differ in terms of whether the sphere of accumulation and its circuit are nationally or internationally linked, the merchant–capitalist class in Egypt is more fully fused with international financial capital because its concrete activities depend more on the security provided by US-led imperialism. After more than three decades of snatching national resources, not only in terms of the sturdiness of the sociological relationship bonding it to finance capital, but also in terms of dollarised losses, this class loses little from forfeiting its production base in the home economy. It does *not* run a branch plant economy at the behest of multinationals resulting from the maturity of the life cycle of the product as did Latin American comprador (central capital shifts commodity production to the periphery after it ages at home and leaves a comprador in charge to repatriate profits). At least in such an instance, factories would be springing up at a higher rate in Egypt, which is not the case. Merchant capital's principal activity is to tap into national resources (national assets and foreign exchange earnings) by ephemeral investment/ speculation, devalorisation of national assets, and the sale of imports to the national economy.

In this depressive cycle, undervaluing people, not their labour power but the actual humans, as if they were low-priced commodities became part of the shift to the merchant mode and its attendant value usurpation process. Capital as a social relationship regulates its metabolic rate of reproduction in relation to the cycle of value destruction and value creation (Meszaros 2005). The context in which this activity occurs is neither the result of individual agency nor the will of some reified agency that runs history. Increasingly, dominant modes of thought relegate historical agency to 'bigger than life' individuals or to static structures whose elements are catalogued in a given unrelated order without the objective determinations of actually existing history (Meszaros, 2011). In addressing past and present developments in the AW, mass media is awash with Arab presidents or kings, bigger than history, who often parade as clowns, or with explications of social phenomena classified as separate historical instances or emanating from non-existent 'past cultural' phenomena.

For instance, jihadists are either a product of the just-here-and-now or they simply relate to separate reconstructed instances in pre-capitalist history that explain their revival. They are not portrayed as a sequel to 'irrational' but purposeful violence under capital. As to the clowning part of Arab leaders, all one has to do is observe the hilarious performance of the two post-uprisings presidents in Egypt (Morsi and Sisi): they inherited a crisis existing within the context of a larger global crisis and guided by the same neo-liberal drivel and 'peace with imperialism cant', which had initially intensified both the national and the global crises. It is not likely that any president kowtowing to the imperialist line would appear as anything other than a clown. This has to be understood from a value formation and destruction optic in which a country the size of Egypt serves value making via commercial exploitation. Unless they shake off the imperialist yoke, all they can do is prostrate or trade the inhumane embargo on Gaza (in part among other things) for a few more month of borrowed foreign savings.

That mainstream's history is reduced to structure devoid of social relations or just inflated personas is not naïve; it is how the conventional social science adopts fascist platitudes as the science of imperialism. For Meszaros (2011), 'without understanding the true character of the hierarchically articulated structural determinations of capital's increasingly more destructive societal reproductive order, with its organic system in which the parts sustain the whole, and vice versa, in their now paralysing circular reciprocity, there can be no significant improvement in these times'. The mainstream analysis writes off history as the dialectic of the discontinuous and the continuous exercised by social humans and the objective (real) social relationship in which they have entered. The social nature of the world into which human beings are born, its class institutions and other social organisations – legal or political – that have for so long oppressed working people and against which working people struggle cannot be overlooked because the historian cannot feel the social relationship or shake hands with it.[26] To reigning ideology, the men and women that make history are biological and not social.

History to Egypt is the hunger, the potential famine and the forthcoming drone or robotic/drone wars that Egyptians can neither shake hands with nor canoodle. This is not the 'elephant in the room,' but is the room itself, in which the destruction of nature and human lives is necessary for the reproduction of the social relationship and the productive power of capital. To use a higher-order generalisation for the sake of perspicuity, capital is nothing less

---

26 More sophisticated concretisation reduces capital to business networks or, in facile fashion, confounds a symptom of the relationship of the capital class for capital itself.

than the corrosive self-consumption of humanity and nature that serves narrow private interests and creates negative social outcomes as opposed to the banality that new technology replaces old technology and imparts progress as in Schumpeter's famous (1942) 'creative destruction'.

Uprising or Revolution?

For an uprising to transmute itself into revolution, class restructuring should translate political gains into social gains. When the power position of the working class weakens, and benefits do not accrue to the labouring masses, the revolution succumbs. Two salient cases characterise the Arab uprisings. The first is the war condition case of Yemen, Syria and Libya, where the offensive to replace a single comprador class with traces of nationalism into a state with several compradorial classes reigning over multiple territories was carried out by outright Western military intervention. The second case, represented by Egypt and Tunisia, is the initial rise of Islamists to power, which occurred without perturbing the class structure of the *ancien regime*. Despite the fact that social conditions worsened after the uprising, ideological Islam and the despondency attendant on post-uprising failure appear to have lowered the threshold at which peoples' distaste for their condition leads to revolt on one hand, and reorganised the ruling class standing in the power structure of the state on the other. Furthermore, the initial Islamist commandeering of the Egyptian uprising led to the re-domination of old bourgeois ideology, of which Islamic ideology is the corporatist epitome (corporatist is not simply the subjugation of the state to corporate interest – it is rather a higher degree in the coordination of capital's power through the state as a result of deeper crises, which involves inhumane measures to discipline the working class; and, as Lenin (1902) pointed out, this could occur because bourgeois ideology is far older in origin than socialist variants, is more fully developed, and has at its disposal more imperialist support and immeasurably more means of dissemination.

In addition to the overarching neo-liberal ideology, which practically shuns all alternatives like a jealous god, the state as an organ of class rule was left intact. The state's 'public power' (of which the deep state is a recycled offshoot), its armed men, prisons, coercive institutions of all kinds, state bureaucracy and a state machinery that has become perfected under capitalism could not have been revamped because the substance of the rising forces was anti-proletarian (Lenin 1916). There was not even a farcical elite circulation à la Mosca: the same faces in public office remained unchanged (for an illustration of Mosca's elite theory see Bottomore, 1964). In Egypt, it can safely be stated that there was neither a successful political transition displacing the merchant-capital-led class nor a redistributive social revolution. The turn from the MB to the military putsch is a nominal change in which the army or real power broker, as foretold by Abdel-Malek (1968), had really never left the political scene.

James Petras's position that the United States sacrificed the dictator to save its class ally has been borne out by the course of events so far (Petras 2011b). During the uprising and afterwards, the United States continued to inject funds to stabilise the situation (DNE 2011). The United States has invested nearly $100 billion in the Egyptian military (conservative estimates capitalised at the annual interest rate of 5 per cent would sum to $96.5 billion, unadjusted for inflation) and security apparatus since the Camp David Accords. As soon as they ascended to power, both the MB and the upper ranks of the Egyptian military readily declared that they would abide by the terms of Camp David. For the broader masses, these accords were landmarks of surrender under which national security and development parted ways and both were lost.

The Brotherhood's rise to power did not emerge as a revolutionary spur of the moment. The organisation was part and parcel of the rule of the comprador class, which later grew into the fully fledged merchant–capital class (Amin 2015). Sadat, following the 1977 'Bread Revolt', selectively released malleable anti-Nasserite 'brothers' and the regime has cohabitated with them ever since (Awadi 2004, Amin 2015).[27] The only significant organised group prior the uprising was the MB (Amin 2015). On the policy side, first the MB and later the Sisi regime have sanctified existing distributional mechanisms. In every aspect, the process of accumulation continues to be one of dispossession and dislocation. Under the MB, the policies of the *ancien regime* were not reversed or adjusted; rather, they gained momentum (UN 2012). The desocialisation of policy and the displacement of labour, either by the import of labour-saving technology or by extra-economic means, accompany growth in the relative surplus population. In the meantime, the fervour of Islamisation, at first, and the revolutionary zeal experience during the July demonstrations in 2013 died down and were followed by despondency and arrests of political opponents. In addition to repression, the restructuring of the ideological instruments of the state to promote a higher dose of pragmatic coexistence with imperialism continue to postpone resurgence. In all the preceding, one

---

27 The Egyptian critic of political Islam, Farag Foda, had accused Sadat's secret police, *Moukhabarat*, of grooming and orchestrating the rise of Islamism in the universities and the countryside to combat the leftist and Nasserite movements opposed to his pro-American openness policies. Foda was assassinated on June 8, 1992, by a radical Islamic group. http://www.almasryalyoum.com/news/details/964111 (viewed 15 June 2016)

may recall the hypothesis that is being developed upon: insofar as value transfers are directly or circuitously materialised in the forms of imperial rents for US-led capital, these presuppose an Egyptian satellite state or a debilitated social formation under the aegis of the imperialist power nexus.

Uprising without Socialist Ideology

The Tahrir Square event and everything that came afterward appears as tragedy without a trace of farce or comedy. The romanticism of Western left discourse about the uprising is incapable of building an alternative ideological model. The daily dependency of the working class on the despotic power structure for earning its keep is not replaced by a system of socialist convictions commensurate with people's sacrifices and longings for long-term social security. The presence of labour–aristocratic elements within the ranks of the Egyptian left, principally as an appendage to Western Marxism but also to some extent developing nationally under the aegis of merchant capital, breeds the sort of consciousness that drops the alternative of armed struggle from the national agenda and capitulates to the illusion of change by liberal democracy. The unthinkably ludicrous part of the picture is that of democratising in the presence of malnutrition with reactionary Islamists leading frequent armed attacks against the state and robbing the left of its disgruntled working class. The material basis of social democracy and its labour aristocracy rest mainly in the pillage of the working classes in the Third World that are partly funnelled by 'democratic' concession to Western working classes. Bourgeois democracy is synonymous with the reasonability side of capital, its states, institutions and ideological structure, which through wage, bribes and identity differentials sows just the right amount of division amongst labour.

In distinguishing between inter-Western working-class schisms and Western-developing world working-class rifts, questions of degree matter. The very idea that any value, in qualitative, quantitative form or as a social relationship (the state of being of value), working its way toward the centre via capital's stabilising relationship of bourgeois democracy, its capital's key mechanism of resilience, is as relevant as the signification of value occurring as a result of the difference between the premature deaths as a result of neo-liberalism, poverty, wars and mortality (death in the absence of morbid causes) as put forth by Sutcliffe (2006). The shorter peripheral life spans are signification of differential value transfers between North and South. Undoubtedly, Arab and African survive with so little, and their lives are extinguished way before the historically conditioned life expectancy. The hold of liberal democracy on the consciousness of vast swathes of Western workers, which vacillates ideologically between social fascism and fascism, is not haphazard. It is rooted in the differential and historical value extraction from the days of chattel slavery to the present wars of imperialism. The late philosopher Lee-Boggs captured the culmination of lopsided development in revolutionary consciousness as such.

> The next American Revolution, at this stage in our history, is not principally about jobs or health insurance or making it possible for more people to realize the American Dream of upward mobility. It is about acknowledging that we Americans have enjoyed middle class comforts at the expense of other peoples all over the world. (2011: 72)

As flows of imperialism raise the wealth and boost the higher wages of central classes, they also underlie the determination of nationalistically based class consciousness. This is not to say that central revolutions are not a possibility through praxis. The problematic of revolution in the centre has to be framed in terms of the material grounds forming consciousness and the difficulties posed by such social conditions. Most developments in Western Marxian theory (Western in the ideological and not in the geographic sense) when following the resource-flow channels, either neglect the social repercussions of imperialist booty or paint it in an incoherent way. Revisions to the Marxian law of value, the state of becoming in the contradiction between exchange and use values as observed in the various stages of the class struggle (of which imperialist war is the epitome), comes to deal more with how prices would revert to value in a fantasy world, without seeing the sociological aspect of how nationalism/sectarianism and politicising cultural distinctions segregate international working people. The rational side of capital, its ideology in practice, must hold back the objective grounds for the unification of the international working class. In a sardonic critique of the supposedly benign prices that will adjust to value leading to 'even' development by a 'progressive capitalism', including the equalisation of wages by the pull of market forces, Weeks (1998) notes that 'while the logic of the law of value implies capitalism is progressive, it is relevant here to recall Oscar Wilde's aphorism that madness is carrying any argument to its logical conclusion'.

That some workers of nations of exceptionalism are 'rightfully' richer on account of technology and cultural characteristics is an idea that replaced the superiority of race with the superiority of culture or machines. The class core of the existential linkages, the real value chain that begins with imperial assault on the periphery and ends with the product on the Western market and, one that unites a child picking cotton in Egypt to a car factory worker in Germany, is purposefully hidden from view. Worse yet, it is at times quantified in terms of prices to show that the whole wealth and lives of the Third World are insignificant. In actuality, value, in its real and qualitative aspect to which the toil and lives of peripheral working classes contribute, is appropriated by the international bourgeois classes and passed in welfare gains mainly to Western working classes (Emmanuel 1972; Cope 2015). A weakened and subjugated Egypt has provided cover for such transfers. Tangentially, I am aware of the interplay of forces that shifted austerity to the North, but as I argue in chapter 6, the threshold for parting with working-class dividedness depends largely on how the class struggle mediates the national or the particular into the international or universal.

In the same way that sectarian politics can arrest the realisation of working-class power in the state, Islamic forms of identity that are petrodollar-funded slice across Arab and Egyptian working classes. In view of socialist decline, current identity politics spawns the inverse of what Lee Boggs (2011) saw in the Black Liberation Movement's extending its struggle to include all sections of the working class – an identity-based struggle that grows out of itself. At the current conjuncture, the same intermediation between identity and class cannot occur because the overarching ideology that was socialism then – and from which peoples' struggles drew strength – has been supplanted by a sort of Meta-ideology that is neo-liberalism.

The funding and dissemination of these divisive modes of identity, such as Copt and various Islamist identities in Egypt, serve the purpose of implosion within the working classes: collapse as a class-for-itself followed by fragmentation. The imperialist selection of Islamic politics for this purpose has historical roots in the collaboration of the MB with the British in Nasser's time and later in the US funding of jihadists in Afghanistan (Amin 2007). Although in real history it was not Islamic ideologies that governed: 'they merely expounded God's opinion' (Rodinson 1978, 73); the mainstream relegates underdevelopment to some undying concepts of Islam. However, modern poor developmental showings are better understood within their specific historical circumstances and as a result of the social forces that have shaped them, or as Rodinson (1978) sees it, as a result of political declassing rather than religious precepts. Political Islamists provide a valuable service to imperialism in that they shift the axis of the struggle into reassessing divine moral values behind underdevelopment as opposed to prioritising the appropriation of a higher share of the social product through anti-imperialist struggle. In relation to the circuit of capital, and that is what really counts, both, the Islamists and Sisi's regime sanctify the rule of the market even more than does neoclassical economics. In any case, given poverty in Egypt, imperialist-guided funding of obscurantism through the Gulf or US aid requires only a small fraction of oil flows. At a foundational level, political Islam does not oppose Sisi's comprador capitalism.

In peripheral formations like Egypt, the crisis of capital is constantly severe and the anti-imperialist struggle as such should have priority over internal squabbles in distributional arrangements nationally. National security precedes the making of social security, although in the ideal state, they complement each other. The struggle is for national autonomy. It is a struggle in which an alliance of social classes under the leadership of the working class against various forms of imperialist encroachment resurrects an inviolability of the sovereign à la Hobbes. At a general, but not exclusive, level the point is: there cannot likely be anything resembling a humanist development in formations integrated with global capital via war encroachment without situating the development agenda in an anti-imperialist context. If anything remotely resembling an egalitarian development agenda were to be applied under the aegis of imperialism, it would only be to meet the objectives of the imperialist ulterior motives of imperialist stabilisation measures.

In Egypt, the imperialist bargain struck with the local comprador under *infitah* expels huge numbers of workers from gainful employment and debilitates social security. In risk terms, the weakness of Egypt lessens the calculated risks for US-led imperialism to penetrate and exploit other dependent formations in Africa and the Middle East. The destruction to developing social formations releases cheapened human and natural assets and lays the social groundwork for the rate of commercial and labour exploitation to hold steady or preferably rise by absolute appropriation. When the production process depends on a growing global network of cheapened inputs, the most vulnerable places in the Third World are deconstructed to be consumed at exponential rates conditioned by the lessened power of the global working class in relation to rising profit rates for capital.

The financialisation stage of imperialism has integrated multifarious concrete capitals whose success is not to be measured only in the quantitative aspect of amassed universal money form or dollars, but more importantly by the degree to which capital subjugates labour by ideological influence.

> The reproduction of labour power requires not only a reproduction of its skills, but also, at the same time, a reproduction of its submission to the rules of the established order, i.e. a reproduction of submission to the ruling ideology for the workers, and a reproduction of the ability to manipulate the ruling ideology correctly for the agents of exploitation and repression, so that they, too, will provide for the domination of the ruling class 'in words' (Althusser 1994, 104).

If one allows oneself to reason teleologically, the latter (the sociological condition) is a precondition of the former (the economic condition). Despite being surrounded by the glitter of ostentatious displays of comprador-class wealth contrasted with the squalor of slums, the ranks of peripheral labour aristocrats parading under liberalism swelled after 1990. Egypt was no exception, especially as many leaders of the revolt expressed anger without any vision of transforming the existing order. Modes of bourgeois democratic governance in the Western hemisphere, which have mostly arisen as reorganisations of the imperialist homeland for the purpose of plunder, became the moral and political standard by which the ransacked Egyptian periphery was to live. Workers earning poverty wages, or idle people who could not afford a decent standard of living, had the choice of voting for the old regime or the Islamists. Ideals of democracy without material substantiation, as in command over value transfers, mystify the comprehension of social processes and apportion blame for de-development to culture, tradition or moral retrogression. As The argument that 'Egyptians did not know any better' is just about bending the moral categorical imperative on the universality of human rights to the utilitarian ends of empire. If Saudis or Egyptians oppress women or inflict hunger, imperialist mouthpieces would wryly posit that 'this is just their culture', when in fact such pain is an existential condition, a concrete universal that knows no national or cultural boundaries. With the left lagging behind as a result of the erosion and decline of internationalist values, there is a vacated ideological space into which imperialism injects the politics of reaction and identity that serve its strategy. Imperialism in the epoch of socialist retreat has the luxury of choosing its enemy (Amin 2010).

In the midst of ideological defeat, the liberal compromise of the Arab left became alien to the broadest sections of the masses. In Egypt, the poorest peasantry and working classes voted radical Salafi groups into parliament next to the MB in the first post-uprising election (Bianchi, 2012). Together, Islamists (the Al Nour party and the MB) occupied two-thirds of the first parliament after Mubarak. The alternative to moderate fundamentalists became the extreme fundamentalists. To express it formulaically – as opposed to viewing it as historically contingent – this retrogression ensues from a history of decline in industrialism and social development and a drop in socialist and humanist values intersecting with the premeditated strengthening of the Salafi doctrine with Gulf petrodollars. Capital's ideological thrust decouples practical modes of consciousness and replaces them with modes of reasoning that shift the mythology of good and evil from class conflict to divine absolutism. A non-existent pre-capitalist or Islamic past is continuously reconstructed, rewritten and packaged in print as if it is science, although no critique of it is acceptable because it is divine, and the fantastic part of the story is that heavenly intervention in worldly affair assumes new heights. The imaginary abounds while the real political force of class vanishes in this mystification.

The discourse splintering the working classes in the Arab periphery applies to the centre with some superficial permutations on a basic principle, which is always to conceptually confound social class with identity. There is no class without identity, but when the real living process by which people earn their keep and recreate themselves is said to be rooted in cultural practices dating back millennia rather than in everyday material ties, as in earning wages to survive, theoretical fatalism comes to presuppose religious fatalism. It is not that culture is pitted against materialism; the two are intertwined and in a totality in which the determining moment lies at the level of the object or the materiality of living conditions (Lukács 1967). However, working-class alliances come apart when the particular circumstances of the struggle do not intermediate the general condition: when Islamist, Coptic and other identity politics reduce the struggle to 'What's in it for me'? The 'me' here does not include every member of the cultural group, but is the false belief each member identifies with to offset the blatant inequality within the cultural group itself. The perception of a universal common good, which would lead the individual worker to see the necessity of bringing the local struggle against imperialism to fruition to the benefit of the whole, is lost in preoccupation with identity-group precedence or perceived insult to the group or its beliefs.

As elsewhere in the AW, sectarian or identity-laced divisiveness in Egypt is lurking beneath the social plane and being fed by uneven development and deleterious dollar funding. In the same way, the attacks on the Copts during the Arab Spring diverted attention from the broader uprising issues, sectarian conflict can be resurrected when the next uprising looms to abort the revolutionary transition. Disaster-stricken and identity-fragmented peripheral formations facilitate value transfer and, in a purely analytical sense, contribute more to value formation via commercial exploitation and absolute, as distinct from relative, surplus value, although these types of value are not differentiable in actuality. Surplus value cannot just be mimicked by the rate of exploitation of central productive labour or the central profits, rents interest and royalties. Where to draw the line between productive and unproductive labour in the formation of value must include the issue of commercial exploitation: the slave-like labour of the Third World, the war industry and the ontological conditions for capitalist reproduction that articulate peripheral modes of production by violence. The moment the Eurocentric optic drops, the Asian sweatshop working class and the invasion of Iraq consuming a significant part of its population in the Western-sponsored war industry, become the productive labour whose value is under-signified by the price that ensues from the power balances of the class struggle.

Destruction of value and the grabbing of value at little or no cost, mostly by violent means, is the mainstay of imperialism in the AW and Africa. Value seizure from defeated social classes, both within a state or as a result of state collapse (in at least one of its value facets) counteracts the tendency of falling profit rates identified by Marx. I am focusing only on specific mitigating factors, for it is beyond the scope of this work to discuss the imbroglio of the tendency of the rate of profit to fall. To be specific, the reduction of the raw materials costs is one counteracting component of the falling rate of profit (Marx 1894), but the engagement of unpaid or lowly paid labour, war-tied-up labour and the huge yet dispensable reserve armies of labour are an a priori condition of capital (the pedestal that was slavery in Marx's words never parted the scene of capital accumulation). Under commercial exploitation, which grinds down the human, material and ecological constituents' production in a peripheral country such as Egypt, the contribution to profits from imperialist hegemony is doubly effective.

More so than lowering the costs of constant capital, which in turn may contribute, *inter alia*, with all the other mitigating factors, to raising profits, commercial exploitation creates huge reserves of labour that pressure wages downwards, including the wages of the central working classes. Commercial exploitation and politically weakened peripheral working classes cement the ideological grounds on which capital increases the rate of social inequality vis-à-vis legal equality before the state; it pushes waged employment closer to forms of slavery. This decline in social rights is what Balibar (1991) should have had in mind when he addressed the making of the terrain for structural and differentiated racism.

In Egypt and the Islamic world, the Islamisation of political culture severs working class unity. Waged work under capitalism is social, and the ties of labour are organic. The positive-sum game of higher wages resulting from the secular trend of rising organic composition of capital and productivity moves in reverse when the working class is divided. A divided class lacks the power to obtain higher wages, as became apparent in Egypt prior to the uprising when real wages dipped significantly. But 'organic' means that the setback suffered by peripheral social classes will also hollow out the power of the central working classes, except for the way the organised dimension of capital – its resilience via bourgeois democracy – bribes central working classes. Account taken of the rising organic composition of capital, and its by-product, continued rising wealth in real history, the concession through democracy to workers of the North must undermine the relative share of the social product in the South. The hegemony of capital and its favoured political identities ensures that at no time will the organic ties across the globe coincide to consolidate the power of global labour. The pizza that was ordered from Tahrir Square to be delivered to Capitol Square in Madison is one such coincidence in real time that capital abhors (Benjamin 2011). Imperialist contamination through Gulf and American aid to abort the struggle and reduce the ripple effect of revolutionary appeal has been under way. Labour aristocrats assume different roles, but at a general level their purpose as interlocutors of capital is to delude working people with the idea of bourgeois democracy and to widen the gap between social being and social consciousness by placing identity over class.

In Egypt, the determining moment in capital accumulation combines dispossession, value grabbing and commercial exploitation bereft of progress in national industrial development. Negative productivity growth implies that diminishing rates of added value are experienced nationally, and the profits of the ruling merchant class accrue from lowering the share of labour and from circulation. 'Circulation, of the exchange of commodities, creates no value' (Marx 1867), and in Egypt, the greater part of additional value is snatched from the life-sustaining resources by which society stabilises itself. The dollar space into which nationally grabbed wealth grows necessitates an alliance of the Egyptian ruling class with the central classes or with classes rooted in the dollar-based international financial structure. On the flip side, working class alliances across the globe remain brittle. The ideological resonance of pizza-buying for Wisconsin strikers, as a token and symbolic gesture, was quelled (Kroll 2011). In any case, if that is the most that happens in terms of global labour solidarity, when dislodging capital requires forms of violent struggle, the working class is back to square one. Capturing value in Egypt for the Egyptian working class necessitates controls on trade, finance and more egalitarian resource redistribution. The chances that measures of this nature would apply without working-class ordained violence in such a strategic place are remote.

Closing Comments

Morsi posited that he needed a hundred days to turn the economy around in Egypt (El Sharnouby 2012). Sisi says he needed longer given the complexity of the task, but three years after he ascended to the highest public office (at the time of writing in 2016), policies have not changed, and living conditions have not improved (Accorsi and Piazzese 2014). In Egypt's negotiations with the IMF, Sisi's ruling class is materially inclined to concede to the loan terms. The headlines from Egypt, however, speak of dwindling wheat stock, rising food prices, fuel and drug shortages and a restive population (Abaza 2013; Saleh 2013; Westall and Perry 2013). Qatar slowed its financial support for Egypt on the grounds that past disbursements did not suffice to relaunch growth, and later withdrew its support for reasons to do with the political persecution of its allies in the MB (Doherty and Saleh 2013). Currently, other Gulf states fill the financial gap needed to sustain the dollar-pegged currency. Ongoing strikes and civil unrest in several cities could spiral into chaos, necessitating the intervention of the armed forces (De Smet and Malfait 2015). The conditions for another uprising are maturing at the level of working-class dissatisfaction and, more important, at the level of ruling-class disarray, which continues to mount. For US-led capital, the dilemma lies in not overstretching its military resources as the domino effect of Arab crises engulfs the whole region, on one hand, and stabilising Egypt long enough to curb the intrusions of Russia (China behind Russia, too) on the other. The benefits of booty from the US surrogate sovereignty over the Gulf, at least for the time being, exceed the gains from capsizing the Egyptian social formation altogether.

Meanwhile, Sisi's measures of stabilisation include the reduction of public expenditure, labour-market liberalisation, further shifts from government-led to private-sector-led investment and export-oriented growth. These policies meet the disciplining conditions imposed by Bretton Woods' institutions, which always arrive under the false pretence of poverty reduction:

> The cause of poverty reduction is best served by more rapid adjustment to fiscal imbalances, rapid adjustment to lower inflation and external deficits and the use of higher interest rates to achieve these ends, internal and external financial sector liberalization, deregulation of capital controls, deep and rapid privatisation of state owned enterprises, and, perhaps the strongest unifying factor – rapid and major opening up of the economy to trade and foreign direct investment. (Kanbur 2001)

If one breaks down the effect of these supposed poverty-reducing polices, we get the following: reducing spending on social programmes; reducing wages, credit and money supply to the working class; opening up trade in food and industry to destroy national agriculture and manufacturing; higher interest rates to supply credit and hold the national currency steady for the national bourgeoisie and, lastly: not that privatisation is ideal, but privatise under an uneven legal and political structure shifts public assets to be liquidated by the merchant class. That is not a theoretical rebuttal. That is what has happened in Egypt and elsewhere in the AW. Generally, poor theory must resort to falsification of fact. The money trail from such policies is anti-working class. If it is a question of the facetious position of waiting long enough for the brilliant outcome to materialise, the working class, unlike World Bank staff, has precious little time to wait.

Prior to the uprising, the World Bank commended Egypt for its fast pace of reform. Past liberalising reforms, however, did not attract developmental investment (plant and equipment), sustain equitable growth or create enough jobs, as the pre-uprising neo-liberal literature claimed they would (as in Dasgupta, Keller and Srinivasan (2002, 90) and Pfeiffer (2000, 113–114). Although the World Bank demands openness, the single most-devastating cause of Egypt's poverty is precisely openness. Had Egypt curtailed openness to recirculate its wealth nationally, it would not have lost nearly as much in value transfers upward and abroad (to its own merchant class and to the dollar domain). The onus of central-bank-funded pegging to the dollar under open capital accounts in addition to exposure in food security leaves the country at the mercy of US-led capital and its Gulf associates.

Just as in the days of Arab socialism, more equitable redistribution, capital and trade controls, multiple exchange and interest rates all remain requisites to shift the development course from its dependency on handouts into a sui generis industrially driven economy. But a reminder: a sounder development strategy might undermine US-led imperialist hegemony. With Syria and Iraq having fallen and Iran staggering, nearly the whole of the region is firmly in the grip of US-led imperialist forces. However, *pax Americana* is different from *pax Romana*. In fact, it should be *bellum Americanum*. The Roman Empire needed stability and population growth to raise tribute, whereas US-led capital raises tribute via productivity growth and by the selective destruction of physical and human assets, especially in vulnerable Third World areas.

Already, US-sponsored and petrodollar-funded Salafi organisations and ideologies infiltrate the lowest segments of society. The stratum of the working class willing to sacrifice the most in anti-imperialist struggle finds its efforts diverted into fuelling the prosperity of capital by expanding the justification of the 'war on terror' or the destruction of value for profits. For the time being, the social forces that shape history are those of capital, and the conditions of working-class struggle appear much more insurmountable than they did before the uprising. Coming to terms with the iron fist of the Sisi regime that has proven more repressive than Mubarak's, and with the even more aggressively blocked ideological horizon for social change, the participation rate in the parliamentary elections of 15 October 2015, was as low as 2 per cent on the first day of voting, with a total participation rate as low as 15 per cent.[28] The despondency that marked the populace after the failed Arab Spring is beginning to hinder the prospects of a socialist resurgence.

28 First Round of Egyptian Parliamentary Elections Ends: Early poll numbers show low turnout in vote expected to bolster clout of country's president, http://www.wsj.com/articles/first-round-of-egyptian-parliamentary-elections-ends-1445281201 (Viewed 21 October 2015). The Egyptian people have turned their back to the election process. http://www.raialyoum.com/?p=332593 (Viewed 21 October 2015).

For the time being, socialist discourse fails to punctuate in the slightest the development debate. However, as the numbing effect of neo-liberal demagogy wears off, which it will inevitably, another potential popular insurrection will gain momentum. The speed of historical time or the time it takes to effect social change in the information age will increase further and overcome the lethargic pace of chronological time. As Marx tellingly put it:

> The more production comes to rest on exchange value, hence on exchange, the more important do the physical conditions of exchange – the means of communication and transport – become for the costs of circulation. Capital by its nature drives beyond every spatial barrier. Thus the creation of the physical conditions of exchange – of the means of communication and transport – the annihilation of space by time – becomes an extraordinary necessity for it. (Marx [1877]1973)

In Egypt, the circulation of exchange value did not by itself generate an expansion in the national means of communication because exchange under the dominant merchant mode shuns the creation of value by industrial or productivity growth. Advanced means of communication, as is the case for much borrowed technology in the Third World, originated abroad. But merchant capital is pure exchange, and an extension of the means of communication to the periphery follows from the inherent growth in technology globally. Just as the first anti-parasitic drugs for malaria reached Africa as English cows contracted a parasitic disease similar to malaria for which the English pharmaceutical industry had developed a medication, the means of communication also reached Egypt to facilitate the role of exchange as a spinoff to the product lifecycle.

But social media and information technology might also facilitate revolt once again. Not that revolutions need an Internet connection to burst into the open, but to the extent that revolutionary deliberations escape the control of capital as actual struggle plus *détournement* (one may extend Debord's 1967 notion of using images and revolutionary language to undermine dominant ideology), another Egyptian revolt may be dubbed an Internet revolution. For that to happen, social space has to collapse into and partly reappear as cyberspace. The speed of the modern means of communication had already made redundant the socialising factory floor of the nineteenth century, which arose as the space to conquer for an all-out revolt. The secular trend of faster circulation, quicker value usurpation and their attendant speedier information exchange found the new platform (factory floor) for working class revolt. Whether the next rebellion will transmute into a social revolution will pretty much depend on socialist ideological spread and development globally.

Chapter 3

THE INFEASIBILITY OF REVOLUTION IN SYRIA

That the Syrian regime had squeezed the Syrian state to an extent that it had jeopardised its very conditions for existence is borne out by the recent uprising and ongoing social and political unrest. The reasons for the ongoing collapse are many. In the literature they oscillate between the purely economic to the wholly political, with shades of synthesis in between. To whichever side of the argument one leans, the Syrian military in alliance with various strata of society is allegedly the perpetrator of the ruin or, literally, the subject of this passage of history. But the most relevant overtone of the uprising to date has little to do with domestic conditions and more to do with the great tectonic collision between the Sino-Russian camp on one side and the Euro-American camp on the other. The world appears to be reliving a proxy war for the division of peripheral formations, resembling to some degree a pre-World War I scenario. Prior to the uprising, the Syrian regime and its associated social class usurped the resources of Syria, deepening its misery and driving it to the point of uprising, doing so with the tutelage of Western powers and World Bank (WB) instructions on liberalisation. Since the uprising, the Syrian regime and its associated class, battered as they are, could not have remained in power this long without the support of the Sino-Russian constellation. Thus, the discourse that conflates the Syrian regime with the subject of history is a miscategorisation and an inadequate conceptual tool for communicating developments in a process. 'The regime is to blame' catchphrase extracts selective details from the historical process in order to provide a less-than-full understanding of the ongoing conditions. It is social science meant for an ideologically biased culpability game, or one that exonerates US-led imperialism from its crimes against humanity.

Tangentially and on ethical grounds, or by Kantian moral equivalence, all parties involved in the making of conflict are implicated. But by an act or reasoned position that mitigates the intensification of the atrocities of the US-led class and its ideology on a global scale as a result of Syria's succumbing to the US-led imperialist camp and the subsequent deepening of the rule of capital, it is only the Syrian cohort realigned with US militarism that bears the burden of responsibility.

At the Kantian equivalence stage, the responsibility is not greater for those whose acts have worse consequences. Responsibility in that sense is unquantifiable. In the historical era of monopoly capitalism, whose principal relationship is capital, the ethical challenge is to motivate the issue historically by asking what revolutionary act of resistance should be carried out to thwart the rule of the US-led capital class, its free market policies, poisonous democracy and human rights cant and accumulation by militarism and finance. Moreover, given the strategic importance of Syria and the region, this conflict and its outcome have daunting repercussions across the globe. The practical, cum ethical, imperative is to situate the Syrian national struggle in an anti-imperialist context.

The notion that a small military clique in a strategic corner of the globe commands history is *prima facie* absurd and, in principle, methodologically flawed because it depicts a partially skewed view of things or a falsification of fact. Neither Syria, as a political entity, nor the very constitution of its internal conditions can be said to be primarily effected by nationally generated forces. As I argue in this chapter, it is not by chance that Syria parted with Arab socialism, and that the allocation of the social product to developmental ends receded after two principal military defeats, in 1967 and 1973; and, at any rate, this was an era of global descent into neo-liberalism. As more Arab countries flew into the US-led 'moderate' orbit (Egypt in particular), the regional balance of forces further tilted against Syria. In spite of its pan-Arab hubris, Syria's weakening security position became glaringly obvious. In a self-serving manner, which coincided with the goals of US-led imperialism, the regime and its associated class turned the state of defeat into ideological defeatism and employed it as an alibi to pass more of the 'pragmatic' concessions that eroded development and enriched the capitalist class. For a long time, the Syrian working population tolerated the heavy toll of austerity as the price for its anti-imperialist position. The state bourgeoisie, however, siphoned off national resources and betrayed the popular sacrifice. Changes to national class formation, specifically, the expansion of the culture-medium for private-sector growth – the free market incubation context – responded to the contiguous demands of US-led imperialism and the ascending Syrian bourgeoisie.

Since the battle of Maysalun in 1920 – which appears to have been more like mass suicide than a military confrontation as a few thousand ill-equipped Syrian fighters confronted a French mechanised infantry division with aerial support outnumbering them five to one – the creation of Syria and the course of its history have been primarily shaped by monolithic extra-national forces. Superior military force still stands out as the foremost component of the power structure with which Syria is faced. In this chapter, I argue that the determining relationship in recent Syrian history represents a cross-border class alliance in which the regime and its class were structural partners of US-led imperialism, until the time of the uprising. As is often the case, class ties of the leading capital interests supersede national interests. In the shadow of a distorted power structure, the Syrian regime and its associated class gullibly internalised the neo-liberal cant, transplanted their reproductive base to the dollarised global market, and thereby became a class whose material and ideological bases are an extension of imperialism.[1] In its latter stages of neo-liberal development, the class in charge of Syria became that part of the cross-border relationship with imperialism whose realisation in war strengthens the US-led imperialist goal of hegemony. It became the class that sacrificed its own social formation to its former imperialist partner, who had already laid down its inauspicious path of class apoptosis. In its desultory unity with imperialism, attracted to and then opposing it, the Syrian regime and its associated class are secondary in relation to the making of Syrian history, in which 'secondary' means that its capacity to guide events is merely a minor derivative of a balance of real global and ideological forces. In its current personification, the regime is left to fend off a concerted global reactionary assault on the national territory.

The regime and its associated class are afforded real, if narrow, margins within which to enact and administer a certain state of affairs, but the historical scene, the context itself, was shaped by the results of an inter-imperialist struggle for the control of the Middle East. The peculiarity of Syria's weakened security-cum-position-of-sovereignty in a highly strategic region implies that the class in charge was appropriating more of its surplus from the geopolitical rents wrung from cross-border relationships. Although every national ruling class enjoys some partnership with extra-national classes, the fact that geopolitical ties determined both the degree of flows into Syria and the productivity of the leading domestic sectors meant that the material basis for national decision-making lay principally in these extra-national relationships. The regime and its associated class were trading not only goods and services, but also the weight of Syria in

---

1 The state of ignorance gripping the upper echelons of the ruling clique can best viewed from the results of the fieldwork conducted by Matar (2016). She recounts how state officials were aghast with the idea that the president studied in the UK, had a British wife, and wanted to become European-like in his ways, as in joining modernity and leaving behind the legacy of the Ba'ath and its socialism. A shallow invidious emulation of consumption patterns typical of developing countries' elite has always been a sign for the onset of a social national catastrophe.

the regional security structure, which in 2015 drew an 'on-the-ground' Russian intervention. That is why, when the regime decided to fully adopt the neo-liberal strategy at home, it also went to the extreme of structurally fulfilling the diktat of US-led imperialism, including its links to the CIA's 'black-site' renditions. It is in this interrelated class context that the regime's margin of manoeuvre and autonomy are defined. In hindsight, as the region falls victim to accumulation by wars of encroachment, Syria was predestined to be flattened by this implacable trend of history.

Conventional propaganda acting as received wisdom posits that the Syrian regime represents the principal agent of contemporary Syrian history. Like the superhuman heroes of Greek mythology, a handful of people in power in a supposedly somewhat secluded state are depicted as the evil force responsible for Syrian political and economic disaster, with resonance disturbing a global balance of power. In parallel, Syria the nation state itself is reified as a prime agent of history, one that was incapable of meeting the challenges of democratisation and modernity for 'inherent' reasons of corruption, culture or a state whose people are innately ahistorical.

In reality, neither the regime nor Syria as a state can be said to enjoy any significant degree of seclusion from the rest of the world. Once the fact of interrelatedness is established, then, one must investigate the determinacy in the inter-relationship. The purpose of this chapter is to read the gradual departure of Syria from the framework of Arab socialism and rebut the received assumption of history constructed on the basis of personal powers. It is to assess recent Syrian history from the point of view of the interconnectedness of the Syrian class structure with imperialism. Equally important is to demonstrate through tracing the circuit of capital or critically reading an account of recent economic history (insofar as it can be documented), that the process of accumulation by encroachment *qua* imperialism that is headed by US-led capital, is the primary subject of the developments in Syria. Unlike most past colonial practice, US-led capital benefits more from a fragmented, devastated and non-sovereign Syrian society than it does from Syria as a cohesive entity. The intermediated relationships of history are the real classes, but the real human beings who personify those relationships and their respective agencies are couched within the historically given forms of social organisation that reproduce the conditions for class rule and value flows. The ruling Syrian military-mercantile class, international financial capital and its governance structures, exemplify the dominant social forms through which the ruling class – the class alliance of national and international agents rooted in the dollar material domain – self-realises. It is through these objective and impersonal class processes that the exercise of ruling-class power holds back necessary social change.

Much has been written about the Assad regime's early political swerve to the right in key historical moments: its containment in 1976 of the Palestine Liberation Organisation (PLO) and the Lebanese National Movement (LNM); its devolution of resources along sectarian lines; and its participation in the 'Coalition of the Willing' in the war on Iraq, to name a few. This chapter, however, mainly focuses on the economic evidence of class collaboration between the Assad regimes (both father and son) and imperialism until the dawn of the uprising in 2011. The collaboration itself ended in 2011 when the US and its allies turned against their partners and decided to bring down the whole of the social formation, as they have done in Iraq.

Subordinately, this chapter addresses the pattern of value divesture as additional proof of an structural class alliance between the Syrian military–merchant class and US-led imperialism, as a result of which national development faltered, contributing in turn to the rise of a war economy and its associated war bourgeoisie, whose essential characteristic is the drawing of surplus through inter-communal fighting. I follow the evolution of resource allocation from the Arab socialist stage to the neo-liberal mode and justify my claim that these neo-liberal developments paved the road to disaster on two counts: the international shift in the global environment toward financialisation, neo-liberalism and militarisation; and the inherent tendency of the Syrian state bourgeois class to grow into a bourgeoisie proper.

A Note on State and Class

The case may be that conceptually no state rises above class to occupy the driver's seat of history. However, for Syria, the collapse of class into state is more pronounced – that is, without the subtle disguise in bourgeois democratic or legal institutions of class power in the state. As a deployable concept, the Syrian state, innately fraught with contradictions and later unravelling, would be less than adequate for capturing the role of social forces in a political process. The Syrian state was already on a downward path, which is post facto proof of the overbearing weight of class over state. The fleeting state autonomy that Poulantzas (1978) claimed to have observed, and which sustains social reproduction at the behest of capital, vanishes to the point where the state reduces itself to a mere instrument of a ruling class continuously subjugated to imperialist pressure. Capital can assert hegemony over society through the state by controlling the destabilisation that results from short-term profiteering. However, that function is not an alternative that the Syrian ruling class chose; it is imperialism that carries out the strategic choices. For the purpose of this chapter also, the subject of history is not an analytical interplay between individualistic agency and structure; it is an articulation of classes reconstituted by imperialist aggression. To effectively analyse this articulation, one must recognise the primacy of class *relationships* over classes considered as aggregations of individuals. As already stated in the introduction, social classes cannot exist outside class relationships, whether in alliance with or opposition to imperialism. Ruling classes are real social relationships in a state of flux whose determination, development, and growth lie in their capacity to appropriate wealth by means of value realisation and dispossession. A capitalist class in the act of expropriating the working class is capital accumulation. Relationships between classes are co-determined by the social relations of production. In Syria, as in many Arab countries, the specificity of value expropriation by dislocation of direct producers and war came to characterise the social formation. By these I mean surplus accrued to the ruling military–merchant class without rising productivity – a monetisation of natural and social assets or as in crushing the social formation to cheapen people and resources. Once the circuits of value are opened, the scope of capitalist development into which nationally grabbed wealth is to flow necessitates an alliance of the ruling class with imperialist classes rooted in the dollar-based international financial structure.

The relationship of the Arab ruling classes with imperialism is only marginally supported by the surplus seized in money form from their respective states. With the obvious exception of the Gulf States, the relatively small amount of money capital drawn from Arab nations in general and Syria in particular by the ruling military–merchant class is not the primary concern of US-led imperialism. With neo-liberal reforms, whatever Syrian dollar assets existed, they were recirculated abroad and eventually held in US Treasury bills. In the Middle East, the core objective of imperialism is strategic control in order to pressure the rest of the world into submitting to imperialism's political and financial order. By contrast, the objective of the Arab ruling classes is to requisition the national accumulation process for the purpose of generating and dollarising wealth from the national economy itself. More often than not, these objectives do not overlap. Although the Syrian military–merchant class and US-led capital co-align their objectives when their earnings are tabulated in dollar form, these classes draw their earnings from differing sources, channels, and practices. Although the dollar joins and universalises two strands of capitalistic social classes, the Syrian merchant-inclined social classes remained subservient to US-led financial capital because they had to dollarise their capital as they grow – the level of submission to imperialism was such that just before the uprising of 2011, the dollar could be exchanged for commodities on the streets of Damascus (Matar 2016). In this uneasy symbiosis (regime and US-led imperialism), the regime's class represents the subsidiary partner, while imperialism generates its rents from the power it draws by debilitating Syrian working-class security and the sovercignty of the very state from which the Syrian bourgeoisie arrogates its wealth. Hence the interests of these two cross-cutting partners were set to diverge.

US imperial rents rise by the degree of strategic control of oil it exerciscs in the Middle East, a process that principally underwrites the dollar as the world's medium of wealth holding (Avramidis 2006, Patnaik 2009). Always within the context of imperialist hegemony, Iran's relative autonomy undercuts the stature of the US empire and its ambition to control the eastern flank of the Gulf. Although prior to the uprising, the Syrian regime's relationship with Iran was 'business-like', Iran's and Hezbollah's anti-Israeli positions had provided a facade of legitimacy to counteract the growing popular dissatisfaction with lower wages and as a result of the regime's growing share of wealth. Post uprising, the stabilisation arrangement that the Syrian regime had instilled at the behest of US-led capital withered. In the new phase of the US–Iran stalemate, the rules of the game changed. More than just the capitulation of the Syrian regime, but the destruction of the Syrian social and physical infrastructure was in the offing. The reintroduction of national proxies of imperialism as partners in the formation of the state is the new mode of recolonisation in the Middle East. US-led imperialism has developed a new pathway to colonial conquests: a weak and fractured state in which its political leverage, principally backed by military means, settles the political process. As the momentum was building against Iran, a Syria that was slowly fragmenting under robber capitalism had to be dissolved. The power of US-led capital does not decline with the destruction of Syria and, unlike the stagism put forth by the astute socialist website 'Lenin's Tomb',[2] the Syrian conflict experienced a single phase: the phase of war without scope for resolution. Given shattered Arab states, the power of US-led capital measured by the degree of its strategic control is at its peak, threatened only by the potential impact of a Russian intervention that is symptomatic of shifts in the global power structure. The notion that the US is weakened or has failed in the region, and that a revolutionary force in Syria could or would erect a pluralist democratic state there (or anywhere in the Middle East) is illusory. It is the unease of China and other major developing nations in relation to their holdings of unsubstantiated dollar-debts and the anti-American measures they exercise that determine whether US-led capital weakens or not.

2 See 'The Syrian revolt enters a new phase'; 24 July 2012 (viewed 5 June 2013) http://www.leninology.com/2012/07/the-syrian-revolt-enters-new-phase.html

The Debate on Reforms

As usually occurs with the imposition of neo-liberal policies, the Syrian ruling class pushed the share and revenues of huge sections of the Syrian working class below the historically determined minimum income. They effectively expanded the objective grounds that contributed to the making of the recent uprising. In most analyses, however, one-sided economic causes, without grounding in a broader politico-economic context, are presented as the reasons behind Syria's slide into the abyss.

The collapse of Arab socialism is attributed to statist economic practices and their alleged outcomes, such as low levels of productivity, resource misallocation, institutional weakness, debt build-up and foreign-exchange shortages.[3] But this is not true. It is as if no one bothered to check the statistical facts as shown by the Annex to chapter 1. Only on account of investment per worker, which rose to $3,117 per worker in 1980 (measured in purchasing-power parity dollars) and later went down to a plateau of $2,000 between 1985 and 2008, the dirigiste past appears far more advanced than the neo-liberal era (Marquetti and Foley 2011). It was during neo-liberalism that productivity growth became negative, unemployment rose, public and private institutions exhibited a marked lack of efficacy, real wages declined and inflation rose significantly.[4] The estimated output capital ratio after 30 years of

---

3 This quote from the Economic Research Forum (ERF) captures the gist of the mainstream message regarding Arab socialism: 'Import substitution strategy in the aftermath of WWII produced enormous benefits in most countries, it also had its limits; the inefficiency of bureaucracy and limits of social programs without enough economic growth resulted in the switch to liberalisation. Most of these countries liberalised on both the economic and political fronts'. See the Economic Research Forum's publication: *The Post-Revolutionary Economic Prospects of Egypt*, http://erf.org.eg/?s=socialism&type=all, undated (viewed 2 December 2015). One ought to note that economic growth in this period was quite high and, therefore, the ERF is falsifying facts. Moreover, 'liberalised', as in loosened the wealth supply channels to the bourgeoisies had indeed taken place, but politically, judging by the monumental failure in human-rights abuse both in terms of depriving people of basic necessities and political representation, seems to be an outlandish remark to have been made. What the mainstream dubs as the authoritarian bargain model, the exchange of economic benefits, welfare and public employment programs in return for consent in an anti-imperialist struggle context, was replaced with what one would call the authoritarian theft model, which is a combination of immiseration and submission to imperialist slaughter. Government spending did not decline under neo-liberalism. It rose per capita, but the lax accountability under neo-liberalism for social waste, as in inefficiency, also rose to meet the private sector's appetite that fed off public spending. Also neo-liberal government expenditure targeted the expansion of the repressive security apparatuses and the funding of wealth conversion into dollars for the wealthy (UN 2009).
4 The Ministry of Finance keeps records of real public-sector wages, which have exhibited a downward trend since 2006 (Barout 2011). Underscored by a rise in informal poverty unemployment, productivity growth is proxied by output per worker and as

gradual neo-liberalism and supposed modernisation was at around 1.05 in the early 1970s and dropped to a plateau of around .95 to 1.0 from 2000 to 2008 (Marquetti and Folcy 2011).

To undermine the credibility of state intervention under Arab socialism, public policies are given a life of their own, deemed inherently catastrophic and assumed to decay naturally – hence, contributing to social breakdown. However, the social collapse occurred *after* the imposition of neo-liberalism. The catchphrase 'running out of steam' because of so much government spending is the tired and empty metaphor that neo-liberals parrot as the reason why Syria shifted gradually to neo-liberalism. Under state dirigisme, and until 1980, social conditions in Syria were on average far better than anything experienced afterwards.

By about 1990, as a result of the first doses of neo-liberalism a decade earlier, the rate of capital accumulation measured by the growth rate began to falter, and state-led investment shrank. The neo-liberal solution was as always to raise the openness level and, also as always, to substitute public investment for private investment. Liberalisation is said to mobilise local and foreign capital and facilitate debt-relief loans and other subsidies from the international community (Barkey 1992; Richards and Waterbury 1996; Hopfinger 1996). Authors like Perthes (1995), Polling (1994) and Sukkar (1994) contend that it was basically Syria's economic crisis of the late 1980s that pushed the regime into pursuing a market-driven economic order. But that crisis actually occurred as a result of the initial swerve away from the socialist model, relaxing currency convertibility measures and the decentralisation of economic decision-making.

Richards and Waterbury (1996) further posit that economic crisis under Arab socialism forces fiscal and political adjustments. They describe the move toward market-friendly transitions as being 'unnatural' because there are some 'interest groups' who are benefiting from the status quo. First, the crisis of Arab socialism was not foremost an economic crisis, but a political one. However, it is a good starting point for the authors to question the behaviour of the bourgeois class as opposed to reifying any policy like the exchange-rate policy, for instance. Yet is it not somewhat 'natural' for capital to grow exponentially and for the state bourgeoisie to make the most out of any transition, especially given its grip on power? Also, because the state bourgeois class can deploy the initial funds

shown in the Annex to chapter 1, it has been quite low despite higher oil revenues prior to the uprising. The efficacy of the public sector is denoted by the declining quality of services (Barout 2011). Inflation can be retrieved from the World Bank database (WDI), however, the real inflation rate according to Barout (2011) has been consistently doctored by the authorities.

necessary to convert public assets into private assets, it will secure the most for itself in any transition. Similarly, one questions why the authors do not probe the macroeconomic context in which bourgeois behaviour proceeds. Implicitly, these authors assume that there is some ideal state of 'perfect' market competition, 'pure' prices allocating resources efficiently, and a 'translucency' of information, which in fact sound as if they belong to some religious mythology of sorts. What is 'natural' is for capital to use its enormous power to devour anything in its pursuit of profit, and not otherwise. In a roundabout way Richards and Waterbury's comments bestow upon economic policies a life of their own: yes they reify the market and its policies and omit the fact that policies intermediate vested interests, which are exponentially expanding capital–*class* interests.

In another moralistic condemnation by second-hand moral values condemning the epiphenomenon of the unethical in market capitalism, Beblawi and Luciani (1987) introduce theories of the *rentier* state (a government that routinely derives a key portion of its income from external rent or export of raw material), and consider the state as the principal recipient and distributor of external rent in the economy. They describe Syria-like economic transformation as being primarily driven by a fall in rent. This fall pushes the state to decrease its role and increase the role of the private sector. The state is viewed as the main facilitator of economic liberalisation as it responds to economic pressures. The liberalisation process happens as an outcome of the interplay of internal challenges like economic deterioration, rather than of international pressure, or more specifically of external political considerations. Probably more so than anywhere else, in an Arab context the state is privately owned; the explanation is not patrimonialism with a ludicrous personalisation of history but the grip of an internationally integrated class on the state, to which real persons in power are appended. The devolution of the share of rents to the working class in an Arab context principally assumes stabilisation functions, whereby rents drive consumption but not do not raise productivity – save the reported astronomical rise in Gulf-state productivity in recent years, which is incidentally not actual productivity growth but increased output per worker (the calculation of productivity includes oil revenue rising as a result of rising oil prices between 2002 and 2015). One is prompted to recall that the class for whom stabilisation proceeds is determined by the hegemony of its leading partner: imperialism. Although the contradiction between the pressures to accumulate and the need to stabilise is not easily containable, the fall in rent can be redressed via more egalitarian distribution or equalisation funds rather than in heightened political or economic repression, the latter of which functions through liberalisation.

Rents are associated with nearly all economic activities. Increasing usurpation by a transforming capitalist class has always been the practice in peripheral capitalist societies. There were no economic exigencies behind the fall in rents to the Syrian state; at the time of transition from Arab socialism to neo-liberalism, productive capacity and investment rates were still high in comparison to the pre-uprising ones (WDI, various years). There were, however, political exigencies. Capacity (measured in modern productive capital per worker), wealth and their associated rents dwindled as a result of neoliberal 'free market' reforms; the persistence of neo-liberalism increased the share of the rich in the real-wealth pie that was growing ever smaller[5]. Types of rent and the social mode of life developing around them – as in knowledge-based to boost productivity or ignorance-infusing by imperialism to boost resource grab – assume their state of being depending on whether they are anchored in the sovereign industrial space or in commerce and extractive activity without much industry tied to the international financial arena. As the global ideological shifts of the 1980s dawned, the opportunity for further rent-making from a redivision of the national income also opened up (raising the rents of the ruling at the expense of the ruled class). The wealthy-biasing reforms stiffened the regimentation of the labour process to the point where workers would gradually forcibly consent to the social structure coming undone as the transition loomed. The mainstream rent literature, which attributes rent grab to some pathological personal drive rather than to an inherent tendency of capitalism, suffers from an illusory disconnect between the formation of social classes and the state.

Rents are congenital to a market economy. The idea that Arab rents are unearned income when financial rents are a blessing that helps the market adjust to equilibrium is not only discriminatory, it undermines what the anti-colonial national struggles were all about, which is the ownership of national resources by the working class. The short-sightedness of such an approach is in the superficiality of collapsing rents into their price forms. Imperialism does not prop up a comprador class only to amass dollar returns from capital flows. The real rents that imperialism seeks are in the differentials between the value that it cheapens with the able assistance of its lackeys and the price it pays for the resources. Yet the mainstream cannot see that the operations of the law of value defining socially necessary labour is not about the manifest quantities of labour and their prices (wages), but about the sedimentary class power shaping the social conditions for exponential profit-making. Does it

---

5 Between 2000 and 2010, the labour force participation rate fell from 51 per cent to 46 per cent (ILOSTAT various years). This is indicative of the high despondency rate related to declining job creation rate. Although the official and rather exaggerated average real wage remained nearly steady, the labour wage share from GDP fell by 7 per cent over the same period.

require too much effort to see that capital regularly deconstructs unions and bombs weaker developing countries to get cheaper wages and resources?

In Egypt, Beblawi became prime minister in 2013 as a result of a military putsch, but neither the acute moral transgression of his soldiers gunning down protestors nor the asphyxiating foreign exchange crisis could halt the rent grab by the Egyptian ruling class. As I have been at pains to point out, ruling classes in the AW are subordinates of imperialism. Hence, to postulate that falling rents lead to policy switches in favour of more openness depends less on what national ruling elites want and more on what damage openness imparts to the imperialistically sponsored regional security arrangement. Rents to the state bourgeoisies from external sources and from superior domestic economic performance were higher under Arab socialism than under neo-liberalism. The cause of the policy switch is not to be found in the quantity of rent rising or falling, but in the broader ideological shifts and in the level of commitment of the class in power to the national economy.

While some analysts stress economic crisis as the main driver of economic liberalisation, others point toward political considerations. Callaghy (1990) and Haggard (1990) adopt the view that in authoritarian, state-controlled regimes, political considerations precede economic concerns, especially when the latter entail higher risks for the political survival of these regimes. These authors argue that political logic supersedes economics, as economic decisions end up being governed by the regime's political considerations. Taking a more synthesising view, Heydemann (1992) contends that the 'political logic of economic rationality dominates', and that authoritarian regimes can actually react rationally to economic crisis, especially when the crisis creates a threat to their security. He adds that 'under these conditions, the logic of politics becomes, in some measure, the logic of economic reform' (Heydemann 1992, 15). In a similar vein, Hinnebusch (2001) posits that in Arab authoritarian regimes like Egypt and Syria, the ruling elite's preoccupation has been to secure both their class interests and regime security. This concern has required compatibility and balance between political and economic logics. He points out that 'while a neo-mercantilist regime subordinates economics to politics, it recognises that national power requires a healthy economic base' (Hinnebusch 1993, 199), because 'usually neither logic can wholly prevail' (Hinnebusch 1994, 98). Eventually, if political logic does not place itself in harmony with economic logic, then economic crisis will unfold. Pool (1993) also draws from some Arab countries examples of how both economic and political imperatives – the latter ranging from political uprisings to external intervention – accompany the process of limited and partial economic reforms. He adds that political liberalisation in some Arab states has been shaped by both economic liberalisation and the 'tactics and strategy of regime survival' (Pool 1993, 50). The transformation is also considered to be a response to neither an internal economic crisis nor a regime's political considerations exclusively. Rather, it is the interplay of political and economic considerations that shapes the transformation process (Niblock 1993; Hinnebusch 2001; Heydemann 2000).

But of course this eloquent *give-and-take* model had already crumpled in the face of reality – as the uprisings arrived. The mainstream purposefully obscures the dominant relationship of US-led imperialism to the ruling comprador classes. It just ignores the tidal ideological wave of neo-liberalism that is woven into every action of capital and, '*right or wrong*', it is the mindset of the class rearranging the measures of value destruction/creation at the behest of the leading global capitalist class. Why emphasise right or wrong? Because in the absence of an effective organised international labour power platform, there is no right or wrong in what US-led imperialism carries out; it makes history as it pleases and even its blunders are assets supporting its course of development. The most credulous remark I have heard recently from one the above authors (to remain unnamed) in a closed meeting with Chatham House rules is that Europe and the United States are at a loss on what to do in Syria; they have nothing to with it. The only measure that *took hold* is the gun of the state security apparatus to offset the disastrous conditions created by a ruling class that pawned its national formation to imperialism. The biggest economic crisis occurred during the uprisings, and maintaining regime stability would have depended on serious reforms steering society away from neo-liberalism. But nothing of the sort happened after the uprising. Neoliberalism is more than the economic policies slotted under it; it is the ideology of financial capitalism, which includes *inter alia* the call for small government and the false dictum that market freedom is social freedom. Realistically, so long as links between the international financial market and the national economy remain, it is not possible to escape neo-liberalism. Once the circuit of value is kept fully charged by open capital flows, it is the financial class that has the last word. Not that economic crises in developing areas easily lend themselves to sequential logical construction; but the distinction between the economic and the political may be analytically overemphasised. It is a political consideration, namely control over the labour process, that holds primacy with respect to the degree, timing and even targeting of reforms. The labour process to be sure is not only about changes to the structure by which direct producers sell their labour power to the capitalist or how capitalists translate labour power into labour in more advanced technical conditions separating manual from mental labour in developed economies or in how super exploitation in the periphery ties to central production, as in Burawoy (1985), it is also the historical commercial exploitation and the wars of colonial aggression that are the stepping stones of the capitalist labour process. When measures of social control over the working class are imposed, the money-form earnings of the ruling class reflect the degree of regimentation and discipline exercised over the working class (the capitalist labour process). When that labour process happens to be in Syria, it becomes – in one minor manifestation of it as compared to imperial power refuelling – another war of colonial aggression dislocating millions of worker-refugees.

The regime's political rationality does not rest solely on internal factors; rather, it is the role that Syria plays (in a highly volatile and strategic region) that more convincingly buttresses the argument for the primacy of politics. But whose politics and whose primacy is it, when the regime is willingly held hostage to international financial capital? As robber capitalism was ransacking Syria under the watchful eyes of the International Financial Institutions (IFIs), pushing the state into self-destructive conflict, not a single anti-neoliberal remark was uttered to arrest the unfolding disaster.

The story of economic exigencies forcing reforms does not provide a complete picture. It has been anecdotally said that Hafez al-Assad would insinuate that the regime cared less for the economy than it did for the politics of stability: 'Do whatever with the economy, but leave the politics to us'. Given the wealth amassed by the military–merchant class, such a statement is truly anecdotal. In any case, if liberalising reforms transform public assets into private assets at a rate that produces a crisis of authority in which the ruling class loses its consensus and is no longer leading but dominates by coercive force alone (Gramsci 1971), then the anarchy of capitalist profiteering has overtaken the rationality of class hegemony through the state. This phase of extreme profiteering value-grab was not deliberate Syrian ruling-class suicide. It was an act of the broader class of international financial capital, to which the Syrian ruling class had hitched itself, self-reempowering by destroying the value of a social formation that might potentially stand as a base of action for the Syrian working classes. But in this era of socialist ideological retreat, to draw a parallel from Gramsci (1971, 556), the great masses have become detached from revolutionary ideologies, and the crisis consisted of the fact that the old is dying and the new cannot be born; in this interregnum a great variety of morbid symptoms appear. The rise of the Islamic State (IS) and other fatalistic politics readying the Islamic world for recolonization are such symptoms.

The post-uprising conflict put an end to the reasoning that relegated the purview of economic decisions to the regime. Heydemann (1992, 17–32) remarks that only when economic crisis represented a serious issue in the sense that it threatened political legitimacy did the regime take measures that would serve and safeguard its security. Moreover, Hinnebusch (2001,

116) observes: 'Elites can therefore, to a considerable extent, determine the pace and scope of reform according to their own goals and interests while adapting it to economic and external exigencies'. As Syria suffered from military aviation congestion over its skies in mid-2016, this nicely synchronised adaptation did not remotely correspond to the way current events have unfolded. Economic reforms were subordinated to the political priorities of imperialism, including regime security and its economic basis for reproduction, which had burst asunder.[6]

I am aware that worsening social conditions may not determine the timing of an uprising; what such conditions do is create the objective circumstances for that uprising. From 1980 until 2000, Syrian free-market reforms were gradual and targeted. Economic liberalisation was conducted under the decisive control of the ruling military–merchant class, and in a way that apparently eschewed threats to the core power structure. Now, despite early reform gradualism, we stand confronted with an appalling social and economic condition that includes war and the shattering of the territorial integrity of the state. In politics, the regime appeared savvy because US-led imperialism tolerated the minor costs incurred as a result of the Assad regime's anti-imperialist posturing. In key regional confrontations and in areas of working-class development and empowerment, the regime did not attempt to crack the the imperialist-imposed ceiling.

This is a matter of historical record. The Syrian military–merchant class in charge actually pushed the limits of resource usurpation to the point that the state was on the verge of crumbling. In spite of being in a state of war with Israel, in which its security foundation was at risk, the Syrian regime squandered the economic and political arrangements that in the Arab socialist past had safeguarded it and the state. Although the prospects that Syria faces are predeterminedly more violent, the regime did the opposite of what Gramsci envisaged for a war of position that would require 'enormous sacrifices by infinite masses of people and a concentration of hegemony and more interventionist government, which will take the offensive more openly against the oppositionists and organise permanently the impossibility of internal disintegration – with controls of every kind, political, administrative, etc.,

---

6 One is aware of how slow market reforms were in the 1990s and how willing was the regime to adapt. In Matar (2016), a senior official had emphatically pointed out that Syria is willing to conform economically in the hope that the United States would allow it WTO membership and more political rapprochement. With wars raging in Iraq, the World Bank was not so eager to recommend very fast reforms such as those that took hold in 2006. Syria's role as a regional 'sponge' that sucks the radical elements that spring on the back of imperialist aggression held priority over pushing the economy to the brink too quickly.

reinforcement of the hegemonic positions of the dominant group' (Gramsci 1971, 495). The historical trajectory of the regime is reminiscent also of Hamza Alavi's point about the excessive practices of a state bourgeoisie, which may bring down both the peripheral state and its associated ruling class (Alavi 1972). But the specific historical reason why a Syrian military–merchant class in charge of the Syrian state would allow the anarchy of capitalist accumulation to erode its stability is that once this class pursues a capitalist mode of appropriation and becomes an extension of imperialism as such, its exercise of hegemony through the state is no longer its own; it has relinquished hegemony to imperialism.

The Neoplatonic tenets of neo-liberalism (I am aware that Neoplatonism may seem a bit strained, but I am using it as in a formal structure of perfectionistic axioms having only remote reference to reality) worked only where they were superseded – in the case of East Asia. In capacity-lacking social formations, neo-liberalism wrought havoc wherever it was applied (UNCTAD 2007). In Syria, neo-liberalism reallocated resources away from and weakened labour, cheapened its value and weakened national capabilities. It transpires that whether piecemeal or all at once, the neo-liberal mantra, once acted upon, delivered a death sentence on Syria as a state residing in an over-determining international environment over which the United States is willing to undertake nuclear war (US Department of State 2013). The Syrian regime misread the essence of imperialist objectives and its own *rapport de force* with imperialism. The regime's stance on the liberation of Palestine, and its contemptuous hubris in relation to other inalienable Arab rights (thinly camouflaged under pan-Arab rhetoric) lost their appeal as millions of Syrian stomachs were hunger-gnawed, and the flight of the Tunisian president in 2011 showed the possibility of regime change. The state was unravelling along two intertwined axes: first, to serve US-led imperialist objectives and, second, as a result of national economic blunders and loss of hegemony by the regime.

Monumental Obfuscation

The history of neo-liberal reforms and their contribution to Syria's uprising and war has to be read in light of two interrelated forms of obfuscation. The first and more primary form is about the process by which the Syrian ruling class, in charge of a country at war, had deluded itself into applying reforms that debilitated its social base and dried up the source from which it draws its rents. As it slowly integrated with imperialism, the regime failed to understand imperialist motives of greater geopolitical control and, instead, believed that its accession into global financial circles could be promoted by a combination of rapprochement with imperialism, on one hand, and the transfer of value and dollarised national assets to the centre, on the other. The second form of obfuscation relates to how the regime deployed its technocrats to numb the consciousness of its population and promote the idea that after neo-liberal reforms, the trickle-down effect would result in major welfare improvements.

Syria is an important player on the Middle East stage. It draws geopolitical rents by virtue of that position. Because of frail defences, it acquired the status of a front-line state against Israel by Arab League consensus and, subsequently, received significant aid from other Arab countries. The Assad regime (father and son) played both sides of the capital divide, drawing rents from national as well as international spheres, with its own merchant-class roots swaying innately toward the larger spaces of US-dominated financial capital. After all, when capital outgrows its national economy, it can only head toward the safety of US Treasury bills. The neo-liberal bent gradually shifted the basis of accumulation of the state bourgeoisie from national industry, protected and controlled by the state, to one of wealth drawn from higher capital share and imports for sale on the local market. The diminution of national industry became a corollary of import-led growth and the implicit terms of war losses to imperialism. To boot, the Syrian state's role in CIA rendition/torture programs, its participation in the First Gulf War, and its later furtive role in squeezing Iraqi resistance, are landmark pro-US-led imperialist positions. But the most important contribution the regime provided to the military face of capital was to furnish it with the conditions for prolonged civil strife in Syria.

The Assad regime was colloquially dubbed the 'let's make a deal' regime. In its early stages, the balance of power of the Cold War created the medium for its survival. In the post–Cold War era, the regime lingered because there was no imperative to immediately end Syria as a social formation by an invasion, as was done with Iraq. Its developmental process, however, was incapacitating and self-defeating; the regime's repression hollowed out the participation of the working class in politics and, in terms of military capabilities, it was literally defenceless. In other words, Syria was doing itself the kind of harm on which imperialism gazed with gloating *schadenfreude*.

Whereas the Sino–Russian strand of capital required a foothold in the Middle East and a more or less sovereign state in Syria, the Assad regime was drawn toward the United States by a drive to secure its loot in US-controlled financial markets. Earlier in 2000, Iran and Russia had practically written off their debts to Syria in an effort to further consolidate their regional positions, but the wealth of the military–merchant class was becoming increasingly dollarised. At the same time, the Syrian military–merchant class promoted private banking and fulfilled World Trade Organisation (WTO) standards despite Syria not being a member of the WTO. Syria's WTO membership was opposed by the United States and Israel until months before the uprising, when the United States gestured its approval of Syria's reform progress and offered the country observer status (WTO 2012).

US-led imperialism had a broader goal, certainly exceeding Syria's $40 billion income (approximate figure for the year 2007 in nominal dollars as per the WDI), its pre-uprising GDP. The regime's strategy failed to peer beyond the facade of the money form and to understand the essentiality of conflict and dislocation in the AW to expanding the resources available to capital globally: financialised rents and socialised value or idle resources at the disposal of capital. Syria is part of the global expanded circuit of capital which, through subjugation, involves the transformation of global value and surplus value into profit, and the transfer of value from the South to North according to the low prices paid for goods produced by cheaper labour in the South (Lauesen and Cope 2015). The power of imperialism and its ability to destroy and create value spans the planet; rising rates of exploitation-cum-profit are the result of the total global capital accumulation process. Both idle and productive assets are elements at the disposal of capital, and both organically contribute to accumulation. This integrated relationship is a condition of being, or an ontological condition, for humanity under capitalism. Retrogression and idleness of resources have been the trademarks of an Arab region that is more like a surplus depository for the more active dynamics of production in other parts of the global South. The agencies of the imperialist class, which create the context in which private capital can boost its earnings, influence the ragged conditions in insecure states, slowing the rhythm of industrialisation and preparing the stage for higher potential earnings through militarisation. The ultimate sovereign in the AW, under the guns of imperialism that, as always, are the *ultima ratio regum* (the final argument of kings) is US-led capital incarnate in the comprador classes kowtowing to its directives, its drones and the dozens of US military bases strewn around the region.

Not that oil is un-strategic, but the hype surrounding the strategic relevance of oil doubly contributes to the social and political underpinnings of global accumulation: first, by keeping all those without strategic control uneasy with respect to an abrupt halt of oil supplies and, secondly, by heightening militarism and increasing global transaction risks, hence raising the rents through rising risk premiums exacted by the US-led dollar-based financial order. The uncertainty surrounding the safety of the oil supply is figured into the costs of financial transactions worldwide. The dislocation of the pauperised Arab masses by war and indirect colonisation resituates the balance of forces whereby the money form and its associated financial system present themselves as real and symbols of power. As market crisis sets in, the imperialist power progressively disengages more of the social material in the Third World for resource-grabbing purposes. This power also fragments and appoints itself as a proxy sovereign in order to reproduce the terms of trade and price ratios in its favour. The enigma that the cost of imperialist wars exceeds the monetary returns from certain ex-colonies occurs because exchange prices are not set by benign market conditions, but by the fact that powerless corners of the Third World cannot negotiate the price at which they valorise their assets. Imperialist wars of recolonisation, especially in the strategic Middle East corner, keep the world tense and create the disastrous social conditions that implicate global production in the destructiveness wrought upon the AW (more on this in chapter 6).

Value as a qualitative category is created by the totality of physical and human material and relationships available to capital, of which the human or crucial element creates the additional surplus value. The dislocated billions in the Third World – let us say the huge tranche whose income is only 5 per cent of world income – by their very poverty form part of the material relationship of capital. The real and ideological pressures that the pauperised and politically disempowered Third World masses exert by reducing production costs via cheapened primary resources and lowered wages are critical for profit-making. Their successful emergence, by contrast, would damage the progress of private appropriation by selective and necessarily uneven capitalist development. Their debilitation by war entails a weakening of their states, such that imperialist military intervention potentially may at any time tip the internal balance between national forces in its favour. Syria is in such a condition.

The imperialist goals had more to do with undermining the state than did the tribute channelled from Syria to international financial circles via neo-liberal policies. Syria's role to US-led imperialism was a *prophylactic* by which it warded off imperialist competitors. The leaders of the regime were historically predisposed toward the war process, and given the intensity of the reactionary assault, there was no option but war. In one early gaffe indicating the mindlessness of key regime figures, the notorious Assad cousin Rami Makhlouf said in a *New York Times* interview that Syria protected and will continue to protect Israel from Al-Qaida (Ha'aretz and Reuters, 2011). During the early stages of the uprising, the regime attempted to bribe the workforce by raising salaries, or to appease the Islamists by appointing Islamic bankers to government positions and allowing women teachers the *niqab*. One ought to note that a remarkable myopia concerning the regime's balancing act vis-à-vis imperialism took hold in the years preceding the uprising, but not with respect to the regime's class and its international ties: for the imperialist class the war was healthy.

More so than that of his father Hafez, the regime of Bashar (since his accession to power in 2000) and the class associated with it infused the cultural sphere with the rhetoric of neo-liberalism and began to speedily dissociate itself from a relatively planned and heavily state-interventionist past. Initially, the reforms were confined to raising private investment and to eroding the subsidies attached to the basic consumption bundle delivered to the working population. But, gradually, the glitz of these reforms began to be visible in ostentatious displays of wealth on the part of the upper echelons of society. The gains to the military–merchant class in terms of control over the labour process, regimentation and repression also rose as socialist work benefits (shorter working hours) were transformed into a more stringent Third World sweatshop environment.

Most reforms were predicated on the rise of private investment. However, in view of uncertainties beyond the instantaneously foreseeable, the private investment rates did not rise sufficiently to offset public investment and the total rate fell (on average, the investment rate fell from 25 per cent in 1981 to 20 per cent in 2010, WDI various years). In addition to the uncertainty that would dampen 'animal spirits', it was unlikely given the paucity of private finance that the private sector would succeed in driving up investment rates. Private undertakings piggyback on public investment and, peculiarly in Syria, privateers expand public finance via their hold on the state to meet their own private ends. The latter case is what occurs in every financialised economy, but the process in Syria was personalised. With low oil prices holding steady until 2002, real growth rates were on average around zero, and unemployment figures reached the two-digit level (UN 2008). Growth would only pick up when oil prices regained momentum in 2003, and this growth was both jobless and inequitable.

Despite this malperformance, the Syrian regime deployed its technocrats to promote liberalisation and to subordinate and control the social process for wealth-grabbing purposes. In 2008, when the financial crisis overtook the planet, the interlocutor of the ruling social class in government announced that their economy was spared and that some $11 billion in investment was forthcoming from abroad.[7] This was a period in which stunted growth in children under five had reached 28 per cent (UNICEF 2013).[8] Instead of

---

7 See http://www.alwatan.sy/dindex.php?idn=128939&fb_source=message (viewed 7 January 2013)
8 See At a glance: Syrian Arab Republic, http://www.unicef.org/infobycountry/syria_statistics.html (Viewed 9 September 2014)

arresting these reforms when their initial dose failed, the regime intensified the neo-liberal arrangements, freeing more resources for transfer into private ownership. To invert Waterbury's remark, it was 'natural' for the regime and its class to continue with the reforms because, in a context of openness that could neither be regulated nor abide by nonexistent free competition, the regime and its class were the prime beneficiaries.

Veering steadily away from national industrialisation, the regime was shredding the virtuous circle productivity growth/welfare, self-reliance and its own support base.[9] The regime snuffed the first Damascus Spring (around 2000) and cloaked its neo-liberal bent with the 'social market economy' proposal of Syrian economist and politician, Issam Al Za'im. Evidently, there was nothing social about these reforms, and Al Za'im was very critical of the process (UN 2007).[10] In the latter phase of neo-liberal reforms under Bashar, the regime lifted price controls on basic commodities, removed most tariff barriers, and further freed the capital account. In one indication of the primacy of labour's subjection to capital, the regime lifted subsidies on certain essential commodities, including heating fuel (upon World Bank advice) but dispersed cash handouts in lieu of subsidies on account of targeting and rationing spending. Despite the fact that the cost of subsidy was lower to the state than the cash disbursement, the aim of this policy was to humiliate and subjugate the workers.

The price of staple commodities rose, and the inflation rate jumped on average to more than 10 per cent from 2006 onwards (the Central Bureau of Statistics of the Syrian government – CBS various years).[11] In the absence of autonomous labour organisation or trade unionism, the corresponding rise in wages was inadequate (Ernesto 2011). By the time of the uprising, the regime had significantly privatised some swaths of previously nationalised agricultural land, widened the income gap, dealt a blow to national industry and promoted import-led growth (Matar 2016). Typically, poverty rose and public health and education plunged in both quality and delivery capacity (Shaoul 2010).[12]

The Central Bank stabilised the national currency with reserves, so that locally amassed wealth denominated in the Syrian pound could be converted into dollars at a stable rate to the advantage of the military–merchant

---

9 Although the figures vary from source to source, the share of manufacturing from GDP in 2011 had declined to 4.6 per cent (UN 2014).
10 Expert Group Meeting on Employment Policies and Economic Development in Countries Including those Emerging from Conflict 19/12–20/12/2007, Damascus.
11 See http://www.cbssyr.sy/index-EN.htm (viewed 3 October 2013).
12 See 'Multidimensional Poverty Index' (MPI), 2011. Online: http://www.ophi.org.uk/wp-content/uploads/Syrian-Arab-Republic1.pdf (viewed 1 January 2012).

class. When the currency is pegged to the dollar, drawing resources from the national economy to steady the currency represents a form of subsidy to the national-money holders – an effort to stabilise their wealth in terms of dollars. By the end of reforms, and just prior to the uprising, unemployment was still rising and real wages were at half their 2006 level.[13] The process of diverting resources away from the interests of working people reached the point in 2009 that nearly 71 per cent of Syrian workers were earning less than S£13,000 (approximately $274) monthly when the average household expenditure on food alone was estimated at S£14,000 (approximately $295) per month (CBS 2009). This decline in living standards occurred in a country where the BBC had reported in the early 1980s that average purchasing power was exceptionally high as compared to other countries in the same bracket of development.

The Syrian Regime: Transformation by Successive Defeat

Unconditional openness in a developing context *wastes wealth*, either through affluent consumption or by diverting capital abroad at prices dictated by the more powerful players in the global markets. Open capital and trade accounts are the gateway by which the military–merchant class converts national wealth into dollars and integrates financially into the global financial structure. How much the outflow of the social product in money or commodity form is constricted by policy or, conversely, how much is diverted into waste in either idle savings or exorbitant consumption, are expressions of the degree of working-class autonomy in and command of the social product. A higher degree of protection and socialisation in Syria reflected the extent to which the state as a sovereign entity erected the necessary safeguards to link development to national security concerns. These are gross benchmarks that apply to all fragile states developing under conditions of war or the threat thereof. Defeats in war and weakened national security impose their terms of surrender, either directly by incorporating the victorious party into the composition of the state (as did Paul Bremer in Iraq), or structurally, with gradual liberalisation. Both reveal at once the regime's proclivity and its supplication to the enemy.

Recall that in the case of Syria, it is not the Syrian outflows *per se* that are of concern to US-led capital, but the value drawn from the security arrangement in the Middle East, to which Syria contributed. Imperial rents are drawn from the strategic control of an oil region. A cursory reading of the economic history of Syria reveals the close correlation between the allocation

---

13 Gross estimates based on calculations conducted on data provided by the Syrian Central Bureau of Statistics (CBS).

of the social product to working-class needs and the degree of security and sovereignty enjoyed by Syria in relation to the balance of forces with Israel and the United States. As consecutive defeats took their toll, the social class structure and political rhetoric shifted to accommodate the allocation of the social product away from working-class living and, hence, weakening national security. The agency that is Syrian class formation lurks only in the shadow of greater imperialist forces and, as such, it is more of an object rather than a subject of history.

Post-Independence Syria

Syria became independent on 17 April 1946. After its defeat in 1948 by a newly established and Western-armed Israel, and a period of political turmoil resulting in the downfall of President Shishakli in a 1954 coup, a state of normalcy emerged, and the only free parliamentary elections in Syrian history took place in 1955. Despite being dominated by more conservative elements, the elected parliament undertook several socialising measures that protected the rights of farmers against eviction, redistributed some state land to peasants and enacted the law of social security. This parliamentary experience was soon to end with the creation of the United Arab Republic on 22 February 1958. Although short-lived, the unity experience entrenched socialisation. Apart from the establishment of agricultural, residential, and consumer cooperatives, the newly founded Ministry of Agriculture and Agrarian Reform confiscated unutilised land and established a number of agricultural cooperatives and collective farms run by peasants (Chouman 2005).

The United Arab Republic ended on 28 September 1961 and, in 1963, the Ba'ath rose to power in a coup d'état. The immediate steps of its National Revolutionary Command Council included nationalising all banks, lowering the ceiling of maximum land ownership, nationalising education, and erecting tariff barriers meant to protect local industry and agriculture. In the year 1965 socialisation measures reached their peak (under Prime Minister Yussuf Zuayyin). This was a period of massive socialisation in land, industrial sector, textile industry, pharmaceutical industries, food production, electricity and cotton. It was also a period in which direct redistribution to the poor was initiated: subsidies and price caps were introduced, and all imports and exports were to be conducted through the state. The main targets of macroeconomic policies were full employment, exchange-rate stability and socialised health and education. The expansion of the public sector to encompass all economic activity represented the prime objective of this regime. The private sector, constituted by construction and contracting, tourism and craftsmanship, was relegated to a minor position trailing the government plan. In typical Soviet style, the five-year plan envisaged the transfer of ownership of production and distribution from the private to the public sphere. It also envisaged a departure from a profit-oriented economy toward an economy based on societal welfare. This epoch constituted the heyday of security and post-independence achievements (Chouman 2005).

The Beginning of Decline

Syria's defeat in the Six-Day War of 1967 represented the first turning point, one which would restructure the internal class formation in a way that was amenable to the diversion of the social product away from working-class and national security interests. In Yussuf Zuayyin's words: 'We knew that Hafez Assad's ascension to power came as a result of the 1967 defeat and arrangements related to Security Council resolution 242' (as quoted in Ismail, 2010).[14] In November 1970, Hafez al-Assad assumed power. As a first step toward the reshaping of the socialised allocation mechanisms, under Article 14 of the new constitution, he decentralised the devolvement of state revenues to departmental heads and enshrined the right to personal and individual private property in the new constitution. Effectively, he personalised the handling of state funds and began to reverse an earlier trend meant to supplant all forms of private property in production. Syria gradually moved from a high output capital ratio investment, high-growth-rate phase into a lethargic phase leading to collapse (WDI growth data shows that the period 1960 to 1980 exhibits 2 percentage points more per-capita growth than the period 1980–2010; and in spite of the fact that from 2002 oil exports pushed growth rates to a high level between 2002 and 2011).

The new class in power, dominated by Assad and his clique, began a two-way process of resource usurpation reflecting piecemeal capitulation. In one devious measure, Hafez Assad relegated the right to exchange national for foreign currencies to various heads of departments in the government. In the mid-1980s, the scramble to exchange the national currency for dollars in neighbouring markets – driven by merchant-class motivation rather than a need to import necessities – resulted in hyperinflation and the collapse of the price system.[15]

---

14 A similar point was made by Hussein El Shafei'i, vice president unde Nasser, about Anwar Sadat becoming president as a result of international pressure on Nasser to choose him as vice president after the defeat of Egypt in the Six-Day War of 1967 (El Shafei'i interviewed by Aljazeera in August 2002).

15 Syria had a national exchange rate against the dollar that it chose itself and thereby allowed it to control the amounts of national currency being exchanged by its citizens for dollars. However, its global transactions, what it buys from the outside world, were determined by the market exchange rate, which is set in neighbouring markets.

Merchants seeking the scarce dollar on the national market resorted to smuggling their paper wealth abroad by means of regime patronage. While Syria's national currency flooded the neighbouring markets, national reserves were being depleted to stabilise the neighbouring market exchange rate. As national money was sent out, the central bank chased it with its dollar reserves to bring it home. The dollar reserves dwindled, putting further downward pressure on the national currency and lowering its exchange value. The difference between the official rate and the market rate skyrocketed, and the state needed more Syrian pounds for dollars to satisfy import expenditures. The national money stock grew many fold under the pretext that national departments needed to import mainly production goods denominated in dollars, but money traders demanded more and more Syrian pounds for dollars. In spite of the fact that consumption needs were nearly fully satisfied by internal production, the lower exchange rate had pushed costs of essential inputs upwards and drove prices up across the spectrum of domestically traded goods. This process was the doing of a state capitalist class dumping the national currency in search dollars and the initial act of socialist deconstruction.

The drop in Gulf aid during the 1980s as a result of Syria's support for Iran in the Iran–Iraq war, was not significant and was also nearly compensated for by Iran and other remittances. The aid may have been thinner, but the remittances were higher (CBS 1980–1990). In any case, this is a faux argument because even if aid had risen, the leakages from money smuggling were rising at such a rate that no reasonable amount of aid would have kick-started the Syrian economy again. Because of Syria's political alliance with Iran, Arab transfers fell from $1.8 billion a year between 1979 and 1983 to $500 million between 1986 and 1988 (Hinnebusch 1993, 188; Drysdale 1982, 7). However, Iran compensated Syria for its losses, especially those related to transit fees on oil from the Iraqi–Syrian oil pipeline (Perthes 1992, 57). In 1982, Iran supplied Syria with a million tons of free crude oil and up to 5 million tons at reduced prices (EIU 1989–1990, 32). One is reminded that, since many in the top ranks of the regime could simply carry out their exchange of dollars for national currency at will – especially as top-ranking military officers carried bigger hauls of national currency across the borders at the behest of merchants – the exchange rate sank along with the growing personalisation of public institutions.

Oddly, the causes of inflation in the mid-1980s were attributed to a monetary policy that tallied with the lowering of the budget deficit (Sukkar 1994). The rising deficit, although remaining manageable, was an effect and not cause, since initially the money supply was rising to satisfy the foreign-exchange demands of state apparatchiks. In other words, the money stock rose to meet the desires of those in a position of power who, under the new constitution, were granted a laissez faire deal with the money supply. It leads nowhere to speak of money supply leading to inflation in a protected and closed economy in which most basic consumption is satisfied by local means. Rising money supply is symptomatic of inflation but not its cause. In a closed economy with dual exchange rates, as Syria's economy was then, money supply grows by the pressure of transaction demands in the national economy, demands that are satisfied by the local currency (the non-tradable sector) and by the demands of foreign exchange in relation to national reserves (the tradable sector). A dual system of exchange was construed on the basis of a dual exchange rate, as if there were dual currencies, some for national use and others for external use. The purpose of these multiple rates was to finance domestic investment by domestic means and protect the consumption bundle from inflation. In Syria, this was all the more possible because imports represented a low 20 per cent of output (an average rate under Arab socialism, in which the import of Soviet weapons at low interest rates or through barter were significant), the capital account was strictly controlled and the ratio of tradable to non-tradable goods was low. Thus, when the general price level rose, including the prices of basic necessities to the consumer, it was not because there was more money chasing fewer commodities (there were no shortages in basic goods); rather it was because monetary policy targeted value transfer from the working population to the nomenklatura through inflation[16]. One can simply imagine the whole picture as such: as inflation rates rose and the labour share of income fell, the remaining portion of income went to the ruling class, which then converted part of its growing share of income to dollars. Pursuant to this debacle, the president's brother emerged abroad, after being pushed into exile, with enough capital to finance the first Arab news satellite channel.

The early failures resulting from resource usurpation under Assad's restructuring were predictably attributed to the faults of the socialist past. However, as already noted, statistical evidence shows that in the

16 In crude estimates for sake of illustration: Between 2000 and 2010, the state created the equivalent of an additional 26.5 billion $ in national currency, which was exchangeable at a fixed dollar rate of about 52 Syrian pounds. The estimated money supply required to meet the transaction demands of the labour force is estimated at roughly $ 4.9 billion. With the trade account being almost balanced as a result of high oil prices, and excluding an estimated 8.9 billion allotted to other government and investment demand spending, a net addition of 12.5 billion dollars was available for the capital class to meet its demands for national funds that could be easily translated into dollars. The monetary policy actually accentuated the income differences and the class divide in society because the assets of the rich were price-inflated. A millionaire holding excess Syrian pounds becomes a real dollar holding millionaire. The real weapon against the working class and the key to this policy is the open capital account.

socialising age Syria grew at a much faster rate than in the liberalising age. GDP per-capita growth rates in Syria registered 3 per cent during 1964–1974. This rate then dropped to 0 per cent during 1975–1995, a period characterised by gradual economic liberalisation (World Bank 2009). The prosperity of the socialist past was alleged to generate its opposite in low investment rates, high unemployment rates, inflation and the sharp decline in growth rates. Privatisation, downsizing the public sector, subsidies and removal of price caps were the alternatives being readied in the background. The circuit of real wealth or value was shifting from working class to ruling class as a result of these policies. The regime was keen to lay blame on the socialist experience, whose top leadership perished in Assad's jails. Yet the early reforms were carried out as if somehow the working population was oblivious to the austerity that came with market reforms. To use a socio-psychological phrase, the working class appeared subliminally distracted by defeatism, and the price of defeat was such that it had to accept national resource divesture as an act of patriotism.

The empirics of resource transfers in the Syrian economy expose the shift in social wealth away from the productive base and working class consumption into resource flight and affluent consumption patterns. These corrosive policies began with the liberalisation of Hafez Assad's 'corrective' movement in 1971. Measures that assigned a limited role to the private sector were advanced selectively and gradually out of concern that a strong revival of the private sector would bring about anti-regime mobilisation by the old bourgeoisie and the bazaar class, which were dominated by Islamic politics and backed by Saudi Arabia. The cliche was a private sector may generate demands for greater political participation and more political liberties from the déclassé bourgeois class (Gambill 2001). The struggle with the Muslim Brotherhood between 1977 and 1982 was another reason for the slow pace of liberalisation under Hafez Assad (Hinnebusch 2001). Assad was not against rooting development in the private sector, but it was the old traditional damascene class that he was against. This class had to partner with the military–merchant class or leave the scene, whereas the professional, wage-earning middle class, whose petty ambitions were not contained by Cabral-like radical socialist measures, and who remained the main beneficiary of the socialist policies of the 1960s with the public sector providing employment, became a gradual loser as of the mid-1980s.

The early liberalisation measures increased the role of the private sector, allowing it to operate in areas previously restricted to the public sector. By 1991, Law No. 10 purported to provide incentives for greater domestic and foreign investment. Couched in the law were lenient profit repatriation measures, unprecedented facilitation of imports, tax exemptions on corporate profit for a seven-to-nine year period and the removal of restrictions on transfers of foreign exchange (Matar 2016). In 2002, the regime adopted measures of partial liberalisation of trade and pricing policy, abolishing the last remnants of the policy of import substitution. In 2007, the regime removed price caps, lowered subsidies on basic consumption items and raised the prices of basic agricultural products. Under the false alibi of the social market economy, the full gamut of openness was undertaken. This was a blatant case of capitalism parading under the logo of socialism.

The Empirics of Cosy Pragmatism

Although Syria's liberalisation started in the early 1970s, it was not until the early 1990s that it received an official proclamation. The need for change at that time was expressed in terms of the need for economic pluralism (*al-ta'adudiyyah al-iqtisadiyah*) (Hopfinger and Boeckler, 1996). This term was used in most of Assad's official statements and refers to the regime's efforts to unite the public and private (a mixed sector) and bring them into the service of the 'national economy' (*al-iqtisad al-watani*).

In the early 1970s, Hafez Assad introduced corporations of the mixed-sector type into tourism and agriculture. Limited trade liberalisation was introduced by opening up to the conservative Arab states and to Lebanon in particular. Authorisations (subject to a quota system) were granted to licensed importers of previously prohibited goods (Hopfinger, 1996). Customs duties on about 190 products imported from neighbouring Arab countries were lifted entirely. Moreover, restriction on the importation of a wide range of manufactured goods was reduced and called the 'exceptional imports system'. Restrictions on cross-border movement of capital were eased, and the opening of bank accounts in foreign currency for nationals and foreigners was also permitted (Perthes 1995). These reforms coincided with the Syrian army's role in quelling the rebellion of the nationalist movement in Lebanon and constraining the more radical elements of the PLO. During the 1980s, the private sector was allowed to retain 50 per cent of its foreign-exchange proceeds (later raised to 75 per cent). These proceeds were then allegedly used to import necessary raw materials and industrial inputs needed for industrial and agricultural production. But, as Matar (2016) has shown, the import structure gradually changed toward consumption and luxury items. The number of private retailers grew from 72,000 in 1974 to 99,000 in 1981 (CBS 1975–1983).

The early liberal set of market-oriented reforms favoured the commercial bourgeoisie, as distinct from the industrial entrepreneurs. The easing of state regulation created a new commercial bourgeoisie intertwined with the regime, or a military–merchant class. The exchange rate decree of 22 April 1980 was a gesture to the merchants, by which they were allowed to acquire their foreign exchange at a lower market rate. However, in addition to devolving the responsibility of handling foreign exchange to government departmental heads, allowing merchants to convert part of their national currency at favourable rates, was another factor that escalated price inflation in the mid-1980s. The quantities exchanged were not as significant as hauling cash in army lorries to nearby Lebanon, but the measure served to cultivate segments of the bazaar class. Moreover, merchants limited the supply of raw materials, machinery and assembly kits and sold them instead on the black market (Barout 2011). The merchants, to the detriment of the industrialists, smuggled from Lebanon more goods that competed with the products of the industrial bourgeoisie (Lawson 1984). The regime further assisted the wealthy merchants by gradually introducing selective custom and tariff measures until they were all lifted in 2006–2007. In contrast to the buoyant mood at the chamber of commerce, the mood was sombre at the industrialist union in Damascus just prior to the uprising (Matar 2016). Although relaxing import restrictions pushed prices up, the profit margin of the merchants was secured (Mora and Wiktorowicz 2003; Longuenesse 1996; Lawson 1989).

In 1985, the value of the Syrian pound in Beirut (the neighbouring market) dropped from 10 S£/$ to 18 S£/$, and continued to slide thereafter (Sukkar 1994, 27). In 1986, a new 'encouragement' rate for non-commercial transactions was introduced and set close to the free-market rate of 22 S£/$ (Perthes 1994, 58). At the end of 1987, the pound was officially devalued from 3.95 S£/$ to 11.2 S£/$. In order to curtail the contraction of the Syrian pound, in September 1986 the government introduced Law No. 24, which imposed severe penalties on smuggling national currency. The principal smuggler was Assad's brother, Rifaat, who hauled excess Syrian cash to purchase dollars at the neighbouring markets (Robinson 1998, 163). Merchants also benefited and played around the multiple exchange rates. For instance, many items that were bought at the official exchange rate of 42 S£/$ were then sold at the free-market rate of 50 S£/$. The difference was pocketed by the merchants (Robinson 1998).

While official figures recorded inflation at unprecedented levels of 60 per cent in 1987, up from 36 per cent in 1986, unofficial figures reported inflation as more than 100 per cent in 1986 and 1987 (Sukkar 1994, 28). Toward the end of the 1980s, this was coupled with official currency devaluation (only the official rate) in order to alleviate the pressure on budget deficits resulting from financing the huge gap between the state-sponsored rate and the market rate. The cumulative effect of lower productivity levels, a trade deficit, budget deficit and inflation precipitated a stagflation crisis from which Syria did not recover. The number of public-sector industrial workers

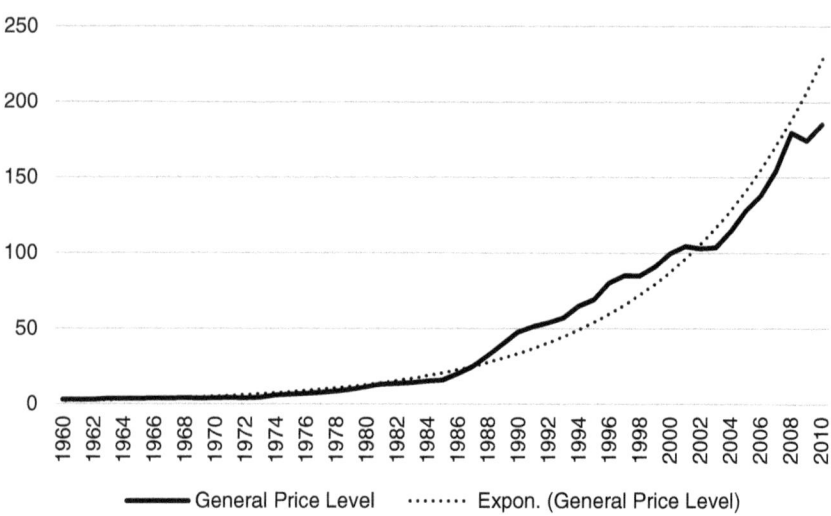

Figure 3.1 General Price Level Index for 1960–2010, General Price Level on the vertical axis against years on the horizontal axis, WDI (base year = 2000)

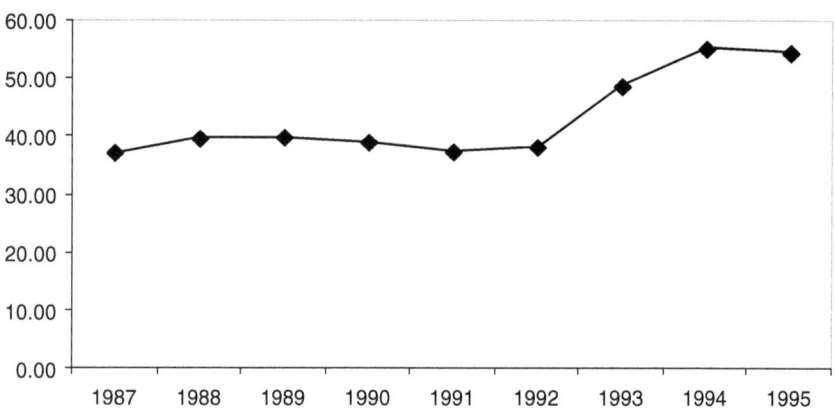

Figure 3.2 Income inequality index for some available years between 1987 and 1995. A higher score on the y-axis represents higher income inequality, while the x-axis represents the years.

Source: Estimated Household Income Inequality Data Set, UTIP 2008.

decreased from about 141,000 in 1985 to 139,000 in 1988, and the number of workers in the public construction sector decreased from about 155,000 to 138,000 in the same years (Perthes 1992, 44). While state employees, farmers and industrial workers suffered from real income losses due to inflation that redistributed income upward, merchants acquired more wealth (Najmah 1986, 323–324).

Regarding unemployment, the growth rate of the population was high as of the 1940s, reaching 3.2 per cent in 1960 and tapering down to 1.9 per cent in 2014 (CBS and WDI various years). To ascribe high rates of unemployment as of the mid-1980s onwards to demographic growth whose rate has tapered down is false. The point is that the rate of job creation declined under liberalising reforms. In terms of proportions, and that is what matters at the macro level, growth receded and went to areas that do not generate decent or high-productivity jobs. Capital productivity did not change, meaning that growth was of the low-technology type. The fertility and growth rate of the population were falling steadily; hence, the supply pressure was diminishing along a time trend. In summary, this could only mean that market reforms cracked the growth-job creation nexus that existed under Arab socialism.

The available data on wages and prices show that while public sector nominal wages rose by about 300 per cent, retail prices rose by approximately 600 per cent from their 1980 level (Perthes 1992, 43). The inflationary momentum, as can be seen from Figure 3.1, continued building long after the mid-1980s. Figure 3.1 also shows that the rate of inflation rose in tandem with the degree of liberalisation. It intensified in the last decade prior to the uprising. In the absence of wage indexing to the general price level, inflation acts as an indirect tax and shifts wealth to the ruling class.

Meanwhile, from the scant data available on income distribution, Figure 3.2 reveals that income inequality nearly doubled in the period ranging from the mid-1980s to the mid-1990s, implying that the reduction in real wages as a result of inflation was significant: scaled projections using trend analysis imply that the gap had widened still further by the time of the uprising. The share of wages out of national income declined from 40.5 per cent in 2004 to 33 per cent in 2009 (Marzouk 2011).[17] A gross estimation accounting of income maldistribution using the category 'compensation to employees' from Syrian national account data reveals that it was less than 30 per cent of the national income at the time of the uprising (CBS 2011).

Another large upward income redistribution occurred as a result of rising oil revenues. The 1990s witnessed the exploitation of new oilfields in the northeast and southeast of the country (Butter 1990). The origin of oil production dates back to the mid-1970s when oil exploration and extraction were permitted to foreign companies on the basis of shared production. During the

---

17 The falsification of data can hinge on the surreal. While real wages were falling under pressure from inflation, between 2006 and 2010, the UN (2014) reported that the yearly average wage rose by nearly 75 per cent in five years: from $1,549 to $2,690.

1980s, Shell discovered a string of fields and continued its exploration with other US–European consortia in different areas of Palmyra, Deir Ez-Zur and the Euphrates basin (MEED 1996). Oil production picked up in late 1986 at a rate of 60,000 barrels per day (bpd), which gradually increased to 200,000 in 1989 and to 300,000 in 1991 (MEED 1996). Major companies, such as Shell, France's Elf Aquitaine and Tullow Oil of Ireland were active during the 1990s (MEED 1996). Foreign oil companies were permitted to use market exchange rates instead of the official rate. Similar agreements were extended for the exploration of gas in the newly discovered fields in the course of the 1990s (MEED 1996).[18]

An estimated 380,000 barrels were extracted daily during the 1990s and, as a result, oil export revenues rose to $2 billion in the mid-1990s (AMF 2002). Between 1994 and 2000, Syria produced approximately 565,000 bpd. Production reached its peak in 1994 at 600,000 bpd, after which production levels tapered down. Pre-uprising production levels are estimated to have been 440,000 bpd in 2006 (OPEC 2007) and post-uprising levels are unknown because of IS control of oil fields. In another gaffe, the regime alleges that figures related to oil revenues are supposedly part of national security and, hence, confidential; however, importers report the amount of oil produced and the costs, which would make it straightforward to estimate such revenues. It is absurd to see such a state of decline in technocratic knowhow in Syria, a country that once boasted intricate input–output models and extensive data collection under Arab socialism.

Accelerated Reforms Beginning in 2000

Syria's economy never really recovered from the 1985 negative shock. Even as oil windfalls boosted the national accounts, the misallocation of resources and rising imports were retarding the social impact of rising oil revenues. As a result of openness, Syria became more vulnerable to internal or external economic shocks. More resources were diverted to low output-to-capital ratio activities – with the exception of oil. The falling investment rate in plant and equipment and basic infrastructure undermined indigenous productive capacity.

A summary of the facts reads as follows: inflation had been rising since the mid-1980s, unions were coopted by the regime, the share of wages was dropping, and the economy moved from public investment-led industrialisation to surplus capture as rent and a commercial mode of economic activity. Just prior to the uprising, most commercial exchange was bereft of a national industrial origin. Industry's share shrank to a quarter of its value in 1970 (UNIDO, various years). Particularly disconcerting is the fall in the composition of

18 For an overview of Syria's oil sector, see EIU (2008) *Country Analysis Brief – Syria*.

industrial machinery imports, particularly die and mold, between 2000 and 2010, which clearly denotes a decline in autonomous industrial knowhow (UN-Comtrade, various years).

The Bashar regime decided to confront the social problems that its neo-liberal reforms had caused – by enacting more intensive and comprehensive packages of neo-liberal reforms.[19] However, this time around, the International Monetary Fund (IMF) was called upon for advice (Barout, 2011).[20] The regime lifted nearly all remaining caps on capital and trade account controls. Customs duties on imports for local manufacturing activities were drastically cut, and laws that had restricted foreign-exchange operations or transactions for almost 17 years prior to the uprising were also abolished. In 2003, Bashar issued Legislative Decree No. 33, which rescinded Decree No. 24 of 1986 and Decree No. 6 of 2000, which had de jure limited foreign exchange dealings in the private sector. Decrees No. 6 and No. 24 were de facto superseded because Investment Law No. 10 had provided investors with exemptions from restrictive foreign exchange laws (*The Syria Report* 2003).

The promulgation of the banking law in January 2001 authorised the establishment of private banks for the first time in 40 years. Since 2001, six private banks have been established in Syria: Bank of Syria and Overseas (BSO), Bank BEMO, Bank Audi, the International Bank of Trade and Finance, Arab Bank and Byblos Bank. Their combined deposits were estimated at $3 billion in 2007 (Moubayed 2007). There were few restrictions on foreign bank operations: 51 per cent of all banks were to be owned by Syrian nationals or companies, and 25 per cent of bank shares had to be controlled by Syrians (Matar 2016). These privileges were usually granted to the new bourgeoisie, rather than to competitive market bidders (Matar 2016). Along with private banking, the Syrian Stock Exchange began operating in mid-2009 as part of the plan to spur the money market.

Prominent figures from the new bourgeoisie were major shareholders in these banks. For instance, leading businessmen such as Rami Makhluf, Nader Qalai, Issam Anbouba and Samir Hassan were the founding shareholders of Byblos Bank (*The Syria Report*, 2010). As to whether these private banks have expanded the availability of finance to private and public investors to facilitate the undertaking of new investment projects, the answer is no.

---

19 As early as 2002, the late Issam Al-Za'im cautioned about the consequences of private sector reform noting that Syria remains in a state of war and the shrinkage of the public sector would have dire consequences. See his lecture on 'Strategy for Reform in Syria', early in 2002, http://www.mafhoum.com/syr/articles_02/zaim/zaim.htm (Viewed March 20, 2015). One may add that as of 2007, the reforms resembled the shock therapy that was applied to the Soviet Union, but with worse consequences.
20 Also refer to IMF's *Article IV Consultation Reports* for 2009a and 2010.

The recent performance of these private banks proved that they have been involved in usury-like transactions as distinct from financing industrial and developmental projects (Barout 2011; Matar 2012).

In 2003, the United States invaded and colonised Iraq, and Syrian exports to Iraq, which had risen via contraband trade during the 1991–2003 embargo, fell drastically. The negative consequences of the war on Iraq further dampened the performance of the Syrian national industry. The immediate collapse of Iraq cost Syria about $2 billion, of which half were gains from the oil pipeline between Syria and Iraq (Spindle 2005). As revenues from exports fell, capital inflows from Iraq rose via remittances and fleeing capital as a result of rising resistance to American occupation. Inflows from Iraq rose from $457 million in 2004 to $803 million in 2005 and to $1.3 billion in 2006 (IMF, 2009). Moreover, remittances from Syrian expatriates (mainly in the Gulf) are estimated to have reached $820 million in 2007 and $850 million in 2008 (*The Syria Report*, 2008). Syrian debts, meanwhile, were on average and throughout Syria's modern history relatively low. Syrian net debt to Russia was relatively small and also serviced at concessional interest rates. The Central Bank of Syria stated that Syria's external debt stood at $6.5 billion in 2007, representing a mere 20 per cent of GDP, and that debt service amounted to a mere 7 per cent of total export revenues. In terms of macroeconomic ratios during 2000–2010, there was a declining debt service-to-debt ratio, higher inflows to GDP rates, and higher savings-to-GDP rates. In spite of this superficially sound picture, spiralling inflation kept on eroding the purchasing power of working people. The real growth rate was on average 6 per cent for the nine years prior to the uprising (WDI various years). Roughly, the profit rates of the ruling class were a cumulative 6 per cent on total income since 2002 in addition to money-form value snatched from the working class as a result of inflation and the declining wage share from income, and the historically accumulated surplus from immiseration of the working class.

But where development counted most, in the area of jobs creation, this oil-driven growth yielded little. There was certainly huge informal poverty-jobs creation but no count of decent jobs creation versus jobs destruction in the pre-uprising decade. Given the shrinkage in the public sector, where real wages took a nosedive, and the swerve away from industry, it is very likely that decent jobs destruction may have exceed decent jobs creation. The principal activity buoying growth was the value added from the sale of additional imported goods on the local market. Imports as a percentage of GDP rose from about 30 per cent of GDP in 1980 to nearly 40 per cent in late 2000 (averages calculated from WDI, various years). With a ban on public-sector expansion in place along with jobless growth (as in decent jobs), real Third

World type unemployment soared, principally in the form of disguised or underemployment (ILO, various years).[21] Ironically, the regime attempted to place the blame for rising prices (inflation) on the pressure Iraqi refugees exerted on demand. However, there was no shortage of supply in the essential items (Matar 2016), and the causes of inflation, a redistribution tool already in use for nearly three decades (beginning 1985), were to be found in two interrelated subsidies for the military–merchant class. The first was the building of national reserves to support their dollar wealth holdings; the second was the removal of price caps, which had in the past disciplined the drive for higher profit rates. Prices were liberalised while sustaining the subsidy to inputs that businesses employed in production, such as energy and labour costs. In summary, there was a circuit of value signified in money form that had favoured the ruling class, which stemmed from a declining labour share (as a result of absent labour representation and inflationary pressure), rising profits from commerce (as it had supplanted the market space previously occupied by national industry) and, ultimately, the money profits in Syrian currency traded for dollars (at fixed exchange rates supported by the revenues of the state).[22]

Misallocating Resources

In every measure of the circulation of capital and the spigots of value, the evidence points to ruling-class usurpation. Income maldistribution, deindustrialisation and demobilisation of real resources abound. Engrossed in the neo-liberal framework of its imperialist partners, as in losing an ideology of its own, Assad's class completely dropped the gradually relinquished many

---

21 Unemployment data as calculated by the Central Bureau of Statistics is of very poor quality. When Syria intensified its cooperation with the World Bank in 2007 following the heaviest dose of reforms, the unemployment rate in Syria was said to have declined from 12 to 8 per cent, and the unreasonable cause that was given by the head of the bureau was that seasonal employment in olive-picking lowered the unemployment rate permanently.

22 To illustrate with the teleology of macro-accounting: while the poor paid more for goods as a result of inflation, the profits of merchants rose in nominal terms as a result of so many more Syrian pounds circulating in the economy. Although there are so many more Syrian pounds, the exchange rate, instead of falling under managed float conditions, stayed put as the central bank drew from its own reserves and exchanged the same amount of Syrian pounds for dollars. Since it is the rich that hold most of the excess Syrian cash, and it is they who exchange it for dollars, such policy taxed the poor through inflation and taxed the state as it converted the same amount of cheaper Syrian pounds for the same amount of dollars and, hence, transformed what should have been nominal wealth to real wealth and literally gave it to the merchant classes.

forms of national security, including the sort of development that would have bettered the living conditions and empowered the working class against imperialism. There are two premises to keep in mind: (1) imperialism is a dynamically aggressive relationship that would not forfeit a moment, which would allow it to bring down Syria's security foundation that includes its developmental capabilities; and, (2) in view of the highly unequal balance of forces, it is necessary to rely on popular resistance and forms of guerrilla warfare, which require a betterment of the conditions of the working class and already had proven worthwhile in the AW and elsewhere. Moreover. the consistent misallocation of resources offers proof of structural collusion between the Assad-led class in Syria and US-led imperialism.

The Assad-led class became a structural partner of US imperialism, a partner that manoeuvred between the poles of placating pan-Arab populism and heeding the hegemony of US-led capital. This class also became a disposable scapegoat whose participation in the weakening of its own social formation enhanced the power standing of US-led imperialism. The Assad regime represented the political form of a state bourgeois class whose process of transformation was co-determined by shifting global ideological currents supressing state autonomy and its inherent tendency to widen its scope in material reproduction. Its historical affinity for world capital progressively exceeded its commitment to its own national working class. More decisively, however, the successive Arab defeats, which were particularly Syria's, were not one-time losses. They were major events whose impact was ideologically deployed to destroy the spirit of resistance. In much the same manner as a Syrian soldier who would have to remove military insignia in order to enter the Quneitra region per the 1973 armistice condition, impoverishing the working population stripped Syria of its ideological symbolism or real momentum for confrontation while attenuating its real sovereignty.

The social reforms carried out in the 1950s and 1960s allowed Syria to develop the internalised value cycle of a nationalistic formation, which effectively combined security and developmental goals in preparation for defence against Israel's superior military capabilities. In the atmosphere of the Cold War, Hafez Assad's regime walked a tightrope of gradually de-socialising Syria without causing undue domestic instability. Although the regime's relationship to society was one of capitalist accumulation through the state, the state as capital's organised dimension disciplined excesses that endangered national bonds. The Assad *père*'s regime assessed Syria's security capabilities (of which Syria's level of development was part and parcel) in terms of the calculated risks they would pose in tilting the balance of forces in a way that would not provoke imperialist belligerence. In any case, the population was filled with anti-imperialist ideology lingering from the anti-colonial struggles, and no Syrian leadership would have been able to walk in the footsteps of Sadat as early as 1978. All the while, the regime did not incite a pre-emptive Israeli or American strike, as did Iraq. It drew some of its rents from its role in the regional stability arrangement – Arab and Soviet aid. The regimes of both father and son may have resorted to asymmetric measures of confrontation, but these, all the same, were not of a serious nature. In crucial issues such as the relationship to the Lebanese and Palestinian resistance organizations and closer ties with Iraq, the regimes well knew where the imperialist taboos lay. One may note that these Assad regimes also contained, absorbed and maintained records of revolutionaries from Kurdistan, Palestine and other internationalist groups that would have grossly disequilibrated an otherwise tense regional environment. It was convenient for imperialism to have a 'pragmatic' figure in Damascus and, at the same time, keep a track record of certain revolutionary movements.

Tangentially, one may suggest that if a more restrained form of profit-making from a growing industrial base had taken hold, the distribution of the social product would have progressed less inequitably, and Syrian welfare could have been better. However, it is a dead end to posit such a hypothetical question when the real forces that shape development are as militaristic as the US-led strands of imperialist financial capitalism. Between putting Syria to work or setting it ablaze, the imperialist choice could not have been clearer. US-led capital's secular tendency to war-making combined with the Russian intervention in Syria is as close as one gets to igniting a global conflict, which, in view of the dictum that all arms races end in war, remains a very real possibility.

From where we stand, any past moment, relation or property of the social condition in Syria appears to explain the uprising. In this overdetermination, the principal social force that laid the grounds for blind accumulation in Syria, with a regime that combined absolute political and economic power, has been the imperialistically set undercurrent of history – the tidal wave of neo-liberalism. Other moments, relations and activities must be understood within this broader context in which the probative condition is the ideological victory of US-led capitalism. Prior to the 1990s, the World Bank's advice was circumspect in relation to how market reforms affect the stability of Syria (Barout 2011). Yet after the 1990s, as the region entered full speed into an accumulation by war mode (as in the string of wars burning across the Middle East) and the military–merchant class itched for dollar wealth after its experience in Lebanon, the WB upped its market mantra for Syria. By 1990, the clique in close association to the regime controlling much of the market, the 'whales' of the market as they have become known in common usage (*AlHitan* in Arabic), was plain to see. This was no fair playing field platform and pushing for further reforms would certainly entail social maladies. This synchronisation of WB reform with war destabilisation cutting across the region could not have been haphazard. It need not be thought of in facile terms of personally orchestrated manoeuvres, as in the mainstream's simplistic conspiracy theory approach as opposed to its alleged value neutral science. Classes do not work that way. Classes as the interrelated relationships whose ideologies institute platforms of actions that primarily reproduce the conditions for the dominant class by formal and impersonal means also reinforce the conditions for the promotion of that class. I do not want to dwell upon the silliness of magnanimous mainstream personal agency, which is more like a psychological illness than social science; all I will say here is that if there were such ingenious good-willed and pope-like characters, why would there be such an objective, impersonal and horrid history for so long and in a class-society context. Liberalisation policy in Syria, slow measures at first and then abrupt in its latter stages (2006–2007), would inevitably resemble the shock therapy introduced in post-Soviet economies and the ensuing calamity.

As the assets of the class in charge of development in Syria came to be denominated in dollars and circulated in the dollar-based financial system, the regime's structural partnership with international financial capital grew. The value of dollar deposits in Lebanese banks alone was estimated at $5–6 billion in 2005.[23] In the final stages of this process of integration with world financial capital, US-led imperialism dumped its Syrian class ally. As the Syrian regime moved away from the last remaining safeguards of Arab socialism (dubbed regulation, as if freeing the market does not regulate it in favour of the ruling class) to neo-liberalism, the rate of transfer of value from the working class to the military–merchant class heightened the threat to national security and stability. The turnaround of the revolt, as mentioned earlier, was sparked by the loosening ideological hold of the ruling class on the state. More so than in less-strategic countries, Syria's descent into neo-liberalism is a form of war-booty galore, not because of the wealth looted from Syria, but because of the imperialist power repositioning, as will be explained in chapter 6. The pre-Assad Ba'ath had consistently represented a state bourgeoisie that safeguarded but disciplined capitalist relations during the absence of a viable national bourgeoisie in the immediate post-independence days. However, it had also stubbornly upheld a populist anti-imperialist position and, in that sense, there was a a roundabout incorporation of the working class into the state. The Assad regime decoupled the working class from

23 Monthly, 2011. *Syrian Deposits in Lebanese Banks: Between Myth and Reality!* 11 October 2011. Available at http://www.information-international.com/info/index.php/themonthly+/articles/682-syrian-deposits-in-lebanese-banks-between-myth-and-reality (viewed 3 February 2014). The amount of deposits by Syrians reported to the Bank of International Settlements was $ 4,618 in 1991 and rose to $ 25,991 billion in June 2008 (IBS Table A6), http://www.bis.org/statistics/bankstats.htm (viewed 2 July 2014).

the political process. However, it could not depoliticise a working class that revolted at a time when US and Saudi-led ideology and funds had nearly taken over the ideological space of the Islamic world.

Closing Comments

When the actual personification of the military–merchant class, duped itself into believing that the pittance earned by financial capital from conducting trade with Syria or capital outflows from Syria was all that imperialism sought, it succumbed to the myopia of dependent capital that often spells its own demise. It foolishly clung to the notion that US-led imperialist forces would be satisfied with the tribute drawn from the Syrian regime's adherence to neo-liberal policy when, in actuality, imperialism draws far bigger rents from the rest of the world as a result of its hegemony over Syria or (now) from a weakened or broken Syria. On the opposition side, the majority were outright allies of US-led imperialism. The moment the war began, the articulation of warring factions that history or the international balance of forces had provided, became the new social relationship governing development, and Islamists who had composed the minority inside Syria prior to the war became the conveyor belts of war funding and making. Others in the opposition were so naïve that they thought they could remove Assad from power and end the war with Israel as their neighbour. The theory of imperialism is principally a war theory, the core of which is that capital wrests power, destroys value, undervalues existing peripheral assets, and grabs resources in order to maintain its rates of profit. The war in Syria destroyed the social and physical structure and left the country weak on the security front.

Imperialist war is not a process that the political establishment of capital can arrest unless there is effective working-class opposition. War and technology are alien to the working classes, endogenous to capital, or fall outside the immediate control of the dominant social classes themselves. To draw future policies or construct a modern Syrian history and policy framework without first positing wars and dislocation amounts to a formal effort without a referent in reality – a sort of theory of efficient history modelled after the phantasm of efficient markets. Victorious imperialist wars have tempered the ideology of resistance to the demands of capital and convoluted it into a form of self-flagellation via Islamism. Much like the fantasy that the adversaries of the Syrian regime promote about the *doux-commerce* nature of financial capitalism and the possibility of a democratic transformation in Syria, the Syrian regime itself was extolling the virtues of free markets and the imminent transition of Syria into a new Arab economic tiger. However, situated in a region where most politics are *realpolitik*-like and war and the heightened threat of war represent principal tributaries of capital accumulation, the Syrian military–merchant class believed that with the services provided to imperialism in stabilisation, rendition, and anti-development, these acts together would ensure its leading-class accession into the global financial club – a sort of class promotion in the international division of wealth. However, times and technologies are changing. The mercantilist mode – selling goods and stocking cash – is quite different from a mode which requires ever-higher quarterly profits from an exponential capital-production process that has to partially shred to pieces its human and natural inputs. The Syrian military–merchant class misconceived the main contradiction as that between Syria's meagre financial wherewithal and the share of US-led imperialism from Syrian dollar flows. As will be detailed in chapter 6, the real contradiction is between variants of capitalist forces: between US-led capital and Chinese and Russian capital that falls under the hammer of the US dollar and consequently strives to partly escape such US hegemony by weakening the US's hold on Syria.

The opportunity to tear asunder the Syrian social formation following the 2011 Arab revolts was unmistakable. The imperialist cohort wasted no time and sacrificed the weakest chain in its structural alliance, the Syrian military–merchant class – and with it, its historical receptacle, Syria. The drawn-out process of destabilisation in Syria reinforces capital's control and the particular share of the US-led financial elite vis-à-vis the other circles of capital. Wars that extend control via the devastation of security in vulnerable peripheral states also expand value beyond the customary value-creation mechanisms. Longer working hours for Syrian workers are insignificant compared to the absolute consumption in the devastation of war of Syrian lives – a form of commercial exploitation. For US-led imperialism, the Syrian uprising was an opportunity to restructure the Syrian formation into a loose social mass in which the central state exercises little or no autonomy at worst, or prolongs the state of conflict at best.

The dominant mode of imperialist control in the AW is not meant to articulate the social formation by the medium of the state, trade and capital flows, but one where a state is engineered to promote the dissolution of the social formation itself. It is a way to wither the political representation of peripheral working classes and, conversely, an inexpensive form of colonialism. The perception that the United States is weaker as a result of leading unsuccessful campaigns in Iraq and Afghanistan is fallacious. It may have weakened as a result of rising China, but not as a result of destroying huge swaths of the Third World. The devastation left behind by US invasions retrogresses the development of working people and writes off their potential threat. Moreover, the profits of the global financial class have been steadily rising in spite of the 2008 financial crisis. Wars contribute to finance, and the US-led financial class draws imperial rents in inverse proportion to the degree to which states in this oil-rich region relinquish sovereignty over their fate and resources.

A cross-border US-led class alliance practises war on the more vulnerable states to mould the social configuration into the form required for undervaluing human and natural assets. That is how victory and/or defeat are to be assessed from a class perspective (as opposed to hallucinogenic nationalism) and not by the cakewalk of advanced armies into semi-starving nations, such as what happened in Iraq. The semblance of a weakened US is misleading because the capitalist class deploying the state to serve its ends is stronger as a result of militarism. Capital is a single whole to the extent that the dollar integrates specific capitalist classes or mediates concrete processes of wealth creation into an abstract one through the dollar. The fetish of national divisions flourishes in the soil of imperialist divisions over resource grabbing; but beyond the mystique of the fetish, as the working class bears the burden of war, it is the working populations in poorer nation states that lose the most. A consistently losing working class is one that is being pushed into a position from which it cannot exercise its social destiny as a subject of history. There are no 'ahistorical peoples', as in the chauvinist language of imperialist social science: there are peoples devastated by imperialist wars, who if they had their say, would prefer to stay out of such European history.

In times of severe crisis and war, the state outdoes itself as the political medium by which capital is reproduced. The scope of business for the military–merchant class of Syria was within Syria. US-led financial capital engages the region as whole (save the Gulf), not for what it can draw from it in money-form gains, but for its debilitation. Value relations, to be sure, precede the money-form making. These are two different modes of accumulation for two incongruous social classes that meet when their wealth coincides in the dollar, but that part company according to how much the immiseration of the Syrian working class contributes to the hegemony of US empire. In this dialectic, many of the physical beings of the Syrian military–merchant class will perish if Syria continues to perish. This was the juncture at which the Syrian regime went too far against its own working classes and against its own interests. It has not yet come to the recognition of the unavoidability of armed conflict and the necessity of war to US-led imperialism. But all along, this un-nationalistic class had misdiagnosed the imperialist drive for war and acted as a surrogate to US-led capital and let the Syrian state be imperialism's medium of repression and exploitation.

To recap, Syria is no ordinary Third World country. It has already extracted some unusual vetoes from China in the UN Security Council and is undergoing a Russian military intervention. For long before the uprising, *the Syrian military merchant class drew its strength from the very defeat of Syria*, and its gradual integration with imperialism over time culminated in deepening the objective grounds for the revolt. The overwhelming firepower of imperialism bolstered the defeatism that the Syrian ruling class needed in order to pass off its reforms under the veneer of pragmatism. Defeatism provided the ideological alibi to forego the goal of combining development with security objectives. It is within this context that imperialist international institutions, armed with a toolkit of neo-liberal policies, began to feed the regime's self-delusion of unrestricted freedom in pursuing its class interests. US-led imperialism's dominant ideology harnessed the blinkered subordinate military–merchant class to undertake the task of self-termination.

Sanctimonious cant derived from international law pervades the discourse on the Syrian crisis. Meanwhile, the war rages, moulding Syria into a shape possibly amenable to other future wars in the region. While US-led imperialism, its liberal Arab intellectuals and its labour aristocracy speak of human rights and democracy, the allies of US-led imperialism in the region channel weapons and jihadists to Syria (Sanger 2012), many of whom are the rejects of Europe, whose prisons exhibit a more than higher proportion of Muslim immigrants. It would stand to reason that the language of resistance to outside jihadist aggression and US-led imperialism in particular, as opposed to second-hand sentimentality, represents a more appropriate angle for addressing the Syrian issue. To speak in Mao Zedong's language of national liberation wars, the contradiction with US-led imperialism is the principal contradiction, while the contradiction with the regime is secondary (Mao 1937). Politically, the language of resistance is about building sovereignty, communal security and national defences. In economic terms, it is about reinstating protectionism, multiple exchange and interest rates and capital controls. In a nutshell, it is the delinking from the international financial market that ensures the recirculation of value within the national economy, which was practised under Arab socialism. For that, a cohesive and sovereign state in Syria is a rudimentary requirement. The fight in Syria is a national liberation war that requires odd alliances against the imperialist-funded jihadists in order to reinstate Syrian state integrity. US-led imperialism stands against autonomous peripheral states more so than do other variants of capital, such as the Russian or Chinese versions. More important, the inter–major powers rivalry is a window for Syrians and other working populations to exercise a certain level of autonomy. The compass of praxis has never swerved from targeting the appetite of the US's appetite for war. These are real priorities, as opposed to one-sided analytical priorities, to make; however, one point is for sure, a weakened state in Syria supervised by US-imperialist drones strengthens the tentacular grip of capital, not only in Syria, but over a planet fast being biologically extinguished by the excesses of capitalism.

Chapter 4
IRAQ – THEN AND NOW

In the two decades following 1958, Iraq leapt from being a country that exhibited one of the highest income inequality and illiteracy rates in the world, to a country with an impressive record of human and social development, including a narrowing gap in earning disparities (Todaro 1979). Economic and human development indicators also attested to faster-than-usual improvements in health, educational and social conditions (AMF various years). That was Iraq then.

When, in Geneva in 1991, US Secretary of State James Baker III warned Tariq Aziz, the deputy prime minister of Iraq, that Iraq would be bombed back into the Stone Age, he probably meant that the United States would deprive the Iraqi civilian population of the right to security of person, water, health, shelter and, more generally, the requirements for decent living.[1] In 2015, Iraq has become a war-plagued and divided territory, and its first prime minister in the Paul Bremer government of 2003, Ayad Allawi, has recently declared that 'the Iraqi people are longing for the days of Saddam Hussein'.[2] This is Iraq *now*.

Between *then* and *now*, hundreds of thousands have died as an immediate outcome of the first US aggression in 1991, the ensuing embargo and the all-out invasion and subsequent colonisation. The war's impact fragmented Iraq as a state. There are territories that are ethnically or sectarianly cleansed under a nominal republic. According to a 2011 report, nearly ten years after the fall of Saddam's regime, and with oil revenues that have increased nearly tenfold as a result of rising oil prices, more than a million orphaned children

---

1 Iraqis Endure Worse Conditions than Under Saddam, UN Survey Finds, by Chris Shumway, *The Standard*, 18 May 2005; and, Daily Living Conditions in Iraq dismal, UN survey finds, UN News Centre. (see recent article entitled 'Food Shortages Gnaw at Iraqis' Stomachs, Morale' Louise Roug, *Times* Staff Writer, 16 June 2005, underscores the horrific conditions in Iraq. And according to the article, 'Shrinking subsidised rations are blamed on corruption, security problems or the US'. Another UN article sways in that very direction, asserting that conditions in Iraq at present are worse than they used to be.
2 Iraqis long for the days of Saddam Hussein, http://www.raialyoum.com/?p=379712 (viewed 26 January 2016).

remained abandoned in the streets of Baghdad (Aljazeera 2011). Rates of birth defects where depleted uranium-laced artillery rounds were fired in US bombardments are significantly high (Al Sabbak 2012; Halliday 2013); what is not so unusual, given how sensitive Iraq is to US-led imperialism, the World Health Organisation (WHO) covered up Iraq's nuclear nightmare (Ahmed 2013). The electric-power crisis has lingered since 2003, and a government report prepared by the advisers to the board in the prime minister's office estimates that Iraq loses billions of dollars annually due to the power crisis (*Shafaq News* 2013).[3] After the 1991 bombing devastation and the subsequent embargo, electric power was restored only few months later and with only national means managed by the government of Saddam Hussein. On the distribution-of-income side, labour's share of national income is estimated at a pitiful 11 per cent, one of the lowest recorded levels globally (Guerriero 2012).[4]

Apart from its Hollywood-style monster movie spectacle, the IS is no anomaly in the region; it nourishes its raison d'être by mauling international law, erasing recognised borders and setting up an ethnically 'pure' government. However, because Muslims inhabit many pluralistic states around the globe, the IS media impact is giving the jitters to the foundations of the modern state system. De-facto, the IS carries out a colonial-hate agenda similar to past forms of cultural imperialism, with the object being to rupture continuity with the indigenous past. IS measures include the erasure of nationalist identity, destruction of historical sites and the cultural heritage, especially in Iraq and Syria. The IS's heightening terror, deeds and rhetoric, would not harm an imperialist capital that principally grows by militarisation such as that of the US.[5] Moreover, whereas material- and human-consuming war rages across huge swaths of the region, US-led imperialism acquired a positive

---

3   The Maliki government in Iraq has removed much of the macroeconomic data and historical time series that were available on the World Bank's WDI database. Obviously, the figure given above is exaggerated and driven by political mudslinging. The losses from waste and rechannelling funds destined to revive electric power are significant.

4   The last year in the sample used by Guerriero is 2009. According to the International Labour Organisation. the last estimate given for the labour share from national income was 21 per cent for the year 2004 (ILOSTAT 2016). This is a very low estimate and indicates extreme income inequality. Since 2004, labour has splintered over unreachable territory and conditions have deteriorated so much that measurements have become impossible. Iraq has removed much of the past data it has provided to the World Bank.

5   The fragmentation of Iraq along purist identity lines represents a threat to many multi-ethnic states. States, such as Russia, face a disconcerting nuisance that may seep through the fundamentalist pipelines.

development in the establishment of a de facto ally in the Iraqi Kurdish region – another loyal land base from which its military arm can further tilt regional battlegrounds. Iraqi Kurdistan has long been an American launching pad of aggression against the Iraqi state, and according to emerging anecdotal evidence, the ruling Iraqi Kurdish class had toyed with idea of erecting a statue of the late Israeli prime minister Ariel Sharon in Irbil.

Under the aegis of US-imposed governments, rising Iraqi oil revenues have funded and entrenched social-identity divisions that so far have produced more sorrow than solace. They did so through the US-reconstructed Iraqi state and its sectarian constitution after the 2003 occupation. To be sure, sectarian identity itself has no being or ontological being of its own; it is a political relationship defined within particular circumstances of the class struggle and in a historically determined social formation. As such, it was constituted by the colonially engineered state and *not* as result of its pre-capitalist historical origins (Amel 1980). Even though feudalism was the womb in which sectarianism was conceived, modern sectarian identity is a product of colonial production relations as opposed to pre-capitalist relations because it is the form in which the colonially spawned bourgeoisie exercises its class power (Amel 1980).

In the new sectarianism of Iraq there is much that resembles the past in form, as the names of Islamic saints (*Walis*) and past symbols reappear anew, but almost nothing in content. More so than any other reconstruction of identity, the current Sunni–Shiite sectarian phenomenon defies the dialectic of continuity and discontinuity. Whereas, in a dialectical relationship the past is sublated, negated and preserved simultaneously, the literal extrication of nearly all contrarian sources of knowledge in Iraq and the erection of an unfalsiable science of sect or ethnicity, put in place an identity whose ridiculously mythologised content bears only the remotest resemblance with the past. With the unchecked reconstruction of identity, divinities, saints and godlike imams are on record to have joined the battles of the sectarian wars. The assentation – the simultaneous discontent and obsequiousness of some under Saddam – has been replaced by unquestionable consent in which sectarian bonds and goals justify ethnic cleansing, at scales previously unseen in the region, by adherence to faith (autonomism-like). With Paul Bremer's constitution designating the control of the social product and oil revenues to Shiites, the condition for permanent civil strife were securely put in place. The sect-sprung bourgeoisie reconstitutes itself via the sectarian rent channel and a higher share of the rent often arises on the basis of inter-sectarian war.

The combination of secluding identity myth from critique by repression, dependency on sectarian war income for livelihood and an individual or collective security that obtains from the sect or sub-sect have circularly supported the post-American war condition. One has to note that competition for loot around the sect drives a self-dividing structure; there are many new inter-sect divisions that were unheard of before. Obviously, while the AW rebelled against abjection and for civil liberties during the Arab Spring, in Iraq, the sectarian divide pre-empted the grounds for revolt. Iraqi workers are suffering worse conditions at the hands of their ruling class, yet they fight each other instead of fighting their oppressor.

In what has become a small world in real time, the supposed US war on terror, a 'positive externality' to capital as a result of the war on Iraq amounts to an assault on the achievements of working people and their civil liberties everywhere. In imperialist power terms, which is the overarching condition for the continued worsening of the status quo as a result of rearing inter-communal conflict dressed in sectarianism, the debilitation of Iraq and Syria strengthened American–Israeli hegemony over the region. Israel has now 'the strongest army from the Indian to the Atlantic Ocean' and most Arab armies are ineffective (Yadlin 2015).

Not only in terms of the rising profit rates of the corporate–financial sector and the ideological power of US-led capital that had allowed it to suppress its own working class wages and segment it, but also in the demonstrable scare-effect arising from its ability to destroy a country and set it on a path of permanent implosion, the Iraq campaign has not downgraded the ranking of the US empire. If anything, the rise of China may have been stunted as a result of instability in Iraq, an area upon which it exercises little control. US-led imperialism, which includes Israel as the regional thrust point, is now interwoven into the governing structure of Iraq and the Gulf states – as much as was any colonial power in the past. An implosive Iraq, subjected to NATO firepower and deprived of sovereignty, not only boosts US leverage over the region and the globe, but beneath the perception of power it is also a process of destruction of physical and human value, a process that disengages unwanted resources from an oversupplied global production circuit. The costs of US and Western aggression – couched under the rubric of humanitarianism – are more than offset by the dual leveraging mechanism of re-establishing power via the demonstration effect, or from the destruction of value that recompose value relationships in capital's favour. The US has to demonstrate its ability to control or to easily win against a potential adversary, which drives the financial world to the safety of the US market. Stripped bare of falsehood, the prices and the sums of financial resources they amount to are the signification of the operation of the law of value in territories like Iraq, whose destruction reduces the control of Iraqi people over their wealth, and their labour and resources (the Iraqi people's) would be assessed in terms of imperialistically determined prices. After the imperialist-sponsored siphoning of the bulk of national wealth, the remaining resources are insufficient for the Arab labouring classes to maintain a minimum historically determined standard of living. The law of value, the tailoring of concrete labouring conditions that go into a labour process to the terms of exchange, spans the acts of consuming people's labour power in production to literally consuming people in wars. This law of value underpins the emergence of the dollar-form as the signification of the ultimate power symbol and has continually favoured US-led capital. As Rosa Luxemburg posited (1913), militarism is a domain of accumulation; but what was not added by her emphatically is that the consumption of human beings in war is itself part of the reproduction of capital. Unlike the targeted killing of fascism, US imperialism is racially and culturally indiscriminate in its process of war as the exercise of power and the representation of power.

As is discussed in the concluding chapter, there are endless ripples to imperialist assaults. But just as a prelude: wars on embargoed and starving Iraqi working people have served to maintain US control of oil supplies through direct military presence further stabilised a financial order in which the dollar remained the world reserve currency and wealth-holding medium; reinforced militaristic, religious and ultranationalist ideologies globally, helped compress the global wage, raised the dollar money supply by the trillions in costs that financial capital held in US debts, taxed the US working class and reduced its share of income, tested new war technology and improved old technology and, ultimately, allowed US-led capital to hold at bay ascendant and competing capitalist powers. In addition to following the descent of Iraq from its socialist period, which is blatantly obvious given its catastrophic condition since 1991, this chapter addresses some issues related to the causality of war and depicts the occupation of Iraq in relation to the imperialist objective of undervaluing Third World assets and raising imperialist rents. This chapter examines Iraq's occupation in terms of accumulation by encroachment, as per Lenin's definition of imperialism (1916).

Causation

On a superficial or media-traded level, the supposed cause of the two wars (in 1991 and 2003) with Iraq swings between the dictatorship of Saddam and the aggression of an American empire. These explanations are working-class stultification efforts that respond to or shape impulsive community moods. Causality in history is multifarious. On the surface, how evidence is interpreted and classified in assessing causation is closely attached to the values and interests of different social classes. A victorious empire may write the salient version of history as it wishes, but in the existing crisis of the imperialist class order, can any version of a victor's history closely reflect the historicity of events? All that is required to answer a question of this nature is to see why mainstream historiography overlooks war making as the *raison d'être* of the institutions and cultural heritage of capital. In the complex and fluid structure of history, there is a set of connected and determining relationships around which all other relationships congregate (Luckacs 1919; Carr 1961). The materially foregrounded and principal relationship in the totality of the historical moment is imperialist aggression. Imperialist assault and its related consequences are a cut above all the other causes; they are the gyroscope steadying global accumulation. They underwrite finance and, subsequently, intertwine themselves ideologically into the subaltern nodes of prevailing consciousness as defeat turns into resignation and sinks into the national *état d'esprit* of the conquered. The very weakness of the peripheral national structure becomes itself an incentive inviting further aggression. Low calculated risks on account of weak self-defence or internal conflict that mounts to resolve the crisis lessen the calculated risk of further imperialist aggression. After starving and bombing Iraq between 1991 and 2003, the country's defences cracked. Iraq's initial bombing and later occupation were dubbed cakewalks. Moreover, as soon as the trappings of the American-instilled political order began to take shape, Iraq's medium of self-reproduction as a social formation became intercommunal conflict.[6] Whereas it required the second-largest US military build-up since World War II to occupy Iraq in 2003, all it takes since the beginning of sectarian violence in 2006 is a small division fighting alongside an Iraqi military faction to tip the internal military balance one way or another.

In a developing-formation context, working-class consciousness transpires according to the forms of resistance the class undertakes vis-à-vis imperialist aggression (Larrain 1994). Analytical reasoning or pedagogy, as in telling people to do what is good for them, is subsidiary to consciousness emerging from praxis in the course of class struggle. How differing class positions are practiced and realigned against imperialism in national liberation struggles – which subjugate identity to class – is how a national working class transcends itself through internationalism. However, more than a decade after the invasion, the positioning of various national (sectarian, communal) forces in Iraq is less against imperialism and more against one another. Mediating these national struggles into a common anti-imperialist position is not an outcome that Iraqis can achieve alone; the state of the struggle worldwide and its

---

6 The United States owes the ingenuity of the application of the sectarian state model in Iraq to France's introduction of the confessional political order in Lebanon in 1920. The sharing of power and rent through the state between various sects created the permanent conditions for civil war in Lebanon.

ideological bearing on Iraq determine whether revolutionary fires will flare again. The Iraqi working classes overcoming their American-imposed divisive identities is synonymous with their reclaiming the channels by which their bourgeoisie reproduces its wealth or with knowing that national liberation cannot be achieved while in the grip of US-led imperialism. Obviously exposing/targeting the sectarian cleavages that underlie the position of the bourgeois class as an infighting relationship subordinated to US-led imperialism as a result of its own weakness is the process that could conceivably allow the working population of the country to climb out of the current quagmire. The Iraqi bourgeoisie is the auto-conflicting historical process by which differing bourgeois instituted in sectarian form relate to each other through violence reared by US-led imperialism. It is possibly the weakest form that a bourgeoisie can assume to protect its national interests and, hence, must exist in least sovereign states. The sectarian war line is the principal characteristic and appropriation mechanism of the Iraqi bourgeoisie.

Tangentially, even though the Iraqi state is in a shambles, the Iraqi people remain 'historical' regardless of the Eurocentric adage that 'people become historical through the state'. All peoples are historical through their forms of organisation and resistance, irrespective of whether the state adheres to imperialist 'standards' of statehood. A state is just another form of social organisation, albeit the one recognised as a society's central institution and whose historical function is the practice of its mediated sovereign rights. Any social form of organisation on the periphery (or for that matter in the imperial centre) is historical according to the degree of its anti-imperialist struggle. The legacy that people are historical only through a European-defined social form is a leftover from the European ultranationalist past of the nineteenth century, which arose via the genocide of many supposedly 'ahistorical' people who are no longer physically around, but whose spirit of resistance will contribute to the demise of the moribund European state system.

The study of history has gone through several phases of development (Mészáros 1995). In the distant past, divine interventions or mythical heroes were valid interpretations of historical development. Historiography has moved further away from these accounts as it began to assess how common will and human volition could be effectively translated via political media and organised political action – epitomised in the political party or the state. That was Hegel's historiography, the height of idealism, wherein the state incarnated the ultimate ethical form of spiritual self-realisation. The investigation of history then moved from the development of ideas to the Marxian notion of development in social relations and their attendant state of consciousness rooted in the development of material conditions. The way society reproduces itself, anchored in its relations of production, became a starting point for analysing historical processes that few could avoid. Scholars were, knowingly or unknowingly, having a discussion with Marx since the inception of such materialist explanations (Mészáros 1995).

Materialist explanations of history, and especially of war, did not begin with Marx. Of course, materialism predates Marxism. For instance, in the mid-eighteenth century Jean-Jacques Rousseau (1762) addressed the strains of economic want and war: '[E]very people, to which its situation gives no choice save that between commerce and war, is weak in itself'. For Rousseau, it is that materially founded weakness that spurs war. Pre–Industrial Revolution aggression occurred because of scarcity in food or the basic needs of society, or a crisis of underconsumption. As underproduction visibly turned into overproduction by the time of the Industrial Revolution, underconsumption crises were more and more relegated to social and maldistribution reasons rather than to natural causes. However, Marx's theory of crisis describes more than just an economic crisis of overproduction. For Marx, capitalism is born faulty and persists in permanent social crisis. Anarchic accumulation and blind competition in the pursuit of profit run amok; maintaining profit rates, extracting surplus value by imposing scarcity of basic goods and underconsumption, and war making are all interrelated facets of the social relationship that is capital. Specific historical circumstances trigger a recurrent fall in a system inherently predisposed to crisis.

Marx's descriptive of the anarchy of production, his 'accumulate, accumulate! that is Moses and the prophets', could be extended to the twentieth-century monopoly age with a twist: as the transfer of value through commercial exploitation from the periphery dips, developed-formation crises become more acute, and their resolutions may entail more aggressive wars. This is the sort of aggression that recreates the conditions for the free or cheaply priced appropriation of human and natural resources; as emphasised all along, it is a re-enactment of early forms of commercial exploitation that included slavery, but that re-enactment now not only engages labour or resources at lowly costs, but also engages labour in war and soldiering with the purpose of extinguishing their lives Unlike the fast-recurring cyclical economic recessions of the nineteenth century, the lower frequency of economic cycle downturns in central economies during the monopoly age stems from the stabilising effect of higher wealth wrought by the historical surplus value and the degree of market power and cartelisation, which allow profits to soar (unused surplus) and delay the onset of new technology or innovation that writes off the costs of old technology (Perelman 1999).[7] Strategic control of peripheral resources often goes

---

7 Monopolies hold prices at a level that allows them to earn extra profits and cover the costs of investment. However, when new technology lowers prices, the ensuing

unmentioned, but it is the foremost constituent of political power, from which all forms of power follow, including market power. In a system originating in violent expropriation, it is the 'power' in the market power that counts. Capital expands by expanding markets and by wars that cheapen or disengage inputs, or that strengthen it (capital) as a social relationship. The resolution of the contradiction arising from the need to meet the rising requirements of the rate of accumulation and the necessity to compete with other circles of capital in grabbing a bigger share of the colonies often involves war making (Lenin, 1916).

The slogan 'the US has to protect its way of life' is possibly the sole rationale available to the leading capitalists; it is now often invoked as pretext for a just war, when in fact under international law (the UN Charter) there exists no such rationale. As to the triggering of wars, many of the incidents in history that have sparked military conflicts are either premeditated or fabricated; concocting the occasion to start a war is a standard practice. This further evokes the question of how an American working class can be so weak so as to be drafted into war. Both the US and Iraqi working classes are victims of the war to varying degrees, but the wage share of the US working class relative to the sinking wages of much of the Third World has historically risen in relation to imperialist conquest (Davis 1960; Emmanuel 1972; Cope 2015). I must caution against an absolutism in conventional wisdom that always sees the Third World as a horde of Stone Age barbarians who are better off only as a result of handouts from Western capitalism. To be sure, subsistence income is a historically determined condition.

US-led capital is a cross-border class alliance that includes many of the social classes linked to it through financialisation or downstream production processes. In addressing this issue, account must be rendered of the state of revolutionary consciousness weakening under systematised violent and neo-liberal assault since the early 1980s and the resultant alienation within American society (Larrain 1979). In view of the crisis in socialist ideology, the same old concerns for job security preoccupy a majority of the working class. Precarious contracts are the standard market practice of the current era, and workers are said to be traumatised (Standing 2011; Bellofiore 2012). The strength of capital's ideology reproduces alienation from the self and the community simultaneously; these are processes that are devolved by the state (Althusser 1971; Meszaros 1970). The ethos of 'every man for himself' grips the social mind, ripping it away from itself and its social context; eventually, the social sickness deepens to the point that while the war rages, people watch the stock market's response to the bombing raids (an inference from Pappenheim

revalorisation and disengagement of non-performing capital tends to accentuate the depth of the fall in the business cycle (Perelman 1999).

1959). The vulnerability of wage labour to market conditions is a relationship that holds above all others in a crisis-laden labour process. Precarious working and contractual conditions, resulting from weakening unionisation and labour's shrivelled political clout in the United States underwrite the distorted balance of power between labour and capital locally and globally. The putative legal or free-exchange relationship between the free labourer and the owner of capital, which conceals beneath it a process of unequal power, resurfaced in successively dehumanising forms at recurrent downturns in the business cycle as acute forms of wage slavery. The inter-differentiated American working-class order, made up of such identities as Blacks, Latinos, 'working class', middle class and so forth, is also a sectional whole in relation to the international working-class order. The remaking of the two-party system itself is not only a reflection of missing socialist alternatives to labour, but it is also a product of the imperial rents that steady the share of labour in American society. In a world of each class for itself, the equilibrating factor in maintaining the stability of sectional working class politics, or the subordination of the working class to capital, is a product of imperial rents.

The destitution of labour is more dismal in developing countries, and capital often indulges in the consumption of the labourer together with his or her labour power in shorter time spans. Even the nominal appearance of level playing fields and fair trade (as in free wage labour) is blighted in a Third World context such as Iraq's. Acute inter-working-class divisions in least-developed countries and the threat of imperialist intervention frequently coalesce to arrest any possible realisation of a universal political expression. To borrow Lukacs's aesthetics' imaginary, American capital has projected its uglier image onto the periphery in material form (Lukacs 1919). Of the many facets of global integration, it is this ability of advanced capital to clone its more repressive traditions in the Third World and simultaneously subject its own labour force at home to a barrage of mythology that severs the organic links of the global working class. In the present epoch, imperialist wars against the poorest people on the globe are less and less questioned by the working classes of the Northern hemisphere.

The large US professional military and the government's capacity to issue large amounts of debt that can be paid off by foreign funds accrued on the basis of imperial expansion can ease the task of moulding American public opinion to withstand the cost of war. Unlike in days past, imperialist armies lose comparatively fewer soldiers, and the public pays less; it watches the war on the screen as if it is a video game (Cui 2005).[8] US-led ideological assault

---

8 The case can be such that even as the fatality rate declines, the rate of severely damaged survivors rises. The cost both financial and social is more and more widely recognised

also targets the Arab population to extinguish any budding forms of revolutionary consciousness. It especially targets any consideration of real measures involving the control of oil or any even partially autarkic policy of more equitable distribution that might lock in national resources. The method by which it has been pursuing this goal, however, involves a show of brutal force that is meant to snuff the spirit of resistance in addition to continuing the Islamisation of identity since the colonial days. On the surface, the assault is combined with 'Western democracy' cant deflecting blame back on the 'inherent despotism of Arab culture'.

In that regard, Israel's disproportionate use of massive violence, the latest of which are the wars on Gaza, is not haphazard; Israel acts as the role model for the United States when it wishes to silence certain forms of dissent, as in the 'shock and awe' and other unsightly forms of overkill strategies. The imperialist purpose is to demonstrate the futility of resistance given the highly uneven military balance of forces. Two weeks before his assassination by Israeli missiles, Hamas leader Abdul-Aziz Al-Rantisi copied a slogan from George Habash, which could be roughly translated as: 'We are winning because our people's resolve to carry out the struggle is unwavering'.[9] Soon afterward, Al-Rantisi was assassinated. Any strand of revolutionary thinking that opens a window of hope for the dispossessed has to be cut short.

Subduing the 'Arab' in neocolonial parlance does not mean swaying the affinity of the subject toward US imperialism. In terms of second-hand psychological emotions, there is more sadomasochism in imperialism than affection or empathy. Although one would avoid farcical mainstream refrains of hearts and minds: the real battle for the heart and mind is not to be won by changing the moods of the broad Arab masses toward the United States; this cliché was aimed at sections of Western audiences whose memory of imperialist pillage is extremely short-term or one whose predisposition is fed with the systemic racism that trails from the colonial era. As much as it can, war propaganda moulds the Western working class into support for war making while

---

as the physically and psychologically mutilated keep coming home to the United States from the endless wars. However, these sacrifices to the sectional class order imply an adjustment to the distribution of the share of labour within the working class. The oscillation between some measure of free healthcare and abolishing abortion rights, for instance, will have no bearing on the bipartisan policy of imperialism, but it will buy into the devotion of lower-income segments of the American working classes to their national identity. The pattern of capital's ideological strength versus the concession made to labour is the dynamic stabilising of the allegiance of the mainly white American working class to imperialism.

9 Article appeared in Al-Quds London, first week of April 2004.

it instils a belief in the uselessness of resistance in poorer peoples abroad. Winning people over is not accomplished on the basis of international democratic debate, for no such democratic platform for debate between peoples of the world has come into being yet.

US-led capital's ideological assault triumphs by converting real human and political issues such as ethnic cleansing or the dispossession of the Palestinian people in 1948 into a theocratic question and a war rooted in mythology. The conversion of fiction into reality can be observed as the US House of Representatives received the speech of Benjamin Netanyahu on 24 May 2011 with 29 standing ovations, in which two particular accolades (standing ovations 15 and 16 respectively) cite biblical references and a 4,000-year-old bond of Jewish people to the Jewish land. In mystifying real issues, imperialist ideology is assisted by three seminal allies in the region: Israel, Iran and Saudi Arabia – seminal, in the sense that none of the ultra-nationalist or theocratic ruling elites of these entities object to the dealings of the free market and the reign of capital. For all the hostility expressed toward Iran by US political leaders, there is no essential antagonism, or a contradiction, based on one country's desire to socialise private property, between Iran and the United States, as was shown earlier in the destruction of the Iraqi national formation when the post-Saddam imperial administration made the decision to divide and further conquer by disenfranchising the largely Sunni Iraqi Ba'ath party while privileging the Shia population and religious parties, a move that Iran backed with money and military support in the sectarian fighting that followed. Wahhabism would not have expanded to the scale it has, had it not been for American- and Iranian-backed Iraqi Shia militias ethnically cleansing Baghdad and other Sunni regions – events largely televised by Aljazeera and other mainstream channels to fan sectarian hatred and boost the ratings of capital through inter-working-class conflict. The war on Iran, if and when it occurs, would not be for market-expansion reasons, but more about the destruction of value and value grabbing. Additionally, all three regimes (Saudi, Israeli and Iranian) seek legitimacy, partially or wholly, via the religious identity channel that has a built-in tendency to collide with its surroundings.

In international law, war is virtually unjustifiable, and the law itself cannot reconcile with virulent forms of nationalism. The United Nations Charter permits war in self-defence and only after approval from the Security Council. Not so long ago, lifeboat ethicists or 'survivalists in a world of scarcity', as opposed to 'a world of abundance and togetherness', introduced the phrase 'protecting our way of life' as a premise that justifies waging war or sinking refugee boats at sea to ensure that Western formations are not burdened with extra costs. As often repeated by the US administration, the pretext for the invasion and occupation of Iraq was to protect the 'American way of life'.[10] Iraq, not by the type of regime it had and not because of Saddam Hussein, but by its very formation and constitution as a viable state was assumed to threaten the way of life of the United States and some of its Western allies. Iraq was not going to invade the great white north, but by developing and industrialising and empowering its working people it would have weakened the channels of imperialist rents to the centre. Pentagon scenarios of plans to invade Iraq were drawn up during the Cold War, according to which US attack planes concealed under Saudi sands will depart from bases in Saudi Arabia and prepare for the invasion of Iraq. One of the generals in charge of such simulations admitted that because the USSR was still around, the chances of a nuclear holocaust had deterred this desire of US-led capital.[11] Intolerance of even semi-sovereign states in the Middle East underpins the relentless intervention and destabilisation.

The post–Cold War ideological victory of capital furnished it with a free hand to promote the 'American way of life', the most visible facet of which is the seclusion of the rich in gated enclaves with private security guards or more generally, in building walls along the national borders – a fortress America for the richer folk. Davis's (1960) explanation of such expansionism rests on an ideology of a frontier Eden or an American history unfolding by manifest destiny, the idea of the uniqueness and superiority of Americanism as a frontier ideology, a frontier developing by unhampered capitalism at the expense of Native Americans and later other peoples around the world. The United States has been a net global debtor in money form for over four decades, but a leading economic and profit rates growth hub for the planet. As the successor empire to European empires, it also enjoys vast power and historical surplus-value privileges that include all the measures of genocide and slavery that blocked the development and industrialisation of the Third World. Foreigners hold an increasing share of US government debt; the four major Asian central banks (Japan, China, South Korea and Taiwan) alone hold over $5 trillion (Hudson 2010, 444). The backing of all this US debt requires the consolidation of hegemony over oil states to counterbalance the money debt (Avramidis 2006; Patnaik 2009).

The pursuit of oil implied that the policy space of many sovereignty-weakened developing Arab states was diminishing. Historical structures – the

---

10 A search for 'protect way of life George W. Bush' will produce nearly 2 million hits on Google. Not all of these of course are George W's, but many are.
11 Interview with an American General responsible for war simulation against Nicaragua and Iraq, Public Broadcasting Service, PBS. http://www.pbs.org/newshour/extra/debate/iraq.html viewed 12 May 2009.

inherited political superstructure, the social geography and the politics, especially anything related to the sheer weight of the US-led security arrangements and firepower, just weighed like a nightmare on small developing states. States like Iraq, Syria or Egypt could no more influence the global decision-making process than a village idiot can influence a town council. The potential of a failed state has come to represent the fate of nearly all Arab nationalist bourgeois classes or socialised states of which, once more, Iraq represented a model of independent nationalism, with certain socialist traits. In fact, unlike Syria and Egypt, being constantly at war, Iraq could not have opted out of Arab socialism even if it wanted to. When it was bombed, sanctioned and invaded, it still had its five-year plans, subsidies and free social services.

At no time since 1958 (Iraq's real independence from British rule), when Iraq was catapulted into the Soviet orbit, has it been at ease when slotted in between monarchical Iran, Turkey, Saudi Arabia and the buffer state, Jordan. A quasi-socialist, anti-American and anti-Israeli state wedged in the midst of these allies of US-led American capital would enjoy little chance of stability. Abdel Karim Qassim (1958–1963), Iraq's first president, brought the Kurdish leader Mustapha Barzani (1958) back from exile in the Soviet Union, and within only few months, the latter resumed a protracted war against successive Iraqi governments supported by the United States and the Shah of Iran, which ended with the fall of the Bakr-led Iraqi government as it ceded its sovereignty over Iraq's only waterway (Shat Al-Arab) to Iran (in the 1975 Algiers Treaty).[12] All along, the Iraqi communist party, which was later to support the American assault on Iraq in 1991, couched narrow sectarian and ethnic agendas under communist hubris and, effectively, fought the idea of closer Arab integration under the pretext of an 'ultra-left internationalist' agenda. Kowtowing blindly to the moderated Soviet position, from the recognition of the partition of mandate Palestine to supporting the United States in its war on Iraq, the Communist Party of Iraq had placed itself objectively in a collaborative position with US-led imperialism, on the basis of the vacuous position that all nationalisms contradict their internationalism.

The Arab integrationist project (opposed by Qassim and the Iraqi communists), insofar as it potentially led to the formation of the anti-imperialist alliance *qua* the United Arab Republic (UAR) joining Egypt and Syria in a single state (1958), represented a much bigger threat to the state of Israel and to US interests than did the Qassim–communist alliance. For the United States, Qassim was considered neutral in foreign policy. In economic policy,

12 United Nations Treaty Series No. 14907 Iran and Iraq Agreement concerning the use of frontier watercourses 1975, and Algiers Agreement of 6 March 1975.

he certainly did not attempt to socialise, as Nasser did extensively in Egypt and Syria, or nationalise oil interests.[13] While Israel acquiesced to Qassim, the United States was uncomfortable with the support he received from the communists and placed more emphasis on the containment of potential communism. Communications between the US embassy in Baghdad and the US Department of State in 1959 show that the United States was comfortable with Qassim's neutrality, but worried about the reach of the communists within his government.

> Qassim's evident resolve to achieve internal stability and adopt effectively neutral stance in foreign relations must contend with persistent regional and world tensions and with inherent instability of Iraq's political, cultural, religious and ethnic make-up. Our hopes for measurable progress toward relative stability and genuine independence are riding on shoulders of one man, whose judgment regarding key factor of Communism is still open to question. (US Department of State 1959)

From post-independence until the end of the Iran–Iraq War, albeit to the dissatisfaction of US-led capital and its allies in the region, Iraq remains in a constant state of war. Trying to cut losses in the early stages of the war with Iran, the Iraqi regime attempted to seek a truce with an intransigent Iranian clergy as early as the first year of the war, but to no avail (Taqi 2008). Much to the dislike of US imperialism, the most viable institution in Iraq, the military, emerged stronger from the Iran–Iraq war and, more significant, backed with a military industry that might potentially violate the ultimate taboo by redressing the balance of forces with Israel. Following the US invasion in 2003, disbanding the Iraqi military was a top priority on the neoconservative agenda. The first trigger for imperial assault was Iraq's efforts to escape the Iran–Iraq war legacy by attempting the impossible, namely to redraw Middle East borders and challenge the foundation of the colonially bequeathed security arrangement by annexing Kuwait. By premeditation or coincidence, that was a welcome opportunity to the victors of the Cold War.

Analysing Iraqi history from the wrong starting point – the point of vilifying and demonising Saddam Hussein – intentionally or not, provided cover for the invasion. By reducing the country to a man, it became easy to destroy the Iraqi social formation through the false rationale of the man's authoritarian rule. This should expose the class whose values are being served in the explanation of historical causality. Many Western liberals have fallen victim

---

13 Law No. 80 of 1961 promulgated by Qassim only expropriated the non-operating concessions of the Iraqi Petroleum Company (IPC) (Dougherty and Ghareeb 2013).

to the erroneous methodological approach of congealing historical developments into the person of an 'insane' or 'evil' dictator at the helm of power in a small developing country. Many liberals, including Noam Chomsky, would criticise US foreign policy and Saddam simultaneously, conflating two separate issues existing on distinct planes of thought, and thereby justifying the invasion. Speaking in 2002, Chomsky said that Saddam 'is as evil as they come, ranking with Suharto and other monsters of the modern era', which draws an image in the public mind that all measures are justifiable against him, including an invasion of 'Saddam', who also happens to be Iraq (Chomsky 2002). In 2015, when asked about ISIS (what I have referred to as the Islamic State all along), Chomsky's answer was that 'the US and Britain invaded Iraq, a major crime that created the background out of which IS grew and developed' (Chomsky 2015). When the liberal moves from the personalist propaganda to the more adequate macro picture of history (the background) to explain the reasons for the rise of IS, the historical background becomes the US invasion – no longer the evil dictator. However, when developing further a picture of the 'background', Chomsky begins to select and falsify the facts. He continues: 'Iraq had already been virtually destroyed, first of all by the decade-long war with Iran in which, incidentally, Iraq was backed by the US, and then the decade of sanctions'. (Chomsky 2015). Although Iraq emerged stronger after the Iran–Iraq war, the falsifications here are many, including no less than that Israel supplied weapons to Iran to continue the war; that before the war, Iraq complained about several Iranian transgressions upon its sovereign territory; that Iraq was Soviet allied and armed; and that Iraq was the most important secular anti-Israeli state in the region.

But let us select a slightly earlier point in history (the background of which Chomsky speaks), such as the toppling of Mossadegh in Iran in 1953 (Abrahamian 2012) and the reinstatement of the Shah and his repressive rule by the United States and Britain. This intervention laid the groundwork for the rise of the first Islamic state in Iran, a state whose constitution and extension into neighbouring countries follows the sectarian line. Iraq complained to the UN Security Council about Iranian incursions into its territory, but its real worry was the sectarian violence in the South led by the parties of the now-governing structure. Also let us consider the reactionary elephant in the revolutionary room: the Iranian clerical regime brutally suppressed and, in many instances, massacred the socialists upon assuming power (Vahabzadeh 2010); it provoked sectarianism in Iraq and Lebanon as early as 1981. The other side of the story is that Iraq was effectively a Soviet-armed satellite and not a Western one. It was not the handshake with Donald Rumsfeld that would turn Saddam into a Western puppet, which was more of a staged Hollywood manoeuvre than relevant history. Given the effectiveness of

Hollywood-style politics, much of mainstream social science should be slotted under film critique or acting and not history. The Soviet Union was already wary of Islamic Iran's anti-communist backlash and its sectarian inroads into its own multi-ethnic society. Baghdad was the most radical anti-imperialist and secularist city in the AW and its destruction was an imperialist 'must'. The 'background' of which Chomsky speaks was altogether the creation of the United States, including the Gulf states lending to Iraq and the channelling of weapons through Israel to Iran to prolong the Iran–Iraq war. The war itself was the value-restructuring relation that imperialism groomed at the behest of capital.

If the history of wars can be explained by the insanity of George W. Bush or Saddam Hussein, then a universal mental asylum would be the functional objective of the peace movement. Systematic human-rights violations originate in a system of social relations that the United States propagates on a global scale. The Iraq war is class-determined (Parenti, 2003). The argument against Saddam and the argument for war on Iraq are separate. Giving the United States a free hand in Iraq is a very serious breach of human rights inasmuch as it breeds the very cause of human-rights violations on a global scale by reinforcing the war-induced international division of labour. Although, by its very essence, Iran is not anti-imperialist, international working-class support for the country ensues from the point of forfeiting another lucrative imperialist war opportunity for the United States, if it decides to bomb. The United States goes to war because its capital must reproduce itself by devouring new territories, resources and people, by destroying to rebuild on its own terms, by hegemonising the social value relations that are the backdrop of production and by controlling and holding off would-be competitors for the seat of empire. Imperialism is a mutating power relationship that is nurtured principally by violent aggression. These are the same old motives of colonialism, which are grabbing and undervaluing Third World assets.

In the legacy of the Middle East and its background, there is so much left over from World Wars I and II that it becomes unreasonable to assign historical agency to the post-colonial state as a state per se or, more ludicrously, to the heads of those states. *Ipso facto*, ample evidence from the post-uprisings states or the trail of collapsing states that the Arab Spring left behind, suggest that the territories laid out as states by intercolonial compromise have staggered under sustained imperialist assaults that have progressively enfeebled their agency.

The British occupied Iraq from the end of the World War I until 1958. Some may argue that it was formally independent, but the British ambassador (circa 1935) related an encounter with Prime Minister Hikmat Suleiman which, besides clearly showing the immense degree of British influence in Iraq, also reflects the weakness of the prime minister's character. The ambassador informed the Foreign Office of how he told Hikmat Suleiman very sharply that his manners were bad. 'When [...] the time came to tell him what was thought about it [the Government's desire to buy arms from-non-British sources] by all in London, I was in some difficulty because I had, as it were, to hold him up with one hand and hit him with the other. I hit him, nevertheless, and the blow was hard – because I took him by surprise. Hikmat was very near resignation and we came to the verge of a complete break when he dined with me a few nights later and I had to give him a jolt about the way the Ministry of Defence (Iraqi) was behaving. When he called on me the next day, he told the Oriental Secretary that, if I meant to hit him again, he would walk out and not come back' (Tarbush 1982, 143–144). The British ambassador was slapping the Iraqi prime minister at almost every encounter, very much like the reported incidents of ministers in the 'sovereign government' of Iraq who were slapped by US Marine Corps officers after the 2003 invasion.

Apart from the major landing in Basra in 1941 to quell rebellious Prime Minister Rashid Al-Kilani, the British landed in newly independent Kuwait in 1961 to aid the state from annexation by the Qassim regime. Palpably, the third major landing occurred in 1990, once again to protect Kuwait from annexation by Iraq. The partition of the Middle East by the Sykes-Picot (1916) Agreement left its indelible imprint at every juncture of recent history. If states are, partly or coincidentally, a form of expression of a people's right to self-determination, then it is safe to say that none of the Arab peoples have commonly or, at least by majority consensus, decided on what they are or what they wanted to be. In hindsight, Arab history is the socially sickening transformation imposed by the superior military power of imperialism. History continues to be imposed by the shackles of an unequivocal US-led military advantage.

In hindsight, the successful blitzkriegs of the Israeli army will suffice as proof of a balance of power favouring Israel. But one may ask what about 'in between Arab-Israeli wars': Were the Israelis always that far ahead of the Arabs in military capacity? Two small paragraphs from the 1958–1961 archives of the State Department illustrate the point. The first earmarks Israel's military superiority and the second shows how the United States contrives to cover up Israel's acquisition of weapons-capable nuclear capacity.

> Undersecretary McGhee expressed understanding Israel's apprehensions arising from its exposed position but commented US has great respect for Israel's military competence and estimates it as being match for some time to come

for any Arab combination. He remarked US has no evidence beyond propaganda statements that Arabs contemplating military move against Israel. He also pointed out that any drastic increase in Israeli armament, particularly to more sophisticated weapons, would likely result in corresponding increase in UAR possibly leading to uncontrolled escalation which might add to rather than decrease instability in region. (Department of State 1962)

Israel's New Atomic Reactor: The Ambassador told the President he believes we can accept at face value Ben-Gurion's assurances that the reactor is to be devoted to peaceful purposes. An inspection of the reactor by a qualified United States scientist can be arranged when the United States wishes, if it is done on a secret basis. Overt examination and announcement of the result to the world will require greater effort, but could be done. [2 lines of source text not declassified] Reid suspects that very few people in Israel knew of the development's true character, possibly not even the Foreign Minister, Golda Meir, until it hit the headlines. (Department of State 1961)

With respect to the latter statement and the docile way the United States addresses Israel's nuclear capabilities, it is relevant to contrast this language with the embargo and other threats the United States makes concerning the current Iran nuclear facilities. Hypothetically, the United States would not object to Iran possessing a few nuclear warheads; the real worry of empire in the region is not the degree of destructiveness that developing-country weapons systems display, it is working-class rule. It is democratisation through empowerment of the working class via political and social rights enshrined in a state, or in mass class-wide organisation and revolutionary ideology that really brings capital to its knees. The type of democracy the United States pushes down the throats of the working population is partial and selective, the image of its own democracy in its age of slavery and genocide of natives, which continues to be reproduced by mainly white voters afraid to lose privilege from integrating with the world working class or from compensating theirs and the victims of their class ancestors.

These pseudo-democratic measures exclude huge sections of the population from representation even though they appear to be represented through the voting system. Standard explanations for undemocratic processes may cite the absence of an unbiased flow of information, the lack of provision for basic needs making social groups vulnerable to manipulation en masse, biased institutions of legal and social rights, a constitution that actually creates sectional groupings as states within a state, a voting procedure that permits the rigging of the process in favour of 'free market' or US-leaning candidates, but most of all, the brittle condition of the state. All these ills are found in Iraq and, together, they obliterate the remotest possibility of a democratic process. The imperialist US-led consortium needs to continuously destabilise the Iraqi social formation and, as such, it must ensure itself the right to count the votes.

If questions of degree were to matter, then the degree to which the balance of forces is tipped against the Iraqi working population should necessitate a new reading of how capital harnesses the resources of underdeveloped Arab social formations. Equally relevant, the features of imperialist practice differ in this region, insofar as the entente prevailing during the Cold War was breached when the UN Security Council was bypassed for the purpose of invading Iraq. That was a rare exception to the rule and, nonetheless, an exceptional explanation of the articulation and the mode of integration of this region with world capital is warranted.

Empirical Note on the Impact of the War

The economic impact of the US-led war on Iraq was a world-significant event. There is considerable evidence in the rates of asset destruction to suggest that past wars in the AW have had long-lasting global economic and developmental consequences. The term 'supply shock' entered economic textbooks after the 1973 Arab–Israeli war. The Arab boycott, a defensive measure against extending Israeli colonisation, was used to demonise Arabs. The rise of petrol prices at the pump could not have had such ample ramifications on inflation had Western governments used a different tax regime to absorb the oil price hike. But already by the mid-1970s the monetarists were calling the shots and allowed runaway inflation to raise interest rates, raise debt burdens, blame Keynesian welfare-intervention, and boost the ideological grounds for imperialist expansion. This was the beginning of the neo-liberal assault on working classes: taxing the central classes and warring against the developing world.

The global recovery from the 1990 recession was, in part, based on the US-led massacre of Iraqis in the 1991 invasion (the massacre was mimicked by the phrase 'shooting fish in a barrel'). The aggression of 1991 occurred at a time when the global economy was still staggering under an incomplete recovery, and military spending boosted economic performance. Since then one still hears of further 'regime change' that may still widen the potential for disaster and, in an auxiliary way, factor the instability into dollar-based international financial transactions. Foster (2006), who is quite reserved in matters of forecasting, says that that the 'doors of hell' have been opened as a result of Iraq's occupation. Looking at all the regional wars around the time of writing in 2015, he was right. Internationally, the undercurrents according to which many major powers opposed the US-led destruction and then invasion of

Iraq remain unchanged, as can discerned from the ongoing Sino-Russian rift with the United States and Russia's direct involvement in Syria.

As a result of continued intercommunal conflict, contemporary social circumstances in Iraq are disastrous in spite of the high oil revenues since 2003. The Kurdish region, which escaped the full trauma of war as a result of its fifth-column alliance with the US, appears to have been willing 'to sacrifice its own people as long as Western and Turkish corporations could fill the coffers of its leadership' (Vltchek 2016). Since 2014, unemployment in Iraqi Kurdistan had reached 50 per cent along with rampant poverty (Vltchek 2016). As early as 2003, top oil-company executives told the United States they will not make large investments in Iraq while the security situation remains so dangerous. In meetings with high-ranking US officials, they have also expressed concern about the lack of political legitimacy for the US-backed authority in Iraq (25/07/2003- FT.com). Fatefully, the reason why Iraqi oil capacity was weaker than Iran's prior to 1958 is also assigned to political instability (Tarbush 1982). The fact that American oil companies are averse to handling the current risks is not so relevant to the United States when compared to the benefits of writing off Iraq as a state and the power it musters, which underwrites the seignorage of the dollar.

Regionally, no matter which way things go, the AW economies have already borne the brunt of the aggression as a result of increased regional tensions and violent spill-over effects because of their geographical proximity as one national formation after another was disrupted and splintered. The invasion of Iraq was also a further assault on the Organization of the Petroleum Exporting Countries (OPEC) and, by implication, through power restructuring, against direct producers of primary commodities everywhere (IWA, 2003). OPEC lost much of its ability to price crude when oil became listed on the futures market in the mid-1980s. Direct-supply conditions now only minimally influence the price, since it can be determined vis-á-vis other listed futures. Moreover, war or warlike conditions, which leave exporting states with narrow margins within which to manage their own supplies, force them to relinquish price determination to American financial markets. With heightened conflicts, the longer-term growth prospects in the AW may also be determined by a combination of high tensions and low to moderate oil prices as has been the case since 2014. Until now, it was possible to offset dire economic consequences with high oil prices; however, increased insecurity implies that much of the oil revenues will go to stabilisation efforts, or worse yet, be sucked into the implacable capital-flight syndrome.

It is really superfluous to bring into the picture the great strides made by Iraq prior to 1980. As shown in the Annex to chapter 1, the average yearly growth rates were closer to 10 per cent. However, the present Iraqi economy is a product of three wars, stringent economic sanctions and years of isolation. Macro relationships are dictated by war exigencies. Available data on Iraq shows that economic performance has been extremely poor since at least 2000. Despite its oil-export revenues – estimated at nearly $700 billion between 2004 and 2014 (OPEC various years)– Iraq's productive capacity is in shambles. Its government currently reports little data: it is an incapacitated economy, and its ability to produce data has been stunted. Also, the regime does not want to show the present imperialist-sponsored state in a bad light. The Iraqi state has no control over large stretches of its own territory. Widespread poverty and a huge number of people lacking adequate access to basic services and resources such as clean water, food, health care, electricity, jobs and sanitation, continue to prevail. The destruction of Tikrit and Ramadi in 2015 show that the Iranian-backed militias, the Iraqi state and the United States through its air cover continued the same old forms of Sunni cleansing under the pretext of fighting IS (Susannah George, for the Associated Press, quoting a United Nations report in 2016). The Sunni–Shiite divide, which so carefully groomed by US-led imperialism, is the goose that lays the golden egg for capital.

Between 2000 and 2004, Iraq's GDP at constant prices is estimated to have been growing at an annual average of negative 10 per cent and recorded a fall to $15,474 million in 2003, the year of the invasion, down from $20,861 million in early 2000 (UN 2005a). In a comparison with other Arab countries, Iraq's GDP per capita in 2003 ranked second lowest to Yemen's (UN 2005a). In 2014, GDP per capita stood at $2401 (WDI, 2014). GDP per capita at constant prices (2000) was estimated at $836 in 2001, declined to $745 in 2002, and to $567 in 2003. It is estimated to have risen again to $884 in 2004. One year after the invasion, daily per capita GDP did not exceed $2.40 per day and unemployment rates, according to official statistics, hovered at the two-digit level (28.10 per cent in 2003, which is said to be underestimated and disguising a measure of about 60 per cent). Should underemployment be considered as well, the degree of underutilisation of the labour force becomes more ominous: underemployment alone adds another 23.5 per cent to the unemployment rate (UN 2005a). Unemployment had increased massively following the disbanding of the Iraqi army and the de-Ba'athification (firing past regime supporters from the public sector) measures from state institutions.

Predictably, given these figures, Iraq's human development indicators are low, for the obvious reason of war. By the time of the invasion, the World Food Programme 2003 Survey (UN-WFP 2004) that covered 16 out of 18 governorates shows that one in five Iraqis (or 4.6 million out of an estimated 22.3 million) suffered from chronic poverty, and that 60 per cent of the population has been relying on monthly food rations. Moreover, 36 per cent of all children (1–5 years old) living in extremely poor households are chronically malnourished. The national average for chronically malnourished children of this age group was 27.6 per cent (UN-WFP 2004).

Personal security and living conditions in Iraq after the 2003 US-led invasion and occupation have deteriorated at alarming rates; a select picture is as follows:

(1) The presence of the American offensive, ongoing kidnapping and criminal gangs were creating huge chaos and lack of security in the country.
(2) UNDP's 'Iraq Living Conditions Survey 2004' estimates that more than half of the population have lived below the poverty line, where the monthly median income of households (constituting an average of 7.8 people) has declined from $255 in 2003 to $144 in 2004 (about half a dollar a day per person). Add to this the ongoing deterioration in health services with a lack of accessibility to drugs and the ruin of hospitals and health centres.
(3) Moreover, illiteracy has become a major characteristic of the poor and extremely poor: 40 per cent of adults in extremely poor households, and 30 per cent of adults in poor households, are illiterate. Life expectancy, which was around 65 years in the mid-1980s, went down to 58 years during the nineties, while the world's average during that period settled at 66 years (UN 2005a).
(4) Another report issued by the US Congress at the end of June 2004 stated that only one governorate in Iraq has access to 16 hours of electricity per day as compared to seven governorates one year before the invasion.[14] To date, power shortages still plague the disconnected country.
(5) On 22 May 2003, the UN Security Council passed Resolution 1483, lifting sanctions on Iraq, phasing out the six-year-old UN oil-for-food program over six months (the program ended on 21 November 2003), and designating a UN special representative to assist Iraq in its reconstruction efforts. On 27 May 2003, the US Treasury lifted most US sanctions on Iraq, thereby implementing UN Security Council Resolution 1483. However, in spite of hundreds of billions spent on reconstruction, conditions remain baleful. Initially, total Iraqi long-term reconstruction costs were estimated at $100 billion. Several times this amount was spent, yet reconstruction stagnated. In one example of how reconstruction is carried out, in November 2003, the US. Congress authorised $18.2 billion for Iraq

---

14 The report referred to the testimony of Samer Shahata before Congress on 15 June 2004. http://www.academia.edu/6753825/Congressional_Testimony_Iraq_Public_Opinion_Toward_the_United_States

in a supplemental allocation aimed at boosting Iraqi development, but only 3.3 per cent of the pledged amount was spent, and much of that was diverted into military-related expenditure, away from priority needs and reconstruction. In one instance of flagrant US-sponsored fraud, a planeload of some 363 tons of cash ($12–14 billion) transferred to Iraq went missing in 2004.[15]

The economic battering during the sanctions and war years: the investment rate fell from 30 per cent in 2000 and maintained an average of around 15 per cent after the invasion. The Iraqi economy suffered from continuous deterioration in output throughout its recent history. It also exhibited low levels of investment and consumption, high unemployment, high inflation, erratic deterioration and fluctuation of the foreign exchange rate (UN 2005a). GDP in constant 1990 prices atrophied to negative 66 per cent in 1991 (war losses) and to negative 22 per cent in 2003 (UN-Statistics Database 2005). The economic situation in 1991 was in a depressive state due to the imposition of UN sanctions. GDP per capita grew at about negative 1 per cent during the eighties and about 0.5 per cent during the 1990s. GDP per capita shrank from $2,200 in the late 1980s to about $488 in the mid-1990s before recovering slightly to an estimated $750 in early 2000 (Table 4.1). Not only did Iraqi GDP collapse, but the value of the Iraqi dinar started spiralling downwards, mainly due to sanctions. In the early 1980s, the official exchange rate was set at ID1 = $3.2, which then collapsed to ID1 = 0.0006 (or $1 = ID1,674) by the middle of the 1990s. In October 2003, a new Iraqi currency, the 'New Iraq Dinar' (NID) replaced the old dinar, and today, the NID hovers at around $1 = NID2,000. This deterioration in the currency and the shortage of the domestic supply of goods, though possibly the least devastating result of the war given the human toll, added to its problematic conditions. Prices grew at an average annual rate of 13 per cent in 1995–2002 as compared to 264 per cent in 1990–1995 (Table 4.2).

Production by Sectors: Between 1990 and 2003, the fall in GDP was also spread across various economic sectors. The oil sector was hit hardest. Compared to 1989, oil output fell by 95 per cent and slightly recovered by 1997, but never to its past levels (Table 4.3). Moreover, Table 4.4 shows that mining and manufacturing shares from GDP, which includes the oil industry,

---

15 How the US sent $12bn in cash to Iraq and watched it vanish. Special flights brought in tonnes of banknotes, which disappeared into the war zone, http://www.theguardian.com/world/2007/feb/08/usa.iraq1 Investigation Into Missing Iraqi Cash Ended in Lebanon Bunker, http://www.nytimes.com/2014/10/12/world/investigation-into-missing-iraqi-cash-ended-in-lebanon-bunker.html?_r=0

Table 4.1 Major economic and social development indicators in the economy over selected years

	1970	1975	1980	1985	1990	1995	2000	2003
GDP at constant 1990 prices (in millions of US$) UN-Stat	15,517	23,478	42,441	31,633	38,356	10,107	17,782	14,952
Population (in thousands)	9,440	11,124	13,238	15,585	17,890	20,536	24,086	27,139
Per capita GDP	1,644	2,111	3,206	2,030	2,144	492	738	551
Unemployment rate (%)								28.1
External Debt (in billions of US$)								125.0
Oil Reserves (in billions of barrels)								115.0
Oil Export Revenues (billions of US$)							17.4	8.4

Source: Central Bank of Iraq; Statistical Bulletin; June 2003; Yearly Bulletin 2003

Table 4.2 Inflation and market exchange rates: 1990–2003

	CPI 1988=100	Inflation %	Rate of Exchange (ID per US$)
1990	161		4
1991	462	187.0	10
1992	849	83.8	21
1993	2611	207.5	74
1994	15462	492.2	458
1995	69729	351.0	1674
1996	59021	-15.4	1170
1997	72610	23.0	1471
1998	83335	14.8	1620
1999	93816	12.6	1972
2000	98486	5.0	1930
2001	114613	16.4	1929
2002	136762	19.3	1957
2003	182741	33.6	1936

Source: Central Bank of Iraq; Statistical Bulletin; June 2003; Yearly Bulletin 2003

Table 4.3 Gross Domestic Product at 2002 prices by sectors (in millions of US dollars)

	1989	1991	1993	1994	1995	1996	1997
Crude Oil	16,637	808	1,063	1,112	1,084	973	5,768
Non-oil	7,420	2,108	2,328	2,191	2,024	2,126	1,962
Total Industries	24,058	2,916	3,391	3,303	3,108	3,099	7,730

Source: MEES Debt, Construction and Economic Diversification, Reconstruction of Iraq 12/7/2004

retreated from 33 per cent in the late 1970s to reach 22 per cent in the 1980s and 3 per cent in the 1990s. On the other hand, non-oil sectors remained quite stagnant in the years following the 1991 war, in which agriculture picked up mostly to constitute 8.5 per cent of GDP during the 1991–2000 period, as a result of the national attempt to boost food supply and dodge the embargo. Manufacturing resumed its activity, but not at the same rate prior to the 1991 war. It fell to 6 per cent in the 1990s due to lack of spare parts under the embargo (Table 4.4).

As a result of Paul Bremer's post-occupation policy of openness in 2003, these shares of industry and agriculture have fallen further, and to make things worse, the IMF stepped in to liberalise. In its first economic review of Iraq in 25 years, the International Monetary Fund stated that it 'believes that the medium term economic outlook for Iraq is satisfactory provided the expansion in oil production goes according to plan and world oil prices remain favourable. The IMF, however, fears significant downside risks to this favourable medium-term outlook, particularly as oil prices are subject to a great deal of uncertainty and the political transformation of Iraq has not reached its conclusion. It therefore believes that it would be important to bolster this scenario with additional revenue measures, particularly by raising the prices of domestic petroleum products. Along these lines, the IMF urges the authorities to quickly reduce government subsidies for petroleum products to free up revenues worth as much as 30 per cent of GDP' (IMF 2005). The IMF has not loaned significant mounts to Iraq. By 2004, the anti-Baathist and sectarian war effort was afoot as assassinations *en masse*, especially targeting scientist and former military cadres by Shiite militias, adumbrated a bleak future for the nation. Recommending the removal of a few billion dollars' worth of subsidies intended to relieve the misery of conflict in a country whose occupation had cost several trillion dollars is indicative of the extent to which the social immiseration *cum* political disempowerment of the Iraqi working class holds priority for imperialism over short-term pecuniary goals. What other purpose does it serve to call upon a state that is being robbed

Table 4.4 Estimates of GDP and selected components at constant 1990 prices (in millions of US dollars)

	1980	Rate (70–80)	1981	1990	Rate (81–90)	1991	2000	2002	Rate (91-00)
Agriculture, hunting, forestry, fishing	4895	17.99%	4990	7595	17.37%	5343	12389	13573	8.5%
Mining, Manufacturing, Utilities		33.68%	5419	9280	22.88%	1474	516	438	3.41%
Manufacturing		8.43%	3693	3389	11.70%	2463	1007	840	6.46%
Construction	4548	6.98%	6438	2788	11.33%	516	191	173	1.95%
Wholesale, retail trade, restaurants & hotels	4097	6.92%	4706	5688	13.11%	2073	4126	4656	26.43%
Transport, storage & communication	3239	5.86%	3281	3464	7.16%	1520	6156	6368	26.47%
Other activities	9844	18.61%	11235	11356	30.09%	6160	3908	3887	22.78%
GDP	42441	100.00%	34811	38356	100.00%	12995	17782	19120	100.00%

Source: UN Statistics database 2005 (Overlapping statistics involving double counting that do not necessarily add up)

by sectarian war, advising it to shrink its spending on the poor, other than shifting the national industrial economy into the inter-working class conflict mode economy? The idea of cutting costs is not about the optimal choice of factors like labour in a mathematical operational problem taught to economics students. This tenet is a sacrosanct class position that says the human toll resulting from cost reduction is justifiable in order to satisfy a positivist efficiency criterion based on maximising profits first. The *modus operandi* over time implies that the pressure resulting from lower prices and demand necessitate labour and other cost reductions in order to maintain profits continuously. In the developing world, such a course of action attenuates the share of wages for the working class; however, in parts of the developing world: it is about encroachment-war making.

Unemployment: Recent official estimates of unemployment are at around 16.4 per cent (WDI 2014); the figure does not include the IS-held territory or the Kurdish Autonomous Region (KAR). In 2003, a survey by the Iraq Ministry of Planning showed that 28.1 per cent of the economically active population, excluding the KAR, were unemployed (COSIT 2004). The female unemployment rate is strikingly higher than that of the male rate, with 30.2 per cent for the former and 16 per cent for the latter, and it remains so (COSIT 2004, ILO 2014).

Recent Oil Production: From 2004 until 2013, oil exports rose; oil revenues constitute around 50 per cent of GDP on average (WDI, various years). Historically, production peaked in December 1979 (3.7 million barrels per day) and in July 1990 (3.5 million barrels). Although under occupation, all ministries were looted, major rehabilitation in the oil infrastructure was undertaken and crude production averaged around 2 million barrels per day in the first 10 months of 2004, which was helpful in making Iraq exports rise to 1.5–1.7 million barrels (ISRB 2004). In 2015, oil production is at 3.1 million barrels per day (OPEC 2015). During the war, seven Iraqi oil wells were set on fire, out of around 1,500 total wells. In this context, one major challenge in maintaining oil-production capacity is Iraq's battle with 'water cut' especially in the South, due to the damage from the incursion of water into oil reservoirs.

Addendum to oil in Iraq: One cannot speak of oil and Iraq just in passing. Oil, the black liquid that gushes out of the ground and burns in northern Iraq, was known in ancient Mesopotamia as the eternal fires of the gods. According to Durant (1935), when Alexander entered Babylon in 331 BCE he tested the black liquid on a young boy by setting him ablaze to examine whether it could be used for military purposes; an ominous beginning indeed. Oil, of which there are huge cheaply extractable reserves in Iraq, is not the sole reason for the colonial drive, but it certainly raises the stakes for imperialism. Oil matters to US-led capital for its strategic control value and, secondarily, for its money value. Oil is paid for in dollars, and it is the United States that issues the dollar. The United States is less affected by higher oil prices; however, net importers are. World oil demand, particularly from China and India, is on the rise. In fact, the GDP per unit of energy used in the low- and middle-income countries rose over the past decade, growing at three-fold that of the high-income countries (WDI, various years). Policies of increased fuel efficiency along with lower-cost fuel-consuming machines (cheap, fuel-efficient cars) have increased demand for more of the cheaper machines and thereby have counter-intuitively raised demand for oil. Although each more efficient machine consumes less oil, as there are more of the fuel-efficient machines, together they consume more oil (Foster 2010). That is not to say that fuel-saving technologies were unsuccessful. They were successful, but not to the point at which strategic global energy policy changed and oil demand began to be curbed (*World Watch* 2005).[16] The oil energy content of every dollar of GDP in the developed world is half of what it is in the less-developed world. But the use of oil derivatives in innovative products and the value added associated therewith have steadily increased. The wedge between the price to the direct producer and what the retailer earns has widened over time, implying greater gains for the Western hemisphere. Klare (2008) argues that the record growth in the 1990s was less 'new economy' and more 'cheap oil'.

Although there was a decline in the rate of use of oil as a source of energy in the more-developed economies (the demand level stayed constant), the energy strategy of the United States did not significantly shift away from fossil fuel. Its shale-oil output lessened its dependency on outside sources for its own consumption, but its strategic control dependency (the crucial part of oil) remains. It is relevant to note in this context that the rise in oil prices since 2002 is principally caused by the influence of speculation rather than a by shortage of supply (Ghosh 2011). The Saudi intervention in OPEC (as early as 1980) at the behest of US-led capital delinked oil prices from the control of the direct producer to further deepen the divide between actual production conditions and finance. Once financialised, oil pricing falls more under the purview of US market deliberation rather than developing country control. Pricing on the basis of Arabian light crude came to an end in 1985 when OPEC's cartel power receded as a result of weakening autonomous Arab and other socialist states. At one point during the 1990s, Kuwait's returns from its fund investment in financial markets were as much as 35 per cent of total revenue (Fasano 2000).

Iraq and the Ugly Face of Globalisation

Globalisation for the AW is minimally about information-age technology, the global village and free trade; it has been more about the belligerence of US-led imperialism. Besides continued dependence on oil exports, declining manufacturing and productivity growth, wars have engulfed most of the region since the invasion of Iraq. Plunges in development and undesirable externalities distinguish the region. For the few successful countries in East Asia, globalisation meant the ability to disperse production, design and distribution around the world under the command of big capital, which (globalisation) becomes effectively private appropriation from both gains in the development of productive forces and from the expansion and exploitation of low-tech processes in the developing world (Andrews 2000). To drain the

---

16 Oil is the single-largest source of energy, accounting for 37 per cent of global energy production. http://www.worldwatch.org/features/security/tf/3

surplus from developing countries via the import of cheap raw materials or through super-exploitation remains necessary; but, on its own, it was never sufficient to revitalise accumulation on a global scale. Imperialism is first about power, then about forced expropriation, per the degree of calculated risk ensuing from aggression upon developing countries, or for organised capital, the imperial rents that will offset the costs of intervention.[17]

In the 1980s, Western capital began to intensify the moving of parts of its production steps, certainly those with lower technological requirements, to the developing world. This also meant the creation of an industrial working class in many parts of the Third World, but the new structure of technology was more labour-saving than during the early phases of Industrialisation, meaning that much unemployment was also being created. Whereas, for most of the twentieth century the industrial working class was concentrated in the developed world, between 1980 and 2010, the industrial working class in the Third World more than tripled in size (ILO-KILM 2014), and it continued to grow – more on the crisis of proletarianisation under war conditions in chapter 5. Sweatshop labour market conditions in the developing world contributed, in addition, to low oil prices during that period, sending corporate profits to their highest levels between 1990 and 2000 (Li et al. 2007).

In the very same period, in security-weak states – in Sub-Saharan Africa and the AW – economic development and the average level of human development declined. Despite slightly rising Arab oil revenues, many of the relevant development indices regressed, and a little over half the population was barely making ends meet (UNDP-AHDR 2003).[18] Globalisation is not the extension of capitalism to the Third World, because the ugliest forms of capitalism already exist there. It is the process by which more advanced capital in the developed countries harnesses or disengages assets and less-productive capital in the developing world, to the requirements of its higher pace of accumulation. In consistent overproduction crises, characterised by underutilisation of capacity and superfluous labour, such requirements partially involve destroying human and natural assets.

---

17 In the relationship of organised to disorganised capital activity, it is always a serious possibility for capital to pursue a path of mass destructiveness as the ideology of neo-liberalism frees the reins of the bourgeoisie to pursue its ambitions for profit-making to a higher degree of contravention of international law and institutions than observed at the present stage in history.

18 The oil price declined and stayed low between 1981 and 2002. During this period, Arab countries increased production to offset the falling oil price; so revenues dipped initially in the early eighties but picked up later. However, it is also during this period that resources and wealth became increasingly channelled via the private sector.

Capital, which is by definition a social relationship centred on private expropriation of socially produced wealth, tends to lend itself to being reasoned or understood because its agents are motivated by vested self-interest; it is not an incomprehensible irrational whole driven by erratic or emotional whim. Where the interests of capital are greater, the risks are greater, the returns are greater and, therefore, the politics are ferocious. Currently, nowhere is this relationship more evident than in the case of Iraq, the AW, and one may add, Central Africa, including the DR Congo. Sitting on a huge reserve of fossil fuels, Iraq has been condemned to receiving the wrath of US-led imperialism, because imperialism's control of strategic energy resources, upon which much of the rest of the world remains dependent, gives it power.

Thus, whereas in the more autonomous parts of the Third World the business of globalisation has been only proletarianisation and re-engaging labour in some form of peace-time employment, in the AW and Iraq, in particular, the old equation still holds: more colonial devastation equals more imperial control and rents, and more war-related employment; hence, the creation of a war-indigent proletariat. Over the decade 2000–2010, little foreign direct investment has gone into manufacturing activity in the AW (UNCTAD-WIR, 2012). Trade structure by commodity groupings barely budged, and oil represented on average about 50 per cent of regional GDP (UN 2005a) – it remained just as high in 2009. Much of foreign investment has focused on raw material extraction, primarily oil. Nothing has changed in the policy of Western capital toward the AW, except that Israel, the old regional gendarme of Western imperialism, is stronger and has a freer hand. The impasse for the AW is huge, and social consciousness is under attack by a combination of Gulf-Islamist ideology and funding, which under the careful eye of imperialism employ the identity-based 'othering' that Iranian-sponsored Shiite militias in Iraq had provided for sectarianism to flourish. There are no formal solutions to such an impasse. There are, however, practicable solutions. To use the standard socialist ideological reply for now: these solutions spring from the revolutionary struggle of working people for autonomy and self-reliance.

Let me begin by posing a series of immediate reflections from facts. To varying degrees, Arab ruling classes are alien to the Arab masses, and external pressures result in their flight toward Western protection. In addition to this class attachment to Western capital, which already shuns any form of developing nation power through regionalism, there can be no common Arab political agenda because the wealth is commerce-derived and its distribution is so skewed that smaller players will lose to the few big capital holders. In their day-to-day survival strategy, the overwhelming majority of Arab regimes have relied more on imperialist backing than their own hegemony via the state. Hence, political stability came to depend more and more on repression and less and less on welfare functions, civil liberties and the formation of consensus through debate. Democracy in a developing formation is about the real human rights, the rights of the working class and its right to a decent living standard, economic and social development and, decisively, its right to self-determination. The latter is a condition that is suppressed by imperialist assault in one form or another.

If globalisation becomes in one aspect the fruition of capital concentration as capital further integrates the periphery, then no culture can be immune to the incursion of globalisation. The universalisation of capital in the dollar form along with homogenisation of diverse commodities and services accompanies acute differences in concrete labour conditions – the chain of value starts from the luxury of Western intellectual or high-tech labour to the dreadful conditions of child labourers and child soldiers. Less pay and more work in Third World sweatshop conditions does not capture the darker side of the global labour process. The labour process gauged in terms of the law of value the historical making of refugees, death related to war and famine and the engagement of Arab and African workers in the war enterprise of imperialism, is the process by which life is squandered to meet the condition of exchange for profits with cheaper inputs. While the industrial proletariat was growing in the Asiatic and Latin continents, the war-indigent proletariat, has also grown as a result of the pressure that an exponential global growth imposes upon the reformulation of the power structure and its related social condition of production. These deteriorating living and social conditions also coincided with the absence of internationalist socialist ideas that unite working people. In the subjection of the culture of resistance to defeat under neoliberalism, the assault of the victor's ideology splinters the resisting ideology into several self-defeating identity forms of political practice. Military defeat reinforced cultural defeat and the creation of defeatism in sectional identity politics. As is blatantly clear from the Iraqi case, minor intra-working class differences were magnified into causes of intra-working class war. To undermine the cultural effects of imperialism, the ascendancy of the old symbols of capital in new meaning and forms, one must undermine capital as means of control, especially in times of severe crisis. The protracted crisis in Iraq, including the war of its working class with itself, has not been able to draw international support to undermine the means of control of capital. The imperialist conduit by which Iraq is globalised, the apathy of other working classes enhancing their lots via the power emanating from the destruction of Iraq, further grinds down the unity and resistance of the Iraqi people and inculpates, not only capital, but also huge sections of the international working class in the Iraqi disaster.

In one facet of this form of control through globalisation by violence, capitalism as an accumulation process also needs to contribute to the detachment of the working classes from each other and the creation of conditions for fetishist consumption demand. It has been doing so very effectively with a culture of consumerism that has sunk into public psyche as if it were biologically determined. The other side of Marx's 'accumulate accumulate, that is Moses and the prophets' is 'consume consume'. This Veblenian competition for conspicuousness in consumption as a social role model is difficult to dislodge because the demonstration of wealth is also a demonstration of power (Davis, 1957). Even the Caliph Abu Bakr Al Baghdadi of IS had a Rolex wristwatch on display during his first publicised sermon. Consumerist emulation for status forms the psychology of a consumer class that sees in affluent consumption its *raison d'être* or an end in itself that defines its own existence. This culture debases many of the cultural values of reasonableness and moderation, especially as it intrudes into conservationist agrarian societies. It follows the edict of capital as it pushes to eradicate deeply encoded values that enshrine the conservation and preservation of nature and replaces them with rising alterations in consumption patterns reflecting the high frequency of shifting communal and personal power patterns in society. These patterns tally, not with human needs, but with the many inflections of power and status recurring in the social order. One may fall back on Debord (1967) and posit that capital's means of control are not to be found only in its capacity to physically repress, but more pervasively, in every aspect of social life as it displaces much of human interaction by introjection into objective spectacular forms of exchange. However, Lukacs (1919) remains clearer and more pertinent in his explanation of such perversions, in the sense that capital imposes its alien value system upon society. The cost-cutting measures at any expense are such value systems. As working classes absorb capital's falsehoods and place short-term stabilisation arising from inter working class divisions above internationalism and its immediate-term gains, many would stand by the wayside as Iraq collapses. Such is the depth of capital's malignancy.

In a Fanonian manner (Fanon 1967), dislocated or déclassée working-class Arabs distinguish themselves culturally and invoke their indigenous symbols of struggle. Given the inward social implosion, many of the ideological guises of resistance that have taken shape under neo-liberalism are socially regressive, especially invoking selective religious text to undermine the rights of women. Internationalist defeatism spawns national defeatism. Instead of particular identities being mediated in a general humanity, rival social identity groups jostle for a position of imperial favour. From the very outset, colonialism and later imperialism bred the Islamist–Salafi alternative to socialism. Although politically, Islamism may appear to be at loggerheads with imperialism from time to time, its doctrine of the free market and of absolute right to private property match those of neo-liberalism – and probably surpass them. Ultra-Islamism *qua* terrorism of the IS type also creates a cheap rationale for permanent war. At this victorious juncture in its history, imperialism wants to fabricate and choose its enemy at low cost (Amin 2010) – an enemy whose final function is to put in place a system of social relations that reinforces capitalist accumulation processes and fuels wars. The social regression and the terror hype arising out of Iraq have relegated some of the bourgeois democratic achievements in the West to the history books. The replacement of Western liberalism by forms of authoritarian practice resembling Islamic-Salafism represents a more welcome and solid ideological basis for the reproduction of Western capital itself.

The virtuous ideological spiral between the IS, Iranian-backed Shiite militias and imperialism is foundational. Paradoxically, the United States bombing IS boosts the popularity of IS among much of the disenfranchised working class and declassés in the Islamic world. Imperialism, from the very outset, has fostered its own convenient brand of anti-imperialist pseudo-resistance, such that, even if Arab countries win more independence and gain more sovereignty but remain governed by Islamists, the long-term losses incurred socially as a result of self-repression will not spread development. Saudi Arabia's culture of social exclusion is a stark example of vast wealth alongside lumpen development. Ultra-Islamism sets off a process of labour dehumanisation that causes working people to inflict reverse development on themselves.

This brings us to the question of the resistance landscape. French communist circles (circa 1960) discussed whether in undeveloped Arab or African formations, a specifically communist party was an appropriate vanguard for the conditions in which struggle is to be taken up (Maggio 2013). The debate arose because Third World-ist communist-party elitism and lack of rapport with local culture relegated pro-Soviet parties to the ranks of a subculture within society. The notion that somehow the struggle for communism as such is better suited to European society is social chauvinism and literally has nothing to do with Marxism. The Western working classes' affiliation with the bourgeoisie is more than modernity and literacy; it occurs through the welfare state, which is its material medium of partnership with capital. The same could be said of the material affiliation of communist parties in developing countries as a consequence of their position within the class structure: as part of the working class whose capital-defined characteristics assign to it a higher share of wages, say because of education (inter-working class differentiation). Pro-Soviet Arab parties have also enjoyed class privileges correlated to their affiliation with the Soviet Communist Party, which also entailed many other benefits.

As the pace of uneven development quickens, bridging the working class divide nationally and internationally has become more difficult. Arab organic vanguards, as per Gramsci (1971), have become scant. The dialectic that relates working-class cultures across national boundaries has come undone. The support of central working classes to their Third World counterparts is more tepid than ever before. The West's facile approach to environmental degradation has prioritised flora and fauna over malnourished children in Iraq and elsewhere. From the 1970s on, central workers' privatised pensions and savings became part of capital. The objectives of social democracy in the battle against capital fell in line behind nationalism. In the international division of labour, the toil of one developing-world working class has been increasingly converted into the loot of another developed-world working class. The callousness of the richer working classes toward spilt blood in the colonies increased and, on the flip side, certain anti-internationalist forms of resistance in the Third World also started to grow. Some ethical works have gone so far as inculpating the Western working classes in war crimes against working Arabs for the established reason that they have voted for leaders who opted for war time and again (Neumann (2002) apportions no blame, but rightly speaks of a shared humanist responsibility to arrest the conflict).

Yet as the world comes closer together in real time, the social and political struggle will inevitably bring world labour together. However, at this restructuring conjuncture, the resolution of a serious inter-working class contradiction is being eschewed by labour. Frank (1982) was prophetic in seeing the rise of working-class fragmentation as a result of the spiral of lacklustre socialist success and the rise of reclusive nationalisms and identities arising from the attenuated forcefulness of national liberation (Frank 1982). 'Religious conviction mixed with nationalist sentiments proposing no systemic resistance to capital are likely to grow in the coming years' (Frank 1982, 165). The dynamic of such failure lies in watered-down 'socialism' or compromised resistance, so that as any conceding anti-capitalist movement growing over time by the handout of capital, lends itself to being manipulated by capital. An opposition to capital with a diluted internationalist component will have its tactics and strategy of resistance moulded into a framework of submissive social democracy. In this epoch, austerity plagues the North while wars and famines are on the rise in many corners of the South, as if in synch. There is a definitive positive correlation amongst the various sections of the working class globally. However, labour is being suppressed by capital at exactly the intermittent moments at which their convergence could be actualised – capital intervenes to make sure that labour does not organise across national boundaries.

The crux of the issue is in the theoretical and ideological compromise to capital, which frames the struggle in a way to overlook the organic links of labour and the unifying conditions of struggle on a planet governed by the same capitalist forces.

Every class culture internalises and philosophises its life processes. If the social scene today appears to be polluted with reactionary elements, the selection from Islam of tenets that assist the population to spiritually cope with the monolithic onslaught of imperialism without anti-systemic resistance should not represent an anomaly. Obscurantist Islam is not only the offspring of capital but also of an anti-Soviet labour aristocracy, which moralised the position of the Afghan mujahidin in terms of a war of national liberation. In the United States – the so-called middle-class could not possibly have disengaged from the Reagan-sponsored mujahidin war because it had already put into place the Reagan administration. The 'let us elect someone to go to war and then dissociate ourselves from the war crimes' is how a class lays the 'moral' grounds for its own continuity. Al Qaeda originated in that campaign and, wanting US forces out of Afghanistan while the country has been destroyed and set on a continuous war path, is another victory for US-led capital. It is just cheaper to leave, but the cause of value destruction goes on while the ideological demonstration effect of the barbarism of the 'others', the Afghan, the Muslim and the Arab, is an ongoing imperialist bonus trumpeted across cultural studies in almost every university. The root of the matter is that the justification for the initial aggression and its ramification have imparted a multi-tiered 'good' for US-led capital and its associated working or 'middle' class – the invasion boosts imperial rents from which a certain payoff in wages accrues to the central working class. The US middle class will continue to earn a slightly higher wage difference (just like that of a foreman, slave catcher or prison guard) as a result of the cheaper wages, resources and inputs that the devastation to the Afghan and the Iraqi people and others imparts to the global power and accumulation structure.

The harsh and highly unequal conditions of the struggle will necessitate the galvanisation and redeployment of all social forces in Iraq and elsewhere into an anti-imperialist stand. The key element to the ideological turnaround is theoretical realism, as in seeing the particular condition in relation to the whole picture, which is one of ruin (Marcuse 1965; Baran 1961). The interlocking of the national struggle with the necessity to defeat capital globally and more or less simultaneously is the practical process that can restore socialist ideological strengths. It will delink the growth of anti-capitalist organisations from the growth of capital, not by bypassing capitalism, which is impossible, but by letting resistance develop at the intersection in capitalist relations whose process of negation breeds capital's self-destruction. Positioning the socialist assault on the intensification of inter-capitalist contradictions is one step by which the self-negation of capital leads to restoration of labour. A lucid statement during the anti-occupation struggles, one that summarises the priority of anti-imperialism in Iraq, is the following.

> The battle of the Iraqi people is the battle of all movements, peoples and nations fighting for their liberation from the imperialist world system led by the US. Therefore, we have to firmly rally behind the Iraqi resistance. If we are able to support their struggle to smash the US attempt to build a puppet regime and to eventually drive out the invaders, it will result into a victory for mankind. It will not only give new momentum to the struggle of the Palestinian and Afghan people, but will lead to a new offensive of the liberation struggles all around the world. (Al-Basrah 2004)

Some demonstrations against sectarianism in Iraq have come to the fore lately (Issa 2015). Sectarianism and reactionary identity politics only appear to have run their course. The breakup of their hold as the ideology of the Iraqi ruling class requires much resistance. That said, resurgence is unlikely without other contingent internationalist factors, especially the working classes of major formations aligning with the embryonic Iraqi resistance.

Sellers (1976) notes that far from being the world's lifeboat, America and the West, lacking any new self-understanding, will turn out to be the world's *Titanic*, dragging down with them the remainder of global society. As to how it will be possible for the developing world to accept any Western values (as in gender-related rights or the alleged democratisation of Iraq) when it is being pillaged by the West, Sellers attaches the condition 'that America and the Western world must reinvent themselves as partners and not enemies of humanity, and only then can such healthy American cornerstones of democratic experience, know-how, and voluntary association come to be accepted by the rest of humanity as gifts no longer suspect' (Sellers 1976). However, unless the material or value channels, the war and poverty inflicted upon the Third World, which feed America and the Western world are exposed, it is unlikely that such a turnaround in working-class consciousness could ever be possible. In the double act of alienation, which provides the grounds for callousness, and the imperial rents that partly buttress central wages, it is difficult to outmanoeuvre the organised dimension of capital that is the watchful eye over capital's stability and rule. A slight hint of rising central working-class awareness invokes a compromise that reins it back to the 'nationalism it merits'. The socialist approach becomes practicable only if the American working classes realise that their ties to world labour supersede their ties to capital.

The most discrete task of all remains in differentiating which 'values are suspect' and which 'are not' in the context of a US-led imperialism that cannot by definition reinvent itself and become a partner of humanity. Not that there is a systematic theoretical approach that explains the pragmatic, or do-as-you-go, US-led imperialism; however, let me just cite a few of the intellectual trappings that arose during the Vietnam War that may serve to illustrate the imperialist drive. The United States adopted three conceptual frameworks for dealing with weaker Third World countries: containment, nation building and the totalitarian approach. Here is James Peck's wry description of what is meant by this language.

> The reverse side of the containment policy was the 'total penetration' approach to foreign affairs, 'diplomacy in depth'. Assist the elites of underdeveloped countries to 'modernise' their societies, demand 'reforms' that undercut the appeal of revolutionaries, and link such nations with the 'international community'. Then revolutionary solutions and 'communists' will lose their appeal. It was, in essence, the Freud plus Santa Claus concept of foreign relations. Persuade countries that underdevelopment was *sui generis* to the society instead of part of a world system which sustains it or an immediate American presence which reinforces it. And then portray a benevolent, gift-giving US bestowing technical assistance for the benefit of others. (Peck 1970; 60–61)

Prior to the invasion of Iraq, there was, in the choreography of war, a meeting of the absurd, the pedantic and the ludicrous. I will illustrate with examples of all three instances in that order.

The Absurd: The Project for the New American Century recommends building US defences (offences really) to the point at which the United States will be capable of conducting multiple types of warfare, probably involving tactical nuclear weapons. 'The United States must retain sufficient forces able to rapidly deploy and win multiple simultaneous large-scale wars and also to be able to respond to unanticipated contingencies in regions where it does not maintain forward-based forces' (Donnelly 2000). As a result of effective armed resistance to the US forces on the ground in Iraq, the current Obama-run war is indeed multiple-stage warfare, but mostly involving drones and aerial bombardment and not many ground troops. Resistance works, but Iran's early role in backing mainly Shiite militias in Iraq thwarted its advance.

The Arcane: Lee Harris, a little-known journalist, wants 'the Arabs to not look the United States in the eye' because had it not been for the United States, that oil under their sands would be useless. Also: the Arabs cannot earn

US dollars, buy weapons, and fight the United States with those weapons. The pedantry appears in his essay 'Our world historical gamble', where a war is necessary for the betterment of the human spirit á la Hegel: 'War is the state of affairs which deals in earnest with the vanity of temporal goods and concerns'. Or, better still, the 'war with Iraq will constitute one of those momentous turning points of history, in which one nation under the guidance of a strong-willed, self-confident leader undertakes to alter the fundamental state of the world' (Harris 2003). It is, to use the language of Hegel, an event that is world-historical in its significance and scope. Such world-historical events, according to Hegel, are inherently *sui generis* – 'they break the mould and shatter tradition' (Harris 2003). Just as Shiite or Sunni militias deploy an Ibn Khaldun-like tribal social solidarity (Asabiyya) as a rallying point for their populations to unite in war, Harris is choosing a few mystical phrases from Hegel denoting a form of ultra-nationalism in which what is good for the nation *qua* tribe is good for its citizen irrespective of where that citizen is situated in the class structure. He has borrowed the motto 'what is good for General Motors is good for America' and dressed it with the old jargon of German idealism. This approach is an admixture of tragedy and farce, because Hegel is presented wrongly, made inaccessible and also quoted out of context.

The Ludicrous: In October 2002, the former commander of US military operations in the Middle East, General Anthony Zinni, explored some of the possible scenarios of a war on Iraq. He listed ten conditions that when realised, would represent the best possible outcome. These ten conditions were: 'first, the coalition is on board; second, the war is short; third, destruction is light; fourth, Israel stays out of it; fifth, the street is quiet; sixth, order is kept; seventh, the burden is shared; eight, the change is orderly; ninth, the military is not stuck; and last, other commitments are met'. 'That is an easy list', he added. 'If we design our strategy and tactics based on this, *everything* will work out'. (Zinni 2002). *Everything worked out as planned indeed.* Plan or not, given the nearly uncontested hegemony of the United States and its neo-liberal ideology, whatever it does works, because there is no one of import to say that it did did not work; everything works in favour of the uncontested hegemon – unless one anecdotally counts the egos of moralising academics, which are extremely potent.

Not all the war party was that obtuse. The best example of American shrewd but unsagacious pragmatism stands out in the many occasions the word 'process' pierces through the avalanche of media drivel. In one of the best examples of sober posturing, a prolocutor for the CIA, when asked what he thought of the 'peace process' in the Middle East, commented: 'Let us not get hung up on the word peace, all we want going is a process'.[19] Why I would like to stop at such a statement is to demonstrate the 'do-as-you-go' imperialist strategy of US-led imperialism. There are no final goals, the very process or act of destruction or deconstruction to politically emasculate developing peoples in the AW and Africa is itself the goal. The process by which the stature of empire is reasserted through war, and by which capital is requisitioned, is in reality the promulgation of violent dislocation to reassert imperialist power. In *America Right or Wrong*, Lieven (2004) makes the point that tracing America's war history on a secular trend shows that neocons are no aberration, and the fact that George W. Bush was re-elected for a second term, was a natural outcome of dominant class politics.

Closing Comment

When Netanyahu was drumming up support for the Iraq campaign, his message was 'If beaten, the Arabs surrender'. As it turns out, in every society, there are social classes that surrender and others that do not. Simplifying social conflict into the Shi'a–Sunni divide is really judging a historical process of defeat by its symptoms – sectarianism is a symptom of defeat repossessed by the bourgeoisie in its act of reproduction. The mainstream definition of class is too static to capture the flow of historical conditions in relation to the material mode of appropriation. The rupture between social condition and identity, as experienced in societies inflicted with sectarianism, is a result of imperialistically sown defeatism.

The struggle against sectarian fragmentation in Iraq represents a challenge for most progressives as the new colonial surgeon's scalpel will not stop at Iraq (Belqaziz 2003). Iran has so far contributed to the status quo. The area of primary interest for Iran is not North, near Pakistan, or South in Lebanon. It is the Gulf, where control of commerce and oil revenues welded an Iranian ruling class to 'theocratic' politics. The Gulf is where the wealth resides, and extracting it requires political leverage. However, Iran's making inroads into the AW via Shi'ism is playing right into the hands of the US's plan to chip apart the region along sectarian lines. Iran has already facilitated US aggression in Afghanistan, and at the advent of the US invasion it even armed and sent into Iraq the Badr brigades. In the past, refusing to end the war with Iraq by divine élan, Khomeini had, knowingly or unknowingly, favoured US-led capital's interests. Iran has delayed all-out resistance in Iraq to US-led empire by keeping a large section of devout Shiites at bay while US occupying forces suffered losses in the so-called 'Sunni triangle'. This is not the result of a

---

19 Interview with PBS on the *McNeil Lehrer News Hour*, 30 January 1990.

personal score to settle with Saddam, it is a social-class act. It is the result of the Iranian ruling classes' vested interests in expanding control and negotiating their position with the United States.

Deconstructing a nation and rebuilding its institutions in a way that guarantees the loss of the indigenous population's control of its oil requires aggression at all levels, including the splitting and fragmenting of the Iraqis and the creation of a pro-occupation proxy army; or, better yet, keeping Iraqis embroiled in a constant state of war. Popular resistance against imperialism, however, will dent the war drive of global accumulation. If Hobsbawm (1994) turns out to be right – that no people can be ruled by a foreign power against their will as per the lessons of the twentieth century – then what has been construed as war booty for US-led capital may turn out to be its nemesis. Where the United States has positioned itself to win the big prize – a regional arrangement that further buttresses the oil/dollar nexus – resistance will quicken the reversal of fortunes. As it has often been remarked, Fukuyama (2005) was again quick to prejudge history when he presumed that US foreign policy seemed destined to rise or fall on the outcome of a war about which everything would be regretted. There is not much to regret so far for the US-led capital class. To date, international resistance to imperialism remains weak. Across history, arresting cultural development in Mesopotamia, as in the Mongol sacking of Baghdad in 1258, appears to be symbolic of setting back all of human development. Until an *élan of uncompromising* internationalist ideology develops from the womb of the current struggles and speaks the language of internationalist solidarity to working people, things can only go on as they are: from bad to worse.

Chapter 5

THE PERVERSE TRANSFORMATION

As mentioned in the Introduction, this chapter addresses the socialisation of labour by neo-liberal means, while the final chapter examines socialisation of labour and resources by means of war. The making of wage labour at ever-faster rates under neo-liberalism is a common characteristic of the AW, and the chapter will examine the issue for all Arab countries. Why should so much attention be paid to the dislocation and pauperisation of labour since the heydays of Arab socialism in particular? Labour power is the principal input into production, and the labourer is both subject and object of accumulation. An understanding of the formation of the labour process through the development of the law of value is rudimentary to understanding the whole process of resource disengagement under neo-liberalism.

More than three decades ago, many envisaged a significant rise in the industrial workforce in developing countries (Amin 1976; Wallerstein 1979; Frank 1982; Arrighi 1982; Abdel-Malek 1963 and 1985). Since then, the rate of proletarianisation globally has soared. In 1950, industrial workers from developing countries composed roughly 30 per cent of the total industrial labour force. In 2010, industrial workers from developing countries represented over 80 per cent of the global industrial labour force (ILO-KILM, various years). In China and the few other newly industrialised Asian economies that enjoy a margin of autonomy in policy, the majority of the newly evicted peasants have moved into high productivity-cum-rising-wage employment. The socialist legacy of China had enshrined certain labour rights that were difficult to undo by the rising capitalist class and that resulted in a steady rise in Chinese labour wages (Weil 2010). For most of the world, however, the transformation has been perverse (Patnaik 2015), and most new wage-labourers either become unemployed or are engaged in low-productivity/poverty-wage informal jobs.

The AW falls into the latter category. Between 1980 and 2010, the share of rural to total population in the AW dropped from about 60 per cent to around 40 per cent. In absolute terms, an estimated 70–100 million people moved from the countryside to urban centres within the Arab region.[1] While

---

1 The estimates vary significantly depending on the method of measurement and the counting of commuters to Cairo. Many daily commuters to Cairo have moved from

this exodus was occurring, the regional rate job creation was falling, and the share of labour in the form of wages fell to around a quarter of national income (Guerriero 2012; ILO 2014). By 2007, the Arab League declared that more than half of the Arab population was living on less than the two-dollar per day benchmark (AMF 2007). The absolute poverty figures (the one-dollar or so benchmark), which were always shown as low prior to the Arab Spring in 2011, were adjusted upward after 2011 (AMF 2012). For a fleeting moment after the Arab Spring, it was difficult to conceal the truth about the depth of poverty.

Under neo-liberalism, basic food production per capita as per the definition of the Food and Agricultural Organisation (FAO) was decreasing, and food imports were rising. Around half the population in the AW was spending more than half of its income on food (WB 2011). When speculation reached the commodity market and basic food prices rose in 2007, more people joined the ranks of the extremely poor. The agricultural sector was shrinking relative to the economy. The productive economy, in turn, was de-industrialising and retreating relative to oil revenues and geopolitical rents. The deconstruction sustained by the productive sectors under neo-liberalism was almost as devastating as war in terms of its social impact. When neo-liberalism could not infiltrate and sufficiently hollow out the development of society, imperialist war completed the job, as was the case of Libya, Syria and Iraq. Massive dislocation and disengagement of real resources, particularly human resources, mark the neo-liberal episode of Arab history. In this chapter, I examine the key component of capital's sustainability: its command of the labour process through dispossession. I discuss the impact of the neo-liberal transformation on the intensification of the proletarianisation process and the subsequent devalorisation of work through the political disempowerment of the working class.

In order to achieve this, I briefly examine how the class of neoclassical models, dual-economy models in particular, are unfit tools for explaining the process of proletarianisation in the AW. Dual-economy models purport to provide an explanation of migration from the less-developed rural sectors in terms of choice and in relation to modern-sector wages. However, in an Arab context, the rationale for migration on the basis of individual choice between two competing sectors is irrelevant. Moreover, the very idea that an individual or a family residing in rural areas is afforded the luxury of choice is insidious doctrine rather than a reflection of historical facts. Whatever choice was available to the individual was subordinate to the choice that was made

rural areas far away from the centre of the city to other rural areas around the city, but ones that still count as rural areas. See more in United Nations (2008a), *The Demographic Profile of Arab Countries Ageing Rural Population*.

by the comprador class in respect to social and macroeconomic policies. The comprador class in charge of development in the AW had a choice between a neo-liberal pattern that universalises and usurps national wealth to be later valorised in dollars, and a strategy based on the recirculation of wealth and the redeployment of real resources for development within the national economy. It chose the former. By doing so, it set in motion a whole dynamic that accelerated the disengagement of direct producers, especially from the land. Peasants and farmers were forcibly dislocated; the choice left to any individual was that of bare survival. The alternatives afforded the individual in the neo-liberal policy context are further narrowed down, by successive violent encroachments on the rights of working people, to two wretched conditions: the abjection of the countryside or the misery of urban squalor.

Although analogies between dual-economy models and structural theories of migration (those that originate in a Marxian framework) are possible in that they both consider the initial disparity in the constitution of the rural and the urban sectors, their differences, however, are conceptually irreconcilable.[2] Whereas in the former, the price mechanism allocates resources efficiently between sectors, in the latter, price becomes one of the many causes by which the less-developed rural economy falls permanently into a peripheral orbit in which its already disadvantaged position worsens. The price of labour (the wage rate) becomes an instrument of repression. For Marxist-type analysis, the premeditated pauperisation of the periphery is generally followed by an outflow of labour. In this chapter, I show that a more pertinent explanation of Arab proletarianisation rests in understanding how the unrestrained immiseration of Arab working classes under neo-liberalism, often degenerating into social collapse, is part of the objective process of reproducing global capital through neo-liberal policies and imperialist politics.

Choice Versus Structural (Marxist) Theory

The received theory in migration literature postulates that a potential migrant coming from conditions of unemployment or underemployment in

---

2 I am distinguishing between structuralism and Structural-Marxism, but at the same time, it is difficult to juxtapose or compare a fluid historical process (Marxism), shaped by a contingent and recurring articulation of social forces, with a static or formal model like that of neoclassical economics. So, for the sake of perspicuity, the structuralist side of Marxism provides a window from which the comparison could be broached. Structural Marxism is actually the radical dependency of Samir Amin and Andre Gunder-Franck, which differs from the Latin American structuralist school. Larrain (1989) provides a complete breakdown of such differences. Meanwhile, as will be seen, I will try to do justice to both schools when informing about their theoretical content.

subsistence-like farming conditions chooses to migrate because the actual or the expected wage and or amenities in the modern sector are higher than those of the rural sector. That people would choose to migrate in order to improve their lot in life appears at first sight as too vacuous a proposition to be debated. Yet the whole of the neoclassical edifice attempts to situate migratory phenomena on the availability of choice and on prices related to higher productivity in the urban areas. Productivity growth in the AW has been more often than not negative, and the mass of unemployed relative to the capacity of the economy has become too large to be absorbed under the conventional efficiency criterion (KILM 2012). The notion that 'choice', as in having multiple options, plays a role in situations in which people have only the choice of survival is a malevolent diversion. It is also meant to promote the neoclassical fairy tale construction that there are two sectors, a rural and an urban, which have entered into a trade relationship from which they both stand to benefit.

Any trade relationship is also a social relationship. Money-form gains or losses to any sector or social class conceal beneath them a social structure engaged in production. But this is no symbolic process of production (as in neoclassical economics); it is a real metabolic process in which resources, including the labour resource, are consumed in the course of action. By ratcheting up its power over rural areas, urban capital draws on a pool of labour whose social cost of reproduction was borne by the hinterland; capital thus grabs an underpriced resource to whose formation it did not contribute. Capital, in its pursuit of profit, must recreate these conditions for cheap inputs in the countryside by all means available. Labour is not cheap but is made cheap by a process of political repression and dispossession, which also entails constructed differential gradations within the non-owning working class (recreating identity differences) and, hence, the socioeconomic heterogeneity of labour. The received theory that the accumulation of capital has a built-in tendency through trade expansion and technological improvement to homogenise the returns to labour is not determined by better machine quality, but by the balance of forces between capital and labour (Sherman and Meeropol 2013). For Marx, although the market tends to equalise wages, the political exercise of capital holds primacy as it exerts counter-pressure in order to fragment labour, otherwise capitalism would be digging in its own grave far too quickly (an inference from Marx 1867).

Under neo-liberalism, free trade and open capital accounts allow values to more readily assume a universal character reincarnated in the dollar as the universal wealth-holding medium. Making developing countries food dependent and underpricing their assets in their own national currencies before their conversion into dollars implies a further differentiation of the developing working class from the central working classes. The assault on the rural sectors of the developing AW is part and parcel of the fragmentation process necessary for extraction of higher surpluses from these peripheral formations and, conjointly, it deprives labour of some of the grounds upon which it can potentially organise itself as a viable political alternative. An extreme analogy of surplus drain resembling such situations would be the case of commercial exploitation based on slavery or of colonial wars of depopulation on the periphery.

The violent aspects of the proletarianisation process, as it occurred in the English countryside two or more centuries ago, were dubbed by Marx as primitive accumulation. The proletarianisation of the English labour force by 'expropriation of the immediate producers which was accomplished with merciless vandalism, and under the stimulus of passions the most infamous, the most sordid, the pettiest, and the most meanly odious' (Marx 1867), resulted in the maturing of capitalism and the reign of European capital as a social relationship globally (Wood 1998). At the beginning of the last century, the proletarianisation process on the periphery was adduced from development by encroachment, the foremost facet of which was colonialism and postcolonial wars. Encroachment by war or otherwise is when the colonists commandeer the political structure of the colonies. Such a form of primitive accumulation was more vicious under colonialism and resulted in massive global dislocation and pauperisation in both absolute terms and relative terms; relative to the historically determined standard of living (Lenin 1916).

For the majority in the Arab working classes, the choices were between two below-decent-subsistence living standards. The historically relevant choices were not made by each individual at any one point in time. As they turned away from dirigisme and Arab socialism, the social class in power decided to introduce violent and nonviolent measures and policies aimed at eroding the very basis of the reproduction of rural life. For countries developing under the onus of conflict, such as Iraq, Syria, Palestine, Yemen, Libya, Somalia and Sudan, the process of expulsion from the home village was materialised in outright aggression, as millions of war-displaced people sought safer shelter. In the absence of military occupation or war, trade openness treaties, displacement laws dispossessing farmers, like Egypt's Law 96 of 1992 (Bush 2015) and macro policies allocating resources away from agriculture, served to uproot the peasantry. Since 1980, the share of investment in Arab agriculture in total investment has fallen continuously, reaching a low of 5 per cent by 2009 (ALO 2010). In Egypt, within a decade, the share of agricultural investment in total investment fell from around 10 per cent to about

Table 5.1 Share of agricultural investment in total investment in Egypt

	(Percentages)
2003	9.4
2004	9.5
2005	7.6
2006	6.9
2007	5.0
2008	4.0

Source: National Planning Institute, Egypt Arab Republic, 2009.

4 per cent (see Table 5.1) (Bush 2007). The rates of malnutrition among children in Egypt and Yemen reached 30 and 45 per cent respectively in 2009 (IRIN 2009). On October 16, 2015, UNICEF reported that half a million Yemeni children face starvation.[3] War and violence since 2011 have magnified the malnutrition problems. These were the results of a concerted and deliberate policy aimed at reconstituting social values for grabbing value by all possible means.

These displacement measures were not a one-time occurrence from which policymakers would soon move away; they were reproduced continuously in real time. The rationale for pursuing displacement stems from the heart of the neoclassical method and its broader ideological form: neo-liberalism. The neoclassical approach postulates that income differences prompt individuals to move, hence, allocating resources efficiently. It also attempts to expand the set of incentives that attract migrants by introducing a variety of other explanatory factors such as the appeal and amenities of cities; at any rate, these non-price incentives also become symbols in an equation and amount to a price explanation or, anyway, to benefits that can be priced. Reducing complex reality to a quantity encapsulated in a price does not answer the question of *why* people move, particularly because prices are themselves an outcome of social relations, which had already included personal and socially intermediated decisions. Was it the intermediated ruling class decisions in the sphere of politics that erected the conditions for the prices to assume a certain nominal value, which is the primal decision behind migration, or was it the decision of the peasant, whose life is determined by these 'given' prices? Obviously, the peasant is a price taker and not the consortium of ruling capital is the price maker.

---

3 http://www.reuters.com/article/2015/10/16/us-yemen-security-children-idUSKCN0SA28W20151016

Some more sophisticated neoclassical techniques trace back individual migratory decisions through time (as in work history surveys). But time cannot be dissected, and individual responses, which are studied at some particular point, do not constitute history. As has often been said, projecting different slides taken at different points in time onto a screen does not reproduce history nor does it recreate the fact that there was a subject of history: that is, the social class in power that was furnishing the conditions for migration by purposefully expelling farmers via neo-liberal policies or war. This is not to say that a class can be reduced to a person plotting in secrecy somewhere to inflict these crimes. Such simpleton clichés running wild in academia are themselves the products of class power. A class is the weight of history, the ideology and the institutions. There is no conspiracy in what it does. The global institutional power platforms are already biased against the weaker national working classes and nations and a product of colonial history. Neo-liberal ideology says it clearly and in colloquial parlance: liberalise or free your resource channels, yet for this 'freeing' to work, your dictator who happens to be part of the global financialised class has to be a good governor. This is not a lie; it is a fictitious remedy. But one thing is clear, the ideological thesis instituting the context for individuals to act contains information, as in foreknowledge, of the consequences of such actions. The 'powerful' need not hide their intentions.

Although there have been a variety of critiques levelled at the neoclassical approach, it remains seminal to migration research. The price-or-choice theoretic framework does not study migratory phenomena because it reconstructs a false reality based on a summation of individual decisions. Apart from its composition–fallacy problem (adding different qualities), this approach does not probe the social history behind the decisions. Any reference to the development of the migratory phenomenon in real time may implicate the social class whose ends the neoclassical discipline serves. Neoclassical economics actually studies something other than the migratory phenomenon; its subject is an arithmetical concoction that bears no relevance to the fact that social interactions like evictions, conflicts, negotiations and bargains subjected to power politics, actually construct prices. If the neoclassical discipline pursued the development of migratory phenomena in real time, specifically as a by-product of the agency of the institutions of capital, and rationalised them, it would inevitably have to question two sacrosanct mainstream concepts: firstly, the terms of trade and its power structure underlying the making of the price system; and, secondly, the systems that interact with irreconcilable contradictions inherent in social formations. The neoclassical perspective has, at whatever cost, to overlook the crux of the issue of proletarianisation, which is the necessary creation of socialised (deprived of its means of production) and cheapened wage labour. By analysing reality away, it avoids incriminating the class in power to which it is subservient. The neoclassical object of study becomes individual choice in a fictitious world of free competition, voluntary unemployment and scarcity – as to what it labels distortions, the infinite externalities; for these there exists a price vector that clears their infinite submarkets.

However, these distortions are actually the fullness of reality that one should refer to when addressing migration. In the neoclassical frame, the flux of market power and its related departures from an ideal but non-existent condition of equal marginal magnitudes, the so-called distortions are actuality; they are priced and subsumed under a general equilibrium framework. If there was a conspiracy on a grand scale, it is not in explaining how the 'democratic' states of the North so frequently commit massacres or genocide in the colonies; it is really how could it be possible that so many prices of so many externalities could be so 'right' such that the infinitely intricate social system gravitates to equilibrium. This is not just a misunderstanding of the concept of equilibrium borrowed from physics and applied to economics, where the mathematics would convey a different account of the economics, as in Mirowski (1989).[4] It is also not on account of an analytical philosophy that distinguishes between the objects of social and natural science; such as an atom, which is the object of chemistry that does not think for itself, in the latter, while, in the former a human being, the object of social science, would be where he or she is today because of where they plan to be in the future. The designation of the object of science as more complex does not make economics less amenable to knowability or less of a science than physics just because it takes longer to explore its laws of development. One can dwell on this point but, as a rule, overly analytical and ahistorical approaches lapse into positivism. Mathematics or physics inevitably become queens of the sciences.

The development of the various branches of sciences are interrelated, and emulation in methods of thought has been taking place since the earliest stages of social development. For instance, Aristotle noted the seminal cyclical movement of social systems and ascribed the causes of decline and fall to lack of equality and justice.

---

4   The use of concepts such as entropy, thermodynamics, Gibbs Free Energy and other complicated mathematical equations would only serve the purpose of illustrating a social condition if it relates the micro conditions to their macro environment in a specifically historical fashion. In other words, without the historical mediation of the particular in the general – that is how agents organise to shift their social conditions – we end up replicating the inanimate atomic structure in society, as in treating human society like a bunch of atoms. As such, this would be more bamboozling ideology than science.

Equality consists in the same treatment of similar persons, and no government can stand which is not founded upon justice. For if the government be unjust everyone in the country unites with the governed in the desire to have a revolution, and it is an impossibility that the members of the government can be so numerous as to be stronger than all their enemies put together. (Aristotle 2014, *Politics*, book 7)

Would such an observation describing cyclical movements not render all the science that followed since a borrower from philosophy? Indeed, it would; but the reason of demonstrating the point with the passage from Aristotle also serves an additional purpose, which is to demonstrate the inevitable instability and changing content of social systems. Whether as a result of injustice or high social entropy, a complex capital-dominated system fraught with contradictions will be explosive at one point in time. Its stabilisation rests on exogenous intervention that includes co-opting of the central and other working classes or redressing profit rates with colonial or imperialist plunder. Theoretical reproduction of this changing reality in thinking, the relation of thought to reality, must deal with categories of dialectics connected with words, such as social classes, composing modes of production, employing wage-slaves via a process of commodification under capitalism, and so forth, rather than with words, themselves, as in supply, demand, equilibrium and marginal productivity (historically transcendent generalisations); it is the logical development of categories, the discovery of the historically relevant phenomena, 'which is guided by the relation in which the elements of the analysed concreteness stand to one another in the developed object, in the object at the highest point of its development and maturity, that discovers the mystery of the genuine objective sequence of the formation of the object, of the moulding of its internal structure' (Ilyenkov [1960] 1982). The relation of words with words only, or one-sided abstract theory, will also remain abstract unless its mediation in the concrete or the thought process by which we relate to historically determined relationships fundamentally changes the nature of the concepts with which we are dealing (categorical understanding as opposed to positivist empiricism). However, in such realism there are no noumena or unchanging ideas across time that suddenly come to life as by-products of themselves and not by the action of social agents in historically defined terms, erecting both new conditions and the new ideas to correspond to these conditions. Each historical phenomenon merits its own explanation by following its development in history and deriving, through intellectual practice, new forms by which we uncover its laws of motion or how things come to be. Systems change, their relations become wholly new and what was for instance a social product derived by submission to the lord's will under feudalism, becomes a social product derived from adherence to market rules under capitalism. In the latter case, subject to the edicts of the market and profit-making, the extra social product that society produces by advanced technology (scale effects) requires pricing the labour power below what is needed for the labourer to maintain a decent standard of living or, often the premature destruction of the living labourer. The surplus product now varies with the varying outlays delivered to the working class as wages. Thus, under the new mature stage, which is capitalism, supply, demand and productivity still exist, but their content, their laws of motion nesting in the contradiction of a social system arising from the commodification of life itself, is now different. All commodities are moneyed, including labour power, in a system ridden by overproduction crises set against the necessity to appropriate higher and higher profits at the expense of the price of labour power (wages of the international working class) and the living security of the working class. Such a system cannot be understood by the epiphenomena of supply, demand and their related price-sums; it is best understood by following the interrelated development of historical *qua* class forces that shape production (supply), consumption (demand) and exchange over time.

The reproduction of the dominant ideology and its neoclassical offshoot occur mainly by de-historicising social science either by stressing discontinuity: things are just as they are now; or by emphasising formal or unrealistic continuity: humans love to consume insatiably across all history. To disentangle Marxist method, the last stages of development can be understood not by abstract concepts that exist in the mind only, but by following the development of a specific condition in time as it shifts from undeveloped (abstract form) to developed (more concrete form) through a specific law of development. In this rationalisation of historical facts in relations to each other and to historical determination within a totality, the logical explanation coincides with the historical; ill-defining historical categories and omitting the primacy of contradiction in social dynamics will necessarily lead to a distorted conception of the essence of the capitalist system.

Moreover, fitting the real (the distortions as per the neoclassical framework) into the formal representation (perfectionist markets) may be admissible for the sake of logical illustration, but only when the initial assumptions denote historically specific phenomena as opposed to theological-like categories of perfectness such as the quasi omniscient and omnipotent economic agent. But neoclassical assumptions are trans-historical, or at times only biological, such that at this level of generalisation, they reference or refer back only to themselves. As shown by Weeks (2014), the principal assumptions of neoclassical economies such as scarcity, perfect competition and voluntary unemployment and so forth are false: for instance, commodities are scarce for many without income, but almost never for the rich or on account of shortages; freely competitive markets and voluntary unemployment are chimerical assumptions that are elevated to the standing of science when they have no referents in phenomenon. Just by making power relations and diametrically opposed contradictions central assumptions of the commodity world, logical ends hold by the determinacy of social relations and their related agencies, but not as a result of the market as *deus ex machina*.

To bring the discussion back to an Arab context, no markets, perfect or imperfect, can display a significant social role in the national Arab formation when imperialist assaults, robbing working classes of their self-rule, destroying their social capital assets and creating conditions for continuous pauperisation sets the logic and the conditions for development. Markets – in the common usage of the term, as in the institution founded to mediate the exchange of namely peacetime commodities – work as addenda to war or to the highly realisable potential for war.

A Comparison with Marxist-Structuralism at a Glance

In the neoclassical framework, the scenario for the wage-pull theory comprises a rural or less modern sector with its associated rural income – a first wage, and a modern sector producing manufactured goods with an associated second wage, which is on average higher than the rural income. Hence, people migrate. What this scenario hides is a process that resolves social contradictions in favour of capital or the more powerful social class. The wage, in more evolved capitalism, acts as the measure that reflects a distorted underlying class and power structure (powerful urban versus weak rural). However, in the neoclassical formal setup, wages are determined by marginal productivities, and each social entity, rural and urban, is supposed to enjoy the same power-standing vis-à-vis the other. Atomised individuals enjoy level playing fields, irrespective of their means and position in society. Such is the imaginary world from which neoclassical theory is derived. These asymmetries are what really needs to be explained. The asymmetries, moreover, are both innumerable and unquantifiable, and reducing them and incorporating them into the formalised mathematical framework leads to theoretical sloppiness instead of academic rigour. By choosing the epiphenomenon of price, the neoclassical method designates a symptom as what is historically relevant instead of looking at the social forces that shape the conditions for the recreation of labour. The method neglects history because it would then have to deal with value, as in the value that mothers impart by bringing to life and caring for labourers as well as all other work that creates labour; and the method does so for a very straightforward reason: to stultify the working class and its potential intellectual allies.

In the Marxist–structuralist analysis of migration, the wage difference, as a symptom of class relations, no longer embodies the allocation mechanism behind the movement of workers; it is the structural difference, the power and development levels, between a modern centre and a rural periphery and the ensuing relation of unequal exchange that motivate migration. In this approach, the level of wealth is determined by productivity, but the wage share is determined by labour's political power. The degree of repression, including the hegemony of capital, has a bearing on the social division of labour and the function of each class in material and social reproduction, as well as on the distribution of social wealth and the form and amount of revenue accruing to each class. In this framework, the individual's prerogative to migrate is being dictated by the deliberately worsened conditions in the rural sector and is, therefore, subsequent to the workings of capital, which create not only the demand for labour but also the conditions for its supply.

As the degree of economic integration between mainly rural and developed-urban economies increases, the process by which uncompetitive economic entities in the rural structure get sifted away picks up speed. What remains in the developing and mainly rural area after its permeation with the scale-cheapened commodities of the modern sector is but a remnant of an infant industry that has been able to support its costs and survive in a changing economic environment. The wages that are taken to represent rural wages, particularly when conducting empirical tests of migratory cases at the macro level, are the wages paid by this surviving pre-modern industry: the wages of agricultural hired hands, of repair- and service-shop employees, small family-run handicraft shops and so forth. However, in reality these are the wages of a subsidiary industry continuously adapting and keeping pace with the new capitalistic condition and, therefore, they are modern enclave wages paid and redistributed within quasi-subsistence farming communities. In the analytical context of the neoclassical wage-based model, these wages should not be different from an industrial enclave wage in the urban centre. The wages that should in actuality characterise the rural wages represent the share of income of the broader and, namely, subsistence farming entities. These incomes are partly constituted in kind (the part of the consumption bundle produced by local means) and partly in measurable money form (which goes to pay for that part of the consumption bundle that is bought on the market). In the case of the AW, farmers came to depend more on goods paid for in currency for their consumption as the squeeze on land lowered the portion of the consumption bundle produced by local means, and the conditions for displacement became pronounced (Kishk 2012). For instance, less and less of the dietary intake of the peasants in Egypt was produced on the farm. As a larger share of food was bought at world market prices and as the costs of daily living rose, the peasantry undertook a gradual exodus from the land (Kishk 2012). In this ongoing process of displacement resulting from increased economic and political subjugation, rural or developing-area labour relinquishes private production means and joins the ranks of wage labour.

From the Marxist–structuralist perspective, the movement of labour from the rural to the urban sector is foreseen as a result of growth in the productive forces along with expulsion measures and the proliferation of foreign capital or merchandise that entails a profound destabilisation of the structure of the peripheral/rural economy. The intrusion impacts the old methods of farming and manufacture, thus generating a mass of unemployed. This process of social restructuring accelerates as the state intervenes with violent and non-violent measures aimed at the complete extirpation of traditional small farming and cottage industries. The violence that the state exercises could be direct or fomented indirectly by accentuating inter-rural differences. Forced farm foreclosures and evictions, massive rolling back of land reforms and other objectionable measures are put to work in the creation of additional members of the proletariat. This latter outcome is a modern re-enactment of Marxian primitive accumulation, which in 'its historical genesis [...] only means the expropriation of the immediate producers, *i.e.*, the dissolution of private property based on the labour of its owner' (Marx 1867). The roots (essence in dialectics) of this expropriation – the socialisation of labour as capitalism creates its 'grave diggers' – are the same: the appearance, the rates of expropriation and the violent measures, their modern manifestation, these correspond to the vitality of financial capital or its higher velocity of exchange drawing the context for faster dislocation. Private property, as the antithesis of social, collective property, exists only where the means of labour and the external conditions of labour belong to private individuals (Marx 1867). The modern rate of wage-labour making is not simply related to uprooting peasants from the land. It is a process and a question of degree by which the higher rate of dismantling all forms of labour autonomy, from bringing down the already established institutions of social security in Western formations to the making of refugees in the South, redress a constant and deepening crisis of capital accumulation.

So far, I have established the following for the Marxian approach: The encroachment of capitalism into the periphery socialises labour and production. That is to say, the dissolution of private peasant forms of property paves the way for turning private farmers into social wage workers. This shift in the labour process accentuates the material basis of the class contradiction because it also enlarges the scope for private appropriation (there are more labourers to exploit at cheap rates). Seen as continuous and growing practice, the release of additional wage workers onto the labour market further suppresses an already low Third World wage, thus shifting the unequal trade relationship more to the advantage of the centre; as such, it increases the rate of surplus drain. This is a tendency inherent in capitalism, the outcome of which is contingent upon the power of the working class in the class struggle.

Neoclassical Chimera

The shortcoming of the neoclassical method is that it considers forms of thought from the standpoint of a formal framework and it ignores the historical content that they may express.[5] It considers paradigmatic suppositions in rigidly isolated forms and not in their interconnection, motion, and development (Davis 1983). For instance, in the theoretical explanation given for labour migration in a dual economy model à la Harris-Todaro, or in the price-incentive migration models that have appeared since, all that emerges is that labour moves because of a difference in expected wages or other related prices making part of the expected revenue stream of the potential migrant. If at any moment another important cause prompting labour to move is discovered – and there are undoubtedly innumerable causes – then wage–price incentives leading to equilibrium falters. Of note in these models, variables other than wages also appear symbolically, once modelled that is, in the form of a price. Because there is a virtually infinite number of social variables that prompt labour to move in differing real conditions, the price-based explanation as a supposedly rigorous system of thought collapses: a case of crude empiricism. As in any other equilibrium approach, including a Nash equilibrium in which the infinite submarkets must all clear somewhat together, it so happens that such a scenario is fairy tale. Short of changing the vacuous assumptions that individuals seek profits or utility, if at any time a theory becomes founded on

5 Unlike the common usage of form and content to mean something relating to the outside and inside, respectively. Form and content are philosophical categories that originate with Hellenistic philosophy and were further developed by Hegel (1830). The content is defined as the set of social relations that are particular to a given historical process. The form originates from the form of thought or idea; but here it means a partitioned historical characteristic and seminal component of content, the mediation of which into content represents the universal law which is common to social formations with different historical processes: e.g., the law of value, wage-labour transformation etc. In Hegel's logic, a law arises when the content becomes transmutable into form and vice versa. This transformation has its equivalent in the concept of becoming, which is the differentiation of the genus. In Marxian terms, it is *the mediation that results from the actual development of an object historically*. Often the categories of form and content are confused for essence and appearance; for an illustration, see Stace (1984).

the erratic elements of crude empirics, the moment the empirical observation changes the theory itself has to completely change. There is nothing wrong with revamping theory to assimilate newly found facts. But this neoclassical theory is stillborn because it is founded upon non-existent assumptions put to work in a formal or ahistorical framework. This is not about the breakdown of transitivity, or the grandiose idea that the individual in the supermarket whose taste for an apple bestows upon it the value that underwrites its price, or the assumption drawn from the dieting advice that the good sensation from eating sweet cakes declines after the first two bites;[6] it is about removing the fact that economic conditions of any sort is a power exercise within a historically *periodised* timeframe. The neoclassical framework is also a theory at odds with initial facts because it pins all its structure on trans-historical platitudes; people may always produce and consume, but the ways and reasons for doing so differ across time, and so these behavioural assumptions are only similar at a superficial level of generalisation or by quantification.

It is not a theory of *anything* to begin with, because all it posits is that there are people out there who want to make money and be happy across history, and they do so with price signals (wages are the price of labour) that lead to social welfare and efficiency. Through quantification and generalisation, the similitude that is expressed in common denominators provided by unit of measure, the outward manifestation of quality reduced to a symbol, may be ascribed to a variety of conditions across time and space. For instance, the labour that leaves the home economy is expressed as the number of workers, which is a product of its own momentum over time and also its interaction with other variables such as poverty at home or wages abroad; but that number tells us nothing about the social forces that distinguish migrant labour as impoverished wage labour. I am not saying one cannot sum over the same unit of measure; I am noting that a theory explaining the social forces behind social transformations cannot be reduced to quantifications that conceal the particularity of each variable and its social decision-making process.[7]

---

6 The blatant shortcoming of such drivel is its narrow scope of application to higher class or richer regions; it applies only to areas where 'cakes' and choices between cakes are available. But its appeal as a device for luring people, especially social science students, to the notion that capital generates wealth, is a powerful co-option tool. Central capital does generate wealth, but it must also reduce its costs by demolishing the assets and political will of working peoples in the lower echelons of its own working classes and the Third World. The necessary concomitance of war and misery with capitalism is not haphazard or the product of very frequent mad errors. They are the systemic product of capitalist class relations and their dominant ideologies.
7 There is a self-differentiating process within and between social or economic variables; they are a product of themselves and they affect each other by qualitative

Changes in labour practices and profit-seeking under capitalism constitute a different story from place to place, not to mention in different previous epochs such as the feudal or the mercantile. In the present epoch of overproduction crises, it involves the purposeful destruction of assets, including human assets, while producing with economies of scale; more and more goods are produced for continuously lower costs to meet a demand dampened by wage suppression.

Modelling can of course serve to spell out complex realities. Models can be better specified algebraically if economic growth is explained, *inter alia*, in terms of the forceful expulsion of labour, the necessity to cheapen labour costs by the most egregious means available to capital, or the utter obliteration of labour power, which is in great part the death rate in imperialist wars or their ramifications in social ills and hunger. The assumptions of such modelling techniques would for instance relate individual agency to its mediated political agency within a context of class power whose contradiction, necessarily but not exclusively, sets the background for the individual to act. Hence, what would be modelled in these overdetermined contradictions where cause is effect and vice versa is the social contradiction itself as the subject and the universal category whose realisation in heterogeneous elements can be reduced and quantified for didactic reasons. Obviously, historical uncertainty cannot be modelled without reduction; reduction to fit the development in mathematics has often been a tool to mask over real processes by the mainstream. But the falsification of conventional modelling lies more with defining the subject as the abstract individual and not the dominant class relationship; a migrant from Syria escaping bombs or another from a hunger-stricken region fleeing the wrath of his or her ruling class's neo-liberal policy is as much a subject of history as lunar eclipses. Still, for self-differentiating and self-negating social conditions, models that better specify their subjects can only momentarily adumbrate real processes.

> change. As such, this state of contingency a priori omits the possibility of modelling becoming theory. This is more than just time incoherence generating an unpredictable shift in time series data. It is about the resultant vector, as per Engels, of all the historical forces in their course of development realising the state of becoming, which is capitalism. Moreover, the mainstream choice of dissecting the social state of affairs by overlooking social contradiction also omits the model as such from serving merely as an illustrative tool. So it is not only that some variables were overlooked and that theory requires their inclusion in a continuous process of falsification to stand on better grounds, or that it is the quantitative relationship of variables to each other that would count as theory; it is in failing to account for the dynamics of history: that is the subject of history – which social relationship is doing what by means of which intermediated agency.

One may further enquire about the interconnections of systems and their development, and how they correspond to the story of rural or urban-sector relations in the neoclassical dual models. The categories of low technical development and low marginal productivity pre-exist in these models. They are given assumptions without a historical basis. Little is known about how this poor rural performance came about or why there should be an interconnection between this particular rural and urban sector. Why is the rural sector becoming poorer when modern means of farming can be scale-economies and modern just like any other industry? Why is there need for exchange, apart from an individual making a choice to migrate? In fact, the sociohistorical conditions that *ex ante* create the necessary environment for migration are absent. To say that the policy and welfare implications for both rural and urban systems are the cause of price-based explanation under a dualistic framework is again not plausible, as in actuality, for welfare and policy implications to be inferred, there has to be first an explanation of how prices are formed and why exchange occurs. If one posits that the individual's decision to leave conditions of near starvation in the countryside and move to the metropolis is really a 'choice' – in other words, if one reduces economics to physics as a positive science and completely neglects the fact that human beings require a historically defined level of subsistence – then in this rather fascist sense, choice, which is the single choice of migrating, exists. Dispensing with sizeable populations so that the market can clear the glut of labour will not explain why this exchange came to be, but it can explain why the welfare of a certain class or 'race' of humans, posited as different from humanity because of inherent cultural or 'genetic' qualities, depends on dispensing with some other humans. In actuality, depleting the hinterland of its labour reserves and swelling the urban areas with formerly rural urban poor occurs as a result of exponential growth in the more powerful sectors that draws in the politically weak sectors and uses them or, more often, abuses them for their resources, including human resources.

Just as important, precious little knowledge is imparted by these models about the relationships within a sector that necessitate any relation of exchange with the other sector. The sum of all the actions of all the migrants, their decisions to move, observed empirically signal something about worsening conditions in the rural sector. However, the migrants are reacting to overbearing historical conditions that engulf the rural sector. The migrants' escape also implies that they could not have determined the direction of development in their home sector. In other words, they have little leeway in improving rural development, because if they had any political leverage, their conditions might not have worsened. The subject of rural-sector history, the class in charge of its development, remains unknown to us in the voodoo of neoclassical economics. Besides, to assert anything about the rural sector from the movement of one of its strata (say the migrant group) is to forget that its movement depends on the amalgam of social forces present within it, especially the role of the landed class and its alliance with the urban bourgeois class. Although over-determination (In a totality in which cause is effect and vice versa, the particular rural condition is best explained in relation to the general capitalistic condition) always prevails, one cannot construct the symptom, which is forcible dislocation, as the cause of migration.

A theory as a system of thought that is meant to capture and explain changes and transformations has, at a foundational level, its own methods of building abstractions. The construction of the abstract can be an aspect of the particular historical condition or a one-sided, trans-historical, more or less common behavioural–biological aspect.[8] It can either be that people under capitalism depend on the market for survival or that people breathe, consume food and work. The latter premises, which are conditions for any state of being across time, constitute a genus of behavioural assumptions in the neoclassical discipline. The method by which the neoclassical school operationalises these hypotheses is actuarial. It measures, in terms of the price form, the response of policies; in this particular instance, the policies one has in mind are aimed at deconstructing the old forms of life and property in the rural sector. In that sense, the mainstream method is akin to an insurance company's search for the premium that has to be developed to calibrate the flow of labour that will satisfy capital accumulation. However, when prices are considered as instantiations of class and power structure – the workings of the law of value – then the actuarial side of neoclassical economics ceases to explain much. For a theory to be pertinent in a given period, it has to be capable of generating a view of the whole, a universal, which is also the sum of diverse phenomena. It is about following the process of reality's self-differentiation and designating the social forces that propel its movement (that is why I can say the sum

8 On one-sided abstraction I follow Ilyenkov's (1960) elaboration of the Marxian definition of the abstract. The abstract is not a trait or a characteristic common to a social condition across time. It is an aspect of the social condition within a determinate historical period. The abstract is not a trans-historical aspect or property of the sensuously concrete, but rather the contrary; the sensuous concrete proves to be only an abstract, one-sided 'embodiment' of the universal. 'This inversion, by which the sensibly concrete is regarded as a form of manifestation of the abstract and general, instead of the abstract and general being regarded on the contrary as a property of the concrete, is characteristic of the expression of value. At the same time, it makes the expression of value difficult to understand. If I say: Roman law and German law are both law, which is self-evident. If, on the other hand, I say: the law, which is an abstraction, is realised as such in Roman law and in German law which are concrete laws, the connection between the abstract and the concrete becomes mystical' (*Capital*, vol. 1, 771).

of diverse phenomena).⁹ For theory to do this, its definition of the abstract is best when it represents social development in motion as a result of social interaction and contradiction and not some denominator (as in how much one 'eats and enjoys oneself') common to living humans across recorded history. An alternative method of theory can be carried out by historical investigations substantiated with a formal reasoning of the social forces shaping development. This allows for diversity in unity, the concrete as it assumes its state of becoming by the law of motion or the abstract, borne by the historically specific dynamics of social development (as in the cheapening of labour power, itself the abstract or the law, being a necessary measure under capitalism coming to fruition in rising proletarianisation, or the concrete). What is general and theoretical is the historical specificity of the class struggle, which defines the dynamics of concrete value relations that culminate in prices – themselves the *abstract* manifestation of value.

At a further remove, a theory would address the relation of the whole to the individual: how agency is devolved from the whole to the individual and their mutual relationship. In the neoclassical method, the individual's agency fuels the migration process. The individual *qua* worker, however, is faced with a worsening economic situation resulting from the actions of hegemonic capital; he or she can respond only by moving or not moving from a situation to which he or she did not necessarily contribute. Individual agency functions to change the bequeathed historical structure of capital via its intermediated forms of political organisation. Individual agency is not the utility-maximising part of *homo economicus*, as in getting satisfaction from a sandwich; it is the individual as political relationship mediated into mass political practice. Rural workers' exercise of power, for instance, could be gauged by the degree of

---

9 Althusser (1968) had remarked that there are no philosophical traces of Hegel in Marx, otherwise Marx becomes Hegelian through and through. That is just philosophical and not logical; Marx's method is owed to Hegel. However, the rigour of philosophical Marxism originates from a rupture with Hegel's epistemology. 'Marx rejected the Hegelian confusion which identifies the real object with the object of knowledge, the real process with the knowledge process. Marx defends the *distinction* between the *real object* (the real-concrete the real totality, which *survives in its independence, after as before, outside the head* and the *object of knowledge*, a product of the thought which produces it in itself as a thought-concrete, as a thought-totality, i.e., as a *thought-object*, absolutely distinct from the real-object, the real-concrete, the real totality, knowledge of which is obtained precisely by the thought-concrete, the thought-totality, etc. Marx goes even further and shows that this distinction involves not only these two objects (thought and real), but also their peculiar production processes' (Althusser 1968). Ilyenkov (1960) preceded Althusser and distinguished between the production process of a given real object, its historical development and the production process of the object of knowledge, which takes place through the method of ascent from the abstract to the concrete in thought.

improvements wrought as a result of equalising their rural development with other sectors.

In view of the urban-rural disparity and the *post facto* evictions, the rural migrant is unlikely to be a politically empowered historical agent. It is by defining the forces mustered by the relevant historical subject (the ruling capital class) for the creation of deteriorating social conditions in the countryside that one moves a theory away from the impertinent into the adequate. Addressing the issue of why any new development in a relationship between two heterogeneous systems (rural and urban) should necessarily arise points to a historically determined universal pattern of development under capitalism. As noted above, capital whose wealth is the heap of commodities as self-expanding value reproduces the conditions for its own expansion by dispossessing the direct producer; but dispossession itself assumes so many forms that the phenomena arising from this process of dislocation are as heterogeneous as actuality itself. One does not arrive at the general law (the universal in theory) by seeking common characteristics in the outcome of dislocation, for there are none unless one quantifies the many forms of abjection dislocation results with the same measure. The universal is the necessary but not exclusive act of dispossession as engendered by the dominant social relationship of capital. More particularly, in relation to the question of migration, theory has to probe the depth of the relationship of exchange of labour services for money wages between a rural and an urban sector and the contradiction that the migration process mediates. It is then that one finds that the universal or law in proletarianisation is the social contradiction between the stratum of private peasants (or semi-proletarianised farmers) and a growing capitalist production process hungry for cheap inputs.

A Non-Price Explanation of Proletarianisation

While criticisms of neoclassical method are many, some areas of relevance to the conditions of proletarianisation in the AW have to be addressed so that concerns over the false primacy of the price system are put to rest. In the Marxist approach, the conditions for the transfers of labour are an undercurrent of development. Each social entity has its own economic content and, therefore, path to development. Some eject many private labourers from the land while others evict them at slow rate. The rate of expulsion depends of the rate of consumption of the internal constituents of production, namely labour power, and the countervailing political organisation of labour, namely the peasantry.

The process of the practice of prevailing ideology, here of neo-liberalism – to counterpoise the Marxist method, as the idea or form becomes content in the process by which the theory of development policy has a certain outcome in development – relegates much of the developing world to a less-than-favourable position vis-à-vis a developed world. Behind that process is a relation of unequal class and power structure from which unequal exchange arises. In the language of pure Latin American structuralism (the original frame of dependency theory), the development of a world capitalist economy has led to its division into a centre specialising in the production of modern industrial goods and technical innovations, and a periphery engaged in the production of raw materials and food. The terms of trade or the ratio of export to import prices for the developing countries is worsening, which in turn, leads to part of what is created in the periphery being drained into the centre. For Prebsich (1950) and Furtado (1964), unequal development principally reflects the unevenness in the technical basis between the developing and the developed world. However, the Marxian tradition posits that the technical disparity between the developing and developed countries is secondary to the sociological relationship of capital, which creates the necessary political environment, ideology and institutions in developing countries to serve the interests of central capital and ensure access to Third World resources. Here is Marx on this issue.

> As soon as capitalist production takes possession of traditional agriculture, the demand for an agricultural labouring population falls absolutely.[...] This source of relative surplus population is thus constantly flowing. But the constant flow towards the towns pre-supposes, in the country itself, a constant latent surplus population, the extent of which becomes evident only when its channels of outlet open to exceptional width. The agricultural labourer is therefore reduced to the minimum of wages, and always stands with one foot already in the swamp of pauperism. (Marx 1867)

The dynamic of the radical dependency theory of development is quite different from simply positing two disparate structures coming in contact at a point in time. For radical dependency, fixing the exchange relationship, tinkering with prices, does not thwart the drive to dispossess labour. It depicts the process of proletarianisation as an ongoing historical condition necessitated by wealth making from central accumulation by industrialisation. A characteristic example of lumpen Third World development and its impact on labour is provided by Frank, a leading radical figure of this school.

The development of industry in Saõ Paulo has not brought greater riches to the other regions of Brazil. Instead, it converted them into colonial satellites, de-capitalized them further, and consolidated or even deepened their underdevelopment. There is little evidence to suggest that this process is likely to be reversed in the foreseeable future except insofar as the provincial poor migrate and become the poor of the metropolitan cities. (Frank 1966)

This industry developing in Saõ Paulo is characteristic of much of what is developing throughout the underdeveloped world. This development assumes its course through growth in the investments of multinational corporations, or through the opening of local markets to foreign commodities. The demand for cheaper labour and the conditions that lead to increasing the number of migrants from the rural to the urban areas follow this cross-border capital concentration. One ought to recall that this is not a hydraulic relation (mechanical-like), but a contingent value relationship in which underdevelopment is considered in view of the historically determined wealth and *rapport de classe*.

The wage, in the Marxist-structuralist view, is ancillary to the basic proposition of different economic structures with disparate technical bases entering into a relation of unequal exchange. This is not because the individual or the wage mechanism falls to some secondary or unimportant position, but because in this context the individual responds to changes in the socioeconomic environment that are formed independently of his or her immediate will. Whereas in the neoclassical method the individual is the nucleus of action or the undisputed agent, in the radical approach, it is the social human being, whose political decision coagulates in class power, that is the agent in the historical context. There are two different types of human beings that we are dealing with, social humanity and *homo economicus*; the latter does not confront the burden of history. From a radical perspective, the whole of the social formation, its political mass in international relations and autonomy, is its historical agency.

In mainstream models, the rural and urban sectors involved in exchange exhibit a functional and positive relationship to one another: they just trade, without ulterior motives. In the radical framework, these sectors are united in an antagonistic relationship. The formation with the stronger power and technical base integrates and subordinates the one with the weaker technical base.

The culturalist label of 'traditionalism' applied to the rural sector is not the reason for its weaker position. Rural areas may still exhibit traditions that linger from the past, but vestiges of yesteryear also linger in modern urban societies. There is no quantitative threshold for a preponderance of pre-modern folk tradition that defines a formation as capitalistic or non-capitalistic. The same also goes for the rate of unemployment. A high or low rate does not designate the degree of capitalism. Capitalism is a historical stage, of which capital is the seminal relationship. Weakened Arab rural formations were incapable of withstanding the assault of imperialism, and the peasantry as subject of history made no significant contribution to bettering its own development. As such, the rural and peripheral areas are not independent, nor do they fall beyond the range of capitalist power and weaponry. The peasants, like their urban working-class counterparts, per Marx's maxim in *The Eighteenth Brumaire*, are 'making history but not as they please'. They become reservoirs of additional resources or wage workers in waiting. Capitalism's higher rates of underemployment and poverty-level rural employment are a manifestation of the permanent social crisis of capital. Full employment of labour under low-productivity conditions does not run counter to the way society has expanded its output. Capitalism in the hinterland operates in a colonial mode – to requalify: the transfers of labour by migration are the necessary outcome of an intensified joint comprador–imperialist assault intended to either permanently disengage resources or to cheapen them to be reengaged at a later stage.

To wait for the fruition of the transformation attendant on expanding commodity exchange in order to categorise a rural formation as capitalist is a misunderstanding that views capital as a stock of commodities rather than a social relationship. The contradiction between the private forms of appropriation and the social forms of production dictates the subjugation of rural to the urban sector and is often reproduced by violent political means. The rural and urban sectors do not require commodity exchange to be united; they *ex ante* have class politics and imperial hegemony to coercively unite them.

> It is otherwise in the colonies. There, the capitalist regime everywhere comes into collision with the resistance of the producer, who, as owner of his own conditions of labour, employs that labour to enrich himself instead of the capitalist. The contradiction between these two diametrically opposed economic systems manifests itself here practically in a struggle between them. Where the capitalist has at his back the power of the mother country, he tries to clear out of his way by force the modes of production and appropriation based on the independent labour of the producer. (Marx 1867)

There is no hybrid mode of production, half capitalist and half pre-capitalist. The higher number of oxcarts side by side with modern lorries does not make half or quarter capitalism, as if capitalism could only be measured against 'Swiss-like' machinery. There is a capitalistically developing rural formation characterised by poor technical advancement, one whose evolution depends on the dynamics of the leading class or class alliance in the more central capitalist areas. The peasantry is part of a working class whose income is derived from the politically determined labour share of income. The uprooting of peasants and their conversion into social wage-labourers (socialisation) ensues in relation to pauperisation and the necessary expansion of the reserve army of labour – a corollary to the expansion of the broader relationship of capital. However, in organic and interdependent accumulation, the rural sector is not of secondary rank just because it constitutes such a low percentage of GDP. Without the sublation (simultaneous negation and preservation) of the hinterland, the historical resilience of capitalism suffers. The rural sector serves as a reservoir of cheapened resources, a reproducer of labour power whose value outlays are borne by the working class, and a repository for capital contingently upon the reign of socialist ideology. In this unity of different social forces, the tendency is for the ruling class alliances to form and to regulate the labour process and its attendant proletarianisation to the demands of capital accumulation.

In the AW, up until independence in the mid-twentieth century, the economy was mainly rurally based. After independence, circa 1950 and until 1980, the apparent structural transformations, specifically those associated with uprooting the peasantry, occur at a rate that is positively dependent on the rate of the imperialist-hijacked national capital accumulation. The national economy grows less by productivity growth that may boost wages and more by grabbing a higher share from cheaply employed workers; hence, more labour is drawn from the rural areas to cheapen wages. The Arab socialist economies invested heavily in agriculture to stem the outflows of labour from subsistence farming. The capitalisation of agriculture had implications for both national and regime security: cash crops and food security buttressed the national economy, and the lower rate of peasant flow to the cities attenuated the growth of shantytowns and urban poverty that would have threatened the regimes.

Under neo-liberalism, transforming the population into a reserve labour pool in subsistence farming and later into wage labour (mostly engaged in impoverished urban employment) incurred the additional cost of disarticulating the rural areas – creating a two-tier rural stratification with a parasitic class integrated as consumers with the centre through the price differential of returns on exchange rates denominations. What was new under neo-liberalism is that the rate of labour dislocation followed the demands of national capital as well as international financial capital. The Marxian category of the reserve army of labour includes all persons of working age capable of working, but unable to work because the economy does not generate sufficient employment.

Then, as now, the colonies and later the peripheries produced huge numbers of labourers. 'But in the colonies [...] the absolute population increases much more quickly than in the mother-country, because many labourers enter this world as ready-made adults [...] and the law of supply and demand of labour falls to pieces' (Marx 1867). Marx wrote this in reference to the many persons forcibly shipped to the colonies or those many of the colony's rural population transformed into bonded labour and, hence, violently put to work. In more recent times, technological advancement and the changing post-independence balance of power (relative autonomy in the periphery) in addition to the importation of labour-saving technology, meant that unlike days past where all the labour was absorbed in low-productivity, slave-like agriculture, a significant proportion of new entrants into the labour market became permanently disengaged from production or eked out a living in low-productivity work in urban areas. More particularly, Arab deindustrialisation and the reduction of public-sector employment and or public investment also lowered the rate of decent job creation. The global crisis of overproduction further implied a cheapening of labour, not simply on the basis of the rule of large numbers (too many people willing to work), but also and more importantly on the basis of a larger redundant workforce whose very abjection cheapens its market-priced labour power even further. The hundreds of millions wallowing in poverty, demonstrating the worthlessness of labour as they are aggressed upon and perish prematurely, serve further the intertwined purpose cheapening and disempowering labour. More so than before, the sordid prospect remains that in the demonstration of imperialist power there is not a number of dead from war and famine that would cause global labour shortages.

In most of the developing world, the proletarianisation process gained momentum circa 1980 with the onset of the neo-liberal age; but in much of that world, wage labourers were created without decent wage-paying jobs (Wallerstein 2011). Exponential growth entailed a higher rate of repression and exploitation of labour. As value became universalised in the dollar – financialised and with profit reported quarterly – drearier conditions of labour in production intensified. The initial stages of the production chain, the stage of producing the raw material where often violence prevails in the developing world, wrought the worst of the contradictions of exponential growth and immiserating exploitation. Increasingly, the subsistence side of the declining rural economy became a social support mechanism for the peasant who is a potential wage earner but is unlikely to ever find a decent wage-paying job. The failure of the rural sector to deliver sufficient social support raised the spectre of crisis, especially as corporate land grab and cheaper food imports from the North degraded the basis for local sustenance and reduced the share of the consumption bundle created by local means (Kishk 2012). In addition to expulsion by violence, the cross-sector ruling class enacted the laws influencing lower amounts of food produced for immediate consumption by the farmers and, subsequently, incentivising their removal from the land.

Autonomy and sovereignty rest upon the command of the working class in the state and the amalgam of living and national securities. Depriving the rural classes of security, including food security, represented another measure that would add to the erosion of state autonomy over policy. There was more than just a commodity mode of integration with the Western world underpinning this relationship. Commodities are traded not only because they are objectified labour, but also because there is a social relation that is itself the historically given context that advances the trade of commodities. The coopting of the Arab bourgeoisie under neo-liberalism – its metamorphosis into a comprador class – was nearly complete at the time of the Arab Spring, and the resultant disarticulation within an Arab formation reinforced the already-dire objective conditions to the point of explosion.

A non-Marxist but structuralist analysis along the lines of the non-radical Latin American dependency theory does not fully account for this relationship of a social entity to itself, including its contradictions and its mode of articulation with the modern sector through rural-urban class alliances (Larrain 1989). The question that concerns the agency influencing the dynamics of modern capital accumulation – its crisis, its demand for cheapened labour, and the ensuing politics of aggression in the hinterland resulting from the interlocking of two separate structures in an exchange relationship – is underemphasised. Moreover, the social contradiction, which is intrinsic to every class society, is overshadowed by the rubric of the nation-state. But a state is a form of social organisation with varying levels of sovereignty and multiple layers of class and security structures. One first should question the relationship of rural or urban labour to its own ruling class. Could there have been social changes in the rural sector as a result of its own internal class antagonisms, changes that steered matters in parallel with the interest of more modern capital, as in the salient case of a partnership of landowning classes with the bourgeoisie? The undertone that structures are somewhat immutable and determined by a trans-historical 'nationalist' sentiment of social classes is the Achilles heel of structuralist non-Marxist dependency theory. The failure of Latin America's import-substitution policies was not a result of the failure of the policy itself; failure was more intelligently attributed to the inevitable collaboration of the Latin comprador bourgeoisie with the capitalist class of the imperialist centre (Larrain 1989). Account was taken of the higher degree of imperialist belligerence – this is what has happened in the AW. The failing of the structuralist approach lies in underemphasising the social context of value formation in a social process imbued with contradictions. Worse yet, import substitution in an Arab context is destined to fail at a quicker rate when the basis for trade, capital flows and foreign exchange rules are almost wholly pre-furnished by the imperialist. The way to expose this failure is through a value-theory-based understanding, which fundamentally changes the rules of intellectual engagement. Such an approach posits a historical reading of the social class and power structure as a precursor to reified policy and price formation.

The Marxian Critique

The proletarianisation process can be encapsulated in the relationship of exchange of labour power, itself a commodity, for other commodities. Examining the issue at this level of abstraction lays bare the social relations that underlie the proletarianisation process. Also, by understanding these relationships from a value perspective, a prognosis could be derived from the tendencies in social relations governing present developments. On the surface, one observes an exchange taking place between a less-developed entity, the less-modernising or rural sector, and the modern developed or urban sector. The former exports or sells labour power for wage goods from the developed entity. The functional relationship between the two formations dictates that one serves a purpose for the other. The rural area pays for part of its trade deficit with the remuneration from remittances.

That labour moves in response to higher wages is a notion that captures only a one-sided aspect of exchange. The moment exchange takes place, the determinants of the functional relationship (labour working for wage goods away from home), and those of the internal rural relationship (expelling the additional stock of labour power from the countryside) are combined in the objects being exchanged. These objects are labour power and wage goods: both are objectified value alienated from their producers. Seen from the optic of the rural areas, the exchange relationship is not about just the last moment when the person moves away to work; it is also about the history of scant work opportunity at home and the cost of maintaining labourers. The social cost of the reproduction of labour, all that moneyed and non-moneyed value that went into supporting the labourer who is unemployable at home since birth, bears no fruit for the suppressed rural sector. The problem as such cannot be reduced to the formal idea that the price of labour power (the wage rate) pulls labour, because the rural sector has already been substantially deconstructed before the allure of urban wages comes into being. Simply, there is a history to the making of the migrant.

Analytically, the question of whether exchange of labour power for wages occurs because rural migrants serve a function for urban capital and are enticed by wages, or because rural labour is vastly unemployed in the rural sector and therefore has to move, appear simultaneously in thought. However, the courses of these developments are not simultaneous. The political and economic dispossession of the rural areas precede the making of labourers whose labour power is readied to be exchanged. The question of causal determinacy is not a statistical exercise ascribing so much to wage pull or labour push; it is about the primacy of historical agency, that particular social relationship reproduced often enough to resituate the grounds beneath the theft of rural labour by modern capital. As Ollman (2003) put it in his 'Dance of the Dialectic', ask not who took the goose from the commons, the question should be who took the commons from the goose.

Empirical studies meticulously describe each case of migration as different, such that there will be as many theories as there are studies. Each case is different, indeed. Yet again, a mere listing of differences obscures the general social dynamics creating the conditions for proletarianisation. The universal dynamic is the *process* of proletarianisation itself, or it is how the law of value asserts itself. For the neoclassical method, this relationship of exchange becomes conceptually discernible only if it is ultimately reduced to a price or wage. But many underdeveloped social formations knew no money system and had no money prices to begin with. Recalling: prices are not given; they emerge on the basis of a distorted power structure. Let us put the question this way: Is it possible for the price of labour to be set so much below what is needed to maintain human life that emigration becomes a survival necessity?

Of course the answer to the question from a neoclassical point of view is that in the atomised world of equilibria, there will be a price, no matter how low, which will clear the market. That low price may also clear the lives of many labourers. But the price system is an epiphenomenon of the social wage system, which is what needs to be explained. To capture the kernel of proletarianisation, I need to document the history of establishing wage labour (the socialisation of rural labour) and the removal of additional labour from land in synch with the demands of capital. To bring this to light, I illustrate the process, from a Marxian perspective of exchange, as the mediation of the contradiction between value and use value or between the social cost of labour (investment in labour) and the productivity of labour. Labour is a qualitatively unique category in that it is both a commodity (labour power, which is what the labourer actually sells) and a producer of commodities – a producer whose rate of contribution to making commodities can be undervalued by the rate of exploitation. But for the moment let us consider only the one aspect wherein labour power (the intellectual and physical activity that workers impart to commodities or services) is a commodity being exchanged for another commodity.

Any commodity is a product of purposeful social activity, and it is at the end of the production process, defined as an objective entity. Each commodity in itself, before it enters into exchange, has two qualities: use value and value. Value, unlike the Ricardian point, is not only some average quantity of labour (as in the average intensive magnitude of labour whereby a given quantity of labour is expended in a given time), which is the Ricardian substance of value: the average physiological input of labour in the commodity. The natural act of labouring is trans-historical. It only presupposes value as socially necessary labour time: that is, the historically given relation under commodity production that socially equalises labour (Rubin 1972). Value as such is the mediation of the commodity's internal contradiction: it is subject and substance. Another way of putting this: value is the inner relation of a commodity *to itself*, outwardly revealed through the relation to another commodity (Ilyenkov 1963). Labour power is useful (in the good it produces or the service it provides; its productivity), but also it has a cost. In the case we are considering, the rural sector's outlay on the human development and maintenance of the labourer in schooling, healthcare and food (moneyed and non-moneyed care) is the cost of reproducing rural labour power, its intrinsic value. This value, to which the urban capitalist contributed nothing, is transferred into the commodities that rural labour produces once it migrates. The same is true of the modern (urban) sector's labour power and commodities. Thus, before exchange occurs, each commodity, as value and the product of value relations, has a dual quality (value or socially necessary labour time and use value) and a relationship to itself. This relationship of the good to itself is a contradictory one. First, the labour-power commodity has an inherent cost in terms of the outlays of labour that reproduce labour; but, second, it has little or no use value to its owner within the squeezed rural social formation wherein it was bred, but has no market into which it can deployed or realised. It is similar to the objectified commodity that the industrial capitalist produces and must sell. To parody the situation from a Marxian angle: exchange (here, the act of migration itself reciprocated by wage goods) mediates internal value contradictions between value proper (the labour time socially necessary to produce the labour power) and the use value that labour power can impart to commodities in the process of production (Marx 1867).

Tangentially, exchange does not just come about in the moment, or when supply-and-demand curves appear on the blackboards of classrooms; exchange is the outward manifestation or phenomenon resolving the inner contradiction found in the actual goods. This again is a historically, or commodity production, specific condition: society has created labourers, and capital has robbed the grounds upon which they could labour. However, the process does not come to rest because labour is being pushed out as a result of the contradiction between value and use value. There is now the problem of exchanging so many different useful and exchangeable commodities for one another. Initially the contradiction that has arisen in the determination of use and exchange values was resolved by the money form of value. Although each of the commodities being exchanged retains usefulness and exchangeability at the same time, the money form, having only exchange value, subsumes use value and mediates the manifold concreteness of exchange relationships. Labour power, like other commodities, sells for money or wage goods.

Marx resolves the antinomies that usually pile up in the formal system of thought by following the development of the object in real time; the contradictions are preserved and ensure a dynamic of movement from one stage to another. Through social forms of organisation, each concrete or particular social condition (like expanding trade or exchange in a particular market) transcends its own barriers by growing into a more universal or abstract form, doing so via the money form. Methodologically, the ascent is historically fashioned, and what became abstract at one point in time will inevitably be perceived as concrete as a result of the persistence of contradictions (the concrete is a manifestation of the abstract, and both are modes of abstractions from an unfolding actuality). Labour power is a peculiar commodity, and it only came into being with the rise of capitalist relations. Although Greco-Roman forms of slavery had included marginal forms of the labourer converging with labour power (Emmanuel 1972), labour power as such became prevalent as a commodity when 'the commodity became money' under capitalism. Labour power, the commodity whose undervaluing results in surplus value, is the most distinguishing feature of capital as an ahistorical social relationship under capitalism.[10]

Marx shows that the money form and the evolution of credit keep on mediating various social contradictions associated with class and with forms of social organisation and distribution (Ilyenkov 1982). In contrast to the neoclassical approach, wherein money becomes a store of value, Marx shows that the money form of value (one of the many forms of value) captures the lopsided power structure and contradictions within the capitalist class system. Money is anything but neutral. For example, the build-up of fictitious capital (the layers upon layers of unpayable debt in the capital markets) has a

---

10 For Marx an hour of average socially necessary labour produces the same value no matter the relative capital-intensity of the particular industry in which a worker is employed, surplus value being exclusively the difference between the value equivalent of the wages paid to the workers and the value of that workers' total output.

non-fictitious impact on the working class (the working class is made to pay for the debts); hence fictitious capital raises in absolute terms the share of the social product accruing to the bourgeoisie (Bellofiore 2009). Money is a measure of value brokered by the dominant classes to regenerate the social conditions for accumulation.

It is necessary for our purposes to examine the conditions that demand the development of the exchange of labour power for a money wage from the internal relationships found in the creation of both labour power and other commodities. This allows for an understanding of the proletarianisation process as part of the permanent crisis of capitalism, which is manifest primarily in a crisis of overproduction and entails the destruction of value and the suppression of use value to pressing exchange conditions – the working of the law of value. One needs to know how these internal contradictions are mediated and resolved, not in thought, but in their actual course of development within a specific capitalist historical phase, which broadly defined is the relationship of capital.

Accordingly, the longstanding immiseration of the rural sector and its economic quarantine recreate the conditions for not only super-exploitation but also for value destruction. This latter category often goes missing in Western Marxist discourse on imperialism because it situates, at the heart of capital accumulation, the killing of the labourer along with his or her labour power. The capitalist crisis of overproduction has an alter image, which is underconsumption. The capping of the economic potential of the rural sector, limiting its propensity for modernisation in order to impoverish it and make its own labour superfluous to it, is partly the automatic reflex, which is underconsumption, or the negative mirror image of a much greater crisis, overproduction. The destruction of small-ownership rights and the socialisation of the rural labour force devalue labour and slam shut the door of labour reabsorption in the rural areas.

This process also scores another point for capital, as the greater autonomy that arises from the domestic production of essential foodstuffs is part of the potential basis for working-class resistance. In rural or underdeveloped areas, the forms of building the reserve army of labour assume the extremes of commercial exploitation (expulsion laws, violence and slave-like conditions); they are part of the ontological conditions for the creation of surplus value from the harnessing of primary inputs at the early stages of production such as raw material and labour. The production process is organic and one in which national boundaries, identity and political reconstructed barriers should not conceal the cross-national input chain that begins with the intellectual production of design, the mining and the creation of the conditions for mining and later the finalisation of the product. At each of these stages, forms of violence and dispossession vary in intensity to reinforce the departure of value from price. The same lives with the same levels of skills with the same value assume a different price or socially denominated values. The disarticulation resulting from the growing redundancy and the associated social rifts deepen labour-force differentiation, which is an indispensable condition of accumulation.

Thus far, three interrelated issues arise from posing the problem in this manner.

The first, as already explained, is that this exchange mediates a contradiction between all the potentially employable rural labour and the limitation for its usability in the rural sector, or between value (the objective category as the stock of labour power) and use-value, employability. The greater the contradiction between these two, the greater will be the necessity for outmigration or exchange abroad to realise the commodity that is labour power. As seen in the next section, the higher the rate of pauperisation of the countryside as a result of its low share of income (not enough for it to reproduce itself), the higher the rate of social dislocation. As mentioned earlier, the share of income of this and other sectors' working classes is decided *not* by productivity levels, but in the course of the class struggle.

Second, the valorisation of use value in a process of exchange determined by the balance of power in a class structure has an implacable bearing on alienation. The extent of alienation will be determined by the extent to which the working class is co-opted and the concomitant extent to which the labour-power commodity, itself produced by labour, stands above and rules over labour 'as an alien and hostile power' (Marx 1844) – the 'fetishism of commodities' side of the Marxian argument. That labour power comes to stand above labour – that is, a worker's potential to put his or her labour power to work becomes more valuable than the worker herself – in a crisis-ridden developing context, amounts to the sort of alienation that commodifies nearly all aspects of human life. In weakened or bombarded formations like contemporary Iraq or Syria, humans themselves become commodities, and the dispensability of labour power (along with the labourer) determines labour's fate. It is not the individual who will be left with a choice of whether to migrate or not; the class in power adopts choices in relation to the magnitude of the reserve army of labour and its bearing on the rate of accumulation.

The third issue is that of the money form. Although a universal equivalent that resolves the contradictions arising in exchange, money conceals within itself the breadth of antinomies in the social system. In particular, by generalising wealth in the form of money, capital further ties the reproduction of the rural land-owning class to its industrial counterpart. Thus, the proletarianisation process occurs not only through the austere measures imposed from outside, but also by the repression of the collaborationist land-owning class whose mode of wealth accumulation depends on money earned from cash crops. Equally important, money becomes an additional instrument by which the reproduction of capital (via its class power rapport) determines the social wealth devolved to each of the social classes in the rural areas. The mystique of the price system and a rationing of the supply of money to rural areas combine to squeeze the rural working population. Through money/price fetishism, the class in power reinforces the rate of exploitation and the rate of impoverishment necessary to create excess labour.

From an analytical perspective, the question as to why there is uneven development in this union of modern sectors and less-developing sectors appears to represent the duality that defines the boundary of the subject. Knowing their differences appears to explain proletarianisation and migration. However, upon a closer reading, these two sectors are separate as well as united. The political hegemony exercised over the rural area links it to capitalism, not via the trade in commodities/labour route alone, but primarily by a social relationship, namely the political reach of capital. Capitalists acquire territory to engage it in capitalist production. The hegemonic relationship of urban over rural is essentially an extension of the social relationship of central capital into the hinterland. It matters little whether the majority of the rural sector was unemployed or employed, recalling the point that a high rate of unemployment (that is, of workers without work) is not what distinguishes a capitalist from a pre-capitalist formation. At any rate, the comparison is unfitting since in pre-capitalist formations almost all are engaged in low productivity work. Capital as self-expanding value needs the power to *potentially* select and engage resources in the process of profit-driven production. However, because accumulation is profit-driven and overproduction is a permanent condition, idle resources also form part of the concomitancy for the creation of value, hence, the vastly idle underemployed rural population. Insofar as the rural sector is socially and politically subjected to the diktat of central capital where the final stages of production culminate, one ceases to observe any separation between two morphologically different social and geographical entities. The capitalist sector sublates the pre-capitalist sector.[11] It stands to reason, therefore, that a diagnosis of the problem will have to address the leading social agency of the ruling class of the modern sector and its subordinate ally, the rural landowning class, which together pauperise rural areas.

11 To sublate means to supersede, put an end to, but simultaneously maintain, preserve.

The Concrete Condition

From the early 1980s on, as the ideology of socialist resistance waned, more people became divorced from their previous ways of making a living and were driven into poverty. They were separated from their private means of subsistence, socialised as labour and deprived of the ideological and organisational means of developing a framework to meet the requirements of decent livelihood. So huge was the exodus from the countryside that the UN began addressing the issue of an ageing demographic profile of the rural population in the AW (UN 2008a).

In the AW, over half of the consumed food bundle is imported, so a rise in food prices can reduce income. The developments in the agricultural sector as per Tables 5.3 and 5.4 show a reduction in the contribution of agriculture to GDP, a decrease in the rate of agriculture employment and persistent higher poverty in the rural areas.

In the past three decades, most Arab countries joined the World Trade Organization (WTO). This period represents a greater openness in agricultural markets and, hence, greater susceptibility to price fluctuations and import surges. Intraregional Arab trade is at around 10 per cent of total trade with the rest of the world, despite the Generalised Arab Free Trade Agreement (GAFTA, in effect as of 1997), which is supposed to promote inter-Arab trade. The comprador class and its cross-border allies ensure that Arab joint and developmental treaties are unmonitored for implementation and that all integration efforts remain ineffective. A more interlocked and interdependent Arab food market would add an element to Arab national and cross-national security that would shift the power dynamic, tilting the base of international negotiations toward Arab countries. But neither the Arab comprador class nor its international partners would support empowering working people in the AW with the freedom that comes from food independence.

In the poorer countries of the AW, the slightest decline in the domestic food supply runs the risk of being translated into a further reduction of per capita consumption. Over the past 20 years, average consumption per capita declined slightly (FAOSTAT, various years). Notably, for the same period, the per capita production of basic foods (the minimum food bundle of FAO) exhibited a downward trend, and the slack in the level of domestic supply was covered by higher imports (FAOSTAT, various years). It may be argued that greater market integration, lower prices, and accessibility of food supplies prevented consumption per capita from falling further and that, under more autarkic conditions, the pervasive problem of malnutrition could have worsened. But autarkic conditions would not have eroded local-production capacity. Excluding the Gulf, Arab agricultural imports were 3.5 times greater than

Table 5.2 Rural and urban populations of Arab countries, 1980–2020 (percentages); figures do not include inhabitants of rural areas around Cairo who do not count as urban residents

Percentage of rural population					Percentage of urban population				
1980	1990	2000	2010	2020	1980	1990	2000	2010	2020
56.2	50.1	46.3	42.6	38.6	43.9	49.8	53.7	57.4	61.4

Source: The Demographic Profile of Arab Countries' Ageing Rural Population, United Nations, 2008a.

Table 5.3 The agriculture sector's contribution to employment and as a share of GDP (%), selected countries and years

	Algeria	Egypt	Jordan	Morocco	Syria	Tunisia	West Bank & Gaza
Employment	1977: 31	1976: 47	1979: 11	1971: 58	1970: 50	1975: 39	1980: 23
	1995: 12	2000: 30	1993: 6	1999: 44	1991: 28	2001: 22	2000: 14
Value Added	1977: 8	1976: 28	1979: 7	1971: 20	1970: 20	1975: 18	1987: 19
	2000: 9	2000: 17	2000: 2	2000: 14	2000: 24*	2000: 12	2000: 8

Source: The World Bank 2004, MENA Development Report, *Unlocking the Employment Potential in the Middle East and North Africa: Toward a New Social Contract* (Selected countries and years).
* The decline of the Syrian agricultural sector began in 2000 with the onset of the second generation of neo-liberal reforms. Morocco and Syria represented the two Arab countries with the lowest rate of dependency on food imports.

Table 5.4 Distribution of rural and urban poverty*

Country/territory	Percentage of the poor in urban areas	Percentage of the poor in rural areas	Percentage of rural poor in total
Yemen	21	40	84
Egypt	10	27	78
Iraq	16	39	...
Jordan	12	19	29
Syrian Arab Republic	8	15	62
Palestine	21	55	67
The Sudan	27	85	81

Sources: World Bank-WDI (2008); for Iraq, Central Organization for Statistics and Information Technology (COSIT) and the World Bank-WDI (2010); and, for the Sudan, FAOSTAT (2007).
* Most of these figures were substantially revised after the uprisings of 2011 and a show a starker wealth–poverty differential.

exports in 2008 (AOAD, 2008).[12] Financing continuously increasing levels of imports under conditions of dwindling savings and balance-of-payments problems adds to the fiscal deficit (save in the Gulf). In countries where food staples are subsidised, higher food prices increase the pressure on that deficit. As things stand, average growth in GDP per capita in most Arab countries has stagnated (over 30 years until 2002 it rose, albeit in a highly unequal distribution way, but the overall average over those 30 years is closer to 1 per cent). More important, as mentioned in the Introduction the working populations' shares of income fell progressively. Together, income inequality dynamics resulting from an inequitable tax regime and from balance-of-payments vulnerability has put the working class in a more precarious position as debts are paid by further reducing labour's income share. Unless investment and protection of the key sector of national agriculture are reinstituted, the financial enslavement of poorer countries will not abate.

Neo-liberal 'market openness' was supposed to release resources from low-productivity sectors and sharpen the comparative advantage of better-performing economic activities. However, productivity growth was more frequently low or negative, and the AW is still far from reaping the full benefits of trade, had those benefits even existed under such arrangements. The combined impact of declining overall economic performance and balance-of-payments accounts implies a quasi-permanent dislocation of domestic labour and resources. Labour released from sectors rendered uncompetitive by an unbalanced pricing arrangement – in particular subsistence agriculture – adds to urban unemployment.

Initially, low-productivity in Arab agriculture had historical roots relating to colonial repression or neglect and antiquated technology. Arab nations, as defined by imperial treaties, emerged outside the centres of industrialisation and, apart from the early phase of post-independence reconstruction, they remained on a path of relative underdevelopment reinforced by lopsided trade treaties. Consequently, their productive capacity suffers from a compounded negative historical bias (deconstruction and low capitalisation by the comprador classes, reinforced by a neoliberal policy overseen by US-led imperialism since 1980). Also disconcerting is that there are indications that food-importing Arab countries, especially the poorer group, are becoming progressively more susceptible to production shortfalls. The possible combination of conflicts and production shortfalls opens the gateway to lower food-consumption

---

12 Imports and exports include basic foods as well as marketable cash crops. See Developments in Arab Agricultural Trade, Arab Organisation for Agricultural development, Statistical Abstract, No. 29. 2009.

levels per capita and accentuates the problem of malnutrition. Although linear trends can only be formally indicative of things to come under unchanging conditions, the trajectories of imports and exports per capita foretell growing dependency on imports (FAOSTAT, various years). Around the mid-1970s, domestic basic food production in the Arab group represented more than three quarters of total domestic consumption (FAOSTAT various years). At the present rate of decline in output and, under constant conditions, by the year 2020 domestic food production will represent less than a quarter of consumption. Maintaining the rate of consumption (food use) at the present level necessarily implies that the volume of imports will have to rise at a slightly higher rate than that in the 1990s. In a nutshell, if the poorer working strata are to maintain a steady level of food consumption per capita, more food will need to be imported because the rate of decline in food production may not be fully countervailed by the rate of growth in food imports. And when so much of the food bundle is imported and bought with meagre national wages, the two-dollar benchmark of poverty becomes meaningless. Food speculated on and priced in dollars and then paid for in the local currency will raise the share of working class income going to food consumption by the exact proportion of rising food prices in the dollar. That is why subsidies represent an indispensable instrument of stabilisation given that food prices have been subjected to speculation and have been fluctuating so violently of late (between 2002 and 2016).

Would it take much to raise per-capita consumption and alleviate malnutrition under the existing structural framework? It should not, because the required handout amount represents a small share of the budget or a share that an insignificant amount of Official Development Assistance (ODA) could offset. However, the quantity of cash or the logistics of food delivery needed to alleviate hunger and malnutrition are not the reason why these problems are not being solved. Hunger, malnutrition and food-intake deficiency are a basic part of the imperialist or social control structure needed to regiment the labour process tailored for capital accumulation, both nationally and globally. The regimentation and repression of labour, or at times, its partial decimation, is what drives the pricing of resources in developing countries far below value, such that when the value and labour of the South are integrated with the production of the North, a higher surplus value and higher profit rate would be wrought as a result of super exploitation.

A reversal of malnutrition requires little in resources but much in class restructuring to perform a *volte-face* in development policy and its associated faulty macroeconomic interface with reality. Under more realistic projections, even if poorer Arab countries experience moderate-to-high rates of growth, this would not offset the rate of decline in the domestic food sector without a balancing and redistributing of the growth across social strata, with particular attention to the expansion of the basic-necessities sector. Under structural adjustment, economic growth came to be based on yet more-unbalanced sectoral performance; however, unlike Hirschman's (1969) adumbration, the leading sector was extractive and exhibited few positive linkages to the rest of the economy. The structure of these import-led economies is more conducive to food dependency because it tends to favour primary-sector exports or cash crops at the expense of the basic food sector.

The net result of these dire food-production conditions, in addition to wars and forcible expulsion from the land, has been intensified proletarianisation. However, the individual's 'choice' – more necessity than choice – to leave rural areas does not come about just because the higher accumulation of the modern centres necessitates the implementation of expulsion policies and the exchange of modern-sector commodity for labour services – it also arises as a result of an innate crisis of the rural system itself (rural–urban ruling-class articulation that botches rural reproduction). The primacy in this class articulation of weak and open systems is imperialism, or the uppermost cluster in the class hierarchy. Imperialist policy or war halts the growth of the rural sector itself by amputating the realisation of value in agricultural employment. There is a requirement to view the issue in terms of value because, as we will see below, a higher signification of value through price in the rural areas signifies shifts in the class structure. To summarise, the theoretical features of proletarianisation are:

- The rural areas – by the extension of imperialist hegemony articulated with the demands of capital – have undergone significant transformations and are not in any sense pre-capitalist.
- The expansion of capital into rural areas requires the reproduction of cheapened labour from those areas. The extirpation of traditional farm labour is accomplished by imposing restrictive measures on agriculture, and by the politics of forcible dislocation.
- The relationship of labour transfers to the urban centre came into being as an exchange relationship under the purview of imperialist hegemony and as a result of fuelling class contradictions within the Arab social formation. Cross-sector ruling class alliances and the violence of class politics exacerbated rural abjection.
- The social costs of reproducing the migrant labour force in the rural areas cannot be reimbursed by remuneration, at least on account of super exploitation, but also the flow of migrants continued unabated; hence, remunerations do not recapitalise the less modern formations to retain labour.

Resituating the Issue

Under the combined impacts of dislocation, neo-liberalism and a secular trend of growing organic composition of capital,[13] the reserve army of labour has become immense relative to existing capacity and the productively employed working population. Where wars are not shortening lives, the passive gains to the working class resulting from cheaper mass-produced medications and vaccines are prolonging life expectancy in conditions of poverty. Imperialist ideologues often assess progress in developing formations from the standpoint of myth, such that regardless of past colonial genocide and war or neo-liberal policies, imperialism has improved the lives of former 'savages' or uncultured creatures in the developing world. But the colonists' own progress is predicated upon limiting or destroying the progress of an otherwise historically more developed Orient, upon whose passing it has accumulated its wealth. Myth aside, the improvements to working-class living standards are best contrasted with a historically rising level of income related to the development of the productive forces, particularly technology. The decline in the share of wages, rising income inequality and negative productivity growth ensure that the historically determined standard of living has also been declining.

The repression attendant upon the wage system, which regulates the quality of life and reproduction of the working class, needs not only to accelerate the pauperisation of national labour but, interrelatedly, it has to cheapen labour as well, as a precondition for the creation of surplus value. Capital flaunts the death, idleness and indigence of labour so as to contribute, by the demonstration effect, to hollowing out the power of the proletariat. As evidenced by conditions in war-torn least-developed countries, the horrors of the wage system implied by the creation of a war-indigent proletariat whose labour representation has been completely wiped out by the blood-drenched politics of identity, become inevitably more intense because of forced expulsion and to higher death rates due to violence and dislocation. In the organic totality that is capital, the immiseration policy deployed by US-led imperialism not only drains the social product but metamorphoses into a self-reinforcing process whereby each successive loss for labour contributes to strengthening the ideological constructs of capital. Recalling, of course, that the share of wages accruing to the working class is reduced by politically fragmenting the labour force.

13 The organic composition of capital is a value relationship wherein the outlays on constant capital, including technological advance, surpass the outlays on variable capital or the labour side of the production process. The progress over time of this relationship displaces labour.

In the AW, the urban poor's living conditions have been battered under neo-liberalism. The segment of the working class obtaining 'higher' urban wages does not drive the exodus from the countryside by invidiousness. The flaunting of the few successful cases of rural migrant exercising psychological pressure as the ideological alibi, misses the scene of the crime, which is: the wage rate itself is a symptom of the dislocation measures exercised upon the rural population in general. Ideological reproduction is antecedent to capital's reproduction. Because of the integrated circuit of production globally, the show of destitute and more displaced workers pressure national and international wages downwards. At the heart of the matter, there are two mechanisms at work displacing labour in the AW:[14]

- First, the politics of imperialism expressed in the economics of the relative and absolute impoverishment of the peripheral areas; and,
- Second, the nearly complete integration that has resulted from the imposition of economic union via neo-liberalism and open-trade treaties.

The urban sector is the sole survival space available after the asphyxiation of rural life. Persistent rural poverty, uneven development and depletion of the rural labour force are *ipso facto* proof that remitted wages do not offset the lost value from the countryside. The low share of income accruing to the rural sector is related to the way this sector was integrated nationally and globally, and also to the power *rapport de classe* behind this integration. The spectrum of integration varies from modernised agricultural production of cash crops to a repository for wars. The rural sectors of the AW swing to the latter case, given that war is a principal conduit of its underdevelopment.

As I have explained, this displaced labour contributes to value creation, but not via value-added work activity in the last stage of production: there are value-added activities at every stage of production. The early stages of

---

14 In imperialistically integrated Arab economies, the creation of central wealth arises less from the engagement of labour in production than from its disengagement, weakening and fragmentation. Value is generated by commercial exploitation or by intensifying the commodification and dehumanisation of labour: first, nationally, through a lower wage share that allows the comprador class to invest more of the surplus abroad; and, second, by the rate at which human life is commodified and made dispensable, thereby reducing the ideological clout of global labour. A hungry, dispossessed and disempowered Arab working population has been redeployed into an act of realisation via self-destruction in imperialist wars. The terms of power, reflecting class power, that underlie the terms of trade and the grabbing of resources for maintaining the global accumulation rate are reproduced by all forms of aggression, including the destruction of life in war.

production involve the disengagement of labour and or employment in work that requires extinguishing life in a reduced time span, such as menial work in unhealthy conditions or wartime employment in soldiering. When value as a social category is what it takes to reproduce society, erecting national boundaries and killing off the other imparts absolute surplus value and, hence, wealth to the imperialist centre. Socially necessary labour time comes into being not only in imperialist centres: every direct and indirect historical condition of moulding value to the requirement of exchange is part of surplus value (Marx 1894). Put differently, in the interrelated and historical process of wealth creation, all the moments of the totality, all subordinate relationships to the core relationship of capital, contribute to value by directly or structurally influencing the production process. That is why, despite hunger-poverty requiring little in money terms to be eliminated, no effort will be made to end it because, in the crisis of overproduction, the setting aside or destruction of resources, including humans, is how a higher rate of surplus value materialises. That is not counterfactual history; it is what happens on a regular basis under capitalism.

Moreover, financialisation has elevated the snatching of wealth in money form via the crushing of the wage shares of income (lower labour share) into the ultimate mode of meeting capital's tendencies of concentration and centralisation of production;[15] the latter two conditions are no longer only concrete, as in setting up huge monopolies in the centre, but through the denomination of international wealth in money form (namely the dollar) they have also become abstract, strengthening the power of the cross-national bourgeoisie. In addition to the rising organic composition of capital, the dual process of profits growth through grabbing from labour income and the higher concentration of wealth in abstract value form (money) fuel the conditions for the further disengagement of socialised labour.

The integration of capital through increased financialisation under neoliberalism accelerates the rate at which the operation of the absolute general law of capitalist accumulation (AGLCA) proceeds. Often in Western Marxist circles, according to Devine (2005), the operation of the AGLCA – the law in which the value composition of capital favours higher productivity and displaces labour – neglects the international connectedness of production. A caveat is called for concerning the raw-material exporting periphery of the

---

15 Financialised capitalism uses the bogeyman of deficits and debts under open capital accounts to raise taxes and reduce labour share. However, when the national currency is freely traded and transferred on the world market, it is no longer national. The international financial centres shift real-value shares in their favour with so little effort by subjecting states to debt peonage.

Third World. Values generated in peripheral formations, or non-moneyed resources hitched to production by capitalism, are formed by violent social processes and transformed into prices within a disproportionate class and power context. Tearing apart old ways of maintaining a living, inflating the ranks of the unemployed, snatching Third World resources and driving people into abjection by means of war and neo-liberal policy – these build the social foundations for quarterly profit rates. The politics of dispossession and imperialist aggression mediate the growing rift between private gain and the redistribution of value in a complex global production structure that surpasses the narrow confines of the nation state.

Working-Class Fragmentation and Identity

In the state of rural poverty of the AW, the 'primacy of politics' – or the idea that to discipline a working class capital may sacrifice moneyed resources by more than it gets directly back from its investment in putting this working class to productive work – acquires more poignancy. This is because these underdeveloped or rural formations matter more as to how they further imperialist interests via the formations' own insecurity than as to how their development might add to value or wealth. Fruitful resistance to imperialism revalorises, through development and rising incomes, not only the underdeveloped formations but also, by implication, the global balance of forces. Successful resistance would also require the antidotes to neo-liberalism, which are expansionary fiscal and monetary policies financed in relative autonomy from the shackles of the international financial structure. In a nationalist capitalist environment, the national ruling classes have to temper their profits by limiting their own integration with world capital. The rate of wealth accumulation of the national bourgeoisie has to be capped by a ceiling that recirculates much of the social product within the national economy – a constraint that demolishes the very *raison d'être* of a comprador ruling class. Hence, for any underdeveloped or rural developmental and anti-imperialist agenda to be put into effect, the class structure of the state will need to be dominated by a working-class political formation that can bridge intra-working-class differences in an alliance against capital.

Unlike this desired outcome, identity-fuelled and inter-working class divisions in the AW have turned into ugly conflicts. Shifting notions of identity, especially Shiite–Sunni, are often presented by the mainstream as constituting fundamental divisions that criss-cross classes. In a gross falsification of history, such identities are assumed to be immutable across time and to form fault lines of bonding and organisation. These identities are taken as evidence that the immediacy of the cultural determinants of class are more pronounced than are economic ones, as if economic determinants are locked into a competitive game with cultural traditions. However, social classes cannot exist outside class relationships that tie them together; analysis of class in diverse social formations must begin at this point. It is within these relationships that class structures, including their history and evolution, are constituted. What a class is and does depends on how it is situated in relation to other classes; foremost of these is the US-led imperial financial class with its ideological power as a class. Multiple fragmenting identities or a single working-class identity rise or fall in relation to imperialist ideological hegemony. In the early twentieth century, the well-known colonial role in segmenting Arab society along identity lines failed in the face of the rising tide of world socialism. The Arab working classes and their inter-divisions mirror the rapport de force, which had recently come to include the retreat of the global left vis-à-vis the rise of imperialism.

The imperialist assault-and-control element is a determining moment (a principal historical relationship), shaping its ideological progeny into identities that divide working classes. In these social relationships, capitalists organise not only their relations to the means of production, but also into distributional arrangements that cement capital as a social relationship. This is the organised dimension of capital, a political process mediating its growing scope of action, in which state power represents the key articulating moment. Working classes, in relation to the dominant class, can maintain their organisation, their history and shared understanding of anti-imperialist or anti-capitalist struggles, and their collective experience, which together influence the cohesion of the working class a whole, including the peasantry. Class does not disappear beneath identity. It exists in relation to other classes and as a relationship to property in which legal arrangements enact the division of labour according to the prevailing structures of political and ideological power. At a very abstract level, class is the mediation of a particular state of being, materialised in the more general political form; this form is divisive in circumstances of defeat and retreat. These characteristics, in their commonalities and differences, are the outcome of the degree of cohesion within a class and of the balance of forces, including ideological ones, within a political structure.

Class is a real constituent of the agency of history, albeit, in its relationship to other classes. These relationships are materially grounded and cannot be wished or washed away by countervailing ideology in the guise of divisive identity. Various cultural attributes and qualities devolve to social groups in relation to the outcome of class struggle. A class, therefore, is the process that divulges the manifold social characters that exist in relation to capital. The repression endured by the working classes in the AW in relation to imperialism and its oil-control agenda emerges as a state of disarticulation between social condition and consciousness manifested in all sorts of defeats at the current historical moment. While working-class fragmentation in terms of religion and other cultural categories is pursued everywhere under the barrage of funding and the ideological warfare of capital, imperialism splinters more malevolently when it targets the intersection at which the ruinous social condition calls for anti-systemic working class action and solidarity. But, at the present stage, the degree to which people in the AW do or do not identify politically as members of a social class is far from exceptional in a comparative sense. And much like others, they do not exist socially outside the class system, either.

While there are precarious, and internally divided, working classes, there are also cases of cohesiveness and revolutionary thrust. Just prior to the uprising, for instance, strikes by Egyptian El Mahalla Workers and the Tunisian General Labour Union (UGTT) represented poles of resistance around which working-class solidarity formed and unified a spectrum of diverse pauperised strata (Cidamli 2008). Only later, in the post-uprising crisis, did political Islam – the historical brainchild of colonialism and imperialistically groomed for the transition – appear as an organised force (Corm 2015). The Islamic political expression in this case was not univocal; it remains contingent upon the instruments and opportunities that emerged from tacit support in imperialist quarters, where the aim is to abort the revolutionary momentum of the uprising. It is not the existence of a social class that should come into question; it is which kind of political action is forming in response to the assault sustained by working people in the AW and, more importantly, in relation to imperialism.

A Closing Comment

Between 1980 and 2015, around a third of the inhabitants of Arab cities were rural migrants. Most of those migrants have joined the already-impoverished ranks of the urban working classes that engage in low productivity, informal and poorly paid activity. In the shanty towns where the social services of the state have been cut back, a politically 'select' group of NGOs caters to these migrants. These are, for the most part, civil-society institutions of Islamic orientation. With the ebbing of socialist ideology, the migrants have been subjected to the doctrine of political Islam that indicts corrupt individuals but not the context in which these individuals operate, which is capitalism. The security apparatus of Arab regimes, the only effective state institution, was careful in its choice of malleable civil-society operatives. More radical groups were constrained, while those that did not question the comprador basis of peripheral capitalism were given full scope. As indicated in chapter 2, after the bread riots of 1977 Sadat cohabitated with the more docile elements of the Muslim Brotherhood; likewise, for some time before the uprising, Western-compliant sections of the Muslim Brotherhood were fully functional under the auspices of American NGOs.

Peasant and working-class property, which was thieved via the state, had become the property of the ruling class. The uprisings of 2011 came and went and, where no war erupted, elections were held, but no one questioned the past thefts of the ruling class. Doubtless, a political process falling in line with the vision and strategy of imperialism, bereft of economic and social rights, will deliver once and again a style of democratisation like that installed by the United States after the Iraq invasion. So long as the ideological apparatus for the realisation of the working class in the state is determined by imperialism, stolen wealth becomes the unquestionable entitlement of the ruling class. Noting that the labour share is too small to revive healthy growth, the principal policy tools that could rebalance the demand side of Arab economies, namely wealth redistribution and land reform, have been subjected to a coup de grace by the neo-liberal avalanche.

In view of the organic interlocking of the global economy, apolitical policy prescriptions focusing on demand-side Keynesianism to rebuild Arab national economies ring hollow. Even desirable more-expansionary fiscal and monetary policies are meaningless without tipping the balance of power and restraining the comprador bourgeoisie. By restraining, I mean least of all, allowing its expansion to proceed only in rationed money form denominated in national currency, without the capacity to transfer national currency abroad, as has been practised under Arab socialism. Arab socialist multiple exchange rates, interest rates and partial-barter trade resituate the rules of the game in favour of the distressed sectors of the economy and working-class incomes.

Regaining development means regaining policy autonomy under conditions of popular sovereignty. The positive relationship between policy space and positive developmental outcome is such a straightforward question that, in spite of its sensitivity, was addressed by the United Nations Conference on Trade and Development (UNCTAD): '[T]he idea of policy space refers to the freedom and ability of governments to identify and pursue the most appropriate mix of economic and social policies to achieve equitable and sustainable development' (2014). Yet, in the typical half-truth type of positioning resulting from the UN's subordination to the dominant imperialist power, it attributes loss of autonomy, in one instance, to 'various legal obligations emerging from multilateral, regional and bilateral agreements' (UNCTAD 2014). This appears as the UN Security Council deals with the possibility of regional wars escalating into global ones, and state sovereignty has become a by-product of a universally democratic international law in which honouring agreements is part of the gentlemanly behaviour of Western nations. Exponential growth through profit making in an open and integrated system calls for a higher rate of social debilitation in its underbelly to feed its objective path: what Meszaros (1995) designated as the metabolic rate of the reproduction of capital. In such an intrinsic relationship, violent forms of the exercise of class power determine much of autonomy. Class power is not the ahistorical person or group in the executive office with megalomaniac individual agency; it is the avalanche that is history, its dominant ideological vortex and monolithic institutions into which Arabs and Africans are born.

Often, social democratic policies skip the baleful conditions in the lowest ranks of the international production order. Looking at the barrage of Keynesian prescriptions as professed by UNCTAD, one would stand in awe at the naiveté of the idea that all countries can expand demand together, complementing each other and all rising into some sort of development heaven; of all things, such scenarios are envisaged with leading private sectors in state and economy. Private profits-determined global capital accumulation, taken as a totality, must raise the standards in one corner of the Third World at the expense of another, either in the First World or another layer of the Third. Absolute democratic Fordism is equivalent to socialism, where profits are publicly owned. Only when profit rates are publicly generated and equally distributed across national boundaries do the interests of the poorest countries positively synch with the outcome of demand reform in any middle-income country. In such a socialist world, exploitation and surplus value would soon vanish.

In reality, middle-income countries such as Brazil, Mexico, and so forth, are being placated by the extent to which misery and war plague the lowest echelons of the international division of labour (e.g., Yemen, Somalia, Mauritania and the Sudan). Without mention of the centrality of class antagonisms, Keynesian mantras obfuscate distributional mechanisms and strengthen the ideological hold of capital. They represent a way for the organised dimension of capital to manage accumulation by war and immiseration inflicted upon the *Lazarus* layers of Third World labour.[16] Worst of all, the

---

16 Even in such basic arenas of humanitarian intervention, as in lending to the hungry, capitalist policy is more about control than mercy. Consider for example the defunct FAO (2001) project that was to create an international lending mechanism to ease the liquidity constraints on net food-importing developing countries, so that when crops fail, they can borrow at concessional rates to buy food. In 2001, the initial fund required only $16 billion to get started, but donors refused to set up such a lending fund, even though it would earn profits, and preferred to see poorer countries borrow at higher rates to keep them under control.

putative reasons for the underdevelopment of the poorest have shifted from genetic to cultural inferiority.

Dispossessing peasants entails a further socialising of labour and production and an intensification of the contradictions of capital. Looking at the crisis of the rural sector in terms of inhibiting the realisation of value (labour power) leading to under-valorisation of labour is relevant to policy and to the building of rural–urban class alliances. A structural transformation dependant on a broad working-class alliance has to engage the new *Lazarus* class in the struggle for socialised production and forms of social property. Although transitions to socialism currently appear illusory, reforms involving a repricing mechanism are not an impossibility. Insofar as the social organisation of the dependent economy and its agricultural sector is concerned, two points arise from the foregoing emphasis on the value contradictions within the rural or underdeveloped sectors: first, there has to be a reinvention of a price system that revalorises labour and capitalises the national economy and the rural regions, with price guarantees and subsidies being part of that reinvention (Bettelheim 1975); second, through socialising agricultural property into collective or small-owned farms in such a way as to ensure that the social interest aligns with the private interest (land reform that combines productivity concerns with personal incentives and welfare). At the national level, retaining the social product for recirculation within national borders involves multilayered price engineering that ensures exchange- and interest-rate policies that lock in resources and an inter-industry price system that enhances output (regulated inter-industry prices). At a subordinate agricultural-sector level, guarantees for agricultural output, financing for agriculture at concessionary rates – and integrating agriculture into the economy via increased investment – represent the optimum strategies.

The fact that commodities can stand above people and dictate the allocation of resources stems from the way use value is valorised by a class structure that pits it against socially necessary labour. When alienated labour power is more valuable than the labourer, the problem cannot be solved by appealing to humanising the labour process. The profit-driven wage system under capitalism cannot be humanised, and if some national working strata appear more secure, it is usually at the expense of other national or extra-national workers. Redundant labour contributes to relations accumulation by its very redundancy or by its engagement in wars, including proxy imperialist wars. By metabolising humanity and nature in an organically interrelated process, one that knows no national boundary and whose mode of growth under financialisation extracts proportionately more of wealth by absolute surplus value, the production of the reserve army of labour not only becomes increasingly integral to the dynamics of capital, but also to its partial destruction.

What has to change, therefore, are the two seemingly unchangeable pillars of capital: the class structure, and the rate of surplus socialisation, both at the source (initial wealth redistribution) and the end product (taxing higher incomes): workers rule under more egalitarian conditions.

For the present, the same laws governing reproduction of society that created the calamity prior to the Arab Spring remain in place. Imperialist strategy continues to aim at further deconstructing the political underpinnings of working-class security, hence cheapening labour. Financial imperialism has expanded debt to the point where the labour of future generations will be commodified and held as collateral to steady the value and the profit rates from the order of fiat money that signifies the wealth of the ruling classes. In this early phase of the twenty-first century the imperialist grip on the economic channels that fuel inter-working class dividedness is ironclad. Now, as before, revolutionary consciousness must rise from outside the narrow boundaries of the economic struggle that only boosts sectional politics (Lenin 1902). Forms of action that mediate the narrow section (the particular) into the organisational whole (internationalist working-class politics) augur the rebirth of a global vision that empowers the Arab working classes and peasantry.

Chapter 6

PERMANENT WAR IN THE ARAB WORLD

This final chapter addresses the role of imperialist war in denying sovereignty to the Arab working masses and thereby sustaining a cheapened valuation of Arab resources for the purposes of metropolitan capital accumulation. The wars visited upon the AW are not an accident of history unrelated to the necessities of world capital. Carved up and remoulded by the continued practice of colonialism, imperialist aggression and re-colonisation, the AW represents an outstanding manifestation of permanent war theory (Luxemburg 1913; Lenin 1916). Oil in its raw form, together with the value of imperial rents wrought from its strategic control, represents a decisive constituent of the global accumulation process. US-led capital's control of oil by means of violence sustains its rate of expropriation and the stature of the US empire. As such, the articulation of the Arab social formation with US-led imperialism – the capitalist class cutting across national boundaries – issues from US-led hegemony and from wars of encroachment to seize the assets of the Arab region. To redress the declining contribution to the circuit of capital arising as a result of autonomous working classes retaining more of the value they created, US-led imperialism and its class allies regularly resort to military aggression. Militarism boosts war-related technological development and financial expansion – and heightens the rates of dispossession cum devalorisation of insecure social formations, in particular, Arab formations. Hence, as Mao Zedong (1938) might have put it in today's context: the AW is articulated with world capital by the barrel of the gun. What the necessity of war to imperialism implies for Arab development is that imperialist belligerence or the serious threat thereof can result in the collapse of the state as a potential medium for working-class representation in the international political order. So far, where war is not already completely ravaging society, poor development outcomes of the neo-liberal genre characterise Arab development.

In this concluding chapter, I address some aspects of the combined condition of war cum botched Arab development as the *necessary* product of imperialist aggression *qua* permanent war. With Israel and the IS in the process of constructing ethnically pure states, effacing internationally recognised borders and flouting the conventions of the international security arrangement, the threats emanating from the region implicate the entire planet. Unless there grows an internationalist alternative from between the fault lines of contradictions, wars will continue to create a sustainable downward social spiral that fragments the working classes along ethnic and sectarian lines. More important, as a result of financialisation, the implications of dehumanising the labour process in one corner of the world reconstitute the power of capital everywhere (Patanaik and Patnaik 2015). For the first time since the postwar period, the declining share of wages in the central labour–aristocratic nations unequivocally shows the organic ties of the global working classes.[1] Their descent is not only coincidentally related to the descent of the bombed nations or the poorest; it is caused by it. There end the flimsy falsehoods of Western labour aristocracy, and here begins the search for a theory of struggle originating from the conditions of starving refugees in war-torn areas.

War and the Comprador Class

Although no state would be the realisation of the political ideal under capitalism, the Arab state has long since lost even the semblance of a supporting role for national capital, and it rarely embodies the rights of its citizenry by intermediation. The imperialist-dominated Arab state has to estrange the working class from its rights. It creates the external constraints on the development of civil liberties, which mostly through repression, as distinct from the salient psychological mind-twisting propaganda, have become internalised by much of the population as self-policing measures. As a higher degree of the motto 'better be feared than loved', the state is an arbitrage by the exercise of violent repression or pacification by direct handout rather than promoting consent by representation and, conjunctionally, wealth through productivity gains. Each Arab formation has a specific identity determined by its own class structure and the rapport of interlocked internal and external forces. As the ruling merchant class integrates with foreign capital, it becomes

---

1 Measuring output per worker in the centre conceals the direct and indirect value transfers from the periphery, which have a positive bearing on the reproduction of the central working classes, and whose transformation into price of production raises the objective levels of productivity in the centre. The fact that the level of real Northern wages declines – or staggers behind productivity, by a large margin, despite such objective grounds that should raise it – could only mean that the Northern working classes are paying the price for the socialist ideological retreat to which they have contributed. This outcome alone should bring into focus the organic ties of labour worldwide.

part of – and materially rooted in – those external forces. It is half-witted to address the national and international class links or their impersonal, objective and historical relationships in terms of quantity or percentages assigned to either internal or external decision makers to apportion blame. Historical class relationships are also the prevailing balance of forces, or the overdetermined history, which obviously has not favoured the working classes in the AW. One cannot overemphasise how misleading it is to conceptualise class reality anywhere in terms of national bereft of international, especially when the circuit of capital is transnational and the quantity of value assessed in a given chronological period is only meaningful in relation to its constituting social relationships developing in social time.[2] As argued in the previous chapter, value is subject–object, it is the physical commodity and the relationships organising the commodity, while classes are interrelated transnational relationships that the Arab merchant class has integrated with the social relationship that is imperialism.

The merchant *qua* comprador class feeds off the conversion of national resources into dollar assets or acts as a henchman for imperialism, serving its strategic positioning objectives. The merchant class in charge of the social formation is an extreme version of the comprador. It holds a necrotrophic relationship with the national economy. It usurps value from the working class without reinvesting in it because it simply does not depend on rising national productivity to enhance its wealth. The inherited despotism of the old feudal formations, unshattered by liberal bourgeois revolutions, and lingering amidst the increasingly severe accumulation crisis, re-emerges in new divisive sectional (ideological) guises to deliver the regimentation of the labour process.

As it has been anecdotally put, the rich Arabs are protected by imperialist air power and may earn more interest on their wealth abroad than on revenues from productive national undertakings. With the exception of the post-independence industrialisation drive, the merchant side of the Arab economy

---

2 Social time is that time in which revolutionary consciousness comes to fruition as a result of the inherent contradiction between subject and object in the course of practice, the rise of revolutionary consciousness as the working class (subject) fights to lay hold to the use value that has been expropriated from it through the private channels of accumulation (object), after which society leaps forward at shorter intervals in chronological time. To parody the meaning of social time with the myth of Sisyphus as retold by Camus: all the quantities of rocks he rolled up the hill for any span of chronological time would have meant nothing until he came to the realisation that the gods have inflicted an unspeakable injustice upon him and that he had to stop them. Social time is that warp in chronological time in which awakening and revolutionary consciousness either arises from the condition of revolt or brings about revolt.

was the only side carefully reared by colonialism; and in the neo-liberal era it had returned to the same position it had occupied in colonial times. However, in an Arab context, the sheer belligerence of imperialism calls into question the usual characterisation of the relationship between a postcolonial formation and the present imperial powers. The frail sovereignty of the Arab state, its precarious development, and its devastation by war constitute a case of development by wars of encroachment as opposed to industrial and trade-based exchange. In the choice between putting people to work for cheap wages or literally cheapening people, US-led imperialism integrates the AW through the latter mode. The condition of actual or potential defeat to the US–Israeli military alliance shapes an easily penetrable Arab environment for such state of play –war making. The calculated risks to imperialism are low and becoming lower. In comparison, the East Asian *cordon sanitaire*, where a stronger correlation between development and security concerns prevails, imperialist capital flows and the influence of a militarily toothless Japanese state were able to pass certain welfare gains as a result of pouring resources into manufacturing and other tradable sectors. By contrast, the bellicosity of a US-led alliance and its sponsored Arab warlords who masquerade as nationalists but whose material reproductive base rests in geopolitical rents and international financial circles, reverse industrialisation-based development. War itself is necessarily but not exclusively the end goal and the linchpin of most social structures in the Arab region.

In addition to the historical momentum of imperialist aggression to redress power positions, the primacy of politics or the sociological character of imperialism involves the act of strengthening the rule of capital by foregoing some intermediate monetary benefits. Although such concerns for power, control and stability of rule are central to the resilience of capital, as sociological relations underlining imperialist practice they hold much more for the AW than elsewhere. This is mainly the result of the imperialist consideration by which the politics of war and, conjunctionally, oil control overshadow the issue of developing the Arab region's productive capacity for the purpose of trade. The circuitous financial-gain channel for imperialism occurs through war, the power derived therefrom and ideological spinoffs rather than trade in civilian end-use commodities.

War in an underdeveloped context is under-valorisation and control through the disempowerment or alienation of humans and resources. There are two factual points that envelop the case of stripping Arab resources from their owners *qua* producers and then cheapening them. First, there is not much for Western powers in trade gains to be accrued from the pittance of moneyed income of the AW, save for the Gulf states whose funds are already under the purview of the dominant financial power. Apart from oil, there is precious little to desire when the share of labour income of non-Gulf Arab counties is less than .5 per cent of world income. Secondly, militarism's spending (military Keynesianism) or, better yet, war spending are ends in themselves because they redistribute real value to the capitalist class and expand financial assets – simultaneously through higher credits (military spending or war debt) afforded to the financial class and austerity. Foster et al. (2008) reasserted the Kaleckian position that US military spending grew because of capitalist empire rather than the need to contain the Soviet threat by soaking up the US's vast surplus and helping stave off economic stagnation. This position was also shared by Baran and Sweezy (1975) and Mandel (1975). As true as this proposition may be, it is secondary to the fact that wars of encroachment capture, destroy or under-valorise real human and physical value in the Third World.

More so in this period of financialisation (the existence of a huge money supply relative to real output) than in previous ones, military spending and its consummation of surplus are insufficient on their own for the expansion of surplus without the actualisation of war. War upon the AW is not to be solely gauged in terms of degree of surplus or a lower rate of accumulation reaching a threshold that vents itself out by enacting conflict. Imperialist war is an inherent sociological condition that steadies the rule of capital in relation to the rate of capital accumulation. Abdel-Malek (1977) cautions against overemphasis on quantification in the explanation of imperialism, especially as the Third World is trivialised because of its low share of dollar output from total world income. Lauesen and Cope (2015) brilliantly capture the value relationship at the root of the imperialist drive in terms of the transformation of values into prices.

> In a world where the market price of goods tends to be global while the market price of labour capacity varies because of class struggle – both historical and contemporary – the result is a redistribution of value from countries with a low market price for labour capacity to countries with a high market price for such. Thus imperialism must be explained in the context of the transformation of value into price. To claim that this shifts the concept of exploitation from the sphere of production to that of circulation, however, is disingenuous. It is human labour that creates value and surplus labour that creates surplus value. However, (surplus) value is not a physical property that labour adds to goods like some kind of molecule incorporated and stored in the product. Rather, value and the transformation of value into market price is the result of social relations between labour and capital and between different capitals. It is the transformation from value to market price that ensures that the accumulation process continues on an expanded scale. This expanded circuit of capital

involves the transformation of value and surplus value into profit, and the transfer of value from the South to North according to the low prices paid for goods produced in the former by the latter. Exploitation does not, therefore, occur in one particular sector of production or national economy; it is the result of the total global capital accumulation process. (Lauesen and Cope 2015)

War as a principal conduit for ensuring that the transformation of value into price responds to the demands of imperialist accumulation. Once the war link in the global production structure is highlighted, the locus of internationalist class struggle should shift to war zones whose value is being stripped away and destroyed. Quantification by the money form of an average quantity of labour time (as in quantity of labour is the substance of value) whose price would revert to its real value or natural price is a Ricardian interpretation of the labour theory of value and not Marx's position. As mentioned in the previous chapter, Marxian labour power – the commodity – is like any other commodity: an inner relationship of value to use, value externally manifested in exchange value, not some arithmetic average of different quantities of labour measured at a specific moment in time. The physiological (quantity) aspects of value only presuppose the historically specific value relations under capitalism because the quantity of labour is determined via moneyed exchange. The process of realising the internal contradiction of a commodity (value or socially necessary labour against use value or labour's productivity) through exchange – as in pricing it with a wage rate – involves all the trappings of history and the class struggle, including no less, imperialist wars. The capitalist has through class power an inherent interest in under-pricing labour power with lower wages. Trying to make value and moneyed profits agree directly and without contradiction is 'much more difficult to solve than that of squaring the circle. [...] It is simply an attempt to present that which does not exist as in fact existing' (Marx 1863). At this stage in the analysis, let us just posit that labour power is a historically, politically and economically determined variable in whose valuation imperialist war is a central component.

Only when value is considered as immediate substance (physiological quantity) – a substance without a history of becoming as per the law of value, or as in an average quantity of labour – can one say that the Occidental working classes are principal wealth producers whose wages are justified by higher productivity; but on its own such an average does not exist and, if it did, it cannot produce surplus value. Obviously people have always worked to produce, but only under capitalism is the allocation of labour determined by the exchange value of the labour power commodity. Typically, Marx always looks for the historical specificity under capitalism to explain its workings. The various concrete labouring conditions have always existed as natural laws for the reproduction of society. However, the social laws of development specific to commodity exchange under capitalism are reflected as the intermediation of the value/use value contradiction in moneyed form (Ilyenkov 1960). In this sense, the law of resolving the inner contradiction of value through moneyed exchange is the universal, which is also a set of heterogeneous elements resolved, not by adding different quantities of labour directly, but indirectly through its appearance in the price system. The contradictions in Marx's system do not end; they resolve into another stage of becoming while remaining preserved and negated simultaneously (more on this thorny topic in the section below on Barbaric development).

While on the same subject of labour power and its value, there are no absolute advantages in productivity across the advanced economies because of the heterogeneity of productive capacities and the class-muzzled criterion by which productivity is assessed and measured. Emmanuel (1972, 424) points out that 'if it were really comparative productivity that determined wages and incomes in general, the underdeveloped countries should have a wage level and a standard of living higher than those of the advanced countries, since their advantage in the exported article is usually greater than their disadvantage in the imported one'. Without distinguishing labour power from the labourer as a commodity and designating the class process of valorising labour power below its value, we will have the Ricardian substance-only labour theory of value, which Marx (1863) thought invalidates the labour theory of value and restores an ahistorical explanation of the sources of profit, namely as in invested capital. Marx (1847) considered labour power as a commodity whose determination follows the rules applied to other commodities, and he eschewed such delusional propositions as: wages are determined by productivity. A similar point was also propounded by Kalecki (1943) and Emmanuel (1972) who argued that wages are determined in the product and not in the labour market – the labour market affects labour only in relation to, and as a subcomponent of, workings of the broader product market.[3] More recently, Cope (2015) argues that although increased mechanisation results in the creation of more use-values per unit of time, only the intensified consumption of labour power can generate added value and, since wages are not the price paid for the result of labour but the price of labour power, higher wages are not the automatic consequence of productivity gains accruing to capital.

3 For Kalecki, the real wage – wages over prices – is determined simultaneously by the macro conditions of monopoly power and resource leakage abroad. However, because the general price level rises as a result of inflation bringing wages down, the power of unions and the working class organisations have to kick in to raise the nominal wage (demand higher wages) to stabilise or raise the real wage level or the purchasing power of workers.

What often goes unnoticed in the debate is that the whole structure of accumulation through war, realising and then raising the surplus, has at its core a value relationship at work. Deploying the huge Western moneyed surplus in military spending is of relevance, but it is only one part of the story. The cycle of *deploy value, destroy/create value and revalorise* in terms of class-power-mediated prices comes full circle as a result of the practice of imperialist war, which also plays a role in ensuring the rule of capital. Without theorising war into the circuit of value, there is only partial theory. As an aside, the law of value as the historical process that manifests itself in different forms of surplus-value-creation moments, includes, as stressed throughout, the continued re-enactment of commercial exploitation, as colonial and imperialist wars that create massive numbers of wage slaves and cheap resources just as in chattel slavery, but on a much larger scale given the death rates from hunger and wars. Violence is central to capitalism, and its conjoint sociological relationships reassert the relationship of imperialist looting time and again. Here one is looking at a historical value-creation process by violent dispossession whose relevance is underplayed in the conventional literature because of Eurocentric overemphasis on dollar-denominated income, which is higher in the developed world largely as a result of imperialist wars of aggression, past and present. One ought to ask the obvious question: Could the dollar itself, or dollar-denominated wealth, be what it is without the colonial or imperialist wars? Reverting to our own Arab and historically contingent setting, war is – by the inalienability of conflict to historical development – key to the relationship of the ruling Arab consortia to imperialism, even if it means the destruction of the assets of the Arab state.

Wars and the permanent arms economy realise moneyed value and reshape the social conditions that produce value. Apart from employing millions in the creation, destruction and realisation of value, the dynamic of war itself nourishes military technology and its civilian spinoffs using mainly public funds. War maintains the technological edge of the US-led capitalist class, whose institutional structure is the US proper; technological advantage is the material basis for supremacy in the international division of labour. Financially, funding for wars expands US indebtedness in the dollar space; hence, the financial assets available for institutional finance to grab from the share of the working class and expand. Enlarged dollar-money supply has in turn to be underwritten by further military expansion and strategic imperialist repositioning. All of these interrelated and self-propelling processes compose the totality of capital into which the war upon the AW has to be explained as a key moment. Having experienced the highest frequency of conflicts globally (SIPRI various years), the AW is already the soft underbelly of capital, highly receptive and regenerative of permanent war, which is a principal stabilising component of capital.

The growth of credit expended on wars entails higher tax levies and lower social spending on the central working classes: the all-too-familiar austerity shifting a higher share of the social product to the capitalist class. In the AW, the war relationship, and its attendant consequences in the surplus drain, commodify human lives – along with its monetised or non-monetised labour power – and realises them in sudden death or shorter life expectancy relative to the historically determined potential. Like technology, violence is endogenous (innate) to capitalism and transpires as a result of the fetishism (estrangement from direct social control) that commands the allocation of resources. Wars literally consume human lives and other valuable resources whose destruction is central to the commercial exploitation of the vanquished periphery.

When value as an internal contradiction is considered in its stages of transformation, or in its state of becoming – as concrete labour assumes – an abstract form in moneyed exchange determined by capital's ideological power, war making subdues peripheral labour to the requirement of central profit making. In the conditions of exchange resulting from shifting power balances, and according to which social values, the value and use-value of labour, conform to ruling-class power or imperialism, the dying Arabs and Africans in imperialist wars become also real producers of wealth. Their premature deaths are the initial building blocks in a production chain that knows no national borders. Commercial exploitation, which unwillingly joined the slave labourer to his or her labour power and extinguished their lives in short time spans, is re-enacted in war that forces Arab workers into self-defence and extinguishes their lives in short time spans. The organised dimensions of capital, its bequeathed culture and institutions, cannot be cultivated or personally commanded to arrest blind competitive accumulation and the violent-death process. On labour's side, as evidenced by the defeat of peace movements in the twentieth and twenty-first centuries, organised labour was also incapable of halting imperialist wars of aggression. Up until this instance in history, imperialist violence has escaped socially responsible forms of control.

Much of the AW is undergoing a dual process of debilitating containment leading to self-implosion or an outright war of aggression. The Arab comprador-merchant class, through its excessive practices, undermines its own security (at times its own security of person), sovereignty and state as part of a healthy apoptosis (a destruction that benefits capital) rendered by the historically given order guiding its alliance with imperialism.

In an Arab context, national economic relations and policies are not afforded the chance to mature and steer politics in line with nationalist concerns. Externally imposed politics appear as a *force majeure*, with development of economic relations subsumed by political objectives; at this historical juncture, with immense global democratic forces bottled up and unable to find a political form of organisation, and with so many wars fragmenting working people, the horizon for the development of nationalist objectives appears elusive. But, as was noted in the second chapter, the higher velocity of exchange has further compressed time and space. Contingent upon a *volte face* in the Eurocentrism of Western communism, just as finance creates booms and busts, the rise and fall of revolutionary consciousness in tandem with class-based organisation may mimic the sharp deviation in the business cycle. In any case, that remains to be born from the conditions of struggle.

Only narrow margins are afforded to nationalist development policies, and the burden of imperialist aggression forces these societies to use their resources for military ends or to comply with the terms of imperialism. The secretion of the comprador class, its subsequent compliance with usurpation-cum-tribute policies packaged as neo-liberalism, and slow economic asphyxiation, are manifestations of class flux during times of socialist ideological retreat. Such complicity in the case of Libya, Syria and Yemen laid the objective grounds for the war economy and its associated class transformations: the rise of the war bourgeois class and the war-indigent proletariat. The 'pragmatism' of surrender to a militarily superior imperialism and its economic policies ensure the exacting of tribute via freer market policies. Conversely, the ideological victory of US-led imperialism over socialism and the Arab working class is not limited to extracting rents from the Arab region. Given oil's strategic value, imperial rents flow from the rest of the globe to US-dominated markets by virtue of US-led imperialism's violent deconstruction of the Arab and surrounding regions.

The rising insecurity of Arab formations after the invasion of Iraq also intensified the rate of resource usurpation from the region (as measured by the rates of labour and capital flights in UN 2008). Not much is left for the local population to use to improve its lot in life. The advance of neo-liberalism as an ideology has compromised past gains and, even though national control of oil has already been lost due to financialisation (oil was listed in the commodity market in the mid-1980s), to add insult to injury, oil privatisation is back on the development agenda.[4] After the Arab Spring's failure to

---

4 Whereas Iran is often slotted as the next candidate for deconstruction by US-led imperialist war, it appears that the Saudi Vision 2030 plan neo-liberal reform may assist in bringing down Saudi Arabia first. The Saudi Vision 2030 plan, a development plan based on private-sector promotion under open private accumulation channels mechanisms and robber-baron capitalism, might deplete Saudi Arabia of all its resources and accentuate the schisms upon which intercommunal conflict spirals. Incidentally

introduce socialisation policy and the dismay that followed, the region has been once more subjected to the full force of colonial war or to even worse anti-development agendas. On a parallel track, with resources being directed to private ends, the speed with which growth in national wealth is evaporating without a trace of development will further abet the cheap funding of jihadist elements that under the guise of adherence to religious law further commodify human life at the behest of capital. There is a real negative dialectic, or a downward development spiral, that is commensurate with the slide in socialist ideology or with the departure of Eurocentric Marxism from the recognition that value theory and class war begin where imperialism does the most harm: the AW and Africa.

With the rise of jihadists violently opposing already sectional/sectarian regimes, the Arab working class holds less and less control over its own destiny. The frailty of the global left is such that all regional powers are either prostrating themselves at the door of the US empire or wishing to submit; but the empire is not accepting 'yes' for an answer for fear of peace breaking out. Meanwhile, the international avarice for control of regional oil has intensified. Open regional conflicts after the Arab Spring have increased, and many of the national authoritarian regimes have further concentrated power by capitalising on the ideological defeat of popular forces after the uprisings. When a social contract with the national proletarians cannot be written, the classes at the helms of these regimes exhibit an inherent tendency to grow by integrating themselves with international financial capital. The underside of this mode of integration is twofold: first, in addition to the destruction and realisation of value en masse by means of war, value-denoted assets (things without owners) become potential cheap material for capital; and, second, the Arab masses are held for ransom by US-led imperialism, along with their own oil, which many around the world will continue to pay for by holding dollars.

an open conflict in the Arabian Peninsula, in view of American self-reliance on oil and the pressure such conflict may exert on China may boost the cycle of accumulation by militarism, value destruction and power restructuring for US-led capital. Contingently upon the flux in the global power balances, or what would the setting of the Saudi Kingdom ablaze deliver in power and value relations to US-led capital, such historical course of events may just be around the corner. Apart from the recent peak in critiquing the Saudi human rights record in the mainstream media, the higher than usual war and spending deficits drawing down the sovereign fund, there is an immense looting party waiting to be had by all those bidding to build the future Saudi Arabia. How Saudi Arabia Wants to Privatize Its Oil but Keep the Profits, http://sputniknews.com/middleeast/20160112/1032998730/saudi-aramco-privatization-pillage.html#ixzz45xIth8Av (viewed 12 February 2016).

Barbaric Development

If, despite vast resources, development still remains poor and capitalism imparts very little progress to the AW, a case of capitalist decadence á la Luxemburg can be argued (Luxemburg 2013). The notion of capitalist decadence, as used in the early twentieth century, signifies descent into barbarism (per Luxemburg's famous statement that the choice for humanity was now between socialism and barbarism); one could approach development outcomes in Arab countries that are exposed to wars as a case of descent into barbarism, especially with so little in international solidarity to arrest collapse. Although the lack of capacity and modern technology imply underdevelopment, the crux of development or the lack thereof could be explained by the success of anti-imperialist fronts composed of national and cross-border alliances. At a rudimentary level, the defining relationship in crystallising (as in palpable proof of) revolutionary consciousness is when labour as the agent of history commandeers the circuits of capital; this is just another way of saying that the degree development is the degree of independence from the wage system or wage slavery. The least-developing countries, principally African and Arab states – where the extraction of raw material is vital to global capital accumulation and the *rapport de force* is detrimentally in favour of the imperialist/former colonist – are areas where the terms *decadence*, *reverse development*, and often also *barbarism* emerge. Insofar as the AW is concerned, the belligerence of US-led imperialism expands in direct proportion to its historical momentum for control and the relevance of oil as a strategic commodity. US dollar seignorage and the oil-dollar standard require that other capitalist circles with territorial/strategic control ambitions be held at bay.

There is unity in the relationship between oil for its own sake and oil as means for furthering control. As to the 'for its own sake' part of the story, at more than 10 per cent of world trade (means of transport ranks second at 3 per cent, using the Standard International Trade Classification (SITC) at the 3-digit level), dollarising oil represents a central goal for US-led capital. On the control side, the energy share from oil of still-rising powers (China and India in particular) in the developing world is twice that of OECD; add to that a high oil-import dependency, and these countries become even more vulnerable to the strategic control element (Foster 2010). Account taken of the scaremongering related to its exhaustion, oil is strategic in its own right as collateral against dollar-seignorage and in how it appertains to all levels of the value-production chain (Patnaik 2008). Nearly all production processes require oil as input. Although humanity may have grown in numbers without such high dependence on oil, the reality is that world population growth has expanded with direct input from oil-condensed energy content, and the sudden withdrawal of such an energy source may precipitate instant crisis, hence the strategic value.

That is why serious discussion on the causes of wars cannot avoid the oil issue. Even when discussants centre on the balancing act of the US economy – Petras (2011a) uses the formula 'Republic versus Empire' to label the contradictory relationship of militarised, financialised American global hegemony to the health of the underlying US economy and the material security of its population – the foremost premise that drives the empire is strategic oil control. Strengthening control over oil resources or, inversely, weakening the popular hold on resources, provides US-led capital with more than adequate leverage on most oil-dependent countries.

The oil-dollar nexus and, in particular, the dollar-priced barrel bolsters the power of the US-led capital class that underwrites the credit needed to maintain the stable dollar as the world currency (Patnaik 2008). This is all the more relevant when financialisation and earnings through financial channels have come to represent more than half of corporate profits by 2010 (Fine 2010). The US-led capital class overstretches both its military reach and its credit/financialisation, and for this it has to re-empower itself. The debts of the United States are not solely the state's debts. As mentioned in the introduction, the debts of the social formation are the sum of private and public debts; however, there are also the global-transaction guarantees that the financial standing of the United States backs, especially as global money supply (mostly dollarised) has grown to three times real global output over the neo-liberal era. The hegemony of the United States over several strategic areas, particularly in the AW, offers its ruling class a vantage point in terms of collateral against the future; the Federal Reserve rate policy sets the tempo of global money transactions. Pricing oil by the dollar and calibrating the level of instability of the AW to how well the US-led financial class assures itself of increasing power, allows it to snatch a higher share of the global financial rents. The US ruling class is the envy of other capitalist classes as it enjoys rents upon rents.

The issue of stability or instability (war) in the AW, its tilting of power balances in favour of the US-led camp, has an objective bearing on the undervalorisation of resources and its positive ideological bonuses to capital. But at the same time it bears upon financial grab just as oil control does. The control of the circular flow of Arab petrodollars for T-bills or weapons sales is secondary to the much more significant category of imperial rents through circuitous dollar-seignorage financial rents from the rest of the world; but because such regional control is key to the ongoing and worsening real-value snatch from the working classes globally (austerity riding on the back of neo liberal ideological strength), aggression against the AW becomes the mainstay of US foreign policy. If it were not for these material undercurrents, the theory of imperialism would become a matter of psychological whim and would lose much of its political–economic grounding.

Accumulation in the age of financial imperialism grows via a two-pronged approach to resolve the constant debacle of overproduction: expansion of civilian end-use commodities and of military/war-spending (Lenin 1916). Crises, whether the downturn of the business cycle in the 2008 financial lapse or in permanent wars, further displace civilian end-use commodity realisation (the role of profits derived from the sale of commodities in the market) and boosts the role of aggressive ventures through encroachment wars. As argued, military spending and war are not only a way of loosening the realisation bottlenecks (the consummation of commodities in their sale and consumption) when surpluses cross a certain threshold, but they are also a way of reasserting capital's hegemony. Because regulating capitalist competition alone would not avert downturns – crisis is a permanent feature of capitalism (Sweezy 1981) unless one eliminates surplus value – permanent war has already been described as the leading practice of imperialism, the means whereby the mounting difficulties arising from the predicament of maintaining profit rates while balancing out the production and distribution sides are resolved (Lenin 1916). Lenin emphasised that militarism represents a key relationship in the global accumulation process under monopoly capitalism, which does not preclude assessing imperialist militarism as action against the tide of revolutionary organisation and consciousness. However, in more concrete terms, Lenin (1916) as well as Luxemburg (1913) posited that war is permanent, because the drive for the division of colonies and spheres of influence for finance capital to maintain accumulation pits global powers against each other (Lenin 1916). In his critique of Kautsky, Lenin (1918) also made the point that these inter-imperialist differences are not reconcilable because war's inherence to capital is part of its state of being and cannot be mediated through inter-imperialist policy that might halt war (ultra-imperialism). Capitalism would be going against its very nature.

Under capitalism, there was no moment at which global accumulation would have gained enough momentum to lift investment and consumption simultaneously. I have in mind the social conditions in the developing world, which is often omitted from a reductionist global business cycle frame of analysis (price-based). In differentiating modern imperialism from its early twentieth-century forms, Foster (2015) sees that financialised capital has a built-in tendency to advance by war 'occurring in the context of what top U.S. foreign policy strategists are calling a "New Thirty Years' War" unleashed by Washington for strategic control of the Middle East and the surrounding regions'. The crisis is further exacerbated because finance disparages the real production process and, as mentioned above, its expropriation of the share of labour takes place by a combination of austerity at home and war abroad. Financial institutions wed themselves closely to the state, as the 'too big to fail' US banks and similar monopolies exercise power to extract value by decreasing the basic-living share of labour. Such unstoppable expropriation can only proceed by mystifying financial processes. Fictitious moneyed debts are bestowed with divine sanctity to the point where few propose social alternatives to irreproachable austerity and encroachment wars. The mass of fictitious capital, that is, the layers upon layers of unpayable debt, which are underwritten by the hegemony of US-led capital, has to flow freely into higher returns low-wage sanctuaries or higher risk cum higher returns areas. The profit rate is gauged against real and financial capital and because so much credit was created for which there is no corresponding real activity, the drive to raise profits becomes ever more aggressive. Although in accounting terms the drain through the open capital accounts was plain to see, in post–Arab Spring states, especially Egypt, not a single thought was given to delinking the national economy from international financial containment through indebtedness. Also, not a thought was given to the fact that it is quasi-impossible for the bourgeois state apparatus, including the whole edifice of mainstream social science, to propagate any truth that may endanger capital's rule. Of the fallacies promoted against socialism, the adage that people have to queue for hours to buy a loaf of bread has become so engrained after so much inculcation by apparatuses of capital that social policy alternatives were completely written off the map of viable alternatives.

In insecure and dependent formations, such as Arab countries, the subordination of state to capital is more definitive. Ruling capital, the association of local to foreign bourgeoisie, is inspirited by imperialist forces in its seizing of the state. The collusion between the state and financially integrated capital manifests itself in persistent deflationary policies at home, the most usurping of which is the stabilisation of the national currency with the dollar under open capital accounts. The vile trinity of weak unions and proletarian power, dollar-pegged exchange-rate regimes and free capital flows erodes the already-low labour share through rising general consumer price levels and dollar-reserves building to guarantee the conversion of a national currency becoming ever so cheap by monopoly pricing, yet converted at fixed rates for dollars. Apart from the Gulf States, the Arab central banks subsidise the wealthier class by maintaining the currency conversion rate from the drawing-down of national assets to keep the wealth of the owning class steady in the dollar.

Let us re-posit the all too well-known fact about the rise of financial capital but deal with another disastrous spinoff of which: financial capital expands more by snatching a bigger share of the existing surplus than by expanding that surplus through larger markets and productivity gains; hence, it requires a stabilisation of the exchange rate to hold the value of its assets steady, and inflation to deprive the working class of a higher share of income. In Arab formations, the alliance of comprador with international financial capital sanctifies capital-accounts openness, despite the pressures that idle reserve and capital outflows exert on the national economy. Not once did the word 'regulation' stand out in the post–Arab Spring policy discussions. The leakage resulting from capital and trade openness cripples national macro policies. It is not that comprador-hijacked Arab countries have a choice any longer; they simply lose control and regiment fiscal spending by reducing primary spending (the sort of spending on schooling and health, which is the austerity dictated by the IFIs), thereby short-changing labour. An unrestrained market mechanism, in the presence of a war-bent imperialist force dominating the political process through its proxies, bleeds national resources to a higher degree by reducing the working-class share of the social product. Consequently, the growing imbalance between working-class consumption and the flight of resources will, contingent on the ideological hold of capital over society and state, contribute to splitting society at the seams – as already happened prior to the Arab Spring.

When US-led capital seizes the oil jugular, it also pressures different contending circles of capital into further acquiescing to its dollar-debt expansion. What simple accounting conceals is that a class in charge of an empire enjoying dollar-seignorage and imperial rents incurs no losses in permanent wars. Borrowing almost indefinitely in its own currency affords it power over its lenders and pushes the lenders to support its military adventurism, as they fear that loss of hegemony over strategic areas may cause dollar devaluation (dollar devaluation erodes world savings). The argument that imperialism has had no vested interest in invading the Third World because it is dollar-costly to the US overlooks the relationship of imperialist subjugation, which is central to the value foundation of the dollar. It also lumps the US working class with its ruling class willy-nilly. In truth, the money form is an appearance that does not explain much on its own. When the British Empire waned after World War I, the pound circulated by US charity (Patnaik 2008). Wars of imperialist conquest are central to the value of the dollar, which is both signification of value and instrument of repression.

Imperialist assaults in Palestine, Yemen, Syria, Iraq and elsewhere restructure power positions and standing and are crucial to accumulation by expropriation. Colonial and imperialist policy in an Arab context de-industrialises the colonised or hegemonised economy and thereby renders it a pedestal to the colonialist's own economy; furthermore, this policy prices the resources and values of the subjected population by its degree of control relative to value. The power behind imperialist price setting and commercial exploitation is not the typical monopoly power related to high entry costs or prohibitive technological know-how. It is brute violence from which historical surplus value has already been amassed by the successor states of colonial powers (Abdel-Malek 1981).

Imperial rents to the US-led financial class are not only significant, but they have become the gyroscope of the system's stability. The power of financial capital had reached such heights by 2008 that it could shift its debts onto the balance sheets of central banks while continuing to borrow and expand even after the crash. After World War II, part of the imperial rents and tribute flows through financial channels to US-led capital continued to act as bribes to central working classes. The often-touted idea of Western labour aristocracy that reform leads to revolution, flopped. Instead, reform led to retrogression in revolutionary consciousness in the centre. It further boosted the wages of central working classes and the wealth of aristocratic nations as per Emmanuel (1972). Once the struggle shifts away from the point of production to the sphere of exchange (circulation), 'the struggle ceases to be fundamentally a class war of the wage workers in resistance to the extraction of surplus value by the exploiters, and becomes a question of merely regulating the exchange process by the state, i.e.[,] of organizing capitalism' (Browder 1933, 35). In circulation, fed partially by war tribute and superexploitation from which the share of wages of western workers' rises, workers and capitalists frequently share the same interests: as in capital growing by imperialist looting and passing some of the gains to allied sections of Western labour. However, when the struggle of workers focuses on the conditions of production, for instance, 'do not bomb Arabs for the oil we use in our cars and factories', by focusing on the point of origin in production the struggle of workers veers closer to an internationalist class war.

The sociological underpinnings of imperialism gained strength as a result of labour's putting nationalism before internationalism and compromise before anti-systemic struggle, combined with capital's awareness of the need to discipline its blinkered competition to ensure the sturdiness of its hegemony. Under neo-liberalism, while the share of global labour fell as a result of international capital becoming homogenised, resistance became divided and less organised. Through economic openness, capital's unhindered progress integrated outlying national bourgeoisies and commodified their countries' resources including in some cases their air and water. In this condensation of power under the leadership of the US financial rentier class, there emerged a new general condition whose causal determination, rooted in the tectonic plates of capital's underlying dynamics, transpire as immediacy in its politics.

Whatever exigencies of accumulation reported in quarterly profit rates dictate, the current nomenklatura of the bourgeoisie introduces changes to the historical legacy of the institutions of the Cold War, freeing its hands for re-writing old international treaties, concocting aggressive new ones and encroachment wars. The higher rate of integration of capital, its homogeneity, also allows it to decide its rate of profit before wages, especially so that no internationally organised labour movement can effectively oppose the status quo with a viable form of organisation and ideological alternative.

History has borne out the point made by Arghiri Emmanuel in 1970, when he posited that it is difficult for the interests of the richer and poorer international labouring classes to converge at a given point in time. Whenever international working class interests converge, through the primacy of politics or the sociological underpinnings of capital, the ruling central class dips into its purse and sows the divisions. The knack for economising, as in trying to tally prices with values at a specific interval in time, should not be over-emphasised as central to the theory of imperialism, which is indubitably sociological (Abdel-Malek 1981). Trends in prices and the money form serve to demonstrate changes in the degree of exploitation but cannot reflect the sum of values in a single period. Emmanuel's (1972) interpretation of unequal exchange is more than just the façade of declining terms of trade; it is the totality of the condition of exploitation, particularly the commercial exploitation of the peripheral formations, which enrobes class in national guise. The other side of Emmanuel's commercial exploitation argument is that peripheral wages are a steep 'under-pricing' of the social cost of reproduction of labour.

The quantification of value by colonial/imperialist criteria and dollar-assessed low productivity should not relegate the developing world to lower-value status. The notion of quantifying value relations according to Western higher technology and higher productivity to justify central higher wages omits the fact that wages and productivity are *a priori* social. Measurement as such is a convention that requires the subjection of social time to a class desired interval in chronological time. What is social and organic is indivisible, and the time from which one begins to measure the net additions of value added in a value chain determines also one's class position. The whole pernicious interpretation of assigning higher value, and therefore wages, to technology-based productivity overlooks the interrelatedness of production and the imperialist savagery, which is circularly a predicate for dollar-based higher central productivity. The dollar, as I argue later, has a value that is determined by imperialist aggression and strategic oil control rather than by some Western technological edge.

In *Capital* volume 1, Chapter 17, Marx (1867) assumed that commodities are sold at their value and that the price of labour power rises occasionally above its value, but never sinks below it. He then theorises that 'the relative magnitudes of surplus value and of the price of labour power are determined by three circumstances: (1) the length of the working day, or the extensive magnitude of labour; (2) the normal intensity of labour, its intensive magnitude, whereby a given quantity of labour is expended in a given time; and (3) the productiveness of labour, whereby the same quantum of labour yields, in a given time, a greater or less quantum of product, dependent on the degree of development in the conditions of production' (Marx 1867). In *Capital*, volume 3, Marx (1894) posits that the reduction of wages below the value of labour power as a way to increase surplus value, mitigates against the tendency of the rate of profit to fall. Not only that, 'wages below value' or superexploitation is the most important factor to allay the tendency of the profit rates to fall. The first proposition from volume 1 illustrates how various interactive forces acting upon the price of labour power and the making of surplus value under selected historical abstractions or one-sided abstractions such as value set at price. The purpose is to demonstrate that wages are the price of labour power, which is itself a commodity produced by the socially necessary labour time invested in it, but one whose price, the wage, even when set at its value creates the condition in which 'relative to surplus-value, the value of labour-power would keep falling, and thus the abyss between the life-situation of the worker and that of the capitalist would keep widening' (Marx 1867). In money form signification, the profit rates rise by depressing the wage rates and inequality is destined to abound. In the second proposition Marx follows up by exposing the workings of the law of value, or 'when science comes in' to document the making of surplus value under more developed capitalism or, one may add, a central capitalism that has already integrated the globe and can, through its class-power exercise, depress the global share of wages of the working class through outright dispossession or intra working-class division via income differentials and ideological means. Smith's (2016, 240) commentary on super-exploitation stresses the significance of pushing wages below the value of labour power in generating surplus value; however, he remarks that Marx 'excludes it from further analysis'. He goes on to note that this exclusion 'was overlooked by orthodox Marxists as they scoured *Capital* for ammunition to use against dependency theory, seizing instead on Marx's comment that higher real wages in England than in Germany and Russia are compatible with a higher rates of exploitation in England, his assumption of a very much lower rate of surplus -value in China than in England, and a few other scattered asides, in order to exclude the blindingly obvious fact of higher rates of exploitation from theory, and in so doing they use *Capital* itself to obscure capitalism's imperialist trajectory and shield it from criticism' (Smith 2016, 240). Whereas the orthodox Marxists have gone to such measures to avoid the obvious condition of wages falling below the value of labour power, they paid little or no attention to how the law of value asserts itself as a means of denying sovereignty to the Arab working masses by war and, in addition to the creation of an indigent or war-indigent proletariat, also sustaining a cheapened valuation of the whole of Arab resources.

Cope (2015) posits that super international wages are wages substantially greater than the global median value of labour power and are received only by the upper echelons of the international working class. In terms of measurement, the average quantity of labour power at a certain point in time cannot be calculated as being worth so many exact dollars. Value is the constantly shifting relationship of internal contradictions within the commodity manifest in class-power brokered prices. The closest one could come to eying the departure of value from price is to follow the relative movement over a trend of prices earned by direct producers vis-à-vis the prices wrought at the final point of sale (Boratav 2001). In the case of wages, the trend in the share of wages that is necessary to satisfy the rising historically determined living standard (not the hunter-gatherer food basket as per Eurocentric definitions) plotted against the accrued lowly share of wages best captures the departure of wages from the value of labour power.

However, as has been shown by Emmanuel (1972), in terms of comparative advantage, the developing world enjoys much higher productivity as a result of producing 'exotic' commodities. He also elaborated Marx's position that the capitalist does not buy labour, but labour power, and whatever surplus may result from an increase in the productivity of labour belongs to the capitalist or the owner of the means of production, not to the worker (Emmanuel 1972, 419). Although Marx subordinated the physiological aspect of labour, its intensity (the quantity of labour expended in a given time) and its resolution in extended labour time (the basic measure of labour) to the social character of value and its bearing on the distribution of labour, in terms of average intensity of labour, with so many sweatshops and wartime production conditions springing up around the world, this would also lead to the conclusion that the occidental working classes are not principal wealth producers whose wages are justified by higher productivity – a productivity that is not *really* theirs. The emphasis on *really* is because the higher share of wages of the higher echelons of the Western working classes are not the result of higher productivity. This echelon is part saver and owner of wealth through the gains of their working class struggle, which were later abused by capital to increase the wage differential within the working class, but as always with capital's incessant attempt to reduce the share of all the workers in income. The political calculus of the sustainability of the central ruling class in the process of co-opting or dividing not only its own working classes, but also developing world working classes, occurs through many divisive measures, of which the war on the AW and the staged terror act deliver a significant boost inter working class dividedness.

The legacy of imperialism has already bestowed Western working classes with a privileged position within the international market, boosted all along by their accent on nationalistic unionism in their class struggle. The premise that production and the wage system are *a priori* social, as opposed to private, allow the higher central wages to be deduced as the illegitimate fruits of imperialism. Just by the reductionist proposition that workers do not own capital and the additional productivity as a result of mechanisation, either the additional productivity should belong to all workers predicating production from the beginning of the process, or the intensity of work should be the basis of productivity and, hence, developing countries' workers toiling in difficult conditions are more productive. Individual productivities can be approximated in prices or quantities, but only as averages indicative of social productivity. Social productivity and the wage system derive from transnational production and class struggles that contribute to regulating the rate of surplus value. In sweatshop economies, the law of value, through the politics of imperialism, operates to ensure that peripheral technology does not gain speed (catches up with Western technology), and wages remain low relative to the demands of central capital. In war economies that are rich with natural resources, such as the Arab economies, imperialist politics ensures a power balance by which the productive capacity of the aggressed formations is debilitated along with the political forms that allows their population to command the ownership of their resources – the ultimate form of this measure is the degree of fragmentation of states. The concrete conditions and the relations constituting the social actuality of the production and wage systems are interrelated and qualitative with an abstract or general quantitative side discernible by measurement convention.

However, it is also that superficial measurement convention which signals to the owning class and sets the criterion for the owning class to allocate resources. In an organically interconnected global production order, the proportional distribution of labour asserts itself, where the interconnection of social labour is manifested in the private exchange of the individual products of labour, by precisely the exchange value of these products (Marx 1868). Moreover, what is socially necessary arises from blind competition, therefore everyday exchange relations cannot be directly identical with the magnitudes of value. As labour's political dividedness grows, so do the conduits for disengaging more labour or engaging labourers in war and accelerating value flows to aristocratic nations. The setting aside or destruction of value is primal to capital, and it is interrelated with the trade-off between inherent technological advance (organic composition of capital) and the requirement to increase rate of surplus value by higher rates of exploitation. Forcibly disengaged labour is also social, and its relationship to capital is a predicate of productivity and the wage rate. Since 'the historic task of bourgeois society is the establishment of the world market, at least in its basic outlines, and a mode of production that rests on its basis [...] and since that task was accomplished with the colonisation of California and Australia' (Marx 1858,103), this predicate of capital (Third World abjection) is real, historical and precedes the signification of wealth in dollar value.

Europe could not have achieved tremendous wealth without reliance on imperialist loot. That the Third World has to remain underdeveloped vis-à-vis the Western formations issues from the same premise as above (the looting of the world) and as per Marx's absolute general law of capitalist development. War in the context of commercial exploitation, just like the extreme condition of slavery that combines the labourer with labour power, realises *cum* wastes labourers and their labour power – realising a commodity is its sale on the market so that it be consumed, but the consumption of labour power in war means also the death of its bearer, the labourer. War itself is a production process with at least this dual purpose: the realisation of the war commodities and the production of new power balances; the latter are the service that war generates for imperialism depending on the outcome of war. The social relationship of capital and its violent facet, imperialism, are reasserted by wars of encroachment. It is relevant to note that the production space is the global interconnected process, and the time frame is the historical dimension beginning with birth of capitalism and the start of surplus value making or historical surplus value. The length and scope of such boundaries of time and space inform the ideological content and inclination of any conceptual framework used by scholars. It is reductionism with the avowed intent to discriminate, and apologetic to speak of capitalist development in one country while neglecting the imperialist-inflicted disasters. Similarly, only by the ideological chimera of capital and reductionism can a quantification of value in this or that corner of the world be used as reason for the division of the social wage to the international working class.

The share of wages under capitalism from the social product is determined by the political power of labour. No matter how productive labour is, without political representation its share of income would drop to zilch. Higher central wages have come about as a result of the sociological relationship of imperialism (stabilising capital) wherein moral and historical factors play a role in maintaining rising wages (Emmanuel 1972): Emmanuel as per Marx considered that the value of labour power has a certain moral and historical element, namely, the determination of wages by class struggle within the boundaries of a conditioned mode of production – let us just say perceived as national or within a national boundary. Obviously, the same ruling comprador/merchant class morality applied to the war-aggressed AW introduces only poverty wages. However, given the broader state of being (ontological state) of capital by which the cheapening of labour power has to proceed, it is superfluous to assign importance to this section or that section of labour according to the quality of its machines; not only because labourers do not own the machines, but *a priori* because, even if supposedly technology-productivity mattered to wages, it is irrelevant to the fact that capital must create wholly disengaged and unproductive labour as a condition for production. The anomaly can be put as such: productivity matters to capital and may bolster the wage rate for a thin group of the global population as a result of selective sharing from higher wealth, but capital must create unproductive resources and idle people in order to maintain its profit rates; the question then can be put as such: with such a trade-off, which sections of the working class deserve to lead revolutionary struggle – the ones being put to work and paid a slightly higher wage or the ones that are poverty employed, bombed or starving? In hindsight, the whole construct that Western unionised labour, posited as a prerequisite for socialist transformation, is tacit complicity with capital to avoid the necessity not only of revolutionary violence in the class struggle, but also the sort of civil disobedience that disrupts the Western class formation. This may be the foolish logical end, but it could not be more foolish than what is happening or what is going to happen given the current balance of forces.

At any rate, capital's class values ascribe inherent rights and entitlements to Western labour. The higher paid echelons of central labour, whose wages and 'consciousness' partly derive from imperialist aggression, is what ensures the worse misfortune of peripheral labour and, with it, the practice that ensures the absolute general law of capitalist accumulation. The difficult part of building an internationalist class struggle is that the social existence of huge sections of central classes, an existence partly funded by imperialist booty, is what determines their consciousness.

The colonising force or imperialism resorts to aggression to block industrialisation in weakened security formations and, subsequently, organises the conquered economy to become a tributary to central production. Note that the value contributions of various working classes to final products are *qualitatively* different (involving different labour processes and intensities) and organically interrelated; Emmanuel underemphasises the value transfer from the periphery per se because of its low-priced value summed up in capital flows. Peripheral capital flows to the centre are only indicative of the part of the social product being siphoned off – sub-Saharan capital flight is but a minute percentage of total capital flows in the centre (UNCTAD-WIR, various years). Apart from the Gulf states, the money value signifying surplus usurpation from Arab countries to the centre appears too insignificant; but the real value, the ongoing historical surplus formation along with the expendability of human lives in war is gigantic. The omission of war-related seized value, especially human lives consumed in wars and austerity politics, invariably lowers any estimate of the surplus value created by the peripheral working class. Apart from its negative ideological by-products upon aggressed populations as a result of defeat, war is a massive super exploitation enterprise that compresses most national, and often international, prices associated with the assets of working classes far below their value. At any rate, the separation lines between absolute and relative surplus value are arbitrary, especially as lives of equal value perish in the periphery as a result of the war industry in its moment of realisation – its consummation of the labourer and his or her labour power in the market of Western militarism.

To recap: there is more to colonialism and imperialism than just the simple argument of accounts and money flow from the AW. Colonising to strip the peripheral nation's working class of the right to exercise sovereignty, through the state, over its human and natural resources also contributes through balance-of-forces channels to setting the exchange prices against the dollar globally. In the case of the Arab working class, its primary commodities are seized by imperialism's employing military capital while, conjointly, this militarisation releases the pent-up surplus in the centre. This condition for the realisation of the central surplus through military aggression forces upon Arab formations a military cost far beyond their means. It creates a wartime mode of life, a war economy, and with it war-related social classes, the war-indigent proletariat. War also shifts Arab civilian wealth into military enterprise. It literally employs and commodifies Arab human labour and destroys its value in a process of modern military production that uses technology far superior to anything else around. War reverses the physical-end process of high-end technology production to culminate in the AW rather than the centre, because literally the bombs are dropped there. The AW is the spatial market where the war with its high technology and employed labour-soldiers and civilians are exchanged and consumed. The irony is that the Western war machine, including its bombs, in its stage of realisation employs both Arab and American soldiers.

In terms of productivity, the historical cycle comes full circle with the engagement of the Arab worker and the consumption of his or her life and labour power by imperialist high-tech bombs. The culture of science to which medieval Arabs contributed, returns in higher technological forms to engage and annihilate modern working Arabs. Just like chattel slavery, the Arab is forced into a war wherein the intensity and the absolute magnitude of the release of labour power as fodder for the superior guns extinguishes lives in short time spans, hence the higher rate of surplus value. War realises value by the destruction of the military commodity itself along with Arab labour power and resituates power relations that are both services of value and at the same time inputs into value relations. The destruction of value by war, not of the product of labour only but also of living labour itself – as in the death rate – is a quintessential condition to devalue labour globally (counting the ideological impact by the demonstration effect). Apart from the immediate impact of war, the value necessary to reproduce the working population is doubly drained by the costs of war and its political effect, which renders the Arab working classes powerless.

Faltering Productive Capacity

Under conditions of war, the rate of productive capital build-up in the AW decelerates. Private investment growth follows prospective returns and the degree of risks associated therewith. However, in the AW, the issue is one of context rather than of individual responses to market signals. The context is the amalgam of the defenceless state, its acute class contradictions, and the war or the impending war. The investment–growth nexus, defined as the 'inducement to invest' and determined by the gap between the prospective rate of profit and the rate of interest, is demand- and macro-context-determined (Kalecki 1972). There are in this, as in any macro accounting framework, salient tautologies and fallacies of composition. The investment-cum-growth rate is dependent on profitability, and as demand rises the returns on investment fall along with the inducement to invest, precipitating a downturn. Under normal risk conditions, as the interest rate falls – indicating lower risks and raising investment – growth would rise as a result of a higher capital output ratio (Targetti and Thirwall 1989). However, because of diminishing returns to factors of production, the growth rate and returns begin to rise at lower rates, so that higher investment begets lower profit rates.

The story changes in a capacity-wanting and war-ridden developing area such as the AW. With respect to capacity, it would require a deficit in the trade account (lack of export market for domestic goods) and falling wages for investment to produce lower returns. In addition to low demand for domestic goods, higher risks and financial costs attenuate the drive for investment – they can switch between various techniques without adding to the stock of capital. These are standard propositions in analytical rationalities, and one may add several variables that would change matters in one way or another, including an exogenous shock (a government push) that would redress the business-cycle downturn.

However, none of these eloquent demand-side issues matter when Arab-type uncertainties are introduced. Not only do diminishing returns reduce reality to class-biased accounting or mathematics but also, in an Arab context, a formalised recipe for investment does not hold for historical reasons. Arab history, its objective and impersonal social forces saturated with violence, instantiates a qualitatively different macro context. With the ever-present potential for war and the complete collapse of states, social time moves so fast that it compresses the intervals required for normal risk-assessment to be carried out. The horizon for planning and investing in long-term projects is uncertain because the working-class's unchallenged vortex of history mediating the crisis of capital in war puts the long term in doubt. This uncertainty eschews the viability of a static analytical framework to think about the Arab conditions. An actuarial assessment of returns in a steady period is not possible, for there are few steady periods. In other words, the risks to capital formation in the AW are serious enough because neither the external political threats nor the internal political and social stability factors allow long-term policy or production planning to take place. One doubts if there is any amount of animal spirits that would meet this challenge.

Violence alters the course, type, and structure of the risks. Institutions – including the state – and capital assets could be wiped out quickly in an act of war. Only very unusual types of animal spirits could deal with the potential of state collapse. The Arab state's potential collapse effaces the future that is necessary for building private industrial strategy. In this context, private investment decisions will be locked into situations in which returns must redress capital costs within short periods, or else money capital turns to capital flight.

With the kind of uncertainties associated with complete collapse, the inducement to invest private capital nearly vanishes. Algebraically measured risks will bear little reference to reality. Under historical uncertainty, coincidence collides with necessity and the probability values of future returns under different states of nature fuse into one – the inevitability of war, and only that. It is not a question of change of degree or magnitude of risk, but rather that investors invest because they are part of the war economy in which they are involved by necessity – a wartime mode of life is predicated by war-related class formations whose reproduction rests in their ties to imperialism and other capital circles with strategic interests in the outcome of the war. Apart from war-capital building, historical uncertainty is the overriding barrier to civilian capital formation. Uncertainty leaves us with three types of national capitals that are willing to invest in the potentially collapsing economy: state capital; the sections of national private capital that cannot move abroad; and the sections of private capital that metamorphose into war agents of imperialist powers, deriving returns from the military economy itself. The many Arab warlords whose conflicting relationship is the war bourgeoisie are instances of the third group.

In these circumstances, the tendencies are for low-productivity capital to rise and for the growth rate to exhibit oil-related high volatility. One cannot wish away war in a war zone. What the mainstream fails to see is that raising investment under these war conditions becomes an operational issue in which Arab countries must ensure actual security (the substance of which is working-class security) in order to ensure investment and growth. That is not a matter of opinion; it is what happened, and it is a matter of fact (recalling long-term average yearly per capita growth rates over three decades are low and declining, while investment quality swerved into the low output per capital ratio). Despite persistent efforts to doctor and beautify the data, even an alien from outer space would read the statistics as tragedy. That is why the persistent efforts of US-led capital agencies – principally the World Bank – to minimise the role of government in the economy were also a premeditated crime meant to minimise the state, that is the potential political form for the organisation of the working class, into oblivion.

What is more, destruction to life and infrastructure, the loss in forgone income and the exodus of the labour force, skilled or otherwise, are not somehow redeemed by peace or reconstruction plans. Wars diminish the socialising space in which universal, as opposed to narrower sectarian or sectional, values can grow. Through the blood-drenched politics of identity, wars create real physical segregation and psychological lines that divide the working population. In the AW, war may appear to have indigenous causes arising from the tragic farce of fictitious Arab sect or clan identity as the sole political form of working-class representation, but in actuality the courses of wars are charted by a transnational historical agency that also steers development. Sectarian and divisive identities thrive when imperialism wins, and this can be traced historically: for instance, mainly Shiite Bahrain in 1970 refused to join mainly Shiite Iran and stuck to its Arabism. Tangentially, there is almost no resemblance between the types of political Islam practiced today and historical forms of Islamic politics. In point of fact, modern day political/economic Islam shares more in its monetary policy with conservative parties in advanced countries than it would have with the central banks of the caliphs, had central banks existed then. The historical agent that is US-led imperialism, intermediated by the transnational class alliances and institutions of war, promotes aggression for its own sake and for oil control irrespective of the humanitarian lip service.[5] More concretely, the historical agents

---

5 It is not at all surprising that 'the intelligence service of Israel considers a potential Sunni-Shiite war in Syria a favourable development for the country and the West,

are the mediation of US-led class power through impersonal and objective social forms, such as the Security Council and the Breton Woods institutions, whose governing structures are already US-biased.

The scramble is on by various capitalist circles to stake a foothold and share control over the region's polity and resources. Geopolitical rents just pour into the region. The paid militias of Iraq, Syria, Libya and Yemen represent a stark case of money flows reproducing war-related classes, divisions and endless wars. The US-led imperialist precondition is that the geopolitical flows be distributed along sectional/sectarian lines to deepen the social rifts. Because the local forces are being marionetted by irreconcilable international forces, the Arab social formation will once more become incapable of maintaining the living security of its population.

Closing Comment

In the AW, war is not the continuation of politics by violent means; it is rather the continuation of violence by means of politics. This inverted catchphrase represents the thesis around which the argument was woven. War, or permanent war, is not exclusive to the AW. For one thing, war afflicts or has afflicted every region of the globe at one time or another, most of them quite recently: it is only 80 years since Europe was left torn apart by World War II. But war appears as an enduring feature of the AW. One might interject that the AW is a strategic corner, so even smaller wars are comparatively blown out of proportion. However, in addition to war's strategic position, a good dose of media hype exaggerates its already strategic relevance. There is a sort of 'Middle East war-media industry' that surrounds events. While IS was burning alive a Jordanian pilot in early February 2015, a machete massacre took place in Eastern Congo but received little coverage in the mainstream media (*Indian Express* 2015). Further in the past, the Six-Day War in 1967 received several times the attention allotted to the much bigger India–Pakistan war at around the same period.

Yet, hyped attention or media sensationalism about the region is not the line of argument one would want to pursue to show that there is a war, more so than in other regions, mediating the crisis of capital. My contention is that war or the long-term prospect of war in the AW is a constant derived from a system of global accumulation and its attendant international relations. In the AW, war has become an end in itself. From the decolonisation wars, the colonisation of Palestine and the regional hot wars of the Cold War to the

according to an email archive of former US Secretary of State Hillary Clinton, released by WikiLeaks 2012-07-23'. https://wikileaks.org/clinton-emails/emailid/12171 (viewed 10 January 2016).

present 'War on Terror', there is but one common denominator, which is that the policies pursued were meant to incite conflict. If any of the big players had sought to defuse tensions, the regional historical trajectory indicates that their efforts systematically failed. The capitalist class in the United States, along with its subordinate international allies, ratchets up its power and that of the relationship of imperialism by dismantling the platforms of resistance of the working classes in the AW, including their states (weakening and fragmenting); hence, continued aggression.

Chossudovsky (2014) rightly proposes that the Arab formation is metamorphosing from a state into a territory as a result of US-led aggression. The Arab state falls at the tail end of a system of international relations that necessitates it to be in a condition that swings between full-fledged conflict and a high degree of tension. The verb *necessitate* is of particular relevance to the permanent-war thesis. This is because, first, there is a high frequency of regional conflicts in the AW – the highest rate in the world (SIPRI, various years), and second but more decisively because of the crisis of central capital, which has to destroy the right of Arab working classes to development in order for US-led imperialism to hold hegemony over a strategic region. Arab development *qua* working class security may potentially entail that communities take charge of their lives in a way that downgrades US-led regional hegemony. This cannot be permitted because of petrodollars and other value transfers from the AW proper and, more conclusively, because of the contribution to US-led power emanating from control of oil as a strategic resource to imperialism; the latter point that US-led imperialism has to deny the Arab working classes their right to development demonstrates the *necessity* (as opposed to fortuitousness) of war to capital. The other point to keep in mind is that US-led imperialist militarism is more about value snatch than the deployment of excess monopoly surplus.

There are no imperialist bombings based on mistakes or wrong intelligence; history is not a series of gaffes or unintended consequences for the leading imperialist class. The objective forces of history, and specifically of accumulation by war, did not represent existential threats to the ruling class: judging by the historical record of exponential growth with rising inequality – mainly driven by loot from imperialist war war-derived technology, war finance and above all by imperialist power emanating from war – one may say that these 'unintended consequences' work wonders for the financial class in charge. Capital's organised dimension rarely forgoes a 'good war'. 'We made a mistake' or 'the consequences were unintended' are a facile personalisation of history – a reading of history as melodramatic farce, featuring the 'heroism' of occupants of the Oval Office trying to bring peace and prosperity to the globe.

Moreover, distortions abound in a context of war and ideological defeatism. In mid-2000, when addressing Arab development, the chief of the Middle East and North Africa Region (MENA) at the World Bank, ended his lecture with the false wisdom that Arabs are to blame for their state of underdevelopment. Many on the liberal left inculcate this false wisdom and apportion blame by national identity and cultural character as opposed to class. The abstract Arab, however, does not exist; an Arab working class does exist. There is no Arab who is so culturally incapable that he or she cannot respond to development challenges any more than there is a culturally incapable sub-Saharan African or Mayan. The notion of the Arab in the abstract is actually an ad hominem ideological attack on real, individual working-class and poor Arabs because it is used to blame them for their situation. Imperialistically propped-up Arab regimes hold steady according to the degree of repression they deploy against Arab working people. Putting into focus the cross-border ties of Arab ruling classes to US-led imperialism, along with a close reading of the balance of forces, underscores the fact that it is the imperialist class that becomes the agency of historical and Arab development.

The ideological descent of the left is post facto evidence of theoretical flaws in understanding the international dimension of the law of value and the role of capital, as it principally divides central working classes from peripheral working classes. Western social democracy, including its left variant, has so far exhibited a failed praxis (joint theory and practice) from which much of the world still reaps the fruits of the bad investment that has been put into the struggle; the fact that one is now at such a deep trough in forms of internationalist workers' organisations and their associated ideology could only mean that much of the left was practically an ally of the right. It had, through its labour-aristocrat practices anesthetised its own working class with idolisation of bourgeois democracy. In a system fraught with contradictions in which the adding-up fallacy never ceases to strike, bourgeois democracy in its distributional facet – that is the main stabilising relationship of an otherwise implosive capital relationship – cannot be applied across all nations (not that it contains the semblance of democracy as applied now). The procedural mode by which the working class realises itself in the state is democratic or not by the share of the social product a working class commands. The deification of the 'voting system', the idolised procedure with which much of the Western left is besotted, is the false justification for the United States to bomb a Third World country, liberalise its economy, eradicate its opponents, enact a constitutional framework that enshrines social segmentation and only then introduce 'universal' suffrage. Along with car bombs ripping through the lives of the innocent, the vote becomes the supplication of the loaf of bread through the leader of the sector or sect.

The reconstruction of the reconstruction of identity by bourgeois ideology has driven working-class consciousness into a state of mythical animism. Such ideology is the progeny of false mainstream science. Twisting the meaning of the real via departure from fact as a result of narrow empiricism or by analysing situations into infinitesimal particles without relating them to the whole, has progressed as uncontested knowledge. Interpersonal comparison, which is vital for scientific development, has become rooted in the same rules and assumptions such that discussions of contentious subjects revert back to the same position without theoretical value added. No one disagrees on the basics, which are only the ideas that serve the ruling class. One can only foresee that such social science may turn out to be a footnote to the Sokal hoax once labour prevails.

The apologetic stance of apportioning blame on the basis of postcolonial nation-building failures in the developing formations presupposes that while colonialism pulls its troops out, it ceases to inflict damage. Colonialism did not just set back the starting point of the AW, it acted out of the necessity to meet the social or metabolic rate of capital's reproduction by sabotaging any or all social programmes. It reinforced Arab retrogression at every point in time, especially, in its alliance with political Islam and Saudi Arabia. A Western left that conceptually segments working-class struggle by its reified national forms and venerates the voting procedure of bourgeois democracy, implicitly assumes an inner benevolence to capital that outweighs the genocides by which it cheapens its inputs – the 'capitalism is progressive' stance behind which lies the justification for capital. In terms of its function as procedure that pays off the central working class from imperialist war booty, bourgeois democracy is anathema to third world development. This tacit adoration of bourgeois democracy is at the heart of reform building toward international working-class divisions and possibly fascism. Arabs and sub-Saharan Africans have had the choice of dying at the hands of healthy, educated Western soldiers, or less educated ones, depending on the social democratic programmes of the welfare state in the North.

As class-based struggle declines, so does revolutionary class consciousness. The catharsis of guilt by a raucous Western left whose platform is provided by corporate capital reinforces the notion that there is a yet-unrealised utopia in bourgeois democracy that is waiting to happen. Such noise emerging from miniscule organisational forms overshadows the fact that the victory of capital was swift, violent and organisational before it became ideological. Just as one of the capitalist world leaders said in 1990 after the collapse of the Soviet Union: we can relax our right to detain individuals without charges because the disciplined-organised communists are no more; all we have now are the Anarchists and Trotskyists. There cannot be serious opposition to capital without uncompromising resistance based on principles that transcend economistic unionism into anti-imperialism, or principles that focus on the sphere of production instead of circulation/distribution.

Postscript

The articulation of the Arab formation with world capital is conducted by aggression involving a disproportionate use of force. Arab socialism failed because of the use of such force and not because it 'ran out of steam'. What does it mean to say that Arab socialism ran out of steam or failed for intrinsic reasons when all the macro variables were healthier compared to the current neo-liberal abjection? As the *lebensraum* of US-led imperialism narrows under pressure from a China–Russia backed Iran in the Gulf, its drive to level any development platform (including state structures) that might serve to position competing capitalist forces in the region, escalates. Historically, realpolitik and military power have been antecedents to all other forms of regional politics; hence, all the more substantiation to the point that the AW is articulated by the barrel of a gun.

However, as the differences of US-led capital with the opposition forces in the AW grow over issues of controlling indigenous resources, so will differences between various global circles of capital, especially nationalist capitals that are subjected to dollar peonage – China in particular, assuming that its capital remains nationalistic for the most part. The pressure that the US faces in the AW from competitors for strategic resources is another reason why Israel cannot integrate with the Arab region. Israel's trade structure is inherently geared to Western markets and does not address the pittance of Arab market demand (Abou-Anaml 2006). After decades of peace with Egypt and Jordan, Israeli trade with these countries remains low – actually insignificant if one discounts Israel's purchase of gas during its past times of dependence on imports (IMF various years). On the other side, the sections of Israeli capital with interests in integrating with the AW, or the tiny peace movement demanding the normalisation of relations with Arab countries, remain inconsequential. The Israeli formation reproduces its living standards (preferred trade partnerships and aid) and much of its *état d'esprit* via imperialist partnering. In turn, the US-led assault on the AW leads to the strengthening of the colonial–settler relationship as it foments enmity as grounds for future wars. When stripped from myth, the Israeli assault on the Palestinians is more about ideologically disarming of the Palestinians and Arab populations of their means of resistance, which would obviously serve to deter value expropriation by imperialism, than about land. Israel's unequivocal gendarme role to imperialism erects an insuperable barrier that separates Arab and Israeli working classes.

Developments within the circles of central capital turn on two interrelated axes: the relationship of US-led capital to itself (principally how US imperial rents are performing in relation to its own economy), and the relationship of US-led capital to other nationally based capitals (how the rest of the world views its holding of the dollar as a precarious affair). US-led capital equates itself with, or differentiates itself from, world capital by the degree of power it enjoys within the international division of labour – its edge in war-driven technology – and the violence exercised upon the periphery, especially the AW. The AW had already tested the limits of inter-imperialist collusion when the United States, by waging war on Iraq in 2003, breached the covenants of international law enacted in the Security Council. There are limits to diluting the national identity of capital, irrespective of the degree to which financial capital has been globalised – the nation is subordinate to capital, but is also a means for the reproduction of capital. The growing dependency of US capital on resources from abroad and on hegemony over oil regions is the bond holding together globally financialised capital with US capital.

Formulaically, the degree of US-led belligerence will rely on the degree to which the dependent growth of US-led capital in its dollar form becomes a liability to other competing world capitals and warrants an orderly or disorderly exit from dollar-held debt. Fundamentally, the liability is the inverse measure of how vital US-led encroachment becomes, particularly in the AW, in securing long-term guarantees to financial capital. Although foreigners hold US debt, and this may potentially infringe on the ownership of US resources, a debilitated AW, held as collateral and policed militarily, will delay the point at which dollar-world seignorage wanes. So long as world capital stabilises the worth of its dollar savings via US-led aggression on the AW, a condition of ultra-imperialism (or a consensus to continuously shift war to the periphery) also emerges; hence, the multilayered complexity of inter-imperialist relations.

In actuality, inasmuch as the growth of US-led capital continues to depend on the expansion of Arab or regional wars, on the pricing of oil in dollars and on a high degree of control over moneyed resource flows globally, differences within the circles of world capital (inter-imperialist rivalry) regarding hegemony over the AW and the division of imperial rents, will also grow. Arab wars are proxy wars, especially the Syrian conflict, which drew Sino-Russian vetoes from the UN security Council and whose funding sends a clear signal that financialisation does not dissipate inter-capitalist differences. Despite its associated perils, the current Russian intervention in Syria is a case in point.

Perceiving the withdrawal of US troops from Iraq, Afghanistan and other assaulted areas in the past as failures of US policy is a political reading, but from a political economic reading, especially in terms of cheapening resources, these campaigns are a bonus for capital. In spite of retreats, the share of capital globally from world income continues to rise. Altogether, capital as ideology, expropriation and materialisation in production (the real relationship that transcends nationalist pretence) stands on firmer ground. Over the last three decades, the real wages of the central working classes have stood still or fallen, and the dehumanisation of peripheral working classes has reached new depths, now possibly spilling over into Southern Europe, Greece in particular.

In the modern financial age, the centripetal pull of working classes and their objective grounds for unity grew from the way their global wage share is drawn more and more as a residual from the pool of finance-capital profits. Financialisation also homogenises concrete capitals more readily as profits are internationalised. Many capitalists, through their ideological and institutional power, take the decision to shrink the wage share and stir inter-working-class enmities. More and more, working classes deal with one complex structure of capital: the US-led sponsored institutions (the organised dimension of capital) and not various disconnected capitals.

In the AW, the missionary work of imperialist-bolstered civil society infusing religious precepts into public culture furthered religious alienation, or the displacement of responsibility for worldly misery to a supernatural power or to human failure to obey divinely ordained precepts. As working people endure harsher conditions, the Islamisation of political life offers a short reprieve to the merchant leading class. In the absence of a socialist alternative model, change as per the 2011 uprising need not imply progress. Imperialist aggression reconstitutes weak peripheral ruling classes as an agglomeration of class allies in which its capital represents the tipping force within the national state – typical of colonialism. As working-class identities split away from the reality of working-class conditions, the leading ruling cross-border class alliance with imperialism gains ground. For the time being, it appears that no matter how baleful the social conditions of peripheral wars and misery – of which there is no shortage in Africa and the AW – the rule of the dominant class will be kept intact by means of the ideological power it possesses, of which Islamist identity pitted against class is the foremost pillar. Once the politics of identity reproduces the bourgeoisies that shapes history, the history that is instantiated as the state of war, more of Arab history and, by implication, global working-class history becomes the over-determination that escapes social control. Labour's share will continue to decline and be distributed in proportion to the degree of working-class power in the state, which is presently weak. In an international division of labour, the power of a peripheral working class is assessed by the extent to which it perforates the state with its political organisations. By implication, and as result of capital becoming more homogenous, the fall of the Arab working class is also the fall of the global working class. It is not at all coincidental that the wage shares in major parts of the world declined after the bombing and destruction of Iraq in 1991.

In an organic-like social order, the religious–ideological mission and the war in the periphery creep back to curtail the benefits and civil liberties of the central working classes. As the divide between aristocratic nations and commercially exploited nations becomes wider, so go the under-valorisation cum commodification of both the human being and his or her labour power. However, by the time the long-term bonds that tie world labour together become visible to the working classes, the intermittent periods presented as opportunities for one section of labour to make gains at the expense of another have been exploited by capital to the detriment of labour, as Emmanuel and Bettelheim (1970) correctly foretold. The epitome of anti–Third World central working-classes' collaboration with capital peaked as they assented to so-called humanitarian bombings that often obliterated whole social formations. The destruction of states, of which the Syrian scenario is the latest, crowns the ideological victory of US-led imperialism. Instead of targeting the superiority of US-led imperialism by focusing on inter-capitalist divisions to induce capital's necrosis, the priority of anti-imperialist struggles in the commercially exploited nations is relegated to moralistic posturing that absolves imperialism from a whole history of genocide.

Imperialism is a complex relationship in which the central nation state is pitted against its own capital; but at the same time, both central capital and its nation state benefit from imperial pillage. With the rise of China, the deepening of the class divide in the United States and the ballooning of its debts as a result of global dollarisation, a downgrading of US imperial standing lies in wait – but only of the nation-state, not of internationalised capital and its consequent violence in imperialism. Defeating capital requires an organised and armed internationalist working class movement. US-led capital has historically responded by dollar devaluation to restructure the shares of wealth of different circles of capital. Devaluing the wealth holdings in the dollar evokes an opposing reaction from foreign dollar holders and a ratcheting up of imperialist aggression, particularly against the AW – to redress imperialist stature. Until the fall of the Soviet Union, the differences over the redistribution of resources amongst the capitalist formations have been mediated, for the greater part, through politically engineered mechanisms against the common foe, the USSR. The rise of unrestrained capital globally was followed by the spread of austerity inward, from the periphery to the centre. The rise of the free market as the uncontested ideology of capital also bolstered fetishism and further alienated the endogenous production of technology and violence from rational social control. In the same way that austerity has migrated to the North, violence has begun its northward march.

BIBLIOGRAPHY

Abaza, D. (2013) 'Price Controls, Currency Devaluation Fuel Drug Shortages in Egypt', Ahram Online, 12 March; viewed 2 July 2014. http://english.ahram.org.eg/NewsContent/3/12/66532/Business/Economy/Price-controls,-currency-devaluation-fuel-drug-sho.aspx

Abdel-Fadil, M. (2000) *Egypt and the World in the Twenty First Century* (Cairo: Dar Ashourouq Publishers).

Abdel-Malek, A. (1961) *Peuples d'Afrique* (Monte-Carlo: Editions du Cap).

——(1967) 'The Crisis in Nasser's Egypt', *New Left Review*, vol. 1 (45), pp. 67–82.

——(1968) *Egypt: Military Society; the Army Regime, the Left, and Social Change under Nasser* (New York: Vintage Books).

——(1971) *The Army and National Movement* [*Al-jaysh wa-al-harakah al-wataniyah*], translated from Arabic (Beirut: Dar-Ibn Khaldoun).

——(1977) 'Geopolitics and National Movements: An Essay on the Dialects of Imperialism' *Antipode* 9 (1), pp. 28–35, viewed 19 September 2014. http://www.praxis-epress.org/CGR/12-Abdel-Malek.pdf

——(1981) *Social Dialectics: Nation and Revolution 2* (New York: SUNY Press).

——(1981) *Changing the World, Taghyīr al-'ālam al-Majlis al-Waṭanī lil-Thaqāfah wa-al-Funūn wa-al-Ādāb* (Kuwait: Central Council for the Arts).

Abernethy, V. D. (2000) *Population Politics* (New Brunswick, NJ: Transaction Publishers).

Abrahamian, E. (2012) *The Coup: 1953, the CIA, and the Roots of Modern U.S.-Iranian Relations* (New York: New Press).

Abou-Anaml, H. (2006) *Alikstad al Israeli* (Beirut: Markaz Dirasat al-Wahda al-'Arabiya).

Accorsi, A. and G. Piazzese (2014) 'Sisi's Economy: Big plans fail to yield results', *Middle East Eye*, 2 October, viewed 20 January 2015. http://www.middleeasteye.net/news/sisi-s-economy-1552381636

Ahmed, N. (2013) 'How the World Health Organization covered up Iraq's nuclear nightmare', *Guardian*, 13 October 2013, viewed 29 September 2015. http://www.theguardian.com/environment/earth-insight/2013/oct/13/world-health-organisation-iraq-war-depleted-uranium

Alavi, H. (1972). 'The State in Post-Colonial Societies: Pakistan and Bangladesh'. *New Left Review*, vol. 1, no. 74.

al-Dawlah, 'Iṣmat Sayf (1965) *Fundamentals of Arab Socialism* (Cairo: al-Dār al-Qawmīyah lil-Ṭibā'ah wa-al-Nashr).

Al Jazeera (2011) 'Iraq's Abandoned Children', 10 May, viewed 17 August 2012. http://www.aljazeera.com/video/middleeast/2011/05/201151041017174884.html

al-Hamsh, M. (2004) *al-Fiqr al-Iqtissadi fi al-Khitab al-Siyassi al-Souri fil al-Karn al-Ishreen* [Economic Thinking of the Syrian Political Speech in the 20th Century] (Beirut: Bisan).

al-Khafaji, I. (1986) 'State Incubation of Iraqi Capitalism', *Middle East Report*, vol. 142, pp. 4–9, 12.

——(2003) 'I did not want to be a collaborator', *Guardian*, viewed 2 July 2014. http://www.theguardian.com/world/2003/jul/28/iraq.comment

Alavi, H. (1972) 'The State in Post-Colonial Societies: Pakistan and Bangladesh', *New Left Review*, vol. I/74, pp. 59–81.

Al Basrah (2004) 'International Day of Action for the Iraqi Resistance', viewed 19 January 2004. http://www.albasrah.net/moqawama/english/022004/action_040204.htm

Albawaba (2004) 'Arab funds invest $21 trillion abroad', 27 June, viewed 7 June 2008. http://www.albawaba.com/business/arab-funds-invest-21-trillion-abroad

ALO (Arab Labour Organisation) (2010) Workshop on Agricultural Rebirth, Damascus, 23–25 November, p. 57.

Althusser, L. (1964) 'Part Seven: Marxism and Humanism'. *Marxists.Org.* https://www.marxists.org/reference/archive/althusser/1964/marxism-humanism.htm.

——(1968) 'Philosophy as a Revolutionary Weapon'. First published in *L'Unità*, 1968, this translation first published in *New Left Review*, 1971;

——(1971) *Lenin and Philosophy and Other Essays* (New York: Monthly Review Press).

——(1994) 'Ideology and Ideological State Apparatuses (Notes toward an Investigation)', in S. Žižek (ed.), *Mapping Ideology* (London: Verso), pp. 100–140.

Al-Sabbak, M., S. Sadik Ali, O. Savabi, G. Savabi, S. Dastgiri and M. Savabieasfahani (2012) 'Metal Contamination and The Epidemic of Congenital Birth Defects in Iraqi Cities'. *Bulletin of Environmental Contamination and Toxicology* 89 (5): 937–944. doi: 10.1007/s00128-012-0817-2.

Amel, M. (1980) *The Palestinian Question in the Ideology of the Lebanese Bourgeoisie* (Beirut: Palestine Research Centre).

AMF (Arab Monetary Fund, various years). *Joint Arab Economic Report* (Cairo: Arab Monetary Fund and League of Arab States).

Ahmad-Amin, G. (2007) *Exposing Theories of Economic Development* (Cairo: Dar Al Shourouq).

Amin, S. (1974 [1957]) *Accumulation on a World Scale* (New York: Monthly Review Press).

——(1976) *Unequal Development: An Essay on the Social Formations of Peripheral Capitalism* (Hassocks: The Harvester Press).

——(1977) *Imperialism and Unequal Development* (Brighton: Harvester Press).

——(1978) 'The Arab Nation: Some Conclusions and Problems', *MERIP Reports*, vol. 68, pp. 3–14.

——(2007) 'Political Islam in The Service of Imperialism'. *Monthly Review* 59 (7): 1. doi: 10.14452/mr-059-07-2007-11_1.

——(2010) 'The Battlefields Chosen by Contemporary Imperialism: Conditions for an Effective Response from the South', MRZine, mrzine.monthlyreview.org/2010/amin070210.html, viewed 14 March 2013.

——(2012) 'The Surplus in Monopoly Capitalism and the Imperialist Rent', *Monthly Review*, vol. 64, no. 3.

——(2015) 'Egypt: Failed Emergence, Conniving Capitalism, Fall of the Muslim Brothers: A Possible Popular Alternative', in A. Kadri (ed.), *Development Challenges and Solutions After the Arab Spring* (London: Macmillan).

Anderson, L. (1987) 'The State in the Middle East and North Africa', *Comparative Politics*, vol. 20, no.1, pp. 1–18.

Andrews, C. (2000) *From Capitalism to Equality: An Enquiry into the Laws of Economic Change* (Oakland: Needle Press).
AOAD (Arab Organization for Agricultural Development) (2009) *Developments in Arab Agricultural Trade*, Statistical Abstract, no. 29.
Argitis, G. and C. Pitelis (2001) 'Monetary Policy and the Distribution of Income: Evidence for the United States and the United Kingdom', *Journal of Post Keynesian Economics*, vol. 23, no.4.
Aristotle (2014) 'Politics', B. Jowett (transl.). *Ebooks@Adelaide*. Accessed 28 July. https://ebooks.adelaide.edu.au/a/aristotle/a8po/.
Arrighi, G. (1982) 'A Crisis of Global Hegemony' in I. Wallerstein *et al.* (ed.) *Dynamics of Global Crisis* (New York: Monthly Review Press).
Avramidis, S. (2006) 'Articulation by the "Barrel of a Gun": Development Under the Threat of War in the Near East', 8–10 December, Historical Materialism Conference, London. http://mercury.soas.ac.uk/hm/pdf/2006confpapers/papers/Avramidis.pdf, viewed 2 March 2007.
Awadi, H. (2004) *In Pursuit of Legitimacy: The Muslim Brothers and Mubarak, 1982–2000* (New York: I. B. Tauris).
Ayeb, H. (2012) 'The Marginalization of the Small Peasantry: Egypt and Tunisia', in R. Bush and H. Ayeb (eds.), *Marginality and Exclusion in Egypt* (London: Zedbooks).
Ayubi, N. N. (1995) *Over-Stating the Arab State: Politics and Society in the Middle East* (London: I. B. Tauris).
Badiou, A. (2001) *Ethics: An Essay on the Understanding of Evil*. P. Hallward (transl.) (London & New York: Verso).
Badiou, A. (2014) 'The Event, Ceasefire,' https://ceasefiremagazine.co.uk/alain-badiou-event/, viewed 5 March 2015.
Balibar, É. (1991) 'Es Gibt Keinen Staat in Europa: Racism and Politics in Europe Today', *New Left Review*, vol. 1, p. 186.
Baran, P. A. (1957) *The Political Economy of Growth* (New York: Monthly Review Press).
———(1961) 'The Commitment of the Intellectual', *Monthly Review*, vol. 13, no. 1.
———(1973) *The Political Economy of Growth* (Middlesex: Penguin Books).
Baran, P. A. and P. M. Sweezy (1975) *Monopoly Capital: An Essay on the American Economic and Social Order* (Penguin Books).
Barout, M. J. (2011) *The Last Decade in Syrian History* [Al-'aqd al-akhir fi tarikh Suriyah: jadalliyat al-jumud wa-al-islah (1–4)] (Doha: Arab Centre for Research and Policy Studies).
Batatu, H. (1986) 'State and Capitalism in Iraq: A Comment', *Middle East Report*, vol. 142, pp. 10–12.
Beblawi, H. and G. Luciani (eds.) (1987) *The Rentier State* (London: Croom Helm).
Bellofiore, R. (2009) *Rosa Luxemburg and the Critique of Political Economy* (London: Routledge).
———(2012) 'Could Be Raining: The Great Recession and the European Crisis', 19 January 2012, PEL Seminar Series at the International University College of Turin.
BelQaziz, A. (2003) *The American Occupation of Iraq. [Markaz Dirāsāt al-Waḥdah al-'Arabīyah]* (Beirut: CAUS).
Benjamin, M. (2011) 'From Cairo to Madison: Hope and Solidarity are Alive', *Global Exchange Organization* http://www.globalexchange.org/blogs/peopletopeople/2011/02/21/from-cairo-to-madison-hope-and-solidarity-are-alive/, viewed 14 March 2013.

Berger, M. (1958) 'The Middle Class in the Arab World', in W. Z. Laqueur (ed.), *The Middle East in Transition: Studies in Contemporary History* (London: Routledge & Kegan Paul), pp. 61–71.

Bettelheim, C. (1975). *The Transition to Socialist Economy*. B. Pearce (transl.) (New York: The Harvester Press Ltd).

Bianchi, R. (2012) 'Egypt's Revolutionary Elections', *The Singapore Middle East Papers*, vol. 2.

Bilmes, L. J. (2013) 'The Financial Legacy of Iraq and Afghanistan: How Wartime Spending Decisions Will Constrain Future National Security Budgets', HKS Faculty Research Working Paper Series RWP13-006.

Binns, P. (1986) 'State Capitalism, Marxism and the Modern World', *Education for Socialists*, no. 1.

Binns, P., and D. Hallas (1976) 'The Soviet Union: State Capitalist or Socialist?', *Marxist Internet Archive*, viewed 2 July 2014. http://www.marxists.org/archive/hallas/works/1976/09/su2.htm

Boratav, K. (2001) 'Movements of Relative Agricultural Prices in Sub-Saharan Africa,' *Cambridge Journal of Economics*, vol. 25, no. 3, pp. 395–416.

Bottomore, T. (1964) *Elites and Society* (London: C. A. Watts).

Browder, E. (1933) *The Meaning of Social-Fascism*. (New York: Workers Library Publishers).

Bsheer, R. (2010) 'Poverty in the Oil Kingdom: An Introduction', *Jadaliyya*, 30 September, viewed 9 February 2011. http://www.jadaliyya.com/pages/index/202/poverty-in-the-oil-kingdom_an-introduction-

Braverman, H. (1959) 'The Nasser Revolution', *American Socialist Internet Archive*, viewed 2 July 2014. 'http://www.marxists.org/history/etol/newspape/amersocialist/amersoc_5901.htm

Buick, A. and J. Crump (1986) *State Capitalism: The Wages Systems under New Management* (London: Macmillan).

Burawoy, M. (1985). *The Politics of Production: Factory Regimes Under Capitalism and Socialism*. (London: Verso).

Bush, R. (2004) *Civil Society and the Uncivil State: Land Tenure Reform in Egypt and the Crisis of Rural Livelihoods* (Geneva: United Nations Research Institute for Social Development).

———(2007) *Poverty and Neoliberalism: Persistence and Reproduction in the Global South* (London: Pluto Press).

———(2015) 'Uprisings without Agrarian Questions', in A. Kadri (ed.), *Development Challenges and Solutions After the Arab Spring* (London: Macmillan).

Butter, D. (1990) 'Syria's Under the Counter Economy', *Middle East Economic Digest*, vol. 23, pp. 4–5.

Callaghy, T. (1990) 'Lost between State and Market: The Politics of Economic Adjustment in Ghana, Zambia, and Nigeria', in J. Nelson (ed.), *Economic Crisis and Policy Choice: The Politics of Adjustment in the Third World* (Princeton: Princeton University Press).

CAPMAS (Central Agency for Public Mobilization & Statistics, Egypt, various years) *Statistical Yearbook* (Cairo: CAPMAS).

Cabral, A. (1969) 'Amilcar Cabral: Brief Analysis of the Social Structure of Guinea'. *Marxist.Org*. https://www.marxists.org/subject/africa/cabral/1964/bassg.htm.

Carr, E. H. (1986 [1961]) 'What is History?', in R. W. Davies (ed.), *The George Macaulay Trevelyan Lectures Delivered in the University of Cambridge, January – March 1961* (Hampshire: Macmillan).

CBS (Syrian Central Bureau of Statistics, various years), *Statistical Abstract*, various issues (Damascus: Government Publication).
CBSE (Central Bureau of Statistics Egypt) General Indicators, Cairo 1952–1970, pp. 200–204.
CBSE (Central Bureau of Statistics Egypt) Government Statistics Year Book (various years) Cairo.
Central Organization for Statistics and Information Technology COSIT (2004) *Results of The Employment and Unemployment Survey 2003* (Baghdad: Ministry of Planning and Development Cooperation) pp. 17 and 27.
Chang, H. J. and I. Grabel (2004) *Reclaiming Development: An Alternative Economic Policy Manual* (London: Zed Books).
Chapra, M. U. (2001) 'Islamic Economic Thought and the New Global Economy'. *Islamic Economic Studies* 9 (1): 1–16.
——— (2014) *Morality and Justice in Islamic Economics and Finance*. (Cheltenham, UK, and Northampton, MA: Edward Elgar Publishing).
Charafeddine, F. (1981) 'Approche Du Socialisme Arabe En Moyen Orient 1945–1970', Thèse de 3e cycle: Philosophie: Paris 10.
Chomsky, N. (2002) 'Will the US invade Iraq?', *Zmagazine*, 1 September 2002, viewed 2 March 2014. http://www.chomsky.info/interviews/20020901.htm
——— (2015) 'America paved the way for ISIS', *Salon*, 16 February 2015, viewed http://www.salon.com/2015/02/16/noam_chomsky_america_paved_the_way_for_isis_partner
Chossudovsky, M. (2014) 'The Global Economic Crisis, the IMF and the Middle East', MEI-NUS Seminar, Singapore, 16 January 2014.
Chouman, A. (2005) 'The Socialist Experience in Syria, the Consequences of its Movement towards the Market Economy, and the Impact of Restructuring and Globalization', unpublished paper.
Cidamli, C. (2008) 'Call for Class Solidarity from Egyptian El Mahalla Workers', *MRZine*, viewed 2 July 2014. http://mrzine.monthlyreview.org/2008/mahalla070408.html
Clark, R. and D. Jensen (2001) 'Neighbourhood Bully: Ramsey Clark on American Militarism'. Interview in *The Sun Magazine*; viewed 30 July 2010. http://www.racematters.org/ramseyclarkinterview.htm
Cliff, T. ([1955] 1974) *State Capitalism in Russia* (London: Pluto Press).
CMES (Center for Middle Eastern Studies, Harvard University) (2011) 'The Role of Economic Institutions in the Organization of Middle Eastern Economic Life in the Modern and Pre-Modern Periods', March, CMES Conference, Harvard.
Cooper, M. N. (1983) 'State Capitalism, Class Structure, and Social Transformation in the Third World: The Case of Egypt', *International Journal of Middle East Studies*, vol. 15, no. 4, pp. 451–469.
Cope, Z. (2015) *Divided World, Divided Class: Global Political Economy and the Stratification of Labour Under Capitalism* (Kersplebedeb, Montreal).
Corm, G. (2015) *Pensée et Politique dans le Monde Arabe: Contextes Historiques et Problématiques, XIXe-XXIe siècle* (Paris: la Decouverte).
Cui, Z. (2005) 'The Bush Doctrine and Neo-conservatism: A Chinese Perspective', *Harvard International Law Journal*, vol. 46, no. 45.
Dasgupta, D., J. Keller and T. G. Srinivasan (2002) 'Reform and Elusive Growth in the Middle-East: What Has Happened in the 1990s?', *World Bank Middle East and North Africa Working Paper Series*, no. 25.

Davis, A. K. (1957) 'Thorstein Veblen Reconsidered.' *Science & Society*, vol. 21, no. 1, pp. 52–85.

———(1960) 'Decline and Fall', *Monthly Review*, vol. 12, no. 6: October.

———(1983) 'Sociology of Poverty', Lecture Series, University of Alberta.

———(1993) *Farewell to Earth: The Selected Writings of Arthur K. Davis* (Vermont: Adamant Press).

Debord G. (1994 [1967]) *The Society of the Spectacle* (New York: Zone Books).

De Smet, B. and S. Malfait (2015) 'Trade Unions and Dictatorship in Egypt', *Jadaliyya*, 31 August, viewed 9 September 2015. http://interviews.jadaliyya.com/pages/index/22526/trade-unions-and-dictatorship-in-egypt

Deutscher, I. (1964) 'Maoism – Its Origins and Outlook', in *Marxism, Wars and Revolutions: Essays from Four Decades* (London: Verso).

———(1967) *The Unfinished Revolution: Russia 1917–1967: The George Macaulay Trevelyan Lectures Delivered in the University of Cambridge, January-March 1967* (Oxford: Oxford University Press).

Department of State (1959–1962) '*Foreign Relations of The United States, 1958–1960 Volume XII, Near East Region; Iraq; Iran; Arabian Peninsula, Documents 199 and 275*: 'Telegram From the Embassy in Iraq to the Department of State', viewed 29 September 2015, Washington, 24 May 1962. http://history.state.gov/historicaldocuments/frus1958-60v12/d199 Washington, 31 January 1961. https://history.state.gov/historicaldocuments/frus1961-63v17/d6

Devine, J. G. (2005) *Marx's Law of Capitalist Accumulation Revisited: Counteracting Tendencies and Internal Dynamics* (Los Angeles: Loyola Marymount University).

Di Maggio, M. (2013) *Une crise d'hégémonie (1958–1981)* (Paris: Éditions sociales).

DNE (*Daily News Egypt*) (2011) 'US gives Egypt $150 mln to help with transition', 18 February, viewed 18 July 2013. http://www.dailynewsegypt.com/2011/02/18/us-gives-egypt-150-mln-to-help-with-transition/

Doherty, R., and Y. Saleh (2013) 'Benefactor Qatar Dampens Talk of Fast New Help for Egypt', Reuters, viewed 2 July 2014. http://www.reuters.com/article/2013/03/11/egypt-economy-idUSL6N0C37N120130311

Donnelly, T. (2000) 'Rebuilding America's Defenses: Strategy, Forces and Resources for a New Century', The Project for the New American Century, September 2000, viewed 5 January 2008. http://www.newamericancentury.org/RebuildingAmericasDefenses.pdf

Drysdale, A. (1982) 'The Asad Regime and Its Troubles', *MERIP Reports*, vol. 110, pp. 3–11.

Dunham, B. (1955) 'Thinkers and Treasurers, Part 1', *Monthly Review Press*, vol. 7, no. 6.

———(1955) 'Thinkers and Treasurers, Part 4', *Monthly Review Press*, vol. 7, no. 8.

Durant, W. (1993) *Our Oriental Heritage: Story of civilization* (New York: MJF Publishers)

Duri, A. A. (1969) *Muqaddimah fi al-Tarikh al-Iqtisadi al-Arabi*. (Beirut: Dar al-Ṭaliiah).

Drucker, P. F. (1964) *Managing for Results* (New York: Harper & Row).

Egyptian Society for Political Economy (1978) *The Egyptian Economy in a Quarter of a Century1952 –1977*, published by ESPE.

EIA Energy Information Administration (2004) *Iraq Country Analysis Brief* (Washington, DC: EIA).

———(2005) *Country Analysis Brief* (Washington, DC: EIA).

———(2008) *Syria Country Analysis Brief* (Washington, DC: EIA).

EIU (Economist Intelligence Unit) (1989) *Syria Country Profile* (London: EIU).

EIU (Economist Intelligence Unit) (1996) *Country Report: Syria*, no. 3 (London: EIU).
EIU (Economist Intelligence Unit) (2008) *Country Profile – Main Report*, 1 July (London: EIU).
El Sharnouby, D. (2012) 'Morsi's 100-day plan to rebuild Egypt', *openDemocracy*, 29 July, viewed 3 November 2014. https://www.opendemocracy.net/dina-el-sharnouby/morsi%E2%80%99s-100-day-plan-to-rebuild-egypt
Emmanuel, A. and C. Bettelheim (1970) 'International Solidarity of Workers: Two Views: The Delusions of Internationalism; Economic Inequality between Nations and International Solidarity'. *Monthly Review*, 22(2). Retrieved 23 February 2015. Accessed at http://archive.monthlyreview.org/index.php/mr/article/view/MR-022-02-1970-06_2
Emmanuel, A. (1972) *Unequal Exchange: A Study of the Imperialism of Trade*. (New York and London: Monthly Review Press).
Ernesto, G. (pseud) (2011) 'Syria Raises Wages to Calm the Situation Following the Killing of Demonstrators', *World News Post*, viewed 2 July 2014. http://world-news-post.blogspot.sg/2011/03/syria-raises-wages-to-calm-situation.html
Fanon, F. (1967) *The Wretched of the Earth*. (New York: Grove Press).
FAO (2001) *Revolving Fund for the Purpose of Implementing the WTO Marrakesh Decision Relating to the Least-Developed and Net Food-Importing Developing Countries*. FAO. http://www.fao.org/docrep/005/y3733e/y3733e0a.htm.
FAOSTAT (Food and Agricultural Organisation, various years), Rome. http://www.fao.org/economic/ess/countrystat/en
Fasano-Filho, U. (2000) 'Review of the Experience with Oil Stabilization and Savings Funds in Selected Countries', *IMF Working Papers Series* (New York: IMF).
Feenstra, R. C., R. Inklaar, and M. P. Timmer (2015) 'The Next Generation of the Penn World Table' forthcoming *American Economic Review*; viewed 1 June 2015 at http://www.ggdc.net/pwt
Fine, B. (2010) 'Locating Financialisation'. *Historical Materialism*, 1, vol. 8, no.2, pp. 97–116.
Foster, J. B. (2006) 'Naked Imperialism: An Interview with John Bellamy Foster', *MRZine*, http://mrzine.monthlyreview.org/2006/foster171106.html, viewed 30 July 2010.
Foster, J. B., H. Holleman and R. W. McChesney (2008) 'The U.S. Imperial Triangle and Military Spending'. *Monthly Review* vol. 60 no. 5, doi: 10.14452/mr-060-05-2008-09_1.
Foster, J. B. (2010) 'Capitalism and the Curse of Energy Efficiency', *Monthly Review*, vol. 62, no. 6.
———(2015) 'The New Imperialism of Globalized Monopoly-Finance Capital', *Monthly Review*, vol. 67, no. 3.
Frank, A. G. (1966) 'The Development of Underdevelopment', *Monthly Review*, vol. 41, no. 2, pp. 37–51.
———(1972) *Lumpenbourgeoisie: Lumpendevelopment* (New York: Monthly Review Press).
———(1982) 'Crisis of Ideology and Ideology of Crisis', in I. Wallerstein (ed., *et al.*) *Dynamics of Global Crisis* (New York: Monthly Review Press) (pp. 109–165)
———(1992) 'Third World War: A Political Economy of the Gulf War and New World Order', *Third World Quarterly*, vol. 13, no. 2.
———(1998) *ReORIENT: Global Economy in the Asian Age* (Berkeley, Los Angeles and London: University of California Press).
Fukuyama, F. (2005) 'Invasion of the Isolationists', *The New York Times*, 31 August, viewed 29 September 2015. http://www.nytimes.com/2005/08/31/opinion/invasion-of-the-isolationists.html?_r=0

Furtado, C. (1964) *Development and Underdevelopment* (Berkeley: University of California Press).

——— (1970) *Economic Development of Latin America: A Survey from Colonial Times to the Cuban Revolution* (transl. S. Macedo) (Cambridge: Cambridge University Press).

George, S. (2016) 'UN Report: Thousands of Ramadi Buildings Damaged, Destroyed'. *Associated Press.* http://bigstory.ap.org/article/948dafc7c5a941ca898f9a21f3f5b969/un-report-thousands-ramadi-buildings-damaged-destroyed%20viewed%20jan%20 17%202016.

Ghareeb, E. and B. Dougherty. (2013) *Historical Dictionary of Iraq.* 2nd ed. (Lanham, MD: Scarecrow Press).

Ghosh, J. (2011) 'Global Oil Prices', *MRZine*, viewed 2 July 2014. http://mrzine.monthlyreview.org/2011/ghosh190711.html

Goodwin, N., J. Harris, J. Nelson, B. Roach and M. Torras (2015) 'Deficit and Debts'. In *Macroeconomics in Context*, 2nd ed., 363–381. (New York: Routledge), 1. http://www.ase.tufts.edu/gdae/Pubs/te/MAC/2e/MAC_2e_Chapter16.pdf.

Gramsci, A. (1971) *Selections from the Prison Notebooks* (New York: International Publishers).

——— (1978) *Selections from Political Writings (1921–1926)*, Quintin Hoare (ed.) (London: Lawrence and Wishart).

Guerriero, M. (2012) 'The Labour Share of Income around the World: Evidence from a Panel Dataset', IDPM Development Economics and Public Policy Working Paper Series, no. 32.

Haaretz Service and Reuters (2011) 'Assad Cousin to New York Times: No Stability in Israel if There's No Stability in Syria', *Haaretz*, viewed 2 July 2014. http://www.haaretz.com/news/diplomacy-defense/assad-cousin-to-new-york-times-no-stability-in-israel-if-there-s-no-stability-in-syria-1.360907

Haggard, S. (1990) *Pathways from the Periphery: The Politics of Growth in Newly Industrializing Countries* (New York: Cornell University Press).

Halliday, D. (2013) 'WHO Refuses To Publish Report On Cancers And Birth Defects In Iraq Caused By Depleted Uranium Ammunition'. *Biblioteca Pleyades.* http://www.bibliotecapleyades.net/ciencia/ciencia_uranium80.htm.

Hallinan, C. (2015) 'The Saudis Are Stumbling. They May Take The Middle East With Them.'. *Foreign Policy In Focus.* http://fpif.org/the-saudis-are-stumbling-they-may-take-the-middle-east-with-them/.

Halpern, M. (1962) 'Middle Eastern Armies and the New Middle Class', in J. J. Johnson (ed.), *The Role of the Military in Underdeveloped Countries.* (Princeton: Princeton University Press).

Harris, L. (2003) 'Our World-Historical Gamble', Ideas in Action TV, 11 March 2003, viewed http://www.ideasinactiontv.com/tcs_daily/2003/03/our-world-historical-gamble.html

Hassan, B. (2005) *The Politics of Surrender.* (Beirut: Dar Al-Rayess).

Haseeb, K. D. (ed.) (1991) *The Future of the Arab Nation: Challenges and Options* (Beirut: Centre for Arab Unity Studies).

Hassan, M., and Sassanpour, C. (2008) 'Labour Market Pressures in Egypt: Why Is the Unemployment Rate Stubbornly High?', *Journal of Development and Economic Policies*, vol. 10, no. 2.

Hegel, G. W. F. (1975) *Hegel's Logic: Being Part One of the Encyclopaedia of the Philosophical Sciences (1830)*, W. Wallace (transl.) (Oxford: Clarendon Press).

Heydemann, S. (ed.) (2000) *War, Institutions, and Social Change in the Middle East* (Berkeley: University of California Press).
———(1992) 'The Political Logic of Economic Rationality: Selective Liberalisation in Syria', in H. J. Barkey (ed.), *The Politics of Economic Reform in the Middle East* (New York: St. Martin's Press), pp. 11–32.
Hinnebusch, R. (1993) 'Syria', in T. Niblock and E. Murphy (eds.), *Economic and Political Liberalisation in the Middle East* (London: British Academy Press), pp. 177–202.
———(1994) 'Liberalisation in Syria: the Struggle of Economic Rationality and Political Rationality', in E. Kienle (ed.), *Contemporary Syria: Liberalisation between Cold War and Cold Peace* (London: British Academic Press), pp. 97–113.
———(2001) 'The Politics of Economic Liberalization: Comparing Egypt and Syria', in H. Hakimian and Z. Moshaver (eds.), *The State and Global Change: The Political Economy of Transition in the Middle East and North Africa* (Richmond: Curzon), pp. 111–34.
Hirschman, A. O. (1969) 'The Strategy of Economic Development', in A.N. Agarwal, and S.P. Singh (eds.), *Accelerating Investment in Developing Economies* (London: Oxford Press).
History of the Communist Party of the Soviet Union (CPSU)(1939). (New York: International Publishers).
Hobsbawm. E. J. (ed.) (1964) *Pre-capitalist Economic Formations* (London: Lawrence & Wishart).
Hobsbawm, E. J. (1994) *The Age of Extremes: A History of the World, 1914–1991* (New York: Pantheon Books).
———(1998) *On History* (London: Abacus).
Hopfinger, H., and M. Boeckler (1996) 'Step by Step to an Open Economic System: Syria Sets Course for Liberalisation', *British Journal of Middle Eastern Studies*, vol. 23, no. 2, pp. 183–202.
Hudson, M. (2010) 'From Marx to Goldman Sachs: The Fictions of Fictitious Capital, and the Financialization of Industry', *Critique: Journal of Socialist Theory*, vol. 38, no. 3, pp. 419–444.
Human Rights Watch (1991) *Human Rights Watch World Report 1992: Events of 1991*. (New York and Washington, DC: Human Rights Watch).
Hussein, M. (1971) *La Lutte de Classes en Egypt, 1945–1970* (Paris: Maspero).
Ilyenkov, E. V (1960) *Dialectics of the Abstract and the Concrete in Marx's Capital Written: 1960; Source: The Dialectics of the Abstract and the Concrete in Marx's Capital* (Publisher: Progress Publishers, 1982).
Ilyenkov, E. V. (1982) *The Dialectics of the Abstract and the Concrete in Marx's Capital*, S. Syrovatkin (transl.) (Moscow: Progress Publishers).
IAIGC (Inter-Arab Investment Guarantee Corporation) (2004). *2004 Report*. Inter-Arab Investment Guarantee Corporation; viewed 6 June 2012 http://www.iaigc.org/index_e.html
Ikram, K. (2006) *The Egyptian Economy, 1952–2000* (New York: Routledge).
IFAD (2001) https://www.ifad.org/documents/10180/53c8e7e4-8cd2-4ac9-8772-22773897e9fd 19 January 2001.
ILO (various issues) *Key Indicators of the Labour Market (KILM)*, 8th ed. http://www.ilo.org/empelm/what/WCMS_114240/lang—en/index.htm
Ilyenkov, E. V. (1977) 'A Contribution to the Problem of a Dialectical Materialistic Critique of Objective Idealism', in *Dialectical Logic: Essays on Its History and Theory* (Moscow: Progress Publishers).

IMF (International Monetary Fund) (2005) *Staff Report for the 2005 Article IV Consultation, 2005 Consultation with Iraq* (Washington, DC: IMF)
IMF (International Monetary Fund) (2009) 'Syrian Arab Republic: 2008 Article IV Consultation', *IMF Country Report No.09/55*, February 2009 (Washington, DC: IMF).
IMF (various years) International Financial Statistics (IFS). http://data.imf.org/?sk=5DABAFF2-C5AD-4D27-A175-1253419C02D1
Indian Express (2015) 'Machete attack by Ugandan kills 23 in DR Congo', *Indian Express*, 4 February 2015, viewed 7 August 2015. http://indianexpress.com/article/world/middle-east-africa/machete-attack-by-ugandan-kills-23-in-dr-congo/
IRIN (Integrated Regional Information Networks) (2009) 'Egypt: Nearly a Third of Children Malnourished', 8 November, viewed 11 March 2012. http://www.irinnews.org/report/86893/egypt-nearly-a-third-of-children-malnourished-report
Ismail, F. (2010) 'Youssef Zein Opens His Closet Secrets after 40 Years of Silence', translated from Arabic, *Al-Arabiya*, viewed 2 July 2014. http://www.alarabiya.net/articles/2005/06/07/13742.html
ISRB (The Iraqi Strategic Review Board) (2004) *National Development Strategy 2005–2007* (Baghdad: The Iraqi Strategic Review Board)
IWA (International Workers Association) (2003) *'Iraq, Oil and U.S World Hegemony'*, 16 March 2003, viewed 18 November 2005 http://www.iwa-ait.org/iraq-II-e.html
Issa, A. (2015) 'Massive protest wave in Iraq challenges sectarianism', Waging Non-Violence Org, 9 September 2015, viewed http://wagingnonviolence.org/2015/09/massive-protest-wave-iraq-challenges-sectarianism/
Issawi, C. (1955) 'The Entrepreneur Class', in S. N. Fisher (ed.), *Social Forces in the Middle East* (New York: Cornell University Press), pp. 116–136.
Jomo, K. S. and E. S. Reinert (2005) *The Origin of Development Economics: How Schools of Economic Thought Have Addressed Development* (New Delhi: Tulika Books).
Juhasz, A. (2004) 'The Handover that Wasn't', *Alternet*, viewed 2 July 2014. http://www.alternet.org/story/19293/the_handover_that_wasn%27t
Kalecki, M. (1943) 'Political Aspects of Full Employment', *Political Quarterly*, vol. 14, no. 4.
——— (1972) 'The Structure of Investment', in *Selected Chapters on the Economic Growth of the Socialist and the Mixed Economy* (Cambridge: Cambridge University Press), pp. 102–112.
——— (1976) *Essays on Developing Economies* (Hassocks: Harvester Press).
Kanbur, R. (2001) *Economic Policy, Distribution and Poverty: The Nature of Disagreements*, IFAD Rome, 19 January 2001 https://www.ifad.org/documents/10180/53c8e7e4-8cd2-4ac9-8772-22773897e9fd
Khuri, F. (1982) 'The Study of Civil-Military Relations in Modernising Societies in the Middle East: A Critical Assessment', in R. Kolkowicz and A. Korbonski (eds.), *Soldiers, Peasants and Bureaucrats: Civil-Military Relations in Communist and Modernising Societies* (London: George Allen and Unwin), pp. 9–28.
Kishk, H. (2012) 'Tadahwur 'anmāṭ al-ghadhā' ladā al-falāḥīn al-fuqarā' wa-al-'ummāl al-zirā'iyyīn al-mu'dimīn fī al-rīf al-miṣriyy: al-'āliyyāt wa-al-natā'ij' [The decline of food production of farmers and agricultural workers in the Egyptian countryside: mechanisms and results], January 2012, Thimar Conference, Amman. http://www.athimar.org/Article-31
Klare, M. T. (2008) 'Barreling into Recession: How Oil Burst the American Bubble', *Alternet*, 31 January, viewed 2 July 2014. http://www.alternet.org/story/75649/barreling_into_recession%3A_how_oil_burst_the_american_bubble
Krogstrup, S. and L. Matar (2005) Foreign Direct Investment, Absorptive Capacity and Growth in the Arab World. The Graduate Institute of International Studies Working Paper, no. 2.

Kroll, A. (2011) 'Tomgram: Andy Kroll, the Spirit of Egypt in Madison', *Tom Dispatch*, viewed 2 July 2014. http://www.tomdispatch.com/blog/175360/
Labica, G., and G. Bensussan. (1985) *Dictionnaire Critique Du Marxisme* (Paris: Presses Universitaires de France).
Lambert, W. G., A. R. Millard and M. Civil (1999) *Atra-Hasis: The Babylonian Story of the Flood* (Winona Lake, IN: Eisenbrauns).
Lapavitsas, C. (2013) *Profiting without Producing' Profiting without Producing: How Finance Exploits Us All* (London: Verso).
Larrain, J. (1979) *The Concept of Ideology* (Athens: University of Georgia Press).
——— (1983) *Marxism and Ideology* (New York: Humanities Press).
——— (1989) *Theories of Development: Capitalism, Colonialism, and Dependency* (Cambridge: Polity Press).
——— (1994) *Ideology and Cultural Identity: Modernity and the Third World Presence* (Cambridge: Polity Press).
Lauesen, T., and Z. Cope (2015) 'Imperialism and the Transformation of Values into Prices', *Monthly Review*, vol. 67, no. 3. http://monthlyreview.org/2015/07/01/imperialism-and-the-transformation-of-values-into-prices/#fn15
Lawson, F. H. (1984) 'Syria's Intervention in the Lebanese Civil War, 1976: A Domestic Conflict Explanation', *International Organization*, vol. 38, no. 3, pp. 451–480.
——— (1989) 'Class Politics and State Power in Ba'thi Syria', in B. Berberoglu (ed.), *Power and Stability in the Middle East* (London: Zed Books), pp. 15–30.
Leca, J. (1988) 'Social Structure and Political Stability: Comparative Evidence from the Algerian, Syrian, and Iraqi Cases', in A. Dawishi, and I. W. Zartman (eds.), *Beyond Coercion: The Durability of the Arab State* (New York: Croom Helm), pp. 164–196.
Lee Boggs, G. (2011) *The Next American Revolution: Sustainable Activism for the 21st Century* (Berkeley, Los Angeles and London: University of California Press).
Lenin, V. (1917) *The State and Revolution*, in *Collected Works*, vol. 25 (Moscow: Progress Publishers), pp. 381–492.
——— ([1902] 1961) *What Is to be Done? Burning Questions of Our Movement*, J. Fineberg and G. Hanna (transl.) (Moscow: Foreign Languages Publishing Houses), viewed 2 July 2014. https://www.marxists.org/archive/lenin/works/1901/witbd/index.htm
——— ([1920] 1964) *Left-Wing Communism: An Infantile Disorder*, J. Katzer (transl.) (Moscow: Progress Publishers), viewed 2 July 2014. https://www.marxists.org/archive/lenin/works/1920/lwc/
——— (1966 [1916]) *Imperialism, the Highest Stage of Capitalism* (Moscow: Progress Publishers).
——— (1918) *The Proletarian Revolution and the Renegade Kautsky*, Collected Works, vol. 28, 1974 (Progress Publishers, Moscow), pp. 227–325.
Li, M., F. Xiao and A. Zhu (2007) 'Long Waves, Institutional Changes, and Historical Trends: A study of the long-term movement of the profit rate in the capitalist world-economy'. *Journal of World-Systems Research*, vol. 13, no. 1, pp. 33–54.
Lieven, A. (2004) *America Right or Wrong: An anatomy of American nationalism* (New York: Oxford University Press).
Lindorff, D. (2015) 'War: Where 69¢ of Each of Your Tax Dollars Goes', *Nation of Change*, 8 February, viewed 26 July 2015. http://www.nationofchange.org/2015/02/08/war-69%C2%A2-tax-dollars-goes/
Liu, H. C. K. (2008) 'Too Big to Fail versus Moral Hazard', *Asia Times Online*, 23 September, viewed 13 October 2013. http://www.atimes.com/atimes/Global_Economy/JI23Dj12.html

Longuenesse, E. (1996) 'Labor in Syria: The Emergence of New Identities', in E. J. Goldberg (ed.), *The Social History of Labor in the Middle East* (Boulder: Westview Press, Inc), pp. 99–129.
Lukács, G. (1967 [1919]) *History and Class Consciousness*, R. Livingstone (transl.) (London: Merlin Press).
―――(1971) 'Preface', in A. Bostock (transl.), *The Theory of the Novel* (London: Merlin Press), pp. 11–23.
Lutsky V. B. (1969) *Modern History of the Arab Countries* (Moscow: Progress Publishers).
Luxembourg, R. (1913) *The Accumulation of Capital*, viewed 5 July 2012. http://www.marxists.org/archive/marx/works/1867-c1/ch30.htm
Mao, T. (1937) 'Selected Works of Mao Tse-Tung'. *Marxists.Org*. https://www.marxists.org/reference/archive/mao/selected-works/volume-1/mswv1_17.htm.
―――(1938) 'Problems of War and Strategy'. 6 Novemenber 1938. Viewed 23 February 2015, https://www.marxists.org/reference/archive/mao/selected-works/volume-2/mswv2_12.htm
Mandel, E. (1975) *Late Capitalism*. (London: New Left Books).
―――(1990) 'Karl Marx' in J. Eatwell, M. Milgate and P. Newman (eds.), *Marxian Economics* (London: W. W. Norton & Company).
Marcuse, H. (2014 [1965]) 'Baran's Critique of Modern Society and of the Social Sciences', *Monthly Review*, vol. 65, no. 10
Marquetti, A. and D. Foley (2011) *Extended Penn World Tables – EPWT Version 4.0*. New York, August.
Marx, K. (1844) 'The German Ideology'. *Marxists.Org*. https://www.marxists.org/archive/marx/works/1845/german-ideology/ch01a.htm.
Marx, K. (1847) *Wage Labour and Capital Delivered*. Neue Rheinische Zeitung, 5–8 and 11 April 1849; December 1847. https://www.marxists.org/archive/marx/works/1847/wage-labour/index.htm
―――(1858) Marx to Engels, October 8, 1858, in Marx and Engels, *Selected Correspondence* (Moscow: Progress Publishers, 1975).
Marx, K. (1863) *Theories of Surplus Value* (Moscow: Progress Publishers).
―――(1867) *Capital: A Critique of Political Economy, vol. 1, The Process of Production of Capital* (Moscow, Progress Publishers).
Marx, K. (1868) Marx to Kugelmann, London, 11 July 1868. https://www.marxists.org/archive/marx/works/1868/letters/68_07_11-abs.htm, viewed 2 January 2013.
Marx, K. (1894) *Capital: A Critique of Political Economy, vol. 3, The Process of Capitalist Production as a Whole* (New York: International Publisher).
―――([1847] 1947) *Wage Labour and Capital*, F. Engels (transl.), viewed 12 January 2013. http://www.marxists.org/archive/marx/works/1847/wage-labour/index.htm
―――(1973 [1863]) *Grundrisse: Foundations of the Critique of Political Economy* (Rough Draft), M. Nicolaus (transl.) (New York: Penguin).
Marxists Org. (n.d.) 'Abstract' in *Glossary terms: 'A-B'*, viewed on 5 March 2012. http://www.marxists.org/glossary/terms/a/b.htm#abstract
Marzouk, N. (2011) 'The Economic Origins of Syria's Uprising', *Al Akhbar Newspaper*, 28 August, viewed 2 July 2014. http://english.al-akhbar.com/node/372
Matar, L. (2012) 'The Political Economy of Investment: A Historical Examination of Domestic Investment Behaviour in Syria', PhD Dissertation, SOAS, University of London.
―――(2016) *The Political Economy of Investment in Syria* (London: Palgrave Macmillan).

Meillasoux C. (1998) Homme et Société: Anthropologie. In *Terrains et engagements de Claude Meillassoux Broché*, B. Schlemmer (ed.) (Paris: Karthala Paris).
Mészáros, I. (1970) *Marx's Theory of Alienation*, viewed on 2 July 2014. http://www.marxists.org/archive/meszaros/works/alien/index.htm
——(1995) *Beyond Capital: Towards a Theory of Transition* (New York: Monthly Review Press)
——(2011) 'The Dialectic Of Structure And History: An Introduction'. *Monthly Review* 63 (1): 17. doi: 10.14452/mr-063-01-2011-05_2.
MEED (Middle East Economic Digest) (1996) *Foreign Aid Substitutes for Self-Reliance*, 24 May (London: MEED).
Meisenhelder, T. (1993) 'Amilcar Cabral's Theory of Class Suicide and Revolutionary Socialism'. *Monthly Review* 45 (6): 40. doi: 10.14452/mr-045-06-1993-10_4.
Mirowski, P. (1989) *More Heat than Light Economics as Social Physics, Physics as Nature's Economics*. (Cambridge: Cambridge University Press).
Mora, F. O., and Q. Wiktorowicz (2003) 'Economic Reform and Military: China, Cuba, and Syria in Comparative Perspective', *International Journal of Comparative Sociology*, vol. 44, no. 2, pp. 87–128.
Moubayed, S. (2007) 'Syria: Reform Balance Sheet', *Arab Reform Bulletin*, vol. 5, no. 2.
Munif, A. R. (1987) *Cities of Salt* (Cities of Salt Trilogy, vol. 1), (New York: Vintage Books).
Najmah, I. (1986) *The Economic Question in the Syrian Arab Region [al-mas'alah al-iqtisadiyah fi al-qutr al-'Arabi al-Suri]*, translated from Arabic, Fifth Economic Tuesday Symposium. (Damascus: Economic Sciences Associations).
Niblock, T. (1993) 'International and Domestic Factors in the Economic Liberalisation Process in Arab Countries', in T. Niblock and E. Murphy (eds.), *Economic and Political Liberalisation in the Middle East* (London: British Academy Press), pp. 55–87.
Neumann, M. (2012) 'Reflections on Kant and Moral Equivalence', *Counterpunch*, 21 November 2002, viewed http://www.counterpunch.org/2002/11/21/reflections-on-kant-and-moral-equivalence/
Ollman, B. (2003) *Dance of the Dialectic: Steps in Marx's Method* (Urbana: University of Illinois Press).
OPEC a (Organization of the Petroleum Exporting Countries, various years) *Annual Statistical Bulletin* (Vienna: OPEC).
OPEC b (various years) *Monthly Oil Market Report* (Vienna: OPEC).
OPHI (Oxford Poverty and Human Development Initiative) (2011) 'Multidimensional Poverty Index (MPI) At a Glance, December 2011', in *Country Briefing: Syrian Arab Republic*, viewed 1 January 2012. http://www.ophi.org.uk/wp-content/uploads/Syrian-Arab-Republic1.pdf
Osman, T. (2013). *Egypt on the Brink: From Nasser to The Muslim Brotherhood (Revised and Updated Edition)*. 2nd ed. (New Haven: Yale University Press).
Owen, R. (2004) *State, Power and Politics in the Making of the Modern Middle East*, 3rd ed. (New York, London: Routledge).
Pappenheim, F. (1959) *The Alienation of Modern Man: An Interpretation Based on Marx and Tönnies* (New York: Monthly Review Press).
Parenti, M. (2003) 'To Kill Iraq', *Michael Parenti Political Archive*, May 2003, viewed http://www.michaelparenti.org/IRAQGeorge2.htm
Patnaik, P. (2009) *Finance Capital and Fiscal Deficits*. News Analysis. Oxford: International Development Economics Associates. http://www.networkideas.org/news/may2009/news21_Finance.htm.

———(2008) *The Value of Money* (New Delhi: Tulika Books).
Patnaik, U. and P. Patnaik (2015) 'Imperialism in the Era of Globalization', *Monthly Review*, vol. 67, no. 3
Peck, J. (1970) 'An Exchange', *Bulletin of Concerned Asian Scholars*, vol. 2, no. 3 (pp. 60–61).
Perelman, M. (1999) 'Marx, Devalorisation, and the Theory of Value', *Cambridge Journal of Economics*, vol. 23, no. 6, pp. 719–28.
Perthes, V. (1992) 'The Syrian Economy in the 1980s', *Middle East Journal*, vol. 46, no. 1, pp. 37–58.
———(1994) 'Stages of Economic and Political Liberalisation', in E. Kienle (ed.), *Contemporary Syria: Liberalisation between Cold War and Cold Peace* (London: British Academic Press), pp. 44–71.
———(1995) *The Political Economy of Syria under Asad* (London: I. B. Tauris).
Petras, J. (1976) 'State Capitalism and the Third World', *Journal of Contemporary Asia*, vol. 6, no. 4, pp. 432–443.
Petras, J (2011A). *Empire or Republic: From Joplin, Missouri to Kabul, Afghanistan*, accessed 5 March 2012. http://petras.lahaine.org/?p=1857
Petras, J. (2011B) 'Washington Faces the Arab Revolts: Sacrificing Dictators to Save the State', 2 July, viewed 15 April 2014. http://petras.lahaine.org/articulo.php?p=1837&more=1&c=1
Pfeifer, K. (2000) 'Does Structural Adjustment Spell Relief from Unemployment?': A Comparison of Four IMF 'Success Stories' in the Middle East and North Africa', in W. Shahin and G. Dibeh (eds.), *Earnings Inequality, Unemployment, and Poverty in the Middle East and North Africa* (Westport, CT: Greenwood Press), pp. 111–151.
Picard, E. (1988) 'Arab Military in Politics: From Revolutionary Plot to Authoritarian State', in A. Dawisha, and I. W. Zartman (eds.), *Beyond Coercion: The Durability of the Arab State* (New York: Croom Helm), pp. 116–147.
Polling, S. (1994) 'Investment Law No. 10: Which Future for the Private Sector', in E. Kienle (ed.), *Contemporary Syria: Liberalisation between Cold War and Cold Peace* (London: British Academic Press), pp. 14–25.
Pool, D. (1993) 'The Links between Economic and Political Liberalization', in T. Niblock and E. Murphy (eds.), *Economic and Political Liberalisation in the Middle East* (London: British Academy Press), pp. 40–54.
Poulantzas, N. A. (1973) *Political Power and Social Classes*, translated from French (London: Sheed and Ward).
———(1978) *State, Power, Socialism* (London: NLB).
Prebisch, R. (1950) *The Economic Development of Latin America and Its Principal Problems* (New York: United Nations Department of Economic Affairs).
Richards, A. and J. Waterbury (1990) *A Political Economy of the Middle East: State, Class, and Economic Development* (Boulder: Westview Press).
Rizq Allāh, H. (1969) *Culture Et Développement En Syrie Et Dans Les Pays Retardés* (Paris: Éditions Anthropos).
Robinson, G. E. (1998) 'Elite Cohesion, Regime Succession and Political Instability in Syria', *Middle East Policy*, vol. 5, no. 4, pp. 159–179.
Rodinson, M. (1978) *Islam and Capitalism* (Austin: University of Texas Press).
Rousseau, J. J. (1762) *The Social Contract* (Book 2) viewed 29 September 2015. https://www.marxists.org/reference/subject/economics/rousseau/social-contract/ch02.htm
Rubin, I. I. (1972) *Essays on Marx's Theory of Value* (Detroit: Black and Red).

Sanger, D. E. (2012) 'Rebel Arms Flow Is Said to Benefit Jihadists in Syria', *The New York Times*, viewed 2 July 2014. http://www.nytimes.com/2012/10/15/world/middleeast/jihadists-receiving-most-arms-sent-to-syrian-rebels.html?pagewanted=all&_r=0

Saleh, Y. (2013) 'UPDATE 2 – Egypt Wheat Stocks Dwindle, Sufficient for 89 Days', Reuters, viewed 2 July 2014. http://www.reuters.com/article/2013/03/13/egypt-wheat-idUSL6N0C56CA20130313

Sayed, M. (2003) 'Models of Development in Arab Thought'. Centre for Developing Counties Research, Jāmi'at al-Qāhirah. Markaz Dirāsāt wa-Buḥūth al-Duwal al-Nāmiyah, Namaizig al-tanmiyah fi-il-fikr al-'arabiyy (Cairo University).

Schumpeter, J. A. (1994) [1942]. *Capitalism, Socialism and Democracy* (London: Routledge).

Sellers, J. (1976) 'Famine and Interdependence', in G. R. Lucas Jr, and T. W. Ogletree (eds.), *Lifeboat Ethics: The Moral Dilemmas of World Hunger* (New York: Harper & Row).

Seymour, R. (2012) 'The Syrian Revolt Enters a New Phase', *Leninology*, 24 July, viewed 19 February 2014. http://www.leninology.co.uk/2012/07/the-syrian-revolt-enters-new-phase.html

Shafaq News (2013) 'Government Report: Iraq Loses USD40bn Annually Due to Electricity Crisis' *Shafaq News*, 14 September 2013, viewed 29 September 2015. http://www.zawya.com/story/Government_report_Iraq_loses_USD40bn_annually_due_to_electricity_crisis-ZAWYA20130914064103/?lok=064100130914&&zawyaemailmarketing

Shaoul, J. (2010) 'Growing Poverty in Syria', *World Socialist Web Site*, viewed 2 July 2014. http://www.wsws.org/en/articles/2010/07/soci-j13.html

Sharp, J. M. (2015) *Egypt: Background and U.S. Relations* (Washington, DC: Congressional Research Service).

Sherman, H. J., and M. Meeropol (2013) *Principles of Macroeconomics: Activist vs. Austerity Politics* (New York: M. E Sharp Inc.)

Shumway, C. (2005) 'Iraqis Endure Worse Conditions Than under Saddam, UN Survey Finds', *The New Standard*, viewed 2 July 2014. http://newstandardnews.net/content/?items=1816

SIPRI (Stockholm International Peace Research Institute, various years). *Yearbook and Military Expenditure Database* (Stockholm: Stockholm International Peace Research).

Slackman, M. (2008) 'Bread, the (Subsidised) Stuff of Life in Egypt', *The New York Times*, viewed 2 July 2014. http://www.nytimes.com/2008/01/16/world/africa/16iht-bread.4.9271958.html?_r=2&

Sourani, A. (2015) 'A Reading in the Position of the Petty Bourgeoisie'. Lecture, Beit Lahm University.

Spindle, B. (2005) 'Syria Confronts a Turning Point: Lebanon Exit Brings a Reckoning with Regional, Domestic Issues', *Wall Street Journal*, viewed 31 January 2006. http://www.wsj.com/articles/SB111498776614921686

Stace, W. T. (1955) *The Philosophy of Hegel: A Systematic Exposition* (New York: Dover Publications).

Stalon, J.-L. (2015) 'We Must Address Political Economy of Growth without Development in Africa', The *East African*, 12 October 2015 http://www.theeastafrican.co.ke/OpEd/comment/Address-political-economy-of-growth-without-development-Africa/-/434750/2910370/-/t1s6bdz/-/index.html

Standing, G. (2011) *The Precariat: The New Dangerous Class* (London and New York: Bloomsbury Academic).

Sukkar, N. (1994) 'The Crisis of 1986 and Syria's Plan for Reform', in E. Kienle (ed.), *Contemporary Syria: Liberalization between Cold War and Cold Peace* (London: Academic Press), pp. 26–43.
Sutcliffe, B. (2006) 'Death and Development', in *Human Development in the Era of Globalization: Essays in Honor of Keith B. Griffin* (London: Edward Elgar).
Sweezy, P. M. (1981). 'Four Lectures on Marxism'. *Monthly Review*. Accessed 23 February 2015 http://monthlyreview.org/books/pb5844/
Taqi, J. M. (2008) 'Who Is More Worthy of Compensation: Iran or Iraq', *Ahewar*, http://www.ahewar.org/, viewed 30 July 2010.
Tarbush, M. A. (1982) *The Role of the Military in Politics: A Case Study of Iraq to 1941* (London: Kegan Paul International), pp. 143–144.
Targetti, F. and A. P. Thirwall (1989) *The Essential Kaldor* (London: Gerald Duckworth & Co. Ltd).
The Syria Report (2003) 'Syria Abolishes 17 Year Old Repressive Forex Law', viewed 4 August 2008. http://www.syria-report.com/news/finance/syria-abolishes-17-year-old-repressive-forex-law
———(2008) 'Remittances to Reach USD 850 Million in 2008', viewed 22 December 2010. http://www.syria-report.com/news/economy/remittances-reach-usd-850-million-2008
Syria Report (2010) 'Byblos Bank Syria to Increase Capital to SYP 6 Billion', viewed 8 November 2011. http://www.syria-report.com/news/finance/byblos-bank-syria-increase-capital-syp-6-billion
Todaro, M. P. (1979) *Economic Development* (Englewood Cliffs, NJ: Prentice-Hall).
Truitt, W. H. (2005) *Marxist Ethics* (New York: International Publishers).
Turner, B. (1984) *Capitalism and Class in the Middle East: Theories of Social Change and Economic Development* (London: Heinemann Educational Books Ltd).
UN (1966) International Covenant on Civil and Political Rights General Assembly resolution 2200A (XXI) of 16 December 1966 (New York: United Nations).
UN Treaty Series (1975) No. 14907 *Iran and Iraq Agreement Concerning the Use of Frontier Watercourses* 26 December 1975 (Baghdad: UN Secretariat)
UN (2003) *Analysis of Performances and Assessment of Growth and Productivity in the ESCWA Region* (New York: United Nations).
———(various years) *Standard International Trade Classification* (New York: United Nations).
———(2004) *Analysis of Performance and Assessment of Growth and Productivity in the ESCWA Region, Second Issue* (E/ESCWA/EAD/2004/2).
———(2005A) *Survey of Economic and Social Developments in the ESCWA Region 2004–2005* (New York: United Nations).
———(2005B) 'Daily Living Conditions in Iraq Dismal, UN Survey Finds', *UN News Centre*, viewed 2 July 2014. http://www.un.org/apps/news/story.asp?newsID=14255#.U9tDyvmSxkg
———(2006) *Survey of Economic and Social Developments in Western Asia* (Beirut: ESCWA).
———(various years) *National Accounts Statistics: Analysis of Main Aggregates, 2004–2005* (New York: United Nations).
———(2007) Expert Group Meeting on Employment Policies and Economic Development in Countries Including those Emerging from Conflict, 19–20 December 2007, Damascus.
———(2008A) *The Demographic Profile of Arab Countries Ageing Rural Population* (New York: United Nations).

——— (2008B) *Survey of Economic and Social Developments in the ESCWA Region 2007–2008* (New York: United Nations).
——— (2009) 'Summary of the Survey of Economic and Social Developments in the Economic and Social Commission for Western Asia Region'.
——— (2011) *National Accounts Studies of the ESCWA Region, Bulletin No. 31* (New York: United Nations).
——— (2012) *Survey of Economic and Social Developments in the ESCWA Region* (New York: United Nations).
——— (2014) *Bulletin of Industrial Statistics for Arab Countries, Eighth Issue* (Beirut: United Nations).
——— (2015) *Survey of Economic and Social Developments in the Arab Region 2014–2015: Summary* (New York: United Nations). http://www.escwa.un.org/information/publications/edit/upload/E_ESCWA_EDID_15_2_SUMMARY_E.pdf
UNESCO (2015) *Institute for Statistics* (Montréal: UNESCO Institute for Statistics).
UNCTAD (2007) *Trade and Development Report 2007* (New York: United Nations).
UNCTAD-*World Investment Report (WIR)* (various years), various issues.
UNCTAD (2014) *Trade And Development Report* (Geneva and New York: United Nations).
UN Comtrade (various) *Commodity Trade Statistics Database*, http://comtrade.un.org/db/
UNDP (2004) *Iraq Living Conditions Survey 2004*. (Iraq: UNDP and Ministry of Planning and Development Cooperation).
UNDP-AHDR (Arab Human Development Reports, various years) http://www.arab-hdr.org/
UNICEF (2012) 'UNICEF Warns on High Rates of Malnutrition among Children in Yemen', *UN News Centre*, viewed 2 July 2014. http://www.un.org/apps/news/story.asp?NewsID=41037&Cr=yemen&Cr1=#.U9sfy_mSxkg
——— (2013) 'At a Glance: Syrian Arab Republic – Statistics', *UNICEF*, viewed on 2 July 2014. http://www.unicef.org/infobycountry/syria_statistics.html
UNIDO (2014) Industrial Statistics Database, INDSTAT4 – 2014 edition (Geneva: UNIDO)
UN Statistics Database National Accounts Statistics: Main Aggregates and Detailed Tables (2005) http://unstats.un.org/unsd/nationalaccount/madt.asp
UN-WFP (2004) *Baseline Food Security Analysis in Iraq* (Iraq: UN Country Office), pp. 27–33.
US Department of State (1959) 'Short-Term Prospects for Iraq', Foreign Relations of the United States, 1958–1960, vol. 12, Near East Region; Iraq; Iran; Arabian Peninsula, Document 210, viewed 16 March 2010. https://history.state.gov/historicaldocuments/frus1958-60v12/d210
——— (2013) 'The 1973 Arab-Israeli War', in Milestones: 1969–1976, last modified 31 October, viewed 28 July 2014. https://history.state.gov/milestones/1969-1976/arab-israeli-war-1973
UTIP (University of Texas Inequality Project) (2008) Estimated Household Income Inequality Data Set, viewed 8 October 2012. http://utip.gov.utexas.edu/data.html
Vahabzadeh, P. (2010) *A Guerrilla Odyssey: Modernization, Secularism, Democracy, and Fadai Period of National Liberation in Iran 1971–1979 (Modern Intellectual and Political History of the Middle East)* (New York: Syracuse University Press).
Vandenberghe, F. (2001) 'Reification: History of the Concept', *International Encyclopedia of the Social and Behavioral Sciences*, vol. 19.

Vatikiotis, P. (1972) *Revolutions in the Middle East and Other Case Studies* (London: Allen and Unwin).
Vltchek, A. (2016) 'Iraqi Kurdistan Is Collapsing. Western Propaganda and "Two Parallel Realities"', Global Research, New Eastern Outlook, 18 February 2016 http://www.globalresearch.ca/iraqi-kurdistan-is-collapsing-western-propaganda-and-two-parallel-realities/5508655
Wallerstein, I. (1979) *The Capitalist World Economy: Essays* (New York: Cambridge University Press)
――――(2000) 'Globalization or the Age of Transition?', *International Sociology*, vol. 15, no. 2, pp. 251–267.
――――(2011) 'Structural Crisis in the World-System: Where Do We Go from Here?', *Monthly Review*, vol. 62, no. 10.
Weeks, J. (1998) CDPR Discussion Paper 0498: The Law of Value and the Analysis of Underdevelopment. London: Centre for Development Policy and Research, School of Oriental and African Studies, University of London.
――――(2014) *The Irreconcilable Inconsistencies of Neoclassical Macroeconomics; Routledge Frontiers of Political Economy*. Reprint Edition (London: Routledge).
Weil, R. (2010) 'What Difference Does a Revolution Make? A Preliminary Contrast of India and China' *Mrzine*, http://mrzine.monthlyreview.org/2010/weil180710.html, viewed 3 November 2014.
Westall, S. and T. Perry (2013) 'Food Price Rises Put Restive Egypt on Edge', Reuters, viewed 2 July 2014. http://www.reuters.com/article/2013/03/13/egypt-food-idUSL6N0C5DKT20130313
Wood, E. M. (1998) 'The Agrarian Origins of Capitalism', *Monthly Review*, vol. 50, no. 3.
World Bank (various years). *World Development Indicators* (Washington, DC: The World Bank).
――――(1995) *Claiming the Future: Choosing Prosperity in the Middle East and North Africa* (Washington, DC: The World Bank).
――――(2011a) *Middle East and North Africa Region, Assessment of the Local Manufacturing Potential for Concentrated Solar Power (CSP) Projects* (Washington DC: The World Bank).
――――(2011b) 'Arab World Initiative for Food Security', viewed 4 June 2013. http://www.wds.worldbank.org/external/default/WDSContentServer/WDSP/IB/2011/05/27/000001843_20110601143246/Rendered/PDF/P126506000AWIFS000PID-000Concept0Stage.pdf
――――(2012) *World Development Indicators (WDI)* (Washington, DC: The World Bank).
WTO (World Trade Organisation) (2012) 'Accession Status: Syrian Arab Republic', last modified 19 March, viewed 17 September 2013. https://www.wto.org/english/thewto_e/acc_e/a1_syrian_arab_republic_e.htm
Yadlin, A. (2015) 'Israel Has No Existential Threat', AlRased, http://www.arrased.net/?siteid=1&langid=5&itemID=56926, viewed 30 July 2015.
Zinni, A. (2002) 'Strategic Implications of a War on Iraq: Best and Worst Case Outcomes', *The Middle East Economic Survey*, viewed 2 July 2014. http://www.mafhoum.com/press4/119P5.htm

INDEX

Abdel-Malek, A. 12–13, 16, 19, 82n7, 104, 253
Abernathy, V. D. 82
absolute general law of capitalist accumulation (AGLCA) 241–42
absolute poverty 6
accumulation: merchant mode of 101–03; proletarianisation as primitive 205; by wars 11–12; *see also* capitalist accumulation; global accumulation
Afghan jihadis 7
Afghanistan 17, 194
agrarian reform 42
agriculture: contribution to employment/share of GDP **235t5.3**; investment in Egypt 205–06, **206t5.1**; productivity 202, 236–37
Al Nour party (Egypt) 110
Al Za'im, I. 137
Alavi, H. 131–32
Algeria 4, **235t5.3**
Algiers Treaty (1975) 172
Al-Khafaji, I. 63
Al-Kilani, R. 176
Allawi, A. 159
Al-Rantisi, A.-A. 169
Althusser, L. 219n9
Amin, S. 16, 19
Anbouba, I. 149
anti-development outcomes 10
Arab integrationist project 172–73
Arab socialism: achievements/reasons for collapse 42, 58–69, 280; and anti-imperialism 60; causes for turnaround to neo-liberalism 33–34; class considerations in 58–59; determinants of relative success of 33; development under 13, 31–37, 70–71; egalitarian distribution under 34, 48–49, 66; and elimination of working-class organisations 49; and exchange rate 47–48, 61; and food security 61n12; growth and social development, *vs.* neo-liberalism 4; growth rates *vs.* neoliberal rates 61; and imperialism 59; investment rate decline 62; and Iraq 63–64; job creation as matching workforce growth 10; means of production under 27, 42–43; as outperforming neoliberal model in economic/social dynamism 13, 29; particularity of 50; population growth under 61; and post-independence state-owned enterprises 60–61; price-caps under 39; private sector under 42–43, 61–63, 64–65; real wage growth under 29; and repression of working population 71; and rise of state bourgeois class 34; security building under 40, 49; and Soviet-style socialism 60; *see also* developing-country socialist regimes
Arab Spring 32
Arab World (AW): dominant mode of imperialist control in 156–57; overview of 4–12; strategic value of 20
Aristotle 208–09, 214n5
Assad, H. 130
austerity 257, 262–63; in Global North 193; taxes as result of 96, 257
authoritarian theft model 124n3
autonomy 33
Aziz, T. 159

Ba'ath party: disenfranching in Iraq 170; in post-independence Iraq 60; in post-independence Syria 139; reform in Syria under 55
Badiou, A. 20
Baker, J. III 159
Balibar, É. 112
Baran, P. A. 19, 70, 253
Barzani, M. 172
Ben-Gurion, D. 177
Bettelheim, C. 283
Black Liberation Movement 108
Bolsheviks 38, 39; *see also* Soviet Union
bourgeois democracy 30, 39, 72–73, 106, 112–13, 278, 279
bourgeoisie: ideology of 41; proxy 12–13; rise of Arab 32–33; transformation into comprador-merchant class 4, 13; *see also* petty bourgeoisie; state bourgeois
boycott, Arab 178
Braverman, H. 34–35, 83
Bremmer, P. 64
Brenner, P. 3
Bretton Woods 36, 87, 114
Browder, E. 38
Burawoy, M. 129

Cabral, A. 49
Callaghy, T. 128
Camp David Accords 7, 33, 46, 48, 56, 77–78, 81, 84, 105
capital: bourgeois democracy as key resilience mechanism of 72–73; fictitious 263; labour dislocation under national 224; reduction in technical composition of 10; as social relationship 40–41, 189; and socialisation 41–42; subordination of state to 263–64; universalising through financialisation 11; as value relationship 239n13
capital accounts, deregulation of 9
capital gains tax 7
capital ideology, role in insidious Western democratic process 72–73
capital-dominated system, theory *vs.* reality of in stabilisation of 209–10

capitalism: and commercial exploitation 15, 15n8; financialised 11, 52–53, 109–10, 250, 282; monopolistic 118, 262; nationalistic, in Iraq 57; as social relationship 223; violence as endogenous to 257; *see also* means of production
capitalist accumulation: absolute general law of 241–42; elements of, in Egypt 113; in privately ordered capitalist markets *vs.* Arab socialisation 46; and state bourgeois class 45–46; war as instrument of value formation under 13–14; *see also* accumulation
capitalist class, difference from merchant class 47
capitalistic ideology 1
Central Intelligence Agency (CIA), and Syria 133
central working classes: and austerity 257; decline in wages among 112, 282; increase in wages among 265; and internationalist class war 265; and organic composition of capital 112; post WWII 265; relationship to developing working class 193, 195–96, 204–05; and two-party system 73; and US-led imperialism 283
Charafeddine, F. 50
China: as holder of US government debt 171; ideology of 26; labour wages in 201; oil demand from 186; relationship with Iran 280; relationship with Iraq 162; relationship with Syria 156, 157, 281; Soviet shift from 39
choice: individual 202–03, 204, 205, 217, 238; lack of 4; Marxist-structuralism *vs.* 203–11
choice theory 207
Chomsky, Noam 174, 175
Chossudovsky, M. 277
civil liberties 34–35, 40
civil rights: role of military in revamping of 55; of working classes 12, 250
Clark, R. 92
class. *see* social class
Coalition of the Willing 121

colonial/imperialist wars, economic effects of 15, 19
commercial exploitation 15, 15n8; through value seizure 111–12
Communist Party of Iraq 172
competition 9–10
composition-fallacy problem 207
comprador-merchant class: redistribution as anathema to 7; rise of 7–8, 11; and war 250–59; war losses, effect on turning bourgeoisie into 4; *see also* state bourgeois
Congo 86
conspicuous consumption 56, 191
consumerism 191; in Iraq 191; in Soviet Union 26; *see also* accumulation; capitalist accumulation
consumption 5, 58; conspicuous 56, 191; underconsumption 166
Cooper, M. N. 61–62
Cope, Z. 253–54, 255, 268
corruption 67
creative destruction 103
culture, relationship to materialism 111

Daesh/IS 192
Debord, G. 1–2, 41
debt: dollarisation and war debt 17; and Egypt 80, 92–93; and Syria 150; total debt service in AW, 1960–1979 and 1980–2011 **75t1.4**; US foreign-held 171, 281. *see also* economic growth
Decent Work clause of the International Labour Organisation (ILO) 6
de-development 58, 87–88, 110; *see also* development
defeatism 35; ideological 5, 191; political failures breeding 35; ruling class use of 157–58; in sectional identity politics 190
defense: building up of US 196; spending on 5, 20–21
deindustrialisation 6–7
demand-side approaches 36
democracy: bourgeois 30, 39, 72–73, 106, 112–13, 278, 279; workers' 40n5
dependency theory of development 221–23, 267

deregulation 9
Deutscher, I. 26
developing-country socialist regimes: and agrarian reform 42; and consolidation of post-independence position 42; nationalisation of large-scale financial/ industrial institutions 42; state control over natural resources 42; *see also* Arab socialism
development: under Arab socialism 13, 31–37, 70–71; and autonomy 33; de-development 58, 88, 110; dependency theory of 221–23, 267; economic/social development indicators in Iraq **183t4.1**; in Egypt 83, 85–86, 99, 102; globalisation effect on economic/human 188; human development indicators in Iraq 159, 180–81; late-developer syndrome 51; Latin America, outcomes in 67–68, 102; merchant mode effect on outcomes 102; national bourgeoisie and poor outcomes 55, 67–69; under neo-liberalism 13; oil revenues effect on social development 4; during post-independence years 12–13; quantitative/qualitative divergences from 12; and security 21; state- *vs.* market-led, under neo-liberalism 25–27; in Syria 133; technical 221, 223–24, 225; as threat to US hegemony 6; war effect on 86, 260–73. *see also* industry
dictatorships 34
dirigisme, state: economic growth rates under 10; investment per worker under 124; role of national agents in 11; unemployment rates under 10
disease, increase in death rates from 3
dispossession, value as formed by historical process of 14–15
dollarisation: and AW ruling classes 12; of national currency 5–6; and ruling classes 12; and war debt 17
dollars, oil exports as priced in 5
Drucker thesis 4
dual-exchange rates 47–48, 142
Dunham, B. 53–54
Durant, W. 186
Duri, A. A. 50

Dutch disease effects 8
economic growth: decline in AW 10; effect of oil prices on 9, 9n5; effect of oil revenues on 4; effect of wages on 17–18; effect on unemployment 11; in Egypt 79, 92–93, 99; GDP per-capita in AW 61, 142, 236; import-led, in Syria 137; under *infitah*/openness 10; oil prices effect on 9, 9n5, 136; oil revenues effect on 4; real per-capita growth 10, **74t1.1**; under state *dirigisme* 10. *see also* debt
egalitarian distribution: under Arab socialism 34, 48–49; as boosting demand, growth, and stock of capital 45–46
egalitarian redistribution 46
Egypt: account deficit relative to nominal GDP 93; agricultural investment in 205–06, **206t5.1**; agricultural production in 81; agriculture, contribution to employment/share of GDP **235t5.3**; and balance of payments 94, 95; banking sector in 100; and bourgeois ideology 104; bourgeois ideology effect on uprisings in 104; Bread Riots in 6, 21, 83, 97; and Camp David Accords 46, 48, 81, 84, 99, 105; causes of uprising in 97–98; cereals imports 92; civil rights of women in 55; commodity prices, rising 85; consumption, private 81; Coptic Christians in 111; and crushing of Nasserist socialisation 83; debt service in **75t1.4**; dependence on foreign savings in **75t1.5**, 80; development in 83, 85–86, 99, 102; dispossession of farmers in 205; distribution of rural and urban poverty in **235t5.4**; divisions among working class in 112–13; dollar pegged exchange rate in 93, 94; dollar reserves in 93; early experience with modern Western imperialism 83–84; economic growth in 79, 84, 92–93, 99; economic history of 79–90; educational services in 82; efficiency in 81; exchange rate in 82, 89–90, 96, 98n23; expansion education in 45n7; food prices in 5, 6, 97; food production in 92; foreign debt 80; foreign direct investment in 92, 92n15; GDP growth rate in **74t1.1**; Gini index, misrepresentation of data 91, 91n13, 91n14; government borrowing 94–95; health services in 82; imports 90; income distribution, labour's share of 85; income inequality in 5, 89, 90, 94, 99; *infitah* (openness) policy 69, 80–81, 82–83, 109, 114–15; inflation in **74t1.2**, 93, 95–96, 98–99; investments in 101; and Islamist identity/ideology 104, 108; labour productivity in 82n6; labour share in 91n13; labour strikes in 244; land issues in 81, 91–92; and liberal compromise of Arab left 110; life expectancy in 81; literacy in 81–82; and loss of cultural regression/loss of socialized knowledge 101–02; macroeconomic policy in 93–100; malnutrition in 92, 206; manufacturing in 4, 55, 82, 82n6; market capitalisation in 92, 92n16; May Corrective Movement in 54; and membership in United Arab Republic 172–73; and merchant mode of accumulation 101–03; military spending in 81; monetary policy in 89–90, 93, 94, 100; Muslim Brotherhood, social/economic policy under 100; and Muslim Brotherhood 104–05; Muslim-Copt clashes in 89; under Nasser, pre-Camp David Accords 81; national bourgeoisie fragility after colonialism 34; oil exports 92; Orabi Pasha revolt in 84; output per worker in **74t1.1**; per-capita growth rate in **74t1.1**; and petro-remittances 46, 90; popularity of Sadat in 54; population growth in 79, 99–100; poverty in 91, 91n13, 97, 114; price capping in 40; private ownership under Arab socialism in 61; privatisation in 85–86; public debt 92–93; real wages in 95–96, 97, 99, 112; remittances 92; rent grab by ruling class in 127–28; reserves in 98; resource allocation in 96–97; revolutionary consciousness

in 106–07; Salafi Islam in 110; security structure under neo-liberalism 86–87; Six-Day War, costs of 80n1; social disarticulation process, overview of 78–79; social media/technology role in 116; social model, early in post-independence 29; and social relations 102–03; social spending in 93; supposed poverty reduction measures in 114; tax contributions 101; terms of trade in 80n2; textile industry in 50, 83–84; tourism in 92; and trade liberalisation 93, 93n17; unemployment in 92, 93, 97; uprising, failure of 104–05; uprising, without socialist ideology 106–13; urbanization in 201n1, 212–13; US military aid to 82n5; value transfers to US-led Empire 84–85; wage decline in 90; wealth distribution in 89; working class, lack of political representation in 95–96; working class differentiation in 89; yearly wages in 91n14
El Mahalla Workers 244
embargo: on Gaza 103; on Iraq 64
Emmanuel, A. 19, 255, 265, 266, 268, 270–71, 283
employment, full 36, 71, 139, 223. *see also* unemployment
England. *see* Great Britain
entrepreneurial class 34, 70
essence, dialectical category of 31, 31n2
exchange rate 43; under Arab socialism 47–48, 61; dual 82, 142; effect of multiple on imports 47–48; and Iraq 182, **183t4.2**; pegging to dollar 52, 94; and Syria 139, 140n14, 145; and working class 48
exports: cereals 61; high-technology, AW share of 100–01; oil 5, 92

failed states 171–72
famine: effect of globalisation on 190; in Global South 193; potential, in Egypt 103
fascism 39, 163, 279; social 38, 39, 72, 103, 106

fatalism: reactionary 2; spiritual 11; theoretical, as presupposing religious 111; *see also* ideology
financial crisis, 2007–2008, reasons for 17
financialised capitalism 11, 52–53, 109–10, 250, 282
FIRE (Finance, Insurance and Real Estate) 101
five-year plans 39–40
Foley, D. 91n13, 101
Food and Agriculture Organization (FAO) 246n16
food dependency 204–05, 238
food prices: in Egypt 5, 6, 97; in Morocco 5; rise under neo-liberalism 237
food production: in Egypt 92; and neo-liberalism 202
food security: under Arab socialism 61n12; under neo-liberalism 234
foreign workers 6
form and content, defining 214n5
Foster, J. B. 17, 178, 253, 262
France: and battle of Maysalun 118–19; and Iraqi oil 57
Frank, A. G. 33, 193, 221–22
free market: anarchy of 18; and dispossessionary tendencies of past 33; effect of ideological shift to socialism/national liberation on 43; ideology of 87; individual money incentive of 26; Islamic 35; and neo-liberalism in Egypt 80; role of national agents in 11; in Syrian context 118
French Communism 192
Fukuyama, F. 199
full employment 36, 71, 139, 223
Furtado, C. 221

Galbraith, J. 91
Gaza 31, 103, 169, **235t5.3**
Generalised Arab Free Trade Agreement (GAFTA) 234
geopolitical rents 276
geopolitical uncertainty 7, 62
Gini coefficient 52

global accumulation: control of oil as pivotal to 33, 134–35, 199, 249; as interconnected social process 69; relationship of war to 262, 276–77; role in fueling North-South working class divisions 72
global income, global working class income as percent of 11–12
global markets, open 138, 263
global working class. *see* international working class
globalisation 187–98; and communist parties 192–93; and consumerism 191; and decline in economic and human development 188; and defeatism in sectional identity politics 190; and East Asia 187; famine as result of 190; and foreign investment 189; and industrial working class 188; and Islam 191–92; refugees as result of 190; and skewed distribution of wealth 189–90; and trade by commodity groupings 189; and working classes 190
Gramsci, A. 37, 130, 131, 193
Great Britain: and Egyptian textile production 50, 83–84; invasion of Iraq by 174; and Iran 174; and Kuwait 176; and Muslim Brotherhood 108; occupation of Iraq by 175–76; real wages in 267
Greece 282
growth: economic (*see* economic growth); effect on social development 4; population growth 10, 61, 79, 99–100; productivity (*see* productivity)

Harris, L. 196–97
Hassan, S. 149
heavy industry: development of 55; investment in 29, 34, 42
Hegel, G.W.F. 165, 214n5
Heydemann, S. 128, 130
high-technology exports, AW share of 100–01
Hinnebusch, R. 128, 130
Hirschman, A. O. 238
historical, peoples as 165
historical materialism 50, 166

historical surplus value 16, 166, 265, 270
Hobsbawn, E. J. 199
human rights 158, 175, 190
Human Rights Bill on right to work 6
hunger: as cause of Arab Spring revolts 32; in Egypt 92, 103, 110; increase in death rates from 3; as social control 237; in Syria 132
Hussein, M. 12–13
identity: identity-based conflicts 7; imperialism effects on sectarian/divisive identities 7, 275–76; religious 104, 108, 111; role in formation of class 110–11; sectarian, in Iraq 161–62, 174–75, 190, 198–99; sectarian, in Lebanon 174; split of working class 52–53, 109–10
ideology: bourgeois ideology 41; capitalistic 1; Chinese 26; defeatist, reversing 1–2; fatalism 2, 11, 111; of financial capitalism 129; *laissez-faire* 80, 141–42; nationalist 20, 36, 68–69, 72, 107, 172, 265; negative 20; shifts to policy turnarounds 2; Wahabi 8
illiteracy/literacy 81–82, 159, 181, 189
Ilyenkov, E. V. 218n8, 219n9
imperial rents 15–17, 18–19
imperialism: ability to destroy and create value 134; do-as-you-go strategy 197–98; effects on sectarian and divisive identities 275–76; financialisation phase of 52–53, 109–10; ruling classes alliance with 12; security/sovereignty maintained by US-imperial coverage 7. *see also* comprador-merchant class
imperialist diktat 55–56
Imperialist war. *see* war
imports: agricultural 234–36; customs duties on manufacturing 149; effect of multiple exchange rates on 47–48
import-substitution: and developing-country socialist regimes 42; failure in AW 227; failure in Latin America 226
income distribution: during Arab socialism 29; in Egypt 85; widest gap in AW 10. *see also* wages

income inequality 4–5; in Egypt 5, 89, 90, 91, 94, 99; rise in 58; in Syria **146f3.2**
income tax 7
India, oil demand from 186
indirect taxation 7
industrial development: under Arab socialism 13; imperialist edict to arrest 8; reduction in 5
industrial labour force 201
industry: decline of 9–10; Dutch disease effects on 8; heavy industry 29, 34, 42, 55; textile industry, in Egypt 50, 83–84. *see also* development
infant mortality, during Arab socialism 29
infitah (openness) policy 4–5, 9–10, 31, 264; economic growth under 10; effect on unemployment 9–10; in Egypt 69, 80–81, 82–83, 109, 114–15; integration of national bourgeoisie under 265
inflation: in Egypt 93, 95–96, 98–99; in Iraq 182, **183t4.2**; in Syria 141–42, 145, 147, 150–51. *see also* redistribution
infrastructure: economic 10; funding through oil revenues 11–12; investment in 42; social, under Arab socialism 13
integration, social, difficulties in 4–5
interest rates 43
intermediate stratum: composition of 32; defining 32, 37; and means of production 30, 32; military parts from 37–38; as social relationship 30; structure of 32–33. *see also* state capitalist states
international division of labour 193
international financial bourgeoisie 34, 35, 36, 60
international financial capital 7, 11; alliance of military with 71; effect on nationalism 35–36; labour dislocation under 224; and merchant-capitalist class in Egypt 102; and neoliberal ruling class 34; and regional conflicts 259; and ruling class in Syria 120, 130, 154; and Syria 154
International Financial Institutions (IFIs) 130

International Monetary Fund (IMF) 148–49
international working class: and central working classes 265; emergence of 71; fall of 250, 283; income as percent of global income 11–12; and Iraq war 168; lessened power of, in relation to profits 109; negative effects of capitalism on 193–94; North-South divisions 72; organised labour movement, as non viable 265–66; severance of Northern working class from 168 *see also* working class
investment: decline in 9–10, 11, 62; foreign, in Syria 136; geopolitical uncertainty effect on 7; in infrastructure 42; in Iraq 182, 187, 189; private, in Syria 136; in Syria 125; war effect on 182, 273–75
Iran: nuclear capabilities 177; relationship with Iraq 170; relationship with Soviet Union 175; sectarian identity of 174–75; Syria, relationship with 123, 141; takes over Shat Al-Arab waterway from Iraq 172
Iraq: anti-imperialism in 175–76; Ba'ath party, disenfranching of 170; Ba'ath refoms, post-independence 60; bourgeoisie, postcolonial fragility of 34; British occupation of 175–76; civil rights of women in 55; and class divisions as result of petro-remittances 46–47; Communist Party of 172; coups in postcolonial 54; debt service in **75t1.4**; dependence on foreign savings in **75t1.5**; distribution of rural and urban poverty in **235t5.4**; Egypt's shift to US, effect on invasion of 86; embargo, US-imposed 64; and failed annexation of Kuwait 176; female unemployment rate 186; GDP growth rate in **74t1.1**; genre of Arab socialism in 63–64; human and social development in 159; impact of IS on 160; inflation in **74t1.2**, 182, **183t4.2**; Iraqi military, US desire to disband 173; liberalisation program, lack of 65–66; major economic and

social development indicators **183t4.1**; manufacturing decline in 4; market exchange rates in **183t4.2**; national bourgeoisie fragility after colonialism 34; and nationalism 172; nationalistic capitalism in 57; neoliberal turn in 33–34; oil revenue increase in 159; output per worker in **74t1.1**; paid militias in 276; parliament seats designated by quotas in 3; per-capita growth rate in **74t1.1**; price capping in 40; and price caps 40; private sector under Hussein 65; pseudo-democracy in 177–78; recolonisation of 64; rural areas, expulsion from 205; sectarianism in 161–62, 174, 190, 198–99; and Shia Isalm 170; social model, early in post-independence years 29; state involvement in economy in 57; and Sunni Isalm 170; unionisation in 168; and US-led imperialism relationship with Iraqi Kurds 160–61; *see also* Iraq, effects of US-led war on; Iraq War

Iraq, effects of US-led war on 159–60, 163, 178–87; access to basic resources 180; birth defect rates 160; destruction of physical and human value 162–63; economic performance 179–80; electric power crisis 160, 160n3, 181; exchange rate 182; fall in labour's share of distribution of income 160; GDP an selected components at constant 1990 prices **185t4.4**; GDP at 2002 prices by sectors **184t4.3**; GDP per-capita 180, 182; health services 181; human development indicators 180–81; investment rate 182; and Iraqi Kurdistan 160–61, 179; life expectancy 181; literacy rate 181; oil industry 179, 180, 186–87; orphans 159–60; person security and living conditions 181–82; poverty rate 180, 181; production by sectors 182–85; reconstruction costs 181–82; strengthened American-Israeli hegemony 162–63; and Sunni-Shiite divide 180; unemployment 180, 185–86

Iraq War 163–78; and Arab integrationist project 172–73; and capitalist ideology 167–68; costs of 17, 168, 168n8; effect on oil industry 179, 180, 186–87; ethics of 63n14; and human rights violations 175; and ideology assault on revolutionary consciousness 168–69; and imperialist aggression 164; and interclass struggle 164; and international working class relations 168; and Iraqi people as historical 165; and materialist explanations of history/war 165–67; and personalist propaganda 173–74; propaganda, effect on US working class 169–70; reasons for 167, 170–71, 197; and theocratic ideology 170

Iraqi Petroleum Compnay (IPC) 173n13

Ireland, oil company of 148

Islam: and free market 35; and globalisation 191–92; Islamic-oriented NGOs 244–45; modern Islamic economics 69n16; Salafi Islam 4, 11, 110, 191–92

Israel: disproportionate use of massive violence by 169; nuclear capabilities of 176–77; on potential Sunni-Shiite war in Syria 275n5; reasons it is impossible to integrate with AW 280; strength of army compared with AW 162

Issawi, C. 80n1

job creation: under Arab socialism 10; decrease in regional rate of 201–02; effect of neo-liberalism on 6–7, 10, 146, 201–02, 225; effect of oil industry on 6, 150; increase, poverty-wage service sector 6–7. *see also* unemployment; wages

Jordan: agriculture, contribution to employment/share of GDP **235t5.3**; distribution of rural and urban poverty in **235t5.4**

Juhasz, A. 64

Kalecki, M. 37, 46, 255, 255n3
Kantian moral equivalence 117–18
Khrushchev, Nikita 25
Khuri, F. 54
Kishk, H. 91–92
Klare, M. T. 187

knowledge production: application to national technology 42; declining, in Egypt 101–02; holding down/sinking of 5, 11; war, effect on 19
Kurds, Iraqi: economic impact of US-led war on 179; US-led imperialist relationship with 160–61
Kuwait: Iraq and failed annexation of 176; returns from fund investment in financial markets 187; wages in, compared to Egypt 82

Labica, G. 30–31
labour power, as commodity 230, 254
laissez-faire ideology 80, 141–42
land reform: and Arab socialism 13, 50; Marxism on 213; and neo-liberalism 245; in post-independence AW 29, 60
Larrain, J. 20, 203n2
late-developer syndrome 51
Latin America: and dependency theory 221, 226; failure of import substitution in 226; poor developmental outcomes in 67–68, 102
Lauesen, T. 253–54
leakages 141, 264
Lebanese National Movement 121
Lebanon 86, 276
Lee Boggs, G. 106–07, 108
Lenin, V. 104, 163, 262
Libya 104, 202, 205, 276
Lievan, A. 198
life expectancy 29, 81, 181, 239, 257
Lindorff, D. 17
literacy/illiteracy 81–82, 159, 181, 189
Lukács, G. 63n14, 168, 191
Luxembourg, R. 260, 262
malnutrition 234, 236–37; alleviating through class restructuring 237–38; in Egypt 87, 206; as social control 237; in Yemen 206
Mandel, E. 253
manufacturing: decline in 4; in Egypt 55, 82, 82n6; investment in 42; in post-independence Syria 55; shares in AW 100
Mao Zedong 158, 249

Marx, K. 116; on anarchy of production 166; on causes of real wage differences among countries 267; on colonial labour, violent transformation into bonded labour 225; on development of socialism 26–27; on equalisation of wages 204; on labour power as commodity 254; on value of labour power 266–67
Marxism: on the abstract 218n8; on class war 2–3; on consciousness-shaping 2; on labour power as commodity 254; materialist explanation of history 166
Matar, L. 44, 131n5
materialism: dialectical 50; historical 50, 166; relationship to culture 111; of social class reproduction 59, 68
May Corrective Movement (Egypt) 54
Maysalun, battle of 118–19
McGhee, G. C. 176–77
means of production: under Arab socialism 27, 42–43; and capitalism 243; and neo-liberalism 207–08; and social class 30, 32, 35; and state bourgeoisie 45–46
Meillassoux, C. 31
merchant capital. *see* comprador-merchant class
merchant class, difference from capitalist class 47
Mészáros, I. 103, 246
middle class, defining 58n11
Middle East and North Africa Region (MENA) 278
migration. *see* rural areas; urban areas; urbanization
military 54–58; alliance with merchant class, neoliberal period 13; alliance with working class, post-independence 12–13; and coups 54; as instrument of change and modernity 55; prioritisation under Arab socialism 49; and radical socioeconomic reform 55; shifting class allegiance of 54–55, 56; social class origins of members of 54–55
modern Islamic economics 69n16

money-value 18–20
monopolies 95, 166, 166n7, 241, 262
Morocco 5, **235t5.3**
Morsi, M. 98, 113
Mosca, G. 104
Mubarak, H. 91
Mujahidin 194
mukhabarat 57
Muslim Brotherhood (MB) 100, 104–05, 108, 113, 245

Napoleonic conquest 83–84
Nash equilibrium 214
Nasser, G. A.: economic/social reform under 55, 81–82, 83; and *intifah*/openness 80; regime as intermediated regime 37; and revolution 83. *see also* Egypt
national bourgeoisie: anti-colonialism by 34; and armed forces 54; and capping of rate of wealth accumulation of 242; effect of poverty-reducing policies on 114; emergence of national bourgeois industrial class 51; and inequity during colonialism 66; integration under economic openness 265; as international financial bourgeoisie 34, 35, 36, 60; and poor developmental outcomes 55, 67–69; state bourgeois class as surrogate 33; *see also* state bourgeois
nationalist ideology 20, 36, 68–69, 72, 107, 172, 265
natural resources, state control over 42; *see also* oil; oil industry
negative ideology 20
neoclassical economics 204, 207–08, 217–18
neo-liberalism: emergence of 43; political repression under 57–58; social and macroeconomic structural shifts under 53–54; *see also* Arab socialism; socialisation of labour by neoliberal means
Netanyahu, B. 170, 198
Non-Aligned Movement (NAM) 85
nuclear capabilities: of Israel 176–77; of Soviet Union 57; of U.S. 196

oil: control of, as pivotal to accumulation 33, 134–35, 199, 249; demand for 186–87; dependence on 10; economic effects of oil prices 4, 9, 9n5, 10, 136; exports 5, 92; as means for furthering control argument 260–62; and oil for its own sake argument 260; production as percent of global energy production 187n16; role in Imperialist war 249; strategic relevance of 134–35; *see also* oil industry; oil revenues
oil boom, 2003 10
oil industry: effect on job creation 6, 150; technological knowledge held down by 5, 11; war in Iraq effect on 179, 180, 186–87
oil revenues: funding of social/productive infrastructure through 11–12; and growth/social development, under socialism *vs.* neo-liberalism 4; increase in Iraq 159; outflows of 8; redistribution in Iraq 60; role in societal divisions 7
Ollman, B. 228
openness. *see infitah* (openness) policy
Orabi Pasha revolt 84
Organisation of Oil-Producing Countries (OPEC) 179, 187
Osman, T. 71–72
output. *see* worker output
overproduction 262
overseas assets 5
Palestine: distribution of rural and urban poverty in **235t5.4**; expulsions from rural areas 205; partitioning of 172; relationship with Syria 132

Palestinian Liberation Organisation (PLO) 121
pan-Arab secularism 8
Paris Club 93, 93n17
Patnaik, P. 94–95
Peck, J. 196
perfect markets 95n20
Perthes, V. 125
Petras, J. 45, 60, 105, 261
petro-remittances 46

petty bourgeoisie: consciousness development and 32; defining 30–31; suicide of 49; *see also* bourgeoisie; state bourgeois
Polling, S. 125
Pool, D. 128
population growth 10, 61, 79, 99–100
Poulantzas, N. A. 30, 70, 121
poverty: absolute 6; Bretton Woods poverty reduction measures 114; in Egypt 91, 91n13, 97, 114; in Iraq as result of US-led war 180, 181; rates in AW 201–02, **235t5.4**; in Saudi Arabia 9; in Syria 137
poverty-wage service sector jobs, increase in 6–7
Prebsich, R. 221
price caps 39–40, 52, 64–65
price theory 207
private property 2, 213
private sector: under Arab socialism 42–43, 61–63, 64–65; in Iraq, under Hussein 65; under neo-liberalism 65; shortcomings, post-independence 67; in Syria 139, 143
privatisation, transition from socialisation 35–36
production in AW: effect of war on 273–76; and geopolitical rents 276; under neo-liberalism 202
productivity: agricultural 236–37; under Arab socialism 48–49; developed *vs.* developing world 268–69; negative growth under neo-liberalism 6, 204; rise of 126; in Syria 124n4. *see also* worker output
Project for the New American Century 196
proletarianisation 46; of English labour 205; as primitive accumulation 205; theoretical features of 238
public sector, post-independence 62

Qassim, A. K. 172–73, 173n13
Qatar 98, 113

racism 26, 43–44, 68–69, 112
reactionary fatalism 2

real per-capita growth: in AW 1960–1979 and 1980–2011 **74t1.1**; lowest rate in AW 10, **74t1.1**; Saudi Arabia 79
real per-capita income, in Saudi Arabia 9
real wages: decline prior to 2011 uprising 90, 112; in Egypt 95–96, 97, 99, 112; in Germany 267; in Great Britain 267; growth during Arab socialism 29; Marx on differences among countries 267; pegged exchange rate effect on 94; public sector, Syria 124n4, 150; recent decline among central working classes 282; in Russia 267; in Syria 124, 147
realism, theoretical 194
recolonisation 56, 57, 64, 123
redistribution: as anathema to comprador-merchant class 7; under Arab socialism 13, 43, 46, 53, 65, 71; in Egypt 104, 113; of oil revenues in Iraq 60; of oil revenues in Syria 147; post-independence period 67; in post-independence Syria 139; regressive under neo-liberalism 46; of surplus value 40. *see also* inflation
refugees: effect of globalisation on 190; effect of Imperialism on 190; Iraqi 150–51; loss of labour autonomy as resulting in 213; Syrian 130
reification 12, 12n7
rent grab: in Egypt 127–28; as inherent tendency of capitalism 127
rentier state 126
research and development (R&D) 18–19
resource allocation: in Egypt 96–97; in Syria 132
resources: under Arab socialism 48; effects of Iraq war on access to 180; idle and productive in Syria 134; misallocation in Syria 151–54; privatisation of 258–59; state control over 42; *see also* oil; redistribution
revolutionary theory 1, 3
Richards, A. 125–26
Rousseau, J.-J. 166
rural areas: depriving of security 226; distribution of poverty in **235t5.4**; expulsion from, by violence 205, 225–26; Marxist-structuralism on

wages 212–13; population statistics, 1980–2020 **235t5.2**; rate of labour dislocation under neo-liberalism 224–25. *see also* poverty; urban areas; urbanization

Russia: and Iraqi oil 57; military intervention into Syria 153, 157, 281; real wages in 267; relationship with Iran 280; relationship with Syria 133, 150, 156, 157, 178–79; socialist workers' state in 39. *see also* Soviet Union

Sadat, Anwar: anti-regime protests as result of reform by 21, 105; and Muslim Brotherhood 245. *see also* Egypt

Sahfei'i, H. El 140n13

Salafi Islam 4, 11, 110, 191–92

Saudi Arabia: culture of social exclusion in 192; economic effects of oil prices on 9, 10; per capita income in 9

Sayfuaddawla, I. 50

Schumpeter, J. A. 103

security: defining types of 33; and development 21; maintained by US-imperial coverage 7, 8; spending on 5

Sellers, J. 195

service-sector jobs, increase in 6–7

Shishakli, 139

shock, instruments of 17

Sisi, A. F. el- 105, 113, 114, 115. *see also* Egypt

Six-Day War: costs of 80n1; defeat of Syria in 140; illiteracy of Egyptian soldiers as security threat to 21

social class: class relationships 122–23; defining 58n11; as historical relationship 30; and means of production 30, 32, 35; role of identity in formation of 110–11; shifting class allegiance of military 54–55, 56; social class origins of members of military 54–55. *see also* state bourgeois

social class reproduction, materialism of 59, 68

social corps 31

social fascism 38, 39, 72, 103, 106, 190

social humanism 38

social rights, and racism 112

socialisation: as anti-systemic and a process of self-negation for capital 41–42; Soviet model of 38–39; transition to privatisation 35–36

socialisation of labour by neoliberal means: and absence of individual choice 202–11, 217, 238; and class relationship effect on identity 242–43; conditions for 231–32; and deconstruction of productive sector 202; and deindustrialisation 225; and dependency theory 221; and dual economy models 202–03; and equilibrium approach 214; and exchange as commodity production specific condition 229–30, 232; and expulsion from rural sector by violence 225–26; and falling job creation, effect on poverty 201–02; and general equilibrium 208; interconnections of systems and developments, as explanation of 217; and Islamic-oriented NGOs 244–45; and Marxian approach to transfer of labour 220–21; and Marxian perspective of exchange 228–33; Marxist-Structuralism compared with 211–14; and migration 203–04, 212, 213, 227–28; modelling, use in explanation of 216; and money form of value 230–31, 232–33; and non-price explanation of proletarianisation 220–27; and overproduction 225; and policy autonomy 245–46; and property theft by ruling classes 245; and radical dependency theory of development 221–23; and rate of dislocation 224–25; rationale for displacement 206–08, 226; and reduction of public sector employment 225; and regaining of development 245; and resistance to imperialism 242; and rise in global proletarianism 201; and rural sections of 204–05; and rural security 226; and rural wages 212–13; shortcomings of neoclassical theory 214–20; shrinking of 202; and technical development 221, 223–24, 225; urbanisation effect on 201; and value/use value relationship

229, 232; and wage system 239–40; and wealth creation contribution to value 239–40; and working class fragmentation and identity 242–44. *see also* socialisation of labour by neoliberal means, concrete condition of
socialisation of labour by neoliberal means, concrete condition of 234–38; agricultural imports 234–36, 237; agricultural sector contribution to employment/share of GDP **235t5.3**; average GDP growth per capita 236; decrease in worker share of income 236; distribution of rural and urban poverty **235t5.4**; food security, lack of 234; inter-Arab trade 234; low agricultural productivity growth 236–37; obstacles to raising per capita consumption 237–38; per-capita consumption/production, decline in 234; proletarianism, theoretical features of 238; rise in food prices 237; rural and urban populations of AW, 1980–2020 **235t5.2**
Somalia 5, 205
Sourani G. 31–32
South Korea, as holder of US government debt 171
sovereignty: diminishment of Arab state sovereignty 20; maintained by US-imperial coverage 7
Soviet Union: collapse of 66; difficulties in transition to modern economy 38–39; and Iraqi oil 57; nuclear capabilities of 57; relationship with Islamic Iran 175; role of ideology in decline of 27; socialism in 43. *see also* Russia
state bourgeois: Arab socialism and rise of 34; and capital as social relationship 40–41; and capitalist accumulation 45–46; and class alliance of military and intermediate strata 51–52; components of 30; consumption by 58; defining 41; effect of weakness of bourgeois class in postcolonial years on 51; and emergence of neo-liberalism 43; and exchange rate structure 47–48; and frail bourgeois class--2 decades following WWII 53–54; ideology of 41; and industrialisation 50–54; and intermediate regimes 37–38; and intermediate stratum 45; and intermediate stratum alliance with military 45–46; and late-developer syndrome 51; and means of production 45–46; and more pronounced class fault-lines under Arab socialism 46–47; orientation toward imperialism 44; predisposition to capitulate to imperialism 43–50; and price capping 39–40; and state capitalist regimes 38; and state-led development 37–43; structure of 43; and underdevelopment 50–51; underlying hypothesis of 36; and weakness of entrepreneurship 53. *see also* means of production; national bourgeoisie
state capitalism, defining 41
state capitalist states 38
structural theories of migration 203
Structural-Marxism, structuralism *vs.* 203n2
subcontracting 65
substitution effect 6
Sudan 5, 205, **235t5.4**
Sukkar, N. 125
Suleiman, H. 175–76
surplus value: as distinct from value formation 111; historical 16, 166, 265, 270
Sutcliffe, B. 106
Sweezy, P. M. 253
Sykes-Picot Agreement 176
Syria: agriculture, contribution to employment/share of GDP **235t5.3**; and agriculture 144; alliance with US-led imperialism 119; and army's role in Lebanon/PLO 144; Asad regimes in 133–38; and Assad-led class partnership with US imperialism 151–52; and banking sector 144, 149; and battle of Maysalun 118–19; and Bazaar class 144; beginning of decline of 140–43; cereal exports 61; characteristics of uprisings in 104; and class relationships 121–23; coups in postcolonial 54; and

customs duties on manufacturing imports 149; debt service in **75t1.4**, 150; and defeat in Six-Day War 140; dependence on foreign savings in **75t1.5**; developmental process in 133; distribution of rural and urban poverty in **235t5.4**; and dollarisation 133, 140–41; and drop in Gulf aid 141; and economic pluralism 144; effects imperialist war on 155; exchange rates in 140n14, 145; expulsions from rural areas of 205; and foreign exchange laws 149; and foreign exchange proceeds 144; GDP growth rate in **74t1.1**; GDP per-capita growth rate 142; general price level index, 1960–2010 **146f3.1**; and geopolitical rents 133; and growth rate 150; under Hafez al-Assad 140–41; ideological defeatism in 118, 143; idle and productive resources in 134; and imports 150; income inequality index, 1987–1995 **146f3.2**; and industrial knowhow 148; and industrial workers 145; inflation in **74t1.2**, 125n4, 137, 141–42, 145, 147, 150–51; and lifting of caps on capital and trade account controls 149; manufacturing decline in 4; and merchant class 144–45; and military-merchant class 155–56; and Muslim Brotherhood 143; and neoliberal reform to confront social problems 148; and oil revenues/production 148; output per worker in **74t1.1**; paid militias in 276; and partnership with international financial capital 154; per-capita growth rate in **74t1.1**; and petro-remittances 46; political rationality of 129–32; process by which ruling class deluded itself into applying reforms 132; rationale of current destruction in 66; real wages, public sector 124n4, 150; real wages in 124, 147; real wealth shift from working to ruling class 142, 143; reasons for ongoing collapse in 117; relationship with Iran 123; relationship with Israel 155; and remittances from expatriates 150; and removal of price caps in 40, 151; resistance strategy against US-imperialist led war 121–23; resource misallocation under Assads 151–54; and resource usurpation 142; revenues from exports to Iraq 149–50; and role of private sector 143; ruling class use of defeatism in 157–58; state-owned manufacturing effect on GDP, post-independence 55; and strategic relevance of oil 134–35; and subsidies for military-merchant class 151; and technocrats 132–33; and tourism 144; and trade liberalisation 144; underestimation of imperialist drive for war 157; and unemployment 145–47, 150, 150n19; and value creation 135; view toward war 135. *see also* Syria, Bashar regime neoliberal reforms; Syria, neoliberal reform debate; Syria, post-independence

Syria, Bashar regime neoliberal reforms 136–38, 148–51; children's health 137; dollarasition 137–38; education 137; foreign investment 136; growth rate 136; import-led growth 137; income gap 137; industry 137; military-merchant class gains 136, 137; oil prices 136; poverty 137; private investment 136; privatisation of agricultural land 137; public health 137; social market economy proposal 137; staple commodity prices 137; unemployment 136, 138; wages 137, 138; worker subsidies/cash disbursements 137

Syria, neoliberal reform debate 124–32; economic crisis, late 1980s 125; efficacy of public sector 125n4; fall in rents 126–28; investment 125; investment per worker under dirigiste past 124; political considerations 128–31; productivity growth 124n4; public expenditure 124n3; real public sector wages 124n4; reasons for collapse of Arab socialism 124n3, 124–26; reasons for shift to neo-liberalism 125; resource allocation 132

Syria, post-independence 139–40; direct redistribution to poor 139; employment 139; exchange rate stability 139; formation of United Arab Republic 139; land socialisation 139; national bourgeoisie fragility 34; private sector 139; public sector expansion 139; rise of Ba'ath Party 139; social model 29; social reform, effect on nationalist formation 152–53; socialised health and education 139; under Zuayyin 139–40
tariffs 65; effect of multiple exchange rates on 47–48; in Egypt under neo-liberalism 93, 137. *see also* trade
taxes: direct 77; effect of war on 257; Egyptian to Ottomans 84; exemptions on corporate profits in Syria 143; indirect 7, 77, 147; military spending 17; as result of austerity 96, 257; and working classes 163, 178, 236
technology: exports, AW share of 100–01; fuel efficiency 186–87; value through 19, 266
textile industry, in Egypt 50, 83–84
theoretical realism 194
trade: decline in intra-Arab 10; deregulation of 9; and Egypt 80n2, 93; embargos 64, 103; Generalised Arab Free Trade Agreement 234; globalisation effect on 189; inter-Arab under neo-liberalism 234; liberalisation of, and Egypt 93, 93n17; and Syria 144; and WTO standards of liberalisation 52. *see also* oil; tariffs
trade relationship, as social relationship 204
trade unions 48, 99, 137, 244
traditionalism 222. *see also* rural areas
Tunisia 97; agriculture, contribution to employment/share of GDP **235t5.3**; characteristics of uprisings in 104; flight of president of 132; labour union in 244
Tunisian General Labour Union (UGTT) 244

uncertainty, geopolitical 7, 62
underconsumption, crisis of 166; *see also* consumption

unemployment 6, 136, 138, 145–47; under Arab socialism 10; decrease, 2002–2011 11; effect of hollow growth on 11; in Egypt 92, 93, 97; female rate in Iraq 186; in Iraq 180, 185–86; lowest rate in AW 10; official *vs.* true rate of 6; openness policy effect on 9–10; under state dirigisme 10; in Syria 124, 136, 138, 145–47, 150, 150n19. *see also* job creation; poverty; wages
unions, trade 48, 99, 137
United Arab Republic (UAR) 139, 172–73
United Kingdom. *see* Great Britain
United Nations, and justification of war 170
United Nations Conference on Trade and Development (UNCTAD) 246
uprisings: characteristics of 104; in Egypt 104–05, 106–13. *see also* Arab Spring
urban areas: distribution of poverty in **235t5.4**; population statistics, 1980–2020 **235t5.2**. *see also* rural areas
urbanization: in AW 201; in Egypt 201n1, 212–13; under neo-liberalism 61n12. *see also* poverty
value: ability of imperialism to destroy and create 134; as formed by historical process of dispossession 14–15; Iraq war, role in destruction of physical and human value 162–63; Marx on value of labour power 266–67; money as medium between use value/exchange value 18–19; quantifying via Western technology/productivity 266; through war and technology rents 15; value seizure under commercial exploitation 111–12; of Western *vs.* Third World lives 39; working class as value creating 32
value formation 13–14; as distinct from surplus value 111; in Egypt 103; role of identity in 111; social context of 227; war as instrument of 13–14
violence: disproportionate use by Israel 169; as endogenous to capitalism 257; expulsion from rural sector by, under neo-liberalism 225–26; inter-working class violence 7

wage compression 6–7
wage-pull theory 211–12
wages: in China 201; departure from value of labour power 268; effect on growth rate 17–18; in Egypt 91n14, 97, 99; Marx on equalisation of 204; Marxist-structuralism on rural wages 212–13; share of wages as determined by political power of labour 270–71; in Syria under neo-liberalism 137, 138; wage-labour relationship under Arab socialism 48–49. *see also* job creation; real wages; unemployment
war: accumulation by 11–12, 13–14, 262, 276–77; and building up of US defences 196; as central to value of dollar 264–65; and colonialism 279; death rates from 3, 216, 273; and decline of revolutionary class consciousness 279–80; and disempowerment 252–53; effect on commodification of human life 257; effect on development 86, 260–73; effect on investment 182, 273–75; effect on knowledge production 19; effect on taxes 257; effect on working classes 2, 272–73; and expendability of human life 271–72; and financialisation 250; functions of imperialist war 13–14; and ideological defeatism 278–79; and imperial rents 265–66; as instrument of value formation 13–14; as means to transfer of value into price 253–54; and necessity of conflict/tension in AW 277; as necessary for betterment of human spirit 196–97; and primacy of politics of imperialism 252; and privatisation of resources 258–59; as production process 270; and productive capacity 273–76; resistance as strategy against 121–23; role in redressing power positions 251–52; role of oil in 249; Six-Day War 21, 80n1, 140; and social spending 257; spending on 253; as strategic control 262; in Syria 121–23, 135, 155, 281; UN justification of 170; underlying reasons for permanent war 276–77; unintended consequences of 277; as unjustifiable 170; and value formation 13–14, 19; as value relationship 256–57. *see also* Iraq, effects of US-led war on; Iraq War
war debt 17
war in, as proxy war 281
Waterbury, J. 125–26, 137
Weeks, J. 210–11
West Bank **235t5.3**
worker output: under Arab socialism 48; growth rates in **74t1.1**; and labour worldwide 250n1; shrinkage in 12
worker socialisation, effect of reduction in industrialisation on 5
workers: Asian workers 6; forcibly disengaged 269–70; foreign 6; *see also* worker output; working class
workers' democracy 40n5
working class: alliance with military during post-independence 12–13; and bourgeois democratic processes 72; civil/national rights of 12; and democracy 73; dividedness by identity 7; effect of war on 2, 272–73; elimination of organisations under Arab socialism 49; and exchange rate structure 48; global (*see* international working class);
and globalisation 188; inter-working class conflict 4, 7; and nationalism 107, 265; results of working class differentiation 7; strata within, compartmentalisation of 59; as value creating 32; and wage-labour relationship under Arab socialism 48–49; *see also* international working class
working class consciousness: based on public property 40n6, 40–41; effect of identity on 7; Marxism on 2; and socialist ideology took a dive 52
World Bank: and minimisation of government role in economy 275; progress of Gini index of Egypt reported to 91; and Syria 150n19, 153
World Development Indicators (WDI) 91
World Health Organisation (WHO) 159–60

INDEX 319

world income, percent earned by rich economies 5
World Trade Organization (WTO): membership of Arab countries in 234; membership of Syria 133–34
World Trade Organization membership 133–34
Yemen: characteristics of uprisings in 104; distribution of rural and urban poverty in **235t5.4**; expulsions from rural areas 205; and intra-regional disparities 5; malnutrition in 206; paid militias in 276; US-led capital, effects of 86

Zinni, A. 197
Zuayyin, Y. 139–40; *see also* Syria, post-independence

www.ingramcontent.com/pod-product-compliance
Ingram Content Group UK Ltd.
Pitfield, Milton Keynes, MK11 3LW, UK
UKHW041916140426
5217IPUK00013B/171